Private Capital Flows to Developing Countries

A World Bank Policy Research Report

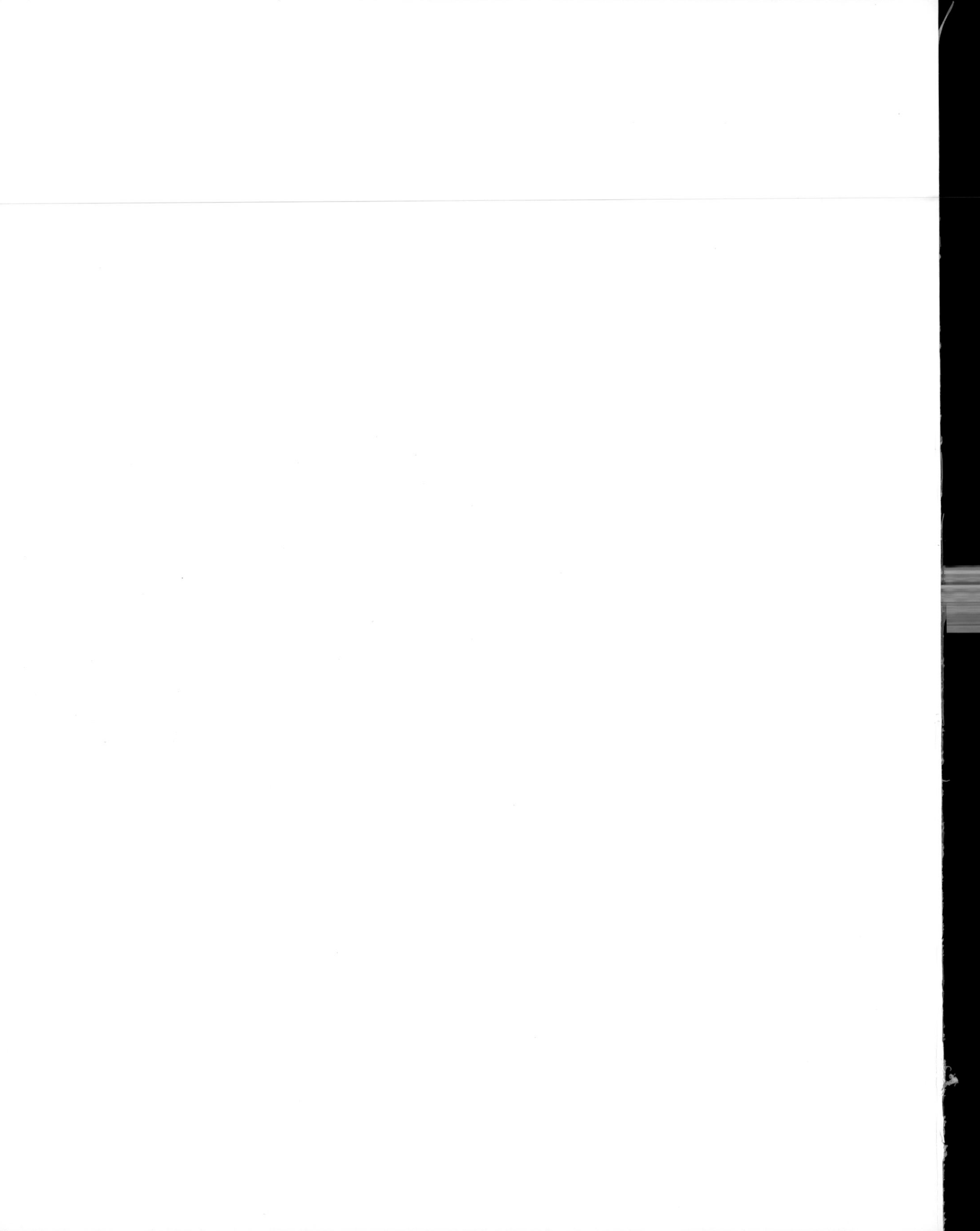

Private Capital Flows to Developing Countries

The Road to Financial Integration

Published for the World Bank
Oxford University Press

Oxford University Press

OXFORD NEW YORK TORONTO
DELHI BOMBAY CALCUTTA MADRAS KARACHI
KUALA LUMPUR SINGAPORE HONG KONG TOKYO
NAIROBI DAR ES SALAAM CAPE TOWN
MELBOURNE AUCKLAND

and associated companies in

BERLIN IBADAN

Published by Oxford University Press, Inc.
198 Madison Avenue, New York, N.Y. 10016

Manufactured in the United States of America
First printing April 1997

Cover photographs: clockwise, from top right: Josef Polleross/The Stock Market; Nadia Mackenzie/Tony Stone Worldwide; Julian Calder/Tony Stone Worldwide; Jane Evelyn Atwood/The Stock Market; D. Stoecklein/The Stock Market

Library of Congress Cataloging-in-Publication Data

Private capital flows to developing countries : the road to financial integration.
p. cm.
Includes bibliographical references (p.).
ISBN 0-19-521116-2
1. Investments, Foreign—Developing countries. 2. Capital movements—Developing countries. I. World Bank.
HG5993.P747 1997
332.67'3'091724—DC21 *97-11785*
CIP

ISSN 1020-0851

∞ *Text printed on paper that conforms to the American National Standards for Permanence of Paper for Printed Library Materials. Z39.48-1984*

Contents

Boxes

Text figures

Text tables

Foreword

FINANCIAL MARKETS AROUND THE WORLD ARE RAPIDLY INTEGRATING into a single global marketplace, and developing countries are increasingly part of this process. The process is being driven by advances in communications and information technology, deregulation of financial markets, and the rising importance of institutional investors that are able and willing to invest internationally. The good news is that developing countries are attracting private capital flows by improving macroeconomic policy and by establishing institutions and regulatory regimes that have increased creditworthiness and promise a more stable environment. Moreover, investors are also becoming more sophisticated in differentiating among countries and their economic fundamentals. Finally, after the Mexican crisis of 1994–95, the international community has realized that more should be done to reduce volatility and risks in international financial markets by improving market disclosure and strengthening coordination among national authorities.

Nevertheless, there remain reasons for concern. First, for the twenty or so countries that have been the major recipients, the management of private capital flows has not proved to be easy. It is not just the volume of flows, but the speed at which such investment pours in—and can be withdrawn—that present particular challenges to these economies. Governments need to build the kind of macroeconomic, regulatory, and institutional environments that channel this private capital into broad-based and sustainable growth. Second, the overwhelming majority of developing countries, in particular the smaller low-income economies, still need to create the conditions to attract private capital and must depend on declining official flows.

This report makes a serious and timely contribution to the analysis of these issues. It explores the nature of the changes that are leading to the integration of developing countries in world financial markets, and it analyzes the policy challenges these countries face in attracting and managing private capital flows. It concludes, for example, that countries receiving large capital inflows should avoid using them to finance large fiscal deficits or consumption booms. The report also includes specific recommendations and warnings on regulatory design that may be useful to developing countries as they seek to maximize the positive contribution of capital inflows while minimizing their potentially disruptive effects.

This book, therefore, will be highly useful to policymakers in developing countries and, more generally, to all development specialists. But it will also be essential reading for members of the global financial community. Investors have seen in recent years how dynamic—and sometimes volatile—emerging markets can be. Understanding these opportunities and challenges is critical for everyone.

The report also comes at an important time for the World Bank. The challenge for the Bank and other development agencies is to create strategies to help developing countries leverage private capital flows so that all benefit. The research presented in this book is an important step in constructing such strategies.

Like previous volumes in the Policy Research Report series, *Private Capital Flows to Developing Countries* is designed for a wide audience. It is a product of the staff of the World Bank; the judgments made in the report do not necessarily reflect the views of the Board of Directors or the governments they represent.

Joseph E. Stiglitz
Senior Vice President
and Chief Economist
The World Bank

April 1997

The Report Team

THE REPORT TEAM WAS LED BY AMAR BHATTACHARYA AND comprised Pedro Alba, Swati Ghosh, Leonardo Hernández, Peter Montiel, and Holger Wolf. Substantial background input was also provided by Andrea Anayiotos (chapter 2), Soonhyun Kwon (measurement of financial integration), Maria Soledad Martinez-Peria (chapter 5), and Michael Pomerleano (chapter 6). The main research assistance was provided by Jill Dooley, Matthew Anderson, and Jos Jansen. Bakhodir Atahodjaev, Madeleine Li-Chay-Chung, and Alok Garg also provided research assistance. Deborah Davis edited the first draft of the study, and Anatole Kaletsky provided editorial input on the summary and chapter 1. K. Anna Kim provided logistical and secretarial support for the overall study, and Hong Vo for chapters 2 and 5. The study was initiated by and carried out under the direction of Michael Bruno and Masood Ahmed. Joseph Stiglitz provided guidance in the closing stages of the study.

The editorial production team was led by Anthony Pordes. The team was assisted by Paola Brezny, Amy Brooks, and Audrey Heiligman. Joyce Gates provided production support.

Acknowledgments

THE REPORT HAS BENEFITED FROM DISCUSSIONS WITH AND comments and contributions from many persons outside and within the World Bank. Special thanks are due to those who have provided guidance and feedback from the inception to the completion of the study. These include Gerard Caprio, Stijn Claessens, Richard Frank, Morris Goldstein, Sarwar Lateef, Diana McNaughton, Gary Perlin, D. C. Rao, Jed Shilling, and Paulo Vieira da Cunha. Special thanks are also due to Mariano Bengoechea, Claudia Morgenstern, Susan Pascocello, Ester Saverson Jr., and Robert Strahota for their extensive feedback on chapter 6. The report also benefited from discussions with Ismail Dalla, Jack Glen, Ross Levine, Millard Long, and Andrew Sheng. We would like to acknowledge support from staff and management of the International Monetary Fund; Sunil Sharma participated in a mission to prepare a background paper, and Donald Mathieson, Anthony Richards, and Michael Spencer provided valuable comments.

The report would not have been possible without the willingness of the private sector to share its perspective on investing in emerging markets. The report has drawn on interviews with many fund managers and pensions funds, information provided by global custodians, and discussions with many others in the financial community. Although they are too numerous to mention, we would like to make special note of the support received from the Frank Russell Company; Citibank, N.A.; the Bank of New York; INTERSEC Research Corporation; and the International Federation of Stock Exchanges (FIBV).

The report drew on background papers or inputs by Reena Aggarwal, Philip Brock, José de Gregorio, Persephone Economou, Ian Giddy, Morris Goldstein, Naoko Kojo, Elizabeth Morrissey, Gabriel Perez-Quiros, Maria Scattaglia, and Charles Seeger. The study has also drawn on a number of country studies that we intend to include in a subsequent volume. The Asian component of the review of country experiences was undertaken collaboratively with the Asian Development Bank (ADB). The study has also benefited from a joint ADB–World

Bank workshop on "Private Capital Flows: Implications for Capital Markets in Asia," and we would like to thank the participants in that workshop. Many individuals in the International Economics Department provided data needed for the study; we would like to make special acknowledgment of the support received from Punam Chuhan and Himmat Kalsi.

Many Bank staff members provided valuable comments, including Noritaka Akamatsu, Suman Bery, Francis Colaco, Uri Dadush, Asli Demirgüç-Kunt, Cevdet Denizer, Hinh Dinh, Daniela Gressani, Norman Hicks, Akira Iida, Ronald Johannes, Johannes Linn, Will Martin, Vikram Nehru, Ngozi Okonjo-Iweala, Guillermo Perry, Thierry Pujol, Zia Qureshi, Jean-François Rischard, Hemant Shah, Robert Shakotko, C. K. Teng, John Williamson, and Roberto Zagha. Finally, we have benefited from comments received at a Board seminar on the draft report.

Data Notes and Abbreviations

Data Notes

HISTORICAL DATA IN THIS BOOK MAY DIFFER FROM THOSE in other World Bank publications if more reliable data have become available, if a different base year has been used for constant price data, or if countries have been classified differently.

- *Billion* is 1,000 million.
- *Trillion* is 1,000 billion.
- *Dollars* are current U.S. dollars unless otherwise specified.

Abbreviations and Acronyms

ASEAN	Association of Southeast Asian Nations
BIS	Bank for International Settlements
C&S	Clearance and settlement (securities)
CPI	Consumer price index
FDI	Foreign direct investment
IFC	International Finance Corporation
IFCI	IFC Emerging Markets Index
IMF	International Monetary Fund
IOSCO	International Organization of Securities Commissions
ISSA	International Society of Securities Administrators
GDP	Gross domestic product
GNP	Gross national product
SRO	Self-regulatory organization

Summary

THE WORLD'S FINANCIAL MARKETS ARE RAPIDLY integrating into a single global marketplace, and ready or not, developing countries, starting from different points and moving at various speeds, are being drawn into this process. If they have adequate institutions and sound policies, developing countries may proceed smoothly along the road to financial integration and gain the considerable benefits that integration can bring. Most of them, however, lack the prerequisites for a smooth journey, and some may be so ill prepared that they lose more than they gain from financial integration. Developing countries have little choice about whether to follow this path, because advances in communications and new developments in finance have made the course inevitable. They can, however, decide how they wish to travel, choosing policies that benefit the economy and avert potential shocks.

This volume describes the forces that have created and that sustain this road, analyzes the benefits and problems likely to be encountered on it, and examines the experiences of those who are farther along on the journey to see what can be learned from them.

The Changing Financial Environment

While the cyclical downturn in global interest rates provided an important initial impetus for the resumption of private capital flows to developing countries in the 1990s, these flows have now entered a new phase, reflecting structural forces that are leading to progressive financial integration of developing countries into world financial markets. The two primary forces that are driving investor interest in developing countries are the search for higher returns and opportunities for risk diversification. Although these forces have always motivated investors, the responsiveness of private capital to cross-border opportunities has gained momentum as a result of internal and external financial deregulation in both industrial and developing countries and major advances in technology and financial instruments.

This process of financial integration is still unfolding. The pace of change will be especially rapid for developing countries, given their more insulated financial markets. Even in the more regulated economies, growing economic sophistication means that financial integration will increasingly not be a choice for governments to make. Markets are making the choice for them. As a result, the financial integration of developing countries is expected to deepen and broaden over the coming decade against a background of increasing global financial integration. As part of this process, gross private capital flows may be expected to rise substantially, with capital flowing not only from industrial to developing countries but also, increasingly, among developing countries themselves and from developing to industrial countries.

Given the continuing decline in investment risks, the higher expected rates of return in developing countries, and the underweighting of emerging markets in institutional portfolios, net private capital flows to developing countries in aggregate are likely to be sustained. The rate of growth, though, will inevitably diminish. There will undoubtedly also be considerable variation among countries, depending on the pace and depth of improvements in macroeconomic performance and creditworthiness. Such basic factors as domestic politics, the availability of resources, and the level of development that has been attained are bound to affect the flow of capital as well, so the process of financial integration can take many courses. In fact, in countries where economic and policy fundamentals are quite weak, the initial manifestation of growing financial integration may take the form of net outflows of private capital.

With changes in the international financial environment, there are likely to be considerable year-to-year fluctuations in private capital flows to developing countries, even in aggregate. These nations are, and will continue to be, highly susceptible to both domestic shocks and changes in the international environment, such as in global interest rates. Nevertheless, flows to developing countries in the aggregate are unlikely to suffer from major reversals as long as the probability of abrupt changes in the international environment remains low. The main risks of volatility and large reversals lie at the individual country level and stem from the interaction of domestic conditions and policies with international factors. And as markets become more discerning, contagion effects of the kind seen after the Mexican crisis are not likely to be long-lasting.

Winning and Losing in an Integrating Market

The experience of nations that have successfully managed financial integration suggests that the benefits of this process are likely to be especially large for developing countries. The direct advantages are twofold: these countries can tap the growing pool of global capital to raise investment, and they can diversify risks and smooth the growth of consumption and investment. The more important benefits of financial integration, however, are likely to be indirect. These include knowledge spillover effects, improved resource allocation, and strengthening of domestic financial markets. In addition, the increasing safety of financial operations in developing markets can support a shift to higher-return investments, with gains for both developing and industrial nations.

As the Mexican peso crisis has so forcefully demonstrated, however, these benefits are by no means assured. In fact, there are large potential costs if integration is not carefully managed. There are two reasons for this. First, although international investors are becoming more discerning, market discipline tends to be much more stringent when investor confidence is lost—a fact that can lead to large outflows—than during the buildup to a potential problem. Second, and more important, many developing countries lack the preconditions needed to ensure the sound use of private capital and manage risks of large reversals. Financial integration can magnify the effects of underlying distortions and institutional weaknesses in these countries and thereby multiply the costs of policy mistakes.

The challenge, therefore, for developing countries is how to exploit the growing investor interest in their markets and so to enter a virtuous cycle of productive financial integration rather than a vicious cycle of boom and bust. In a virtuous cycle, integration and access to external private capital lead to increased productive investment, momentum for policy and institutional reform, and greater resilience to potential instability. In contrast, when the necessary macroeconomic fundamentals are lacking, banking systems are weak, and domestic distortions are pervasive, countries may experience capital flight rather than capital inflows, or they may be unable to use inflows efficiently—with very high costs in terms of growth and instability.

The Lessons from Evolving Experience

This report provides perspectives on how developing countries can respond to these challenges, drawing on the evolving experience of the more rapidly integrating countries. Although the agenda confronting policymakers is necessarily broad and complex, ranging from macroeconomic issues to the so-called plumbing of markets, a number of strategic themes emerge from this study.

- *Given the growing trend toward financial integration, developing countries need to vigorously pursue policies that will enable them to benefit from global capital flows and avoid the associated dangers.*

There is broad consensus—based on lessons from country experience and the considerable literature on the sequencing of reforms—that the most important prerequisites for successful financial integration are a sound macroeconomic policy framework, in particular a strong fiscal position, the absence of large domestic price distortions (for example, those arising from import protection), a sound domestic banking system with an adequate supervisory and regulatory framework, and a well-functioning market infrastructure and regulatory framework for capital markets. All these are key elements of the broader policy agenda that developing countries need to adopt in any case, and financial integration only makes their pursuit more urgent, for several reasons.

First, progress on these prerequisites will help improve a country's creditworthiness and attractiveness to foreign investors. Second, these preconditions will encourage capital flows (such as foreign direct investment) based on long-term fundamentals rather than short-term returns. Third, attainment of these preconditions will ensure that capital inflows are well used, ultimately determining whether countries can reap the benefits from financial integration and avoid its risks. Fourth, the more robust a country is with regard to these preconditions, the greater will be its latitude in responding to surges and volatile flows.

- *How countries respond to the initial surge of capital inflows, which is often associated with the opening phase of integration, will largely deter-*

mine their success in dealing not only with overheating pressures but also with potential vulnerability.

Countries have typically used a combination of policies to respond to large surges of capital inflows. Capital controls, when combined with other policies, appear to have been at least partially successful in reducing the magnitude of inflows and altering their composition. Sterilized intervention has been the most widely used instrument and has been generally successful as an initial response in curbing the growth of base money and building up reserves. Most important, countries that have resisted real exchange rate appreciation by placing greater emphasis on fiscal tightening have tended on average to have lower current account deficits, a mix of absorption oriented toward investment, and faster economic growth.

The main lesson for macroeconomic policy from recent country experience is that a heavy reliance on fiscal policy, supported by sterilization and some nominal exchange rate flexibility—and in the more extreme cases by temporary taxes or controls on inflows—can be an effective response to overheating and can reduce the likelihood of vulnerability to large reversals of private capital flows. More generally, countries are likely to suffer a loss of investor confidence when the real exchange rate is perceived to be out of line, the government's debt obligations are large in relation to its earning capacity and external reserve position, fiscal adjustment is perceived to be politically or administratively infeasible, or the country's growth prospects are bleak.

- *There is much merit in curbing lending booms associated with capital inflows while addressing the underlying weaknesses in the banking system.*

The banking system plays a dominant role in the allocation of capital in a developing country, and the health of this system largely determines whether a country will be able to exploit the benefits of financial integration and avoid its pitfalls. In many developing countries, banking systems have only recently been deregulated, incentives for banks are distorted toward excessive risk taking, banks are poorly capitalized, and adequate prudential regulation and supervision capabilities have not yet been established.

Addressing the underlying weaknesses of the banking system becomes more urgent in a globally integrated environment because banks can increase lending more easily and incur greater risks. The standard tools for bank monitoring and supervision are rendered less effective. Institution building, removing incentive distortions (for instance, in the form of excessive insurance), and strengthening bank supervision capabilities are therefore crucial.

Since reforms of the banking system will take time to implement, it will probably be necessary to curb the lending booms associated with capital inflows by using macroeconomic policies, as well as more targeted restrictions, such as raising reserve requirements or adopting risk-weighted capital adequacy requirements. This will help alleviate overheating pressures resulting from surges in capital inflows and will reduce the vulnerability of the banking system.

- *Development of well-functioning capital markets will reduce risks of potential instability as well as attract the growing pool of portfolio investment.*

Investors are concerned with the unreliability of emerging markets in three main areas: market infrastructure (where the consequences include high transaction costs, frequent delays in settlement, and outright failed trades); protection of property rights, in particular those of minority shareholders; and disclosure of market and company information and control of abusive market practices. Unfortunately, there are no simple solutions to preparing capital markets for financial integration, which requires concerted action across a broad array of areas to improve market infrastructure and the regulatory framework.

International standards for market infrastructure provide excellent medium-term benchmarks for emerging markets, although they need to be tailored to fit individual country circumstances. The experience of the more advanced emerging markets, especially those in Asia, indicates that it is possible to improve market infrastructure in a relatively short period by leapfrogging to state-of-the-art systems. This experience, however, together with the not infrequent weaknesses in emerging market financial intermediaries, also suggests two cautionary notes. First, improving the speed of settlement and custody functions should not be achieved at the expense of reliability. Second, despite the importance of promoting competition among financial intermediaries, membership standards in key capital market institutions should be set high to bolster market safety and improve investor confidence.

A regulatory model based on disclosure and self-regulation is gaining wide acceptance in emerging markets because it has strong advantages over direct government regulation. But government regulation and oversight are still essential, and the state can play a crucial role in capital market development in partnership with the private sector, providing the basic legal structures, for example, and fostering vital market institutions. Given the weaknesses in the regulatory systems of many emerging markets and their susceptibility to "reputational risk," the tradeoff between market development and effective regulation required to develop and maintain market confidence is less pronounced than is sometimes thought.

Emerging markets should also promote the development of domestic institutional investors. By mobilizing significant amounts of resources, these investors can serve as a counterweight to foreign investors and thereby assuage fears of excessive foreign presence; they also reduce the vulnerability of domestic capital markets to foreign investor herding, and their presence may reassure foreign investors about the nation's respect for corporate governance and property rights.

All these policy and institutional initiatives to attract foreign investors and contain the potential negative impact of financial integration on capital market volatility will significantly help the development of domestic capital markets. In turn, there is increasing evidence that well-functioning capital markets make an important contribution to the overall growth process.

- *Developing countries need to build better shock absorbers and develop mechanisms to respond to instability because they will remain highly vulnerable to economic disturbances for some time.*

Growing financial integration may require three types of shock absorbers. First, the level of international reserves needs to be established in relation to the variation in the capital account, rather than in terms of months of imports, since the level of gross flows is higher following integration. For countries where investor confidence is less firm, there is a case for an even larger cushion of reserves. International reserves can also be buttressed with contingent lines of credit, as Argentina has done recently. Second, financial integration heightens the need for fiscal flexibility, which in turn will depend on the level of public debt, among other things. Third, there is strong merit in building up cushions in the banking system. Authorities should use periods of credit boom to increase bank capitalization and provisioning requirements as a way to promote sound banking practices and increase the resilience of banks.

Even with these shock absorbers, countries need to have well-delineated mechanisms that enable policymakers to deal with crises promptly and effectively. This is particularly important for the banking system, where delaying actions intended to contain a crisis will only increase its cost.

- *International cooperation between regulators and adequate disclosure of information at all levels are increasingly important to ensuring safe and efficient markets.*

The globalization of financial markets, along with new forms of investment and the growing prevalence of financial conglomerates, increases the number of channels that transmit systemic shocks across borders and sectors and the speed at which these shocks travel. At the same time it reduces the transparency of the marketplace.

Despite the worldwide integration of financial markets, the authority of regulators has remained mainly national in scope. In a global marketplace, it is difficult to assess the risk exposure of financial intermediaries, and such complex operations as derivatives trading make risk evaluation even more uncertain. To address these problems, regulatory authorities from industrial countries are increasingly cooperating and coordinating with one another. In addition, to reinforce market discipline, these regulators are emphasizing the supervision of the quality of risk management by financial firms (rather than the position of a firm at a particular moment in time) and improved disclosure practices.

In this new environment, reducing information asymmetries across borders will have a significant payoff for emerging markets. At the macroeconomic level, more accurate and timely disclosure of country information would decrease the likelihood of cross-country contagion of financial shocks. Adequate disclosure of the risk profile and financial status of financial intermediaries would increase the effectiveness of market discipline and facilitate supervision by regulators. And for regulators, there will be a large payoff in coordination and information-sharing agreements, with both industrial and other emerging markets, in particular with those likely to share financial institutions and sources of financial shocks.

CHAPTER 1

The Main Findings

THERE CAN BE NO DOUBT THAT DEVELOPING countries have entered a new age of globalized private capital. Consider these facts:

- Net private capital flows to developing countries exceeded $240 billion in 1996 ($265 billion if the Republic of Korea is included), nearly six times times greater than they were at the start of the decade, and almost four times more than the peak reached during the 1978–82 commercial bank lending boom (figure 1.1).[1]
- Private capital flows now dwarf official flows in terms of relative importance. They are now five times the size of official flows. This is remarkable, since only five years ago official flows to developing countries were larger than private flows.
- Developing countries are now a much more important destination for global private capital. Their share of global FDI flows is now almost 40 percent, compared with 15 percent in 1990, and their share of global portfolio equity flows is now almost 30 percent, compared with around 2 percent before the start of the decade.
- The importance of private flows has also increased markedly in the economies of developing countries, from 4.1 percent of domestic investment in 1990 to almost 20 percent in 1996.
- There has been a remarkable broadening in the composition of private capital flows (figure 1.2). Whereas traditional commercial bank lending used to account for more than 65 percent of all private flows, FDI has now emerged as the most important component of private capital flows, and starting from a negligible level

Figure 1.1 Private Capital Flows to Developing Countries, 1975–96
(net long-term international private capital flows)

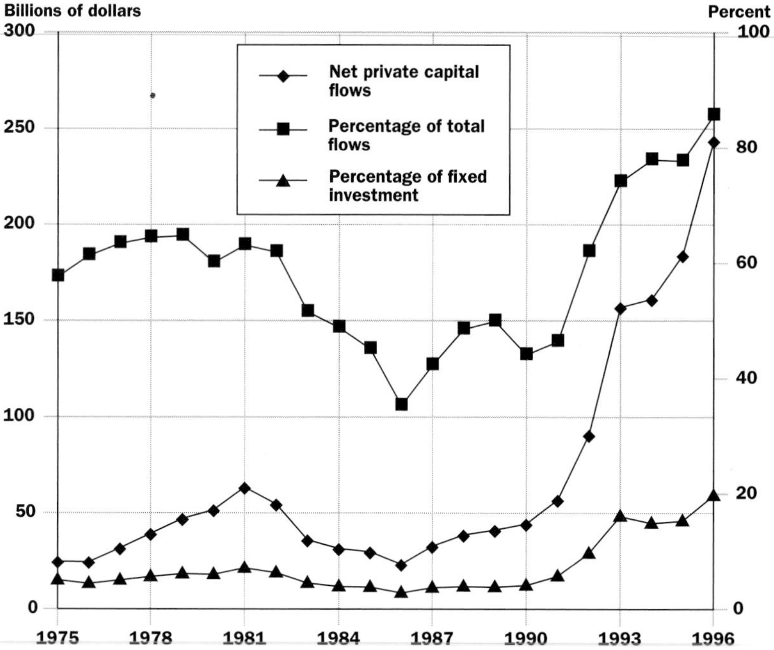

Source: World Bank data.

Private capital flows to developing countries have surged during the 1990s.

in 1989, portfolio flows—both bonds and equities—have increased sharply so that they now account for more than a third of total private capital flows.

- The flow of private capital has also shifted on the recipient side away from governments to the private sector. Borrowing by the public sector now accounts for less than a fifth of total private flows, so that the bulk of these flows to developing countries is passing through market channels.
- Private capital flows to developing countries have proved to be surprisingly resilient. Despite the increases in U.S. interest rates in 1994 and the Mexican crisis in 1995, private flows increased a further 55 percent during the past three years.

Just as private capital is flowing into developing economies, the financial markets that channel this tide of investment are becoming increasingly integrated. More than a century ago, the great scholar and

Figure 1.2 Composition of Net Private Capital Flows to Developing Countries, 1980–82 and 1995–96

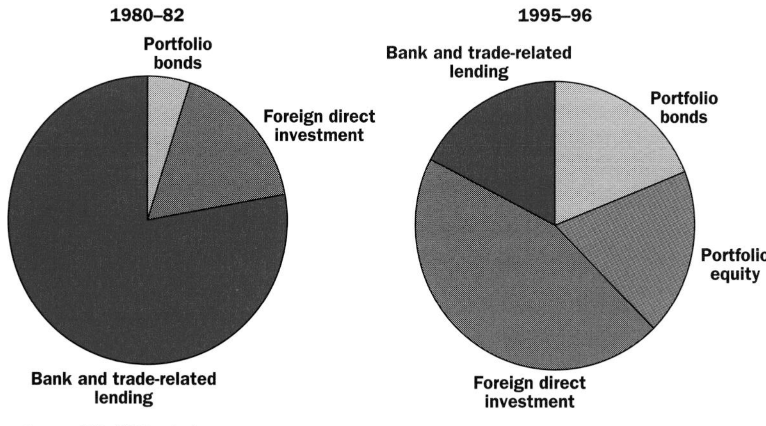

Source: World Bank data.

As FDI and portfolio flows have grown, bank and trade-related lending have declined in relative importance.

practitioner of finance Walter Bagehot noted the beginnings of this trend toward integration, observing that "the same instruments which diffused capital through a nation are gradually diffusing it among nations." Prescient, he went on to warn that while "the effect of this will be in the end much to simplify the problems of international trade . . . for the present, as is commonly the case with incipient causes whose effect is incomplete, it complicates all it touches" (Bagehot 1880, p. 71). The current wave of financial integration, however, differs from its counterpart of the late nineteenth century in at least three respects: its geographic scope, the extent and depth of integration, and the speed with which markets can now react.

Developing countries vary considerably in the rate at which they are integrating with global financial markets as well as in the amounts of private capital they have attracted. Only a dozen countries—all of which are rapidly integrating with international financial markets—accounted for about 80 percent of net private flows to developing nations during 1990–95, and less than a score accounted for 95 percent (figure 1.3). In these countries, private capital flows have been very large in relation to the size of their domestic economies, constituting as much as 5 percent of gross national product (GNP) in some surge years.

In contrast, most developing countries are just starting the process of financial integration and have so far received much smaller amounts of private capital. In fact, 140 of the 166 developing nations account for

Figure 1.3 Concentration of Private Capital Flows, Selected Developing Countries, 1990–95
(net long-term international private capital flows)

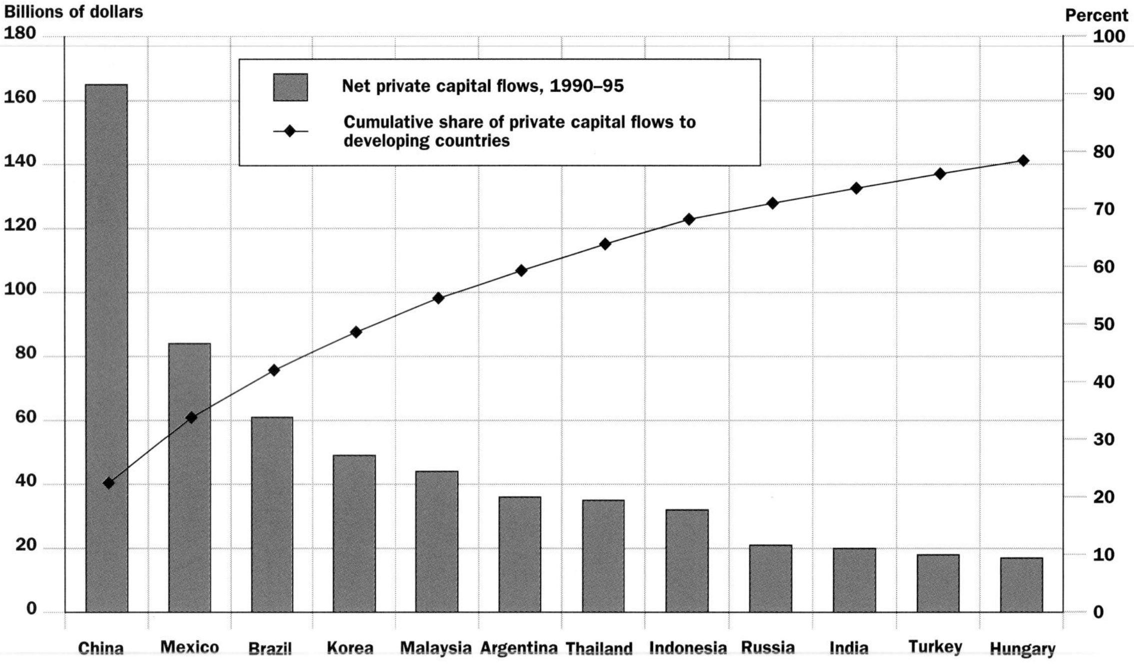

Source: World Bank data.

A dozen countries accounted for about 80 percent of net international private capital flows.

less than 5 percent of private capital flows to such countries. These differences, however, become less stark when scaled by GNP and when private transfers and other unrecorded private flows are taken into account (figure 1.4). In the case of the Middle East and North Africa and South Asia, such flows are more important than recorded private international capital flows, suggesting that integration is proceeding through several channels.

The chapter briefly describes the setting in which the process of financial integration takes place, and chapter 2 examines this background in greater detail. In the next section, we outline the benefits of financial integration, a topic covered more thoroughly in chapter 3, as well as the risks and potential costs of integration. The last part of this chapter explores the lessons from developing nations' recent experience with global financial flows and provides recommendations for sound policies and institutions, summarizing the material covered in depth in chapters 4 through 6.

Figure 1.4 Composition of Net Overall Private Capital Flows by Region

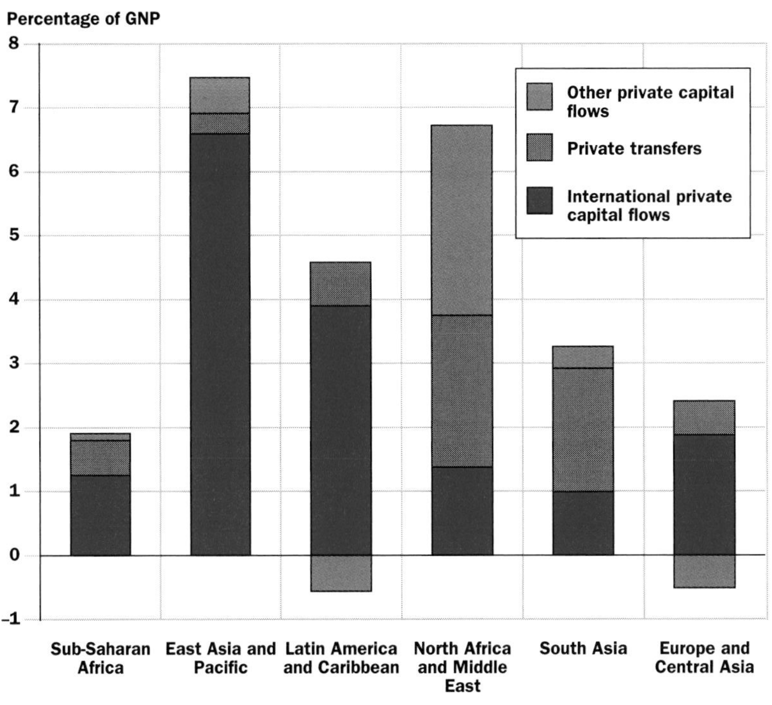

Source: IMF, *International Financial Statistics* data base; World Bank data.

But when economic size and all types of private flows are taken into account, private capital does not flow as disproportionately to a few developing countries.

A New Age of Global Capital

TWO PRIMARY FORCES ARE DRIVING INVESTOR INTEREST IN developing countries and leading to their increased integration: the search for higher returns and the opportunity for risk diversification. Although these underlying forces have always motivated investors, the responsiveness of private capital to cross-border opportunities has gained new momentum as a result of internal and external financial deregulation in both industrial and developing countries and major advances in technology and financial instruments. Figure 2.1 in chapter 2 summarizes the process under way.

In industrial countries two key developments have increased the responsiveness of private capital to cross-border investment opportunities. First, competition and rising costs in domestic markets, along with falling transport and communications costs, have encouraged firms to look for opportunities to increase efficiency by producing abroad. This is leading to the progressive globalization of production and to the growth of "efficiency-seeking" FDI flows. Second, financial markets have been transformed over a span of two decades from relatively insulated and regulated national markets toward a more globally integrated market. This has been brought about by a mutually reinforcing process of advances in communications, information, and financial instruments, and by progressive internal and external deregulation of financial markets. An important facet of this globalization of capital markets has been the growing importance of *institutional investors who are both willing and able to invest internationally.* For example, total assets of pension funds at the global level are estimated to have increased from $4.3 trillion in 1989 to $7 trillion in 1994, while, at the same time, the share of nondomestic investment in their portfolios rose from around 7 percent in 1989 to 11 percent in 1994. Together, these two factors have resulted in an increase in total international investments by pension funds from $302 billion in 1989 to $790 billion in 1994.

In developing countries, the environment is also changing rapidly. Since the mid-1980s, several countries have embarked on structural reform programs and increased openness of their markets, through the progressive lowering of barriers to trade and foreign investment, the liberalization of domestic financial markets and removal of restrictions on capital movements, and the implementation of privatization programs. There have also been major improvements in fiscal performance and the sustainability of external debt.

Although the perceived risks of investing in emerging markets remain relatively high, the more stable macroeconomic environment, growth in earnings capacity (both output and exports), and a reduction in the stock of debt in many countries (following the implementation of the Brady Plan) are leading to a decline in such risks and an increase in the expected rates of return in the major recipient countries.[2]

The second force behind the structural trend in private capital flows is investors' desire to diversify portfolio risks. Investors can benefit from holding emerging market equities because returns in emerging markets tend to exhibit low correlations with industrial country returns—that is, they tend not to move in tandem with those of industrial countries. By holding an asset whose returns are not correlated with the returns of another asset, investors can raise the overall return on their portfolios without a commensurate increasing in risk (variance).

Developing countries have begun to offer investors significant opportunities for risk diversification that arise from the low correlation between rates of return in emerging markets and industrial countries. This opportunity for portfolio diversification in emerging markets is a relatively recent phenomenon. The combined market capitalization of the 18 major developing countries that constituted the International Finance Corporation (IFC) Emerging Markets Index (IFCI) in 1996 was, at $1.4 trillion, 14 times higher than it was in 1985. Although still much lower than that of industrial countries as a ratio of gross domestic product (GDP), the average market capitalization of these countries rose from 7 to 40 percent of GDP during the period. Turnover ratios reveal the same trends, increasing approximately twofold between 1985 and 1994. As a result of this growth, financial markets in developing countries are now beginning to provide foreign investors with significant opportunities to diversify into investments that have good prospective returns and low correlations with their investments in industrial country markets.

Growing Investments and Financial Integration

As a result of these changes, developing countries have seen a strong surge in private capital flows of all kinds. FDI has responded most vigorously to the improving economic environment in developing countries. The driving factor for FDI has been the sustained improvement in domestic economic fundamentals. The nature of the FDI flows has also changed. In the 1970s and early 1980s, resource extraction and import substitution were the primary motives for FDI in developing countries. In contrast, a high proportion of FDI flows now going to developing countries can be characterized as being efficiency seeking, associated with the globalization of production. Commercial bank lending, which accounted for the bulk of private flows in the late 1970s and early 1980s, has also made a strong comeback.

But most striking has been the growth of portfolio investment flows. Whereas developing countries attracted barely any portfolio flows a decade ago, in the past five years they have received almost 30 percent of all the equity capital moving across national borders worldwide. Given its growing importance as a channel of financial integration, we focus primarily on portfolio investment in the analysis of international capital flows.

The driving force behind the portfolio flows of the 1990s has been institutional investors. The initial impetus for the globalization of institutional investment was probably the cyclical decline in global interest rates. But as improvements in economic fundamentals and creditworthiness began to take hold, and as the new investors became more familiar with emerging markets, the emphasis has shifted to long-term rates of return and opportunities for portfolio risk diversification. As a result, institutional investors have become an increasingly important segment of the investor base in emerging markets and their influence seems certain to grow.

Among institutional investors, mutual funds led the surge in investments in emerging market equities. In 1986 there were 19 emerging market country funds and 9 regional or global emerging market funds. By 1995 there were over 500 country funds and nearly 800 regional and global funds. The combined assets of all closed- and open-end emerging market funds increased from $1.9 billion in 1986 to $10.3 billion in 1989 to $132 billion at the middle of 1996. International and global funds are also allocating increasing proportions of their portfolios to emerging markets, leading to a large increase in the total exposure of mutual funds to these markets.

These trends have meant that emerging markets are accounting for a rising proportion of international investment by mutual funds—more than 30 percent of new international investments by U.S. mutual funds went to emerging markets during 1990–94. Since international investment itself has been rising, the share of emerging market assets in total mutual fund assets has risen quite sharply. The exposure of U.S. open-end mutual funds to emerging markets rose from just $1.5 billion in 1990 to $35 billion in 1995, or 14 percent of international exposure (figure 2.9, chapter 2).

Pension funds have followed suit, investing through mutual funds or directly on their own account. Even though they began to invest in emerging markets more recently, allocations of U.S. pension funds to emerging markets are now comparable with those of mutual funds, with some of the bigger pension funds investing considerably larger proportions (figure 2.11, chapter 2). Indeed, U.S. pension fund investments in emerging markets, including investments made on their behalf by mutual funds, have been an important factor in propping up investment flows to emerging markets during 1994 and 1995. As with mutual funds, most pension fund investments in emerging markets are in the form of portfolio equities.

The rapid growth and changing composition of private capital flows reflect the increasing financial integration of developing countries with international financial markets. In the 1980s, private sector lending was mostly in the form of bank lending to sovereign governments. The bulk of private capital flows now is to the private sector and is increasingly taking place through channels that link markets for capital in developing countries with their international counterparts.

Since direct measures of financial integration for developing countries are not available, we have constructed an indirect measure, using three separate elements: a country's access to international financial markets, its ability to attract gross financing, and the breadth of access to financial markets (box 1.1).[3] These indexes are then used to evaluate

Box 1.1 Measuring Financial Integration

TO ASSESS THE DEGREE TO WHICH COUNTRIES are financially integrated, we have used several measures to construct an overall index of integration. We computed the index for the periods 1985–87 and 1992–94 in order to evaluate the degree of integration that has taken place since the mid-1980s.

The first measure looks at a country's access to international financial markets. This is provided by the country risk ratings of the Institutional Investor Survey. Ratings of less than 20 are categorized as low, ratings of greater than 50 as high, and ratings in between as medium.

The second measure looks at a country's ability to attract private external financing computing the ratio of private capital flows to GDP. Since financial integration implies the *linking of markets*, however, not all flows were weighted equally in this measure. Thus, a country receiving private flows primarily in the form of FDI is likely to be less integrated with world financial markets than is a country that receives flows in the form of portfolio and commercial bank lending. Portfolio flows were therefore given a weight of 5, bank flows a weight of 3, and FDI a weight of 1. Using these multipliers, countries whose flows amount to less than 10 percent of GDP were categorized as low, countries whose flows exceed 20 percent were considered high, and countries in between were categorized as medium.

The third measure looks at the level of diversification of a country's financing, based on the composition of flows. The composition matters because different components of flows have different effects on financial integration: FDI benefits local suppliers, who may turn to foreign equity investors to obtain financing for expansion; banking inflows, which lead to a deepening of the financial system, may enhance the liquidity of stock markets and thus increase the latter's attractiveness to foreign investors; and so forth. A significant participation in all three forms of flows is desirable for balanced integration. Countries receiving a minimum of 5 percent of total flows for each type of flow were categorized as high. Countries that received a minimum of 5 percent in two types of flows were categorized as medium, and the remaining countries were categorized as low.

These measures were then converted to an overall index of financial integration. As box table 1.1 shows, developing countries as a group have become more integrated since the mid-1980s. The number of countries in the *relatively* highly integrated category has increased sizably, as has the number of countries in the medium category.

A similar conclusion is suggested by the declining usage of convertibility restrictions and multiple ex-

(Box continues on the following page.)

Box Table 1.1 Change in Degree of Financial Integration

1985–87				*1992–94*			
Korea	*High*	Suriname	Low	*Thailand*	*High*	Tunisia	Medium –
Malaysia	*High*	Togo	Low	*Turkey*	*High*	Ecuador	Medium –
Thailand	Medium +	Tanzania	Low	*Brazil*	*High*	Kenya	Medium –
Cameroon	Medium +	Swaziland	Low	*Argentina*	*High*	Cameroon	Medium –
India	Medium	South Africa	Low	*Korea*	*High*	Egypt	Medium –
Colombia	Medium	Peru	Low	*Indonesia*	*High*	Togo	Low
Niger	Medium	Paraguay	Low	*Malaysia*	*High*	Mauritania	Low
Kenya	Medium	Sierra Leone	Low	*Mexico*	*High*	Myanmar	Low
Papua New		Senegal	Low	*Hungary*	*High*	Nicaragua	Low
Guinea	Medium	Dominican Rep.	Low	*Ghana*	*High*	Tanzania	Low
Indonesia	Medium	Costa Rica	Low	*Chile*	*High*	Senegal	Low
Mexico	Medium	Congo	Low	*Pakistan*	*High*	Sierra Leone	Low
Egypt	Medium	Ghana	Low	*Philippines*	*High*	Venezuela	Low
Chile	Medium	Gabon	Low	Mauritius	Medium +	Niger	Low
Sri Lanka	Medium –	El Salvador	Low	Panama	Medium +	Nigeria	Low
Philippines	Medium –	China	Low	Colombia	Medium +	Zambia	Low
Côte d'Ivoire	Medium –	Benin	Low	Jamaica	Medium +	Guatemala	Low
Ecuador	Medium –	Bangladesh	Low	India	Medium +	Burkina Faso	Low
Mauritius	Medium –	Algeria	Low	Peru	Medium	Guyana	Low
Morocco	Medium –	Burkina Faso	Low	Papua New		Guinea-Bissau	Low
Pakistan	Medium –	Brazil	Low	Guinea	Medium	Gabon	Low
Nigeria	Medium –	Bolivia	Low	Morocco	Medium	Costa Rica	Low
Turkey	Medium –	Lesotho	Low	Zimbabwe	Medium	Congo	Low
Tunisia	Medium –	Jamaica	Low	Côte d'Ivoire	Medium	El Salvador	Low
Uruguay	Medium –	Madagascar	Low	Uruguay	Medium	Dominican Rep.	Low
Zimbabwe	Medium –	Mauritania	Low	China	Medium	Haiti	Low
Argentina	Medium –	Mali	Low	Sri Lanka	Medium –	Madagascar	Low
Trinidad and		Hungary	Low	Suriname	Medium –	Lesotho	Low
Tobago	Low	Guyana	Low	Swaziland	Medium –	Mali	Low
Panama	Low	Guinea-Bissau	Low	Honduras	Medium –	Algeria	Low
Zambia	Low	Guatemala	Low	Paraguay	Medium –	Bangladesh	Low
Nicaragua	Low	Honduras	Low	South Africa	Medium –	Bolivia	Low
Venezuela	Low	Haiti	Low	Trinidad and		Benin	Low
Myanmar	Low			Tobago	Medium –		

change rates. While in 1985 some 60 percent of International Monetary Fund (IMF) members imposed restrictions on current account transactions, by 1995 less than a third of members employed such restrictions. In the same period, the use of capital account restrictions decreased from 80 to 70 percent of IMF members, and the use of multiple exchange rates declined from 30 to 16 percent of members.

the degree of financial integration of various countries and changes that have taken place between the two periods 1985–87 and 1992–94.

The index of financial integration in box 1.1 provides only a broad indication of the degree and change in financial integration. Nevertheless, two main conclusions emerge from the results:

- Developing countries as a group have become more integrated since the mid-1980s. The number of countries that are classified as highly integrated increased from 2 in 1985–87 to 13 in 1992–94, whereas the number of countries classified as moderately integrated increased from 24 to 26.
- However, most developing countries are still in the very early stages of financial integration.

The Prospects for Private Capital Flows

The structural changes underlying capital flows to developing countries are continuing to unfold at both the domestic and the international levels, and there are several reasons to believe that they will spur growing financial integration and the expansion of international capital movements in the years ahead:

- Structural reforms taking place in developing countries are, in some cases, just beginning to produce positive results.
- Technological change and financial innovation will continue to reduce transaction costs and make distant markets more accessible.
- Financial deregulation and competitive pressures will lead to greater emphasis on maximizing returns and diversifying risks.
- Demographic shifts are becoming a major factor behind the long-term movement of capital from the industrial to the developing world.

Although it is difficult to speculate on the course of future innovation and technological change, competitive pressures and increasing integration will probably continue to reduce transaction costs and make distant markets more accessible to small as well as large investors. Such innovations will make policy-induced barriers less effective, spurring even more deregulation and competition. The pace of change will be particularly rapid for developing countries, given their nascent financial systems.

Developing country markets are indeed becoming more open and attractive to foreign investors as these nations implement macro- and microeconomic policy reforms. These reforms, in turn, are likely to increase the productivity of investment. On the expectation that developing countries will continue to strengthen their policies and that the external environment will remain favorable, developing countries are likely to grow at almost double the rate of industrial countries, providing significant opportunities for investors (figure 2.12, chapter 2).

As financial deregulation gathers speed worldwide, a far larger universe of investors will seek to diversify their portfolios by investing in emerging markets. Despite the recent increases, the share of emerging markets in the portfolios of institutional investors remains small—well below their share in world market capitalization. Even in the United States, where institutional investors have increased their exposure to emerging markets more rapidly, mutual funds and pension funds are estimated to hold an average of only 2 percent of their portfolios in emerging markets. For most other industrial countries these shares are much smaller. Given that the share of emerging markets in world market capitalization is currently around 10 percent and is expected to rise, the scope for benefits from further portfolio diversification is substantial.

As a hypothetical illustration, given the current correlations of returns between emerging markets and an international portfolio, investors could simultaneously increase expected rates of return and reduce the risks (variance) in their overall portfolio by increasing their holdings of emerging market assets up to 41 percent of their international holdings—compared with their current allocations of around 12 to 14 percent (figure 2.4, chapter 2). Although such a large reallocation represents an upper bound of possible gains and is not even feasible under present market conditions, it nonetheless illustrates the potential for further risk diversification.[4]

The demographic shift under way in industrial countries is an important new factor that will provide further impetus to these underlying trends. Industrial countries now have a pronounced bulge in their demographic structures, reflecting the aging of the baby boom generation and declining birthrates (figure 2.13, chapter 2). This will lead to a steady rise in the proportion of elderly to active population in all industrial countries, although the pace of this increase is most pronounced in Japan. This is in sharp contrast to the situation in developing countries, whose clearly pyramidal structure reflects a much younger population.

There are three broad implications of this difference in demographic patterns. First, the aging of populations in industrial countries could lead to an increase in savings in the short to medium term. Second, aging and the associated slowing of labor force growth are likely, other things being equal, to exert downward pressure on the rate of return to capital relative to that of labor in industrial countries.[5] Given the demographic structure prevalent in developing countries, the reverse can be expected there. Thus, differences in demographics are likely to reinforce the differentials in the expected rates of return to capital between industrial and developing countries. Both these factors should provide a stimulus for capital to flow to emerging markets. Third, and perhaps most important in terms of its impact, the aging of population in industrial countries is leading to pressures for pension reform.

The growing recognition of the burden that pension obligations under the current system will place on fiscal positions in industrial countries and the need to address the problem during the next 10 to 15 years is beginning to spur pressures to reform the existing pension systems. In particular there are pressures to (a) move away from pay-as-you-go (PAYG) systems and toward more funded systems; (b) privatize pension schemes, through an increasing reliance on private employer and individual schemes—the so-called second and third pillars of old age security (World Bank 1994)—as well as through greater private sector management of public pension schemes; and (c) deregulate the investment allocations of pension funds to enable them to earn higher returns on their investments. All three factors are likely to result in greater response to investment opportunities in emerging markets.

The United Kingdom and the United States have been at the forefront of these shifts, but even in the United States, prospective changes in Social Security and corporate pension plans could have a large impact on asset allocation. Japan and most of continental Europe are also beginning to establish market-oriented schemes. For instance, in Japan, the government has begun over the past three years to implement a series of reforms that is expected to lead to greater international diversification and greater demand for emerging market equities.

Although the pace of change in individual countries is uncertain, the direction is clear. Global pension assets are likely to rise substantially and with a growing trend toward international diversification. Holdings of international equities, in particular, are expected to increase from their very low levels in most countries (figure 2.15, chapter 2).

Pension funds, therefore, are likely to be a major force in the demand for portfolio equities from developing countries. Today pension funds hold about $70 billion of emerging market assets. This amount could rise very considerably over the next decade.

What do these trends imply for future flows to and financial integration of emerging markets?

- First, financial integration of developing countries is bound to deepen and broaden over the coming decade. Indeed, given the changes that are taking place at the international level, the progressive financial integration of developing countries appears to be inevitable.
- Gross private capital flows to developing countries will rise substantially, with capital flowing not only from industrial to developing countries but, increasingly, among developing countries themselves, and from developing to industrial countries.
- There is likely to be considerable variation among countries, depending on the pace and depth of improvements in macroeconomic performance and creditworthiness. Indeed, in countries where economic and policy fundamentals are very weak, an initial manifestation of growing financial integration may take the form of net outflows of private capital.
- Fourth, given the growing importance of institutional investors, a larger proportion of these flows than in the past will be in the form of portfolio flows—especially equities.

Benefits and Risks of Financial Integration

LIKE FREE TRADE, FINANCIAL INTEGRATION HOLDS SUBSTANTIAL benefits for individual countries and for the global economy as a whole. And as in the case of trade, the gains for developing countries are disproportionately large. Large, too, are the risks and potential costs that accompany financial integration.

The Gains from Financial Integration

The benefits of financial integration arise in two main ways. First, financial integration can boost growth, by raising the level of investment and by improving the returns on investment, through knowledge spillover and market efficiency effects. Second, integration allows individuals to insure themselves against adverse developments in their home economies by diversifying their assets and tapping global markets to smooth temporary declines in income. These effects are summarized below and are considered in detail in chapter 3.

Financial integration can boost investment in developing countries by severing the link between local savings and investment. The potential gains from higher investment vary from country to country depending on the relative profitability of investment opportunities and on the difference between the domestic and the world cost of capital before integration. A notional indication of the magnitude of these gains can be seen from the following illustration. If capital inflows reach 3 to 4 percent of GDP (a typical figure for current large capital importers), the growth rate, based on typical capital shares and capital output ratios, would increase by about half a percentage point (Reisen forthcoming). This temporary growth effect is by no means negligible—an increase in the growth rate from 1.5 to 2 percent reduces the period required for output to double by 12 years—yet it is dwarfed by the range of growth rates among developing economies, showing that the successful tapping of foreign capital markets is only one of many ingredients in a successful growth strategy.

Integration may also boost growth by shifting the investment mix toward projects with higher expected returns because of the improved ability to diversify the higher risks typically entailed in higher-return projects. The quantitative significance of a switch to higher-return investments in the wake of integration depends on three factors: the technological lag of a particular country, risk tolerance on the part of the country, and the speed with which existing capital can be reallocated. Simulation studies (Obstfeld 1992) suggest that the gains are very large. The size of gains reflects the magic of compound interest: even small increases in growth have first-order-level effects over time. For the economies lagging farthest behind current best practice, the gains comprise both catch-up and the global efficiency gain, while the leading economies benefit from only the latter change. Yet even for these relatively advanced economies the benefits of higher output and hence consumption growth rates are very significant: a well-managed integration is a win-win situation.

A third and more immediate channel through which financial integration can raise growth is through FDI. There is empirical evidence to suggest that a dollar of FDI raises the sum of domestic and foreign investment by more than a dollar; thus FDI complements rather than substitutes for domestic investment. More important, cross-country evidence suggest that FDI is substantially more efficient than domestic investment. Overall, the growth benefits come primarily through this latter channel, the quality rather than the quantity of investment.

Integration enhances the depth and efficiency of the domestic financial system, with important positive feedback to investment and growth. Greater openness of the banking system can yield significant efficiency gains, even for industrial countries. And the gains from knowledge spillovers, deepening, enhanced competition, and the stimulus given to improvements in the institutional and supervisory framework are likely to be much greater for developing countries.

Even more than in banking, foreign investment has been a driving force of change in the development of capital markets in developing countries. Most directly, financial integration enhances the role of capital markets through its effects on depth and liquidity. This positive association can be clearly seen in figure 3.2, chapter 3, which shows that countries that have received the largest portfolio inflows have experienced the largest increase in market capitalization. The scope for further improvements in the efficiency and functioning of capital markets in many emerging markets is very large. Bid-offer spreads are much higher in developing countries than in industrial countries, suggesting that these indirect benefits associated with financial integration could go substantially farther in reducing the cost of capital to firms and reducing risks to investors.

In addition to these spillover effects on the banking system and capital markets, integration can promote better macroeconomic policies. Although integration increases the costs of policy mistakes in the short term, and increases the constraints on the conduct of macroeconomic policy, the market discipline that comes with integration can be a powerful force in promoting prudent and stable macroeconomic policies, with large benefits over the longer term. For instance, Indonesia's decision to open its capital account almost three decades ago has been an important element underpinning its track record of prudent and responsive macroeconomic policies.

Apart from boosting growth through these direct and indirect channels, the increased opportunities for risk diversification with integration can bring gains in the form of higher and less variable consumption. Integration reduces the volatility of consumption by allowing a better diversification of portfolios and by permitting international borrowing and lending to offset temporary income movements. Integration can also boost consumption by permitting a shift toward a portfolio with higher expected returns—the mirror image of the shift toward investment projects with higher expected returns. The empirical evidence suggests that while there is substantial scope for risk diversification, the primary gains do not come through the reduction of risk per se, but rather through the ability to raise average portfolio returns (and hence consumption growth rates) as a consequence of diversification.

The Risks of Financial Integration

Despite the large potential benefits, there is widespread concern among policymakers that growing financial integration and increased reliance on private capital flows might render emerging markets more susceptible to volatility—including large reversals in capital flows. The decline in portfolio flows, following the interest rate increases in early 1994 and the Mexican peso crisis, was seen as a stark reminder of the potential for such volatility.

Such fears are not without foundation, especially for countries with weak fiscal policies, badly managed or overprotected banking systems, and highly distorted domestic markets. International capital flows can act like a magnifying glass on the domestic economy, multiplying the benefits of well-structured reform programs but also increasing the costs of poor economic fundamentals and policies that are unsound.

At the aggregate level, private capital flows to developing countries are less likely to suffer from major reversals. As noted, private capital flows to developing countries have demonstrated a remarkable degree of resilience. Portfolio flows have also shown an impressive recovery from the aftershocks of the Mexican crisis. Despite the large drop in the first half of 1995, portfolio flows recorded only a small decline for the year as a whole, and a significant increase in 1996 to levels that exceed the peak reached in 1993.

The sustained increases in private capital flows in the face of recent shocks suggests that markets have entered a more mature phase (see World Bank 1997). Governments have demonstrated an awareness of and ability to respond promptly and aggressively to changes in market conditions. And markets have become more able to discriminate among countries on the basis of their underlying fundamentals. This does not mean that there will not be year-to-year fluctuations in private flows in response to changes in international financial conditions. But private flows to developing countries in the aggregate are less likely to suffer from a widespread or prolonged decline of the kind seen after the debt crisis.

However, at the individual country level, volatility of flows and potential vulnerability to reversals remain a serious concern. There are three separate elements of this concern: large surges in the inflow of capital in the early stages of integration; susceptibility to large reversals, as recently experienced by Mexico; and, more generally, the increase in volatility as a country becomes integrated.

Surges. Virtually all major recipients of private capital flows saw a surge in private capital flows during the 1990s, although there has been considerable variation among countries in the timing, duration and magnitude of the surge (table 1.1). These surges have been extremely large in relation to the size of the economies; more than half of the countries shown in table 1.1 received annual inflows averaging more than 4 percent of GDP. Chile, Malaysia, Thailand, and until 1994, Mexico, experienced the earliest, and cumulatively among the largest, surges of private capital flows in the 1990s. At the other end, South Asian countries typically experienced the surge after 1992—generally in a smaller form. Eastern Europe also experienced the surge after 1992, but the magnitude of the inflows has been very large, even compared with flows to the largest recipients in Latin America and East Asia. While low international interest rates were a common factor underpinning the surge in private capital to developing countries during 1990–93, discrete changes in perceptions of creditworthiness and the resulting stock adjustment in international portfolios mean that surges in private capital are a likely feature of the early stages of integration.

Reversals. With the growing importance of private capital flows has come the threat of major reversals of these flows. A number of countries have seen such reversals (figure 1.5). Turkey and Venezuela were the first to experience major capital flow reversals in the 1990s, in both cases following a loss of investor confidence in government policies. The reversal of private capital flows in the case of Mexico was notable in two respects: its size and its triggering of reversals in several other countries, most markedly in Argentina and Brazil. These

Table 1.1 Net Private Capital Inflows to 20 Developing Countries, 1990s
(net long-term international private capital as a percentage of GDP)

Country	*Inflow episode*[a]	*Cumulative inflows/GDP at end of episode*	*Maximum annual inflow*
Argentina	1991–94	9.7	3.8
Brazil	1992–95	9.4	4.8
Chile	1989–95	25.8	8.6
Colombia	1992–95	16.2	6.2
Hungary	1993–95	41.5	18.4
India	1992–95	6.4	2.7
Indonesia	1990–95	8.3	3.6
Korea	1991–95	9.3	3.5
Malaysia	1989–95	45.8	23.2
Mexico	1989–94	27.1	8.5
Morocco	1990–95	18.3	5.0
Pakistan	1992–95	13.0	4.9
Peru	1990–95	30.4	10.8
Philippines	1989–95	23.1	7.9
Poland	1992–95	22.3	12.0
Sri Lanka	1991–95	22.6	8.2
Thailand	1988–95	51.5	12.3
Tunisia	1992–95	17.6	7.1
Turkey	1992–93	5.7	4.1
Venezuela	1992–93	5.4	3.3

a. The period during which the country experienced a significant surge in net private capital inflows.

Source: World Bank data; IMF, *World Economic Outlook* data base; IMF, *International Financial Statistics* data base.

episodes of capital flow reversals in the 1990s were typically not larger in absolute magnitude, or in relation to GNP, than similar episodes during the debt crisis. What is common to most of these reversals (except for Malaysia during 1993–94, where it was attributable to the authorities' attempts to restrain very large inflows) is that they were triggered by a lack of confidence in domestic macroeconomic policies.

Volatility and herding. Apart from the vulnerability to major reversals, countries have been concerned about increased volatility associated with private capital flows, especially portfolio flows. Integration can give rise to greater volatility in two ways: first, it can expose economies to new sources of shocks in the international economy, and second, it can magnify the effects of domestic shocks (figure 1.6). These

Figure 1.5 Large Reversals in Net Private Capital Flows
(short-term and long-term international flows)

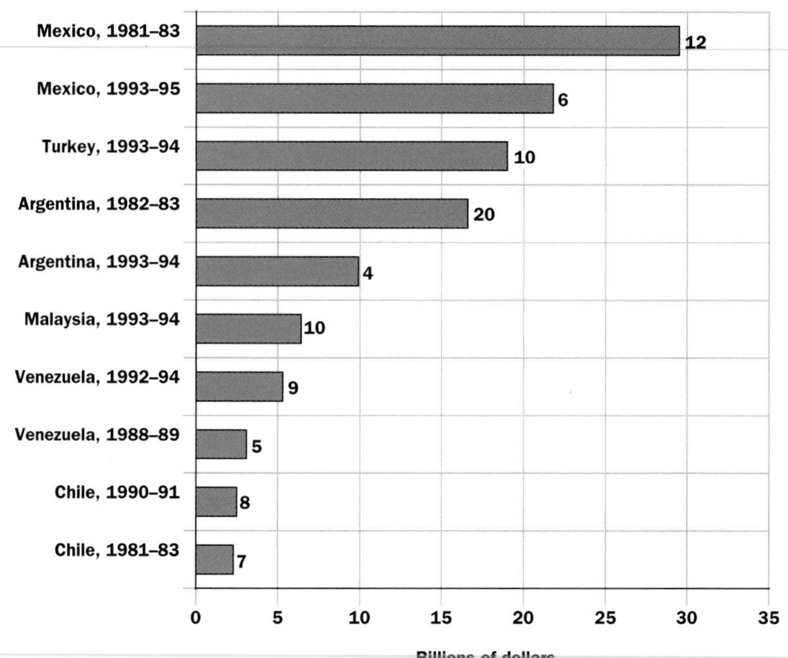

Several developing countries have experienced major reversals of private capital flows.

Note: The figure to the right of each bar indicates the magnitude of the reversal as a percentage of GDP.
Source: IMF, *International Financial Statistics* data base; World Bank data.

concerns become all the more important because the degree of policy autonomy declines with growing financial integration.

The main international sources of volatility are changes in asset returns (interest rates and stock market returns) and potential investor herding and contagion effects. Shifts in asset returns affect capital flows by altering the fundamentals, whereas investor herding and contagion effects may change investment in a country even if fundamentals are unchanged. We find that although portfolio flows to emerging markets remain sensitive to changes in international interest rates, there has been some decline in the degree of sensitivity as country-specific factors have become more important. There is also some evidence to suggest that emerging markets are prone to foreign investor herding, but the experience of countries that began the process of integration some time ago suggests that the peak of such herding behavior is relatively short-lived.

Figure 1.6 Sources of Volatility in Emerging Markets

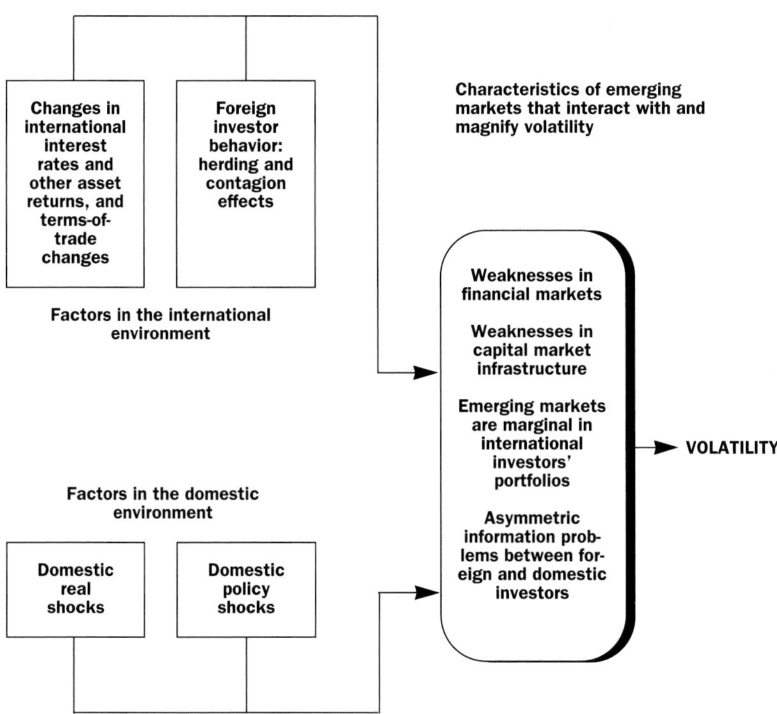

Both domestic and international factors can precipitate volatility in an integrated market.

Finally with regard to contagion, the experience of countries following the Mexican crisis suggests that pure contagion is a relatively brief phenomenon; international markets were able to differentiate among emerging markets, so that those countries with the strongest economic fundamentals saw a resumption in flows quite quickly.

On the domestic side, developing countries are more susceptible to real and policy shocks than industrial countries, and these shocks, in turn, will result in greater volatility of capital flows and asset prices and returns in a more integrated environment. In addition, there are also several characteristics of emerging markets that could possibly magnify international and domestic shocks in the early stages of integration. Financial and capital markets in developing countries suffer more from incomplete and asymmetric information, and from other institutional weaknesses, than do industrial country markets. In this environment, the potential for investor herding is greater, and domestic investors may be influenced by foreign investors, leading to even greater volatility. Emerging markets are also still quite marginal in international investors' portfolios, making them more susceptible to fluctuations in international financial conditions.

All of this suggests that developing countries are likely to be subject to a greater degree of volatility in the early stages of financial integration. However, overall volatility of reserves and private flows has shown no systematic increase in the 1990s (figure 1.7). This is probably because developing countries' exposure and vulnerability to real shocks may have come down during this period. What is striking, however, are the significant differences in volatility between countries and types of flows (tables 1.2 and 1.3). Asia generally shows less volatility, and has reduced its volatility by more, than Latin America, suggesting that country conditions remain the primary determinant of volatility. Of course this does not necessarily suggest that the observed volatility of flows is detrimen-

The volatility of reserves has not increased systematically in the 1990s.

Figure 1.7 Changes in Volatility of Reserves, 1980–89 and 1992–96
(coefficient of variation based on quarterly data)

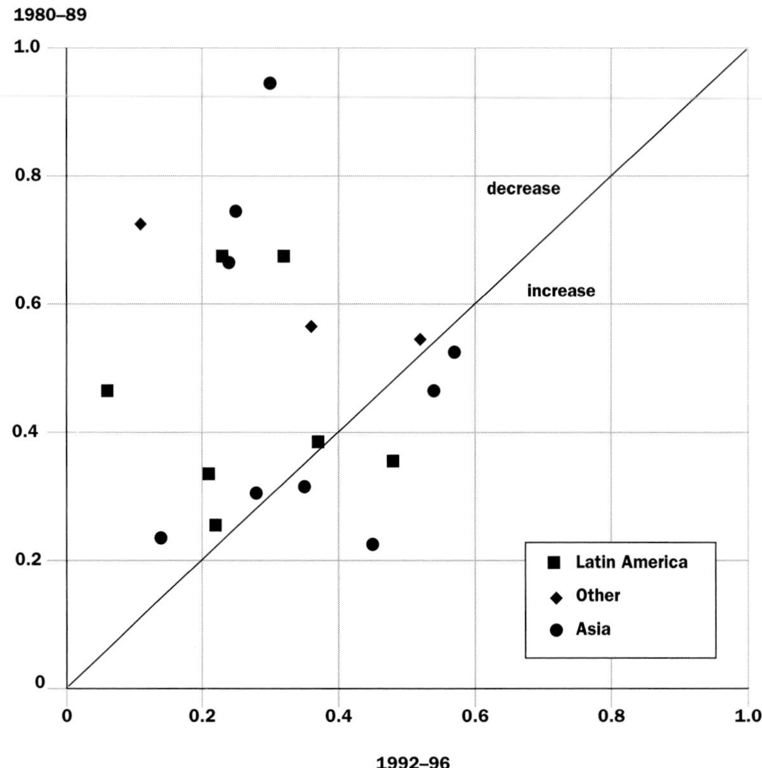

Source: IMF, *International Financial Statistics* data base.

Table 1.2 Volatility of Private Capital Flows from the United States, 1980s and 1990s
(based on quarterly net flows)

	1980s			1990s		
	Billions of dollars			Billions of dollars		
	Average level	Standard deviation	Coefficient of variation	Average level	Standard deviation	Coefficient of variation
Latin America						
Total private capital flows	4,177	8,013	1.92	6,685	13,943	2.09
Direct investment	421	1,495	3.55	3,216	2,084	0.65
Foreign securities	−285	397	1.39	1,923	3,393	1.76
Nonbank	−74	1,359	18.41	449	5,906	13.15
Bank	3,896	8,366	2.15	1,116	11,223	10.06
Africa and Asia						
Total private capital flows	1,031	2,558	2.48	3,550	5,285	1.49
Direct investment	411	816	1.99	1,570	875	0.56
Foreign securities	−203	505	2.48	1,226	1,793	1.46
Nonbank	−12	193	15.87	408	938	2.30
Bank	1,049	2,093	2.00	367	4,493	12.24

Source: U.S. Department of Commerce, *Survey of Current Business;* U.S. Treasury Department data.

tal in all cases, since this volatility could be in response to, and therefore could offset, real shocks such as a terms-of-trade deterioration.

In terms of different types of flows, FDI is the least volatile. Portfolio flows show a higher degree of volatility, but the level of volatility has tended to come down. The volatility of bank flows has gone up relative to

Table 1.3 Volatility of Capital Flows, Selected Countries, 1980s and 1990s
(coefficient of variation of quarterly flows)

	Overall capital account		Foreign direct investment		Portfolio investment	
Country	1980s	1990s	1980s	1990s	1980s	1990s
Argentina	1.28	1.09	1.01	1.26	43.60	2.96
Indonesia	0.93	0.70	0.82[a]	0.39	3.38	1.61
Korea	334.24	0.92	1.22	0.59	4.55	0.87
Mexico	3.85	0.66	0.47	0.62	3.34	1.25
Pakistan	0.71	0.65	0.68	0.30[b]	1.39	0.76
Philippines	1.21	0.75	1.79	0.99	0.68	0.30
Sri Lanka	0.55	0.61	0.36	0.76[b]	0.68	0.30
Thailand	0.78	0.33	0.83	0.23[b]	0.68	0.30

a. 1981–88.
b. 1990–93.
Source: IMF, *International Financial Statistics* data base.

the 1980s, in part because net flows have become relatively small. These differences can be explained by the fact that FDI investments are more costly to reverse, and hence are more responsive to long-term fundamentals, than short-term fluctuations. Portfolio flows, on the other hand, are quite sensitive to short-term differentials in rates of return, and hence to changes in interest rates. Moreover, unlike FDI investors, portfolio investors can divest themselves easily of their stocks of equities or bonds.

Finally, it is worth noting that while volatility—meaning variation around an average level—has tended to come down, or at least not increase, in the majority of countries, the absolute magnitude of variation is now much greater, since the average level of flows is higher. Consequently, the potential impact of such volatility on the domestic economy is also much greater than it was during the 1980s.

In sum, factors in the international environment do contribute to potential volatility in flows and asset prices in emerging markets. Since emerging markets are still quite marginal in foreign investors' portfolios, these markets remain quite susceptible to cyclical conditions in industrial countries. And since foreign investors are still relatively unfamiliar with emerging markets, these markets are also more prone to investor herding than are industrial countries. The main risks of volatility and large reversals, however, lie at the individual country level and come from the interaction of domestic policy and economic conditions with international factors.

As argued below, most developing countries lack strong macroeconomic, banking sector, and institutional underpinnings, and hence remain vulnerable to potential instability and reversals of flows. While international investors are becoming more discerning, market discipline tends to be much more stringent when investor confidence is lost—triggering large outflows—than during the buildup to a potential problem. Financial integration can therefore magnify shocks or the costs of policy mistakes, leading to greater instability.

Policy Challenges and Emerging Lessons

MOST DEVELOPING COUNTRIES ARE STILL A LONG WAY from establishing the rigorous preconditions needed for successful financial integration. The importance of sound macroeconomic policies as the key prerequisite for external financial liberalization has been recognized for some time but cannot be stressed enough. The need to eliminate large price distortions has also been recognized, leading to the recommendation that the current account should be liberalized before the capital account. There is now also growing awareness of the importance of financial sector preconditions and their interaction with the macroeconomic environment as a central element of successful integration. Developing countries also face a daunting institutional agenda of banking and capital market reform, since a much higher proportion of capital flows will be intermediated through these markets. All these are key elements of the broader policy agenda that developing countries need to adopt in any case, and financial integration makes their pursuit more urgent.

For many countries that are not attracting private capital flows, the main task is to make rapid progress in establishing these preconditions and eliminating other constraints that may be impeding foreign capital flows. The experience of Sub-Saharan Africa shows that countries which have made more progress in establishing stable macroeconomic conditions, adopting outward-oriented policies, and addressing other constraints to private investment are beginning to attract significant private capital flows (box 1.2). Since policies to attract private capital flows overlap with the broader agenda for private sector development, on which there is now broad consensus, we do not dwell on it in this study. Instead, the remaining sections focus on the challenges that developing countries are likely to face in the early stages of financial integration, given that it will take time to establish all the rigorous preconditions needed for financial integration.

Macroeconomic Management in an Integrating World

While increased financial integration may provide substantial macroeconomic benefits for developing countries, the integration process also carries with it some difficult macroeconomic challenges. Policymakers in these countries have been concerned with three types of problems:

- The potential for macroeconomic *overheating*, in the form of an excessive expansion of aggregate demand as a consequence of capital inflows.
- The potential *vulnerability* to abrupt and large reversals of capital flows because of changes in creditor perceptions.

Box 1.2 What Is Constraining Foreign Capital Inflows to Sub-Saharan Africa?

THE RECENT SURGE IN INTERNATIONAL PRIVATE capital flows to developing countries has largely bypassed Sub-Saharan Africa (excluding South Africa), but the region's small share masks significant differences among countries and the types of capital flows they receive.

Countries with positive per capita growth (PPC countries) received larger flows than countries with negative per capita growth (NPC countries). Growing economies also showed an improving trend, especially when private transfers are taken into account. The CFA countries (the members of the African franc zone) suffered larger and more sustained declines in private flows during the 1980s than did non-CFA countries. In contrast, private flows (including transfers) to the non-CFA countries recovered significantly in the second half of the 1980s and increased further during 1993–95.

Underlying the aggregate trend in private flows to Sub-Saharan Africa are also quite marked differences in trends for different types of flows. A detailed examination of these different types of flows yields insights into the factors constraining private capital inflows to Sub-Saharan Africa.

Foreign direct investment. FDI has shown a significant increase since the late 1980s for the non-CFA countries and the PPC countries in the factors constraining private capital inflows to Sub-Saharan Africa. For some of these countries (such as Angola, Botswana, Ghana, Mozambique, and Uganda), FDI as a percentage of GDP in 1994–95 compares favorably with that of recipient countries in Asia and Latin America.

Despite these promising trends, most countries in Sub-Saharan Africa have received very modest amounts of FDI. This has been the case despite the fact that rates of return on FDI have generally been much higher in Sub-Saharan Africa than in other developing regions. During 1990–94, rates of return on FDI in the region averaged 24 to 30 percent, compared with 16 to 18 percent for all developing countries. This suggests that risks are perceived to be higher in Sub-Saharan Africa than in other regions or that foreign investors face greater impediments there than elsewhere.

Experience in other regions has shown that investors choose countries with stable political and economic environments. Open markets, minimal regulation, good infrastructure facilities, and low production costs are also key factors in attracting and holding foreign investment. Bringing these factors together has proved difficult for many countries in Sub-Saharan Africa. Specifically, the main constraints that have impeded the flow of FDI to Sub-Saharan Africa include the prevalence of civil strife, macroeconomic instability, low economic growth and the small size of domestic markets, inward orientation and burdensome regulations, slow progress on privatization, poor infrastructure, and high wage and production costs. Conversely, countries that have addressed these weaknesses have begun to see a payoff in increased FDI. For instance, several countries that have seen an end to civil conflict (such as Angola, Mozambique, Namibia, South Africa, and Uganda) have benefited from large increases in FDI inflows during the 1990s. Similarly, countries that have made progress in reducing macroeconomic instability have enjoyed some success in attracting private FDI inflows.

Private loans. Unlike other developing regions, where commercial bank lending has shown a sharp turnaround in the 1990s, such lending has remained either negative or at very low levels for most Sub-Saharan African countries. In part, this has occurred because most African countries have not yet restored their access to financial markets. In contrast to creditworthiness ratings in other regions, which have shown a marked improvement in the 1990s, creditworthiness ratings for Sub-Saharan African countries have remained much lower, on average, and are only just beginning to see some improvement. The main factors believed to have contributed to Sub-Saharan countries' generally low levels of creditworthiness are high political risk, weak growth and export performance, macroeconomic instability, and high levels of indebtedness.

Portfolio equity flows. Although portfolio investment flows to Africa (with the notable exception of South Africa) are still extremely small compared with flows to other emerging markets, there are encouraging signs of growing investor interest. Since 1994, more than 12 Africa-oriented funds, with a total size of more than $1 billion, have been set up. Initially, the focus of these funds was primarily the South African market, but the base has been broadening to include a growing (though still limited) number of other African countries, including Botswana, Côte d'Ivoire, Ghana, Kenya, Mauritius, Zambia, and Zimbabwe. This growing pool of portfolio investment is already perceived as bringing important benefits, including improved liquidity, greater incentives for privatization, and increased pressure for policy reforms and improvement of the financial infrastructure.

A number of factors are, however, still seen as constraining portfolio investment: investors view political instability and weak macroeconomic fundamentals as the most important impediments. They also see many structural weaknesses that inhibit investment and believe that a reduction in transaction costs is critical. The establishment of an efficient securities trading system and the presence of international custodians are important elements of the financial infrastructure that is needed to attract foreign investors. Many investors say that corruption in the public sector, including the judiciary, not only increases transaction costs but also as acts as a deterrent in its own right. The supply of assets is still very limited, and in addition to the public companies already listed on stock exchanges, the number of private firms listed needs to be increased. In some cases, privatization of public assets offers the best avenue for increasing the supply of assets in the economy and attracting foreign investors.

Challenges ahead. With many Asian and Latin American countries growing rapidly and moving far ahead of most African countries in terms of putting in place the financial infrastructure needed to absorb foreign capital efficiently, most African countries will have to undertake speedy policy and structural reforms to attract private flows. Market discipline is likely to be severe in the initial stages, and countries that backtrack on reform will find that their access to international capital is limited and that such capital will be provided on costlier terms.

While microeconomic factors—poor infrastructures, shaky banking systems, thin financial markets, weak regulatory frameworks, dearth of human capital, slow pace of privatization, and corruption—are difficult to quantify, the macroeconomic factors used in the empirical analysis we have carried out (see Bhattacharya, Montiel, and Sharma 1996) yielded clear-cut conclusions. In Sub-Saharan Africa, economic characteristics like output growth, openness, relative stability of real effective exchange rates, low external debt, and high investment rates have encouraged private capital flows. The first three of these have been crucial in attracting FDI, the last two in attracting foreign private loans.

- The more general, longer-term implications of financial integration for the conduct of macroeconomic policy. As integration advances further, policymakers will have to manage the increased macroeconomic volatility that may prevail when the economy is more exposed to external shocks. In addition, they will need to face these and other shocks with reduced policy autonomy.

Policies to avert overheating. The initial manifestation of growing financial integration in many developing countries was a large one-

Table 1.4 Surges in Private Capital Flows to 20 Countries: Policy Responses and Outcomes

Response and outcome	*Argentina*	*Brazil*	*Chile*	*Colombia*	*Hungary*	*India*	*Indonesia*	*Korea*
Magnitude of the surge (net private capital flows as percentage of GDP)[a]	2.8	3.0	5.8	4.8	14.8	1.8	1.8	2.3
Policy response								
Reduce net inflows of foreign exchange								
Controls on inflows		x	x	x		x	x	
Liberalize capital outflows			x	x		x		x
Trade liberalization			x	x		x	x	x
Reduce official borrowing			x		x			
Float/appreciate exchange rate			x	x				x
Reduce impact on monetary aggregates								
Sterilized intervention		x	x	x		x	x	x
Higher reserve requirements			x	x		x		x
Reduce impact on aggregate demand								
Fiscal contraction	x		x			x	x	x
Outcomes[b]								
Average annual GDP growth (percent)	9.1	3.1	5.7	1.6	7.5	−0.7	2.2	-2.5
Consumption (percentage of GDP)	4.4	3.6	−8.5	4.1	6.4	−1.7	−5.2	1.1
Investment (percentage of GDP)	0.6	−2.0	10.2	0.9	1.6	−1.3	5.7	4.7
Current account deficit (percentage of GDP)	1.8	0.6	−4.9	4.9	9.8	−1.2	0.2	5.0
Reserve accumulation (percent)	23	75	−1,970	−22	29	1,820	80	−11
Average annual inflation (percent)	−801.1	−93.5	−4.1	−4.8	−5.5	0.1	1.3	0.8
Real exchange rate (percent)	91.7	7.4	−25.5	14.7	18.9	−30.8	−29.4	4.4

a. This is the annual average for the surge period.

b. All figures represent the change in the surge period compared with the preceding period of equal length, except reserve accumulation, which is expressed as a percentage of the capital account surplus.

Source: World Bank data.

way net flow of capital, magnified by favorable cyclical conditions in world financial markets. Since such flows have been large relative to the size of the economies of recipient countries (table 1.4), macroeconomic overheating has been a potentially serious problem.

In contrast to what happened during the commercial lending boom of the 1980s, however, virtually all recipient countries in the 1990s have resisted allowing the current account deficit to widen by the full magnitude of the incipient inflows. Countries have taken three broad approaches to addressing the potential overheating problem:

Malaysia	*Mexico*	*Morocco*	*Pakistan*	*Peru*	*Philippines*	*Poland*	*Sri Lanka*	*Thailand*	*Tunisia*	*Turkey*	*Venezuela*
9.4	5.3	3.5	3.6	6.4	4.3	6.5	5.5	9.9	5.1	3.0	2.7
x	x						x	x			
x	x		x		x		x	x			
x	x		x		x		x	x			
		x			x			x	x		x
					x						
x	x		x		x		x	x			
x					x		x				
x	x				x			x			
4.0	2.9	−3.3	−2.3	3.3	2.2	8.5	2.0	3.9	0.5	1.4	−5.0
−1.8	6.7	0.8	−2.0	3.1	6.1	11.3	−1.9	−11.2	−1.4	−0.5	6.8
4.8	2.4	−1.1	1.0	−4.0	1.7	−11.1	2.2	13.4	2.6	1.3	6.8
2.9	7.1	0.1	0.9	1.4	0.7	3.9	−0.2	2.3	3.7	1.4	14.6
49	0	93	59	67	79	39	105	59	−28	31	−85
1.4	−74.4	0.1	1.7	−79.1	−3.1	−146.7	−2.2	−1.1	−2.2	5.0	−2.7
−24.5	20.0	−6.5	−9.0	120.9	−10.7	37.9	0.6	−18.9	0.6	1.0	9.8

- *Reducing the net inflows of foreign exchange.* Countries have deployed a number of policies toward this end, including controls on capital inflows, the liberalization of capital outflows, trade liberalization, reduced official borrowing, and appreciation of the nominal exchange rate. The majority of countries attempting to cope with the effects of integration have eschewed direct controls on capital inflows, but a significant minority have continued to maintain capital account restrictions, and new capital controls in some form have been adopted by several countries, in particular those receiving the largest flows (for example, Brazil, Chile, Malaysia, and Thailand) or those that were constrained in their ability to use other instruments to contain overheating (such as Indonesia).

  No country made wholesale changes in its foreign exchange regime. Bands were introduced by Chile, Colombia, and Mexico, but only those of Chile and Colombia seemed designed to accommodate some nominal appreciation in response to capital inflows. More recently, some of the Southeast Asian economies, notably Indonesia, Malaysia, and Thailand, have moved toward greater flexibility in their exchange rate regimes but have resisted significant nominal exchange rate appreciation. Among the other measures listed, reduced official borrowing, trade liberalization, and liberalization of capital outflows were adopted by several countries during the surge period, but these reforms have been of lesser importance. The liberalization of capital outflows may, in some cases, actually have abetted inflows by enhancing credibility.
- *Reducing the impact of reserve accumulation on monetary aggregates.* Since most countries have maintained an officially determined exchange rate, the central banks have had to intervene to defend the parity in the face of large inflows. Virtually all recipient countries, therefore, have had to contend with the monetary impact of a substantial buildup of external reserves. In order to curb the creation of high-powered money, virtually all countries undertook sterilized intervention in the foreign exchange market. A few countries (Chile, Colombia, the Philippines, and Sri Lanka) also raised reserve requirements to reduce the potential multiplier effect on the expansion of broader monetary aggregates.
- *Reducing the impact of inflows on aggregate demand.* In addition to tightening monetary policy, a majority of countries appear to have

tightened fiscal policy in response to inflows, but to very different degrees. In Latin America, Argentina, Chile, and Colombia relied most strongly on fiscal adjustment, whereas virtually all East Asian countries used the tightening of fiscal policy as a cornerstone of their macroeconomic policy response to capital inflows.

Given the scale of the inflows and the accumulation of reserves in the 1990s, most recipient countries have been remarkably successful in curbing inflationary pressures. A majority of countries managed to reduce inflation during this period, and where there was an increase, it was relatively modest. This reasonably favorable outcome was achieved despite an acceleration in GDP growth in most of these countries.

The current account deficit widened in most countries in the post-surge period, as was to be expected, but there were substantial differences in the magnitude of these increases. Hungary, Mexico, and Venezuela saw the largest increases in the current account deficit as a ratio to GDP, whereas Chile actually saw an improvement in its current account balance, with other countries falling in between. There were also substantial differences in the composition of absorption. For some countries, notably Chile and the East Asian countries, a widening in the current deficit (where it occurred) was primarily reflected in an increase in investment. This orientation toward investment was associated in these countries with faster economic growth. In contrast, the composition of absorption was more skewed toward consumption in Argentina, Colombia, Hungary, Mexico, Peru, and Poland. This pattern of absorption was strongly correlated with the degree of real exchange rate appreciation. In particular, an increase in the consumption-to-GDP ratio was associated with real appreciation (figure 4.3, chapter 4).

The differences in the composition of absorption and the appreciation of the real exchange rate between these two groups of countries appear to have been due largely to fiscal policy. Countries that significantly tightened fiscal policy—including Chile, Indonesia, Malaysia, and Thailand—also reduced their share of consumption in GDP during the inflow period. Moreover, all of these countries actually achieved a substantial depreciation in the real exchange rate during the inflow period. Chile and Indonesia also curbed their current account deficits. While the current account deficit increased in Malaysia and Thailand, these two countries also experienced very substantial rises in the share of investment in GDP, as well as in their rates of economic growth, in association with the arrival of capital inflows.

In sum, developing countries have been able to date to counter most of the symptoms of overheating by adopting a wide range of policies. There have been some common elements in their policies, as well as some important differences that have produced different macroeconomic outcomes. In particular:

- Several major recipients have employed new capital controls in the face of large inflows, with at least some degree of effectiveness in reducing the magnitude of inflows and altering their composition.
- Sterilized intervention was used by virtually all countries to offset the impact of reserve accumulation on monetary aggregates. Sterilization appears to have been generally successful in curbing the growth of base money, but less effective in preventing asset inflation. Beyond this, there were significant differences in the policy mix.
- At one end were a group of countries that resisted real exchange rate appreciation and, toward this end, placed greater emphasis on fiscal tightening. These countries were not only able to avoid substantial real appreciation but tended on average to have lower current account deficits, a mix of absorption more oriented toward investment, and faster economic growth.
- At the other end were a group of countries that used the nominal exchange rate as a nominal anchor, with relatively greater reliance on monetary rather than fiscal policy. These countries typically experienced both consumption booms and larger real exchange rate appreciation.

The major policy lesson to be derived from cross-country experience in dealing with surges in capital inflows is that the policy mix employed to combat overheating also has a major effect on the performance of the real economy and its ability to benefit in the long term from capital flows. In particular, a heavy reliance on fiscal policy, supported by sterilization and some nominal exchange rate flexibility—and in more extreme cases by temporary taxes or controls on inflows—can be an effective response to overheating and can also improve the balance between domestic investment and consumption and reduce the risks of an overappreciated real exchange rate and an unsustainable deficit in the current account.

Policies to limit vulnerability. In addition to responding in a particular way to inflows of private capital, a country can be more or less vulnerable to large reversals of private capital flows, depending on its underlying economic and political conditions. The factors affecting investor confidence, and hence the creditworthiness of countries in the new international setting, are not yet well understood, in part because investors are still in the process of discovering emerging markets.

This study uses the Mexican crisis to examine the relationship between macroeconomic performance and vulnerability, by assessing how the incidence and severity of "the tequila effect" (contagion) emanating from Mexico was linked to macroeconomic performance in other developing countries. Our key findings are that some of the initial interpretations of the crisis, which attributed Mexico's vulnerability solely to its high current account deficit, are not well supported by the cross-country evidence. Instead, as shown in table 1.5, the countries that were less vulnerable to the Mexican crisis tended to be those that had avoided real appreciation and imposed a tight fiscal policy during their inflow period, thereby achieving a larger share of investment and more rapid growth than they would have done under different policies. The Mexican crisis and its effect on other countries also highlight at least

Table 1.5 Impact of the Mexican Crisis on Selected Developing Countries

Indicator	*More affected group*[a]	*Less affected group*[b]
Change in stock prices[c]	−22.5	−3.5
Current account balance (percentage of GDP)[d]	−3.5	−3.2
FDI/total private flows[e]	39.8	36.3
GDP growth (percent)[e]	3.4	7.7
Inflation (percent)[e]	361.2	11.4
Central government balance (percentage of GDP)[e]	−4.1	0.6
Debt/exports[d]	273.8	123.5
Debt/reserves[d]	879.0	296.8

a. Countries in this group include Argentina, Brazil, India, Mexico, Pakistan, Turkey, and Venezuela.

b. Countries in this group include Chile, Colombia, Indonesia, Korea, Malaysia, and Thailand.

c. Between December 1994 and the end of March 1995.

d. 1993.

e. Average for 1988–93 period.

Source: IMF, *World Economic Outlook* data base; World Bank data.

four important conditions in the initial environment that could affect subsequent vulnerability:

- Inflation and inflationary expectations at the time of integration can constrain the choice of policy mix. In particular, concerns about inflation often have led governments to adopt a nominal exchange rate anchor, which in almost all cases has led to substantial real exchange rate appreciation.
- The magnitude of external and domestic debt has a direct bearing on investor confidence and also affects the room for fiscal maneuvering and monetary tightening in the face of balance-of-payments pressures.
- As the Mexican crisis has so forcefully demonstrated, the maturity and composition of public debt is as important as the size of the debt. The inability to roll over debt could lead to large capital outflows, especially when a country is vulnerable to shocks, so excessive reliance on short-term debt is risky. The currency composition of debt also matters, because with foreign-currency-denominated debt, the government assumes the risk of an exchange rate devaluation.
- The health and resilience of the banking system are crucial to ensuring the sound use of capital inflows and avoiding vulnerability, as discussed below. A weak banking system can increase vulnerability through too much and too risky domestic lending and by severely limiting the authorities' ability to raise interest rates in the face of a loss of reserves—as happened in Mexico in early 1994.

The most important lesson for policymakers is that creditors (both domestic and foreign) can be expected to take their capital out of a country when they think that a policy change could impair the value of their investments. Thus, vulnerability will arise when the perception is created that a devaluation, nonpayment of public sector debt, or the imposition of restrictions on capital outflows is about to occur. Such expectations are likely to arise when the real exchange rate is perceived to be out of line, the government's debt obligations are large in relation to its earnings capacity and external reserve position, fiscal adjustment is perceived as politically or administratively infeasible, or the country's growth prospects are bleak. From the perspective of creditors, therefore, a high share of investment in absorption and a strong record of growth, a low stock of government obligations coupled with demonstrated fiscal flexibility (in the form of small deficits and low inflation), and a real exchange rate broadly perceived to be in line with fundamentals all augur well for future debt service. From a policy perspective, countries need to have an exchange rate policy that avoids substantial appreciation of the real exchange rate and responsible fiscal policies. For countries that are vulnerable to shocks, it is particularly important to have fiscal flexibility as well as a debt structure with longer maturity and an adequate cushion of reserves.

A final macroeconomic policy lesson is that governments need to move forcefully in the face of shocks and loss of investor confidence. Governments therefore should monitor warning signals and take prompt measures to prevent a large loss of reserves; these measures include tightening monetary policy and adjusting the exchange rate. Countries with nominal exchange rate anchors face special constraints. They must either take draconian fiscal measures or allow interest rates to climb to very high levels, with adverse impact on the budget and investment.

Macroeconomic management in the long term. The two macroeconomic challenges of overheating and vulnerability are likely to be particularly important during the transition to financial integration, when international investors are adjusting their portfolios and when policy credibility is not yet well established in the capital-importing countries. However, new macroeconomic challenges will continue to arise even when the process of integration is well advanced. In particular, financially integrated developing countries will find themselves operating in a very different macroeconomic environment—one in which capital movements are highly sensitive to changes in prospective foreign and domestic rates of return. The macroeconomic consequences of domestic shocks (including changes in policies) will be altered, and the country will also be faced with new types of shocks arising in international financial markets.

This new environment may thus be characterized by ongoing volatility, to which policymakers will need to respond, but with a reduced degree of policy autonomy. Developing country experience to date provides only limited insight about these longer-term implications for macroeconomic management, since most countries are still in the early stages of financial integration. There is, however, a growing body of analysis and empirical evidence from more integrated economies that provides relevant lessons for developing country policymakers.

First and foremost is the importance of responsible and flexible fiscal management. Financial integration places a premium on short-run fiscal flexibility, which provides an effective instrument for stabilizing domestic aggregate demand in response to external shocks in an environment where it is increasingly difficult to restrict capital movements and hence rely on monetary policy. Fiscal policy can also substitute for exchange rate policy as a stabilizing device. Equally important, a stable perception of fiscal solvency becomes crucial for preventing the domestic public sector itself from becoming an important source of macroeconomic shocks (through perceived changes in solvency) and for providing the latitude for fiscal policy to play a short-run stabilizing role.

The second important policy lesson is that exchange rate management remains possible and that crawling pegs, in particular, remain an exchange rate option for developing countries that become closely integrated with world capital markets. However, the scope for deviation from fundamentals, as well as from commitment to the announced regime, is much reduced under these circumstances. Managed rates are certainly capable of generating macroeconomic volatility in this environment, but they generally have not done so. Moreover, an active exchange rate policy does not imply a loss of control over the domestic price level. Countries that have managed the exchange rate with the objective of maintaining competitiveness—and thereby achieving stable or depreciating real exchange rates—have not exhibited deteriorating inflation performance in the context of capital inflows.

Third, the ability to conduct independent monetary policy becomes increasingly difficult if the government wishes to target the nominal exchange rate. Nevertheless, the experience to date suggests that there is scope for sterilized intervention as a short-run stabilizing tool despite increased financial integration. However, sterilization does carry a fiscal cost, especially where credibility is not well established.

Fourth, the evidence on capital controls suggests that they have been able, temporarily, to affect both the level and the composition of capital inflows in the early stages of integration. In the early stages of integration, recourse to capital controls may be warranted for two reasons. The first is on the grounds of prudential restrictions on external borrowing and lending by domestic financial institutions, especially when it is not possible to remove underlying financial sector distortions that lead to explicit or implicit guarantees. The second is as a transitional device to preserve monetary autonomy pending the reforms required to permit the use of fiscal policy as a stabilization instrument. But experience suggests that capital controls become progressively less effective as a country becomes more integrated and that they have not been able to prevent either large capital outflows or inflows when there is the potential for significant arbitrage profits.

Managing the Financial Sector in a More Integrated World

A country's ability to maintain the health of its banking system and capital markets will determine, to a large extent, whether it will be able to realize the benefits of financial integration and avoid its pitfalls. Financial integration makes it imperative for developing countries to move much more aggressively to reform the domestic financial sector, because risks and losses are potentially greater in an integrated environment. However, because of the time needed for such reforms, and the high costs of financial distress, there is a strong case for trying to contain lending booms associated with the early stages of financial integration when the banking sector is weak and for establishing a mechanism for crisis management.

Banking system reform. The risks of distress in the banking system increase with financial integration in three ways. First, increased foreign competition can reduce the franchise value of banks sharply in the short run, inducing domestic banks to invest in a risky manner. Second, banks are able to expand lending much more quickly and thereby incur risks in their portfolios that they may not be able to manage. Third, circumstances can change much more quickly with financial integration, creating macroeconomic and financial sector distress that carries high economic and social costs. In addition to the direct costs of bailing out failed banks, the sudden loss of liquidity in the banking sector can amplify economic downturns. Such distress can severely set back reforms, as was the case with several Latin American countries following the debt crisis of 1982.

Recent difficulties faced by the banking systems in Argentina and Mexico have highlighted the importance of a sound banking system in ensuring macroeconomic and financial stability in a more integrated environment. In this regard two contrasting facts stand out. First, banking systems in developing countries play an even more dominant role in financial intermediation than in industrial countries (figure 1.8). Second,

Figure 1.8 Banks' Share of Financial Intermediation, Selected Developing and Industrial Countries, 1994
(assets of the banking sector as a percentage of assets of all financial institutions)

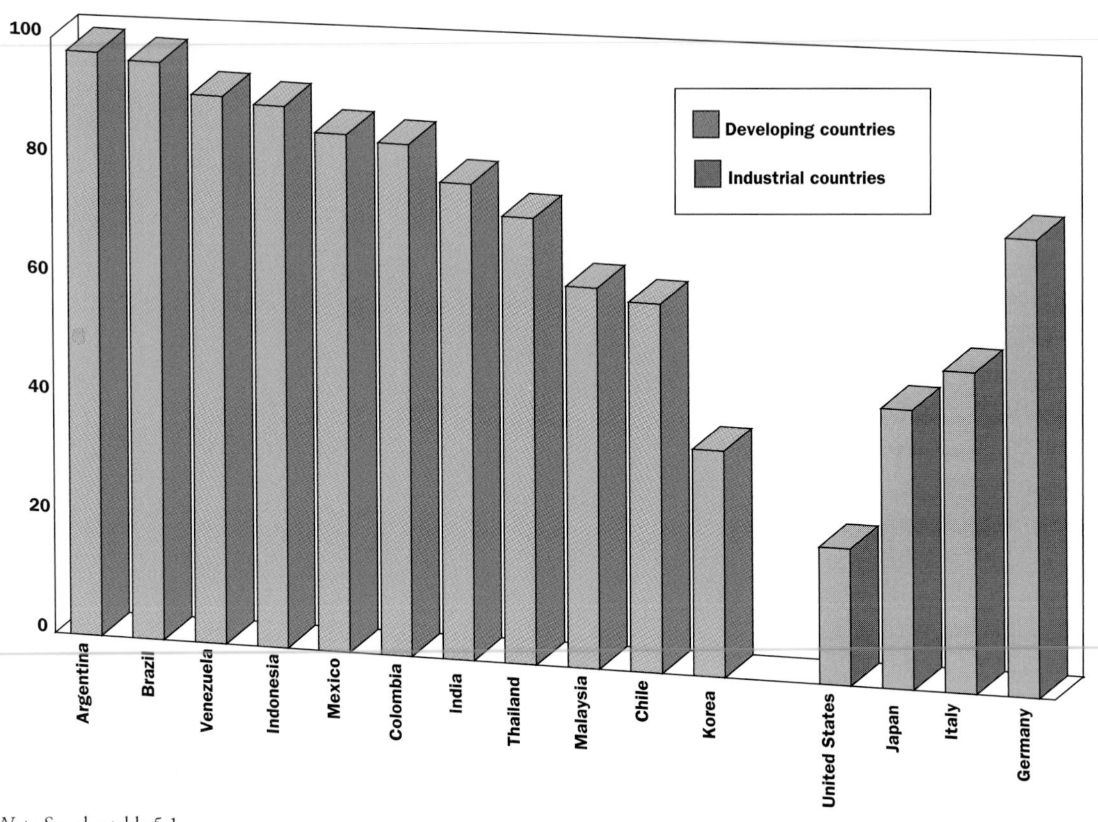

Note: See also table 5.1.
Source: BIS (1996) and World Bank staff estimates.

Banks in developing countries play a larger role in financial intermediation than banks in industrial countries.

the health of the banking system is much weaker in developing countries (figure 1.9). In many instances, the banking systems have only recently been deregulated, the incentive framework is distorted toward excessive risk taking, banks are poorly capitalized, and the prudential regulation and supervision capabilities have not yet been established. Increased openness of the financial system under these circumstances poses considerable danger that capital inflows will be inefficiently intermediated (directly and indirectly) and that the banking system will incur additional risks, thereby not only undermining the benefits of capital inflows but potentially magnifying macroeconomic and financial sector vulnerability.

Figure 1.9 Health of Banking Systems
(percentage of total rated banks)

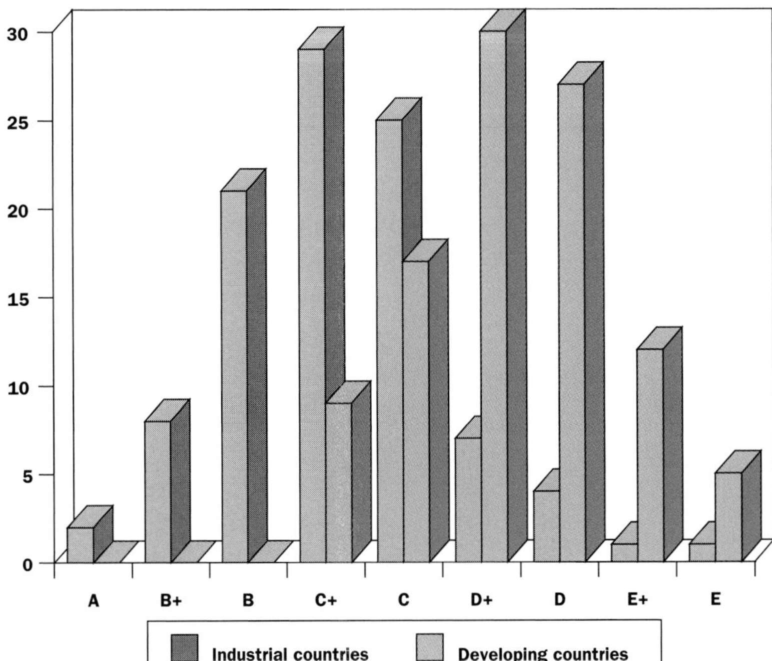

Source: Moody's Bank Financial Strength Ratings for Selected Countries, May 1996.

Banks in developing countries are generally weaker than banks in industrial countries.

Since the process of financial integration is usually associated in its early stages with economic reforms and improvement in prospects, it is often accompanied by a surge in capital inflows. The resulting increase in aggregate demand, rise in asset prices, and easier access to funds can trigger a rapid expansion in bank credit. In turn, the surge in bank credit can reinforce these effects, leading to potential macroeconomic and financial sector vulnerability. This potential vicious cycle occurs because the increase in bank lending finances an increase in aggregate expenditures, accelerating output growth. The increase in output growth, in turn, reinforces economic agents' expectations and induces both firms and households to borrow and spend more. The increase in aggregate expenditures also appreciates the real exchange rate, aggravating macroeconomic vulnerability. Meanwhile, domestic residents' nominal wealth rises because of the appreciation of the real exchange rate and the increase in asset prices. The increase in nominal wealth adds to the surge in households' expenditures.

A weak and inadequately regulated banking sector aggravates this process by lending for consumption and speculative purposes, such as portfolio investment, or by financing a construction boom. By granting more credit for portfolio investments or real estate, the banking sector helps to push asset prices upward, increasing the value of nominal wealth. This can be a self-perpetuating process if banks use inflated assets as collateral in granting new credits. Consequently bank portfolios may become increasingly exposed to sectors prone to boom-bust cycles, such as real estate, and may suffer large losses in case of a deflation in asset prices. This increased exposure to fluctuations in asset prices, or to sectors highly sensitive to variations in interest rates, increases the vulnerability of the banking sector as a whole.

The fragility of the banking system can also become an important constraint for macroeconomic policy. For instance, in both the Mexican and the Venezuelan financial crises, authorities were reluctant to raise interest rates in the face of a loss of international reserves, because of concerns about the effects of such action on the health of the banking system. A weak banking sector can also amplify economic downturns as banks are forced to call in loans or widen spreads to cover losses. In the extreme case of a banking crisis, there may be large fiscal repercussions, since the costs are typically absorbed by the public sector.

Unsettled macroeconomic conditions, in turn, can have severe repercussions on the domestic banking system. Developing countries are more prone to suffer from large macroeconomic swings, given that they are more susceptible to real and financial shocks and that these shocks tend to be large in relation to the size of their economies. But inappropriate macroeconomic management and policy mix can also contribute to macroeconomic and financial sector vulnerability. For example, an overvalued exchange rate that raises the expectation of devaluation can undermine the health of the banking system by leading to high real interest rates and an increase in the stock of nonperforming loans, as was the case in Chile and Mexico in the early 1980s. Similarly, excessive reliance on monetary restraint in the implementation of a stabilization program can also adversely affect the banking system. Fiscal policy also plays a critical role, not only in ensuring macroeconomic resilience but in avoiding excessive taxation of forced lending by the banking system. The importance of macroeconomic conditions for the banking sector is underscored by the fact that most major banking crises have been preceded by a deterioration in the macroeconomic environment (Kaminsky and Reinhart 1996).

There is growing recognition that it is the dynamic interactions between macroeconomic conditions and the banking sector that lead to boom-bust cycles and the risks of macroeconomic and financial sector vulnerability. These risks increase in an integrating environment, since, as noted, banks can expand lending more quickly and in larger amounts, circumstances can change more swiftly, and markets react faster. The likelihood that the process of financial integration in its early stages will lead to a vicious cycle depends on the initial conditions in the recipient country and the policy response to the surge in inflows. Weak initial conditions in the banking sector, including the regulatory framework, and an accommodating macroeconomic policy stance increase the probability that macroeconomic and financial sector vulnerability will increase with the surge in inflows (figure 1.10). An important challenge facing developing country policymakers, therefore, is how to manage the joint process of external financial liberalization and domestic financial sector reform, especially where macroeconomic conditions are still unsettled.

To distill lessons for banking sector reform in the face of growing financial integration, this study draws on a number of different country episodes during the 1980s and 1990s, when countries received substantial capital inflows as a result of integration.[6] A number of important conclusions emerge from our review of country experience:

Figure 1.10 Capital Flows, Lending Booms, and Potential Vulnerability

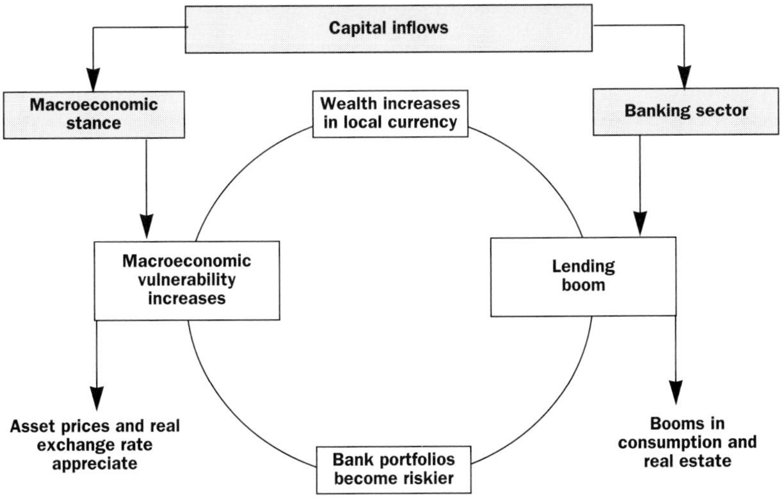

Capital inflows can lead to a vicious circle that increases economic vulnerabilities.

First, countries that received substantial capital inflows as part of the process of financial integration typically experienced lending booms. For the country episodes analyzed, bank lending to the private sector as a share of GDP increased from an average of about 29 percent during the years prior to the inflows, to an average of about 41 percent during the years of large capital inflows (figure 5.1, chapter 5). These lending booms are typically associated with an expansion in aggregate demand, significant asset inflation, and, in several cases, an appreciation of the real exchange rate.

Second, countries that had the largest lending booms typically saw a significant increase in macroeconomic vulnerability, measured by a widening of the current account deficit, above what would be expected on the basis of the size of the inflows; a consumption boom relatively larger than what would be expected given the size of the inflows; and a lower level of investment than would be expected given the size of flows.[7] It is striking that every one of these country episodes with symptoms of increased macroeconomic vulnerability ended in a banking crisis.

Third, lending booms are often associated with an increase in financial sector vulnerability, despite the fact that booms tend to improve bank profitability and hence offer the opportunity for the banking sector to strengthen its resilience to shocks. Yet in the majority of country episodes, banks showed a deteriorating shock absorption capacity during the lending boom period. Countries that did not improve conditions in their banking sectors during the inflow period, but rather allowed bank lending to increase without addressing underlying weaknesses, generally experienced a banking crisis later on. Only in three of the country episodes, namely, Chile, Colombia, and Malaysia during the early 1990s, do we find that banks consistently improved their resilience to shocks as measured by, for example, improved liquidity, higher capitalization rates and loan loss provisions, lower stock of nonperforming assets, and reduced exposure to foreign exchange risk. Other Latin American countries during the early 1990s, namely, Argentina, Brazil, Mexico, and Venezuela, have shown an overall increase in banking sector vulnerability, while Indonesia, the Philippines, and Thailand have shown a deterioration in some indicators and an improvement in others.

Fourth, all of the countries in which lending booms were associated with an increase in financial sector vulnerability, and in which macroeconomic vulnerability increased or remained constant, experienced banking crises (figure 5.9, chapter 5). Countries with the largest lending booms were typically the ones that saw the most significant increase in vulnerability, especially of the financial sector. In contrast, countries that took action to restrain the lending boom, or that pursued prudent macroeconomic policies, fared well and avoided major crises. Furthermore, countries that improved their macroeconomic stance—such as Indonesia, the Philippines, and Thailand—managed to avoid or at least delay banking crises despite some worsening in banking sector vulnerability.

This review of country experience, therefore, suggests that lending booms in the early stages of financial integration are often a manifestation of underlying weaknesses in the banking system that, if unchecked, can lead to increased macroeconomic and financial sector vulnerability. These vulnerabilities, in turn, negatively reinforce one another and in almost all cases lead to a costly banking crisis. A strong macroeconomic policy stance can help, at least temporarily, to avert a banking crisis, even with a lending boom and weaknesses in the financial sector. Based on these findings, the report draws the following conclusions for managing the banking sector in a more integrated economy:

Extremely weak initial conditions in the macroeconomy and the financial sector may warrant a cautious approach toward external financial liberalization. As the recent experience in Venezuela vividly illustrates, weaknesses in the banking sector combined with poor macroeconomic fundamentals can, in an integrated environment, quickly lead to a very costly banking crisis (exceeding 10 percent of GDP).

Financial integration puts a premium on vigorous reform of the financial sector. Although there is still some debate about the sequencing of financial sector reform, there is broad consensus about its urgency in a more integrated setting and about the importance of undertaking a comprehensive reform of three main elements: financial infrastructure and institution building, the incentive structure, and the regulatory and supervisory framework.[8]

The main institutional building blocks are sound accounting standards and practices, auditing, improved disclosure, and the legal framework. But special attention must also be devoted to bankers' management and risk assessment skills. These skills are often eroded after domestic financial liberalization but become all the more important in an integrated environment.

The incentive structure becomes particularly important to discourage excessive risk taking by bank owners and managers, and more broadly to encourage sound bank practices and close monitoring by large depositors. For instance, as shown by the Chilean experience of the early 1980s, and more recently by Mexico, explicit guarantees for foreign exchange can induce banks to increase exposure to foreign exchange risk. Another common distortion comes from explicit or implicit deposit insurance, which can lead to excessive risk taking by depositors and banks. Speedy elimination of these distortions will ensure that market discipline complements the monitoring of banks by domestic supervisory agencies, which may often be imperfect in the early stages of financial integration.

The regulatory and supervisory framework needs to address five aspects that are particularly important with financial liberalization: (a) strengthening banks' profitability and capitalization, (b) restricting connected lending, (c) improving public disclosure, (d) careful screening of bank applicants, and (e) tightening asset classification and loan loss provisions. Virtually all developing countries have now adopted capital requirements that meet or even exceed the minimum standards under the Basle Accords. However, most developing countries have ratios in the same range as industrial countries, despite facing a much higher degree of risk and a more volatile environment (Goldstein and Turner 1996, Hausmann and Gavin 1995). Sustained efforts to strengthen supervision along these lines will not only reduce the possibilities for unsound lending but will also help build a shock absorber in the banking system so it can weather macroeconomic swings that may be associated with increased financial openness.

In regard to the timing of reforms, the inflow period is likely to be associated with lower interest rates and an upturn in growth, and therefore is an opportune time to push ahead with financial sector reform.

A strong case can be made for containing the lending booms associated with the early stages of financial integration. Lending booms can be curbed through a combination of macroeconomic and banking sector policies. As already noted, a combination of tight fiscal policy and an exchange rate policy directed toward maintaining competitiveness has proved to be the most effective means of restraining aggregate demand and shifting its composition away from consumption and toward investment, particularly in the tradable sector. While monetary policy can play an important complementary role in targeting inflation, a tight monetary policy can induce additional capital inflows, especially where fiscal policy is less stringent.

Possible policies targeted at the banking sector to contain the lending boom include (a) increasing banks' capitalization requirements, weighted by the risk of bank assets, as in Chile; (b) raising provisions against loan losses, as in Chile in the 1980s and Mexico more recently; (c) raising reserve requirements, as in Malaysia; (d) imposing ceilings on commercial bank lending; and (e) imposing restrictions on commercial banks' external borrowing, as in Indonesia and Thailand.

The first two policies can be implemented more easily during a lending boom, when banks' profits increase, but in order to be effective they need to be implemented within a consistent incentive and regulatory framework. This is so because bank managers tend to hide their financial problems by underprovisioning nonperforming loans—and, therefore, overstating their banks' capital—especially during periods of financial distress. The last three policies have been used very effectively to contain lending booms, but by implicitly taxing the banking system, they introduce distortions that lead to disintermediation in the medium term.

Countries should establish mechanisms that enable policymakers to deal with a banking crisis promptly and effectively. Delaying actions intended to contain the crisis will only increase its cost. Many countries start reshaping their institutional framework—a lengthy and difficult process—at the same time that they are integrating with the rest of the world. During this period, domestic financial markets will experience strains that, if not properly managed, may lead to systemic crisis and large economic losses. One important aspect of bank supervision and regulation, therefore, is crisis preparedness and management. Given the greater volatility and responsiveness of financial markets in an integrated environment, and the potential for larger losses, the need to detect and contain a banking crisis at an early stage becomes even more urgent. For this, there is a need for good and reliable information, to allow for prompt decision-making and swift corrective action by bank supervisors. In particular, bank supervisors need to carefully monitor off-balance and offshore operations and the extent to which these are used as a device to hide non-performing assets and bypass domestic regulations. The practice of lending to third parties abroad—who then relend the same funds to a related domestic party—has been used in some instances to bypass domestic regulations against self-lending. This occurred, for example, in Chile during the early 1980s and Venezuela during the 1990s. More broadly, there is a need for better information about banks' risk assessment and management, self-lending, portfolio concentration, foreign exchange exposure, and currency mismatches. Such information can help policymakers take preemptive actions and may provide the basis for contingency planning, which, in turn, can help reduce delays and also trial-and-error policies in the event of a crisis.

Crisis management involves the allocation of losses and the management of failing institutions—that is, whether and how to intervene in ailing banks. In an integrated environment, policymakers need to intervene promptly and decisively in ailing institutions in order to contain the crisis and impose losses on the parties responsible: the bank owners and managers. Although rigid rules can help policymakers resist the opposition of interest groups affected by the intervention, they can also force the intervention and liquidation of viable institutions (Goldstein and Turner 1996). Thus, good judgment and discretion are needed in managing a banking crisis, and in many instances policymakers may choose to follow a more heterodox approach rather than a strict application of rules and pure orthodoxy.

The allocation of losses will most likely be biased toward the less protected and less informed groups—small depositors, small shareholders, and taxpayers—in an integrated setting, since large depositors, bank owners, and managers will often be able to move funds offshore. Thus, the need to intervene promptly is even more urgent if the objective is to impose maximum losses on the largest market participants, those who have greater incentives to be well informed and for whom it is cheaper—proportional to their investment—to move funds from onshore to offshore locations.

Finally, a cautious macroeconomic stance becomes even more important when managing a banking crisis under the more stringent conditions imposed by integration, especially in the presence of a currency or quasi-currency board.

Preparing Capital Markets for Financial Integration

Given the changing investor base, a growing proportion of flows to developing countries is being channeled through their capital markets in the form of portfolio equity capital. These investments, which represent an important opportunity for developing countries, have been accompanied by a spectacular increase in activity in their equity markets. Table 3.1 in chapter 3 illustrates the spillover effects of portfolio investment on domestic trading activity. But while the improvements in many emerging markets have been noteworthy, most of these markets are still in the early stages of development and need to close the gap separating them from more advanced capital markets to be able to compete in an integrating world. And they need to compete for new issues and investors not only with the more advanced markets but also increasingly with other emerging markets.

To this end, developing countries face two main tasks:

- First, they must implement policy reforms and strengthen institutions to make their markets more attractive to foreign investors and reduce the risks of capital market instability. While investors are attracted by the potential for rapid growth and high returns, they are discouraged by operating inefficiencies, by the lack of reliability of market institutions and infrastructure, and by regulatory frameworks that increase transaction costs and reduce transparency.[9] Improvements that increase the attractiveness of emerging markets for foreign investors also serve to reduce volatility and risks.
- Second, authorities in developing countries need to deal with the new regulatory concerns resulting from globalization. These concerns, which also relate to the banking sector, are reviewed in the last section of this chapter.

This policy agenda is not new, in that it includes many of the policy and institutional reforms essential for developing capital markets in a more closed economy. Domestic and foreign investors generally welcome the same institutional and policy improvements, which also diminish volatility and risks irrespective of whether they originate from domestic or external sources.

Improving market infrastructure. As cross-border flows increased during the 1980s, there was considerable debate on best practice in market infrastructure and how to harmonize systems across countries.[10] The landmark efforts in this area were the Group of 30 (G-30) initiative in 1989 and the 1995 workshops organized by the International Society of Securities Administrators (ISSA). The G-30 recommendations and suggested ISSA revisions are summarized in box 1.3.

Partly in response to foreign portfolio investment, emerging markets have made major strides in improving their infrastructure and now meet many of the G-30 standards (table 6.4, chapter 6). Twelve out of the 16 markets included in table 6.4 now have central depositories, and the remaining four—India, Indonesia, Pakistan, and the Philippines—are all scheduled to have them by mid-1997. Many emerging markets,

Box 1.3 Best Practice in Market Infrastructure

Matching. The matching system should be integrated with the clearance and settlement (C&S) system, and all trades by direct and indirect (institutional) participants should be matched at most by T+1 (one day after trade).

Clearance and settlement. Settlement should be accomplished by a delivery versus payment system of good quality with same-day funds (that is, final delivery of securities takes place only if final payment is made); there should be real-time gross settlement or a netting system that meets stringent risk control standards, depending on the characteristics of the market; and the rolling settlement system should have final settlement occur by T+3.

Depository. There should be one independent central depository managed for the benefit of the industry, broadly defined, and if more than one depository exists, they should be interlinked; there should be an independent registry or registries; and immobilization and dematerialization should be encouraged, and the legal framework revised, if necessary, to permit this.

especially in Asia, have also adopted computerized trading systems to increase market transparency and the capacity of the market to handle the surge in activity that accompanies financial integration. These improvements are remarkable. A key lesson that can be drawn from recent country experience, especially in Asia, is that it is possible to achieve rapid progress and in some areas leapfrog to state-of-the-art systems with a sustained and well-organized effort.

At the same time, country experience also suggests that the G-30/ISSA benchmarks are objectives to be attained over time and tailored to country circumstances. For example, the shortening of the settlement cycle to the G-30 benchmark of T+3 (the third day after the trade) has been a key focus of this effort. But the emphasis on speed may not be fully justified. Foreign investors care less about G-30 speed standards than about reliability. Malaysia, one of the more successful emerging markets, illustrates this point very well: although settling only at T+5, it has been able to achieve one of the more reliable settlement systems in the developing world.

Similarly, developing countries need to give greater emphasis to reducing systemic risks in their securities markets. With respect to international benchmarks, least progress has been made in achieving delivery versus payment in the settlement process. With central depositories, the delivery side of the equation is generally working well. It is on the payment side that delivery versus payment seems to fail, perhaps because of weaknesses in the domestic banking and payment systems. Market authorities in developing countries should also consider setting strict membership standards for clearinghouses and other focal points of transmission of systemic risks. High entry standards are particularly important until other risk reduction systems become fully operational at the clearinghouse and until the brokerage industry strengthens.

Despite the major improvements in market infrastructure and performance in recent years, there is still a gap between emerging and mature markets. As shown in figure 6.3, chapter 6, industrial countries are more efficient by a factor of 10 to one regarding the average number of days it takes to collect dividends, 20 to one regarding the average number of days to register, and two or three to one regarding trades that settle with a delay. The width of the gap varies widely among emerging markets. For some countries, such as India, the gap is very striking. Other markets, such as Korea and Mexico, have a performance close to or even better than that of industrial markets.

Legal and regulatory framework. Constructing and reinforcing the regulatory framework is essential for emerging markets to attract foreign investors and reduce systemic risk. Investors are most concerned with protection of property rights (including minority shareholder rights) and transparency. For example, investors want both macro data on economic prospects and micro data on corporate performance, to be able to make informed investment choices. Improving disclosure will not only address investor concerns but will also reduce the susceptibility of the market to volatility resulting from incomplete or asymmetric information.

Unlike market infrastructure, however, there are no clear-cut criteria for a sound regulatory framework, and institutional structures and practices in industrial countries vary considerably depending on historical antecedents. There is, nevertheless, a growing convergence toward the so-called self-regulatory organization (SRO) model, one based on public disclosure, on self-imposed market and industry discipline, and on better internal risk management by financial firms themselves.[11] The key elements of this model are discussed in box 1.4.

The SRO model faces a number of potential problems in emerging markets: the institutional and human capital may be insufficient to en-

Box 1.4 Principles of the Self-Regulatory Model

FIRST, THE PURPOSE OF THE REGULATOR IS NOT to substitute for the market in helping investors to make investment decisions, but to ensure that the incentives and structure of the market are consistent with efficiency, fairness, and safety. The regulatory framework should ensure that timely and accurate information is available, so that investors can judge the merits of alternative investments, hence the regulatory emphasis on disclosure and eradicating fraud. The regulator should prohibit insider trading for fairness reasons, and because such practices have the negative externality of discouraging investors and savers from participating in capital markets.

Second, market participants, rather than government, should have the main responsibility for establishing and enforcing market rules and regulations. The rationale is that participants have an interest in ensuring that markets are fair and efficient and are better able to judge how to make them so. In practical terms, this means that self-regulatory organizations (SROs) such as the exchanges, broker-dealer associations, and accounting and auditing associations will bear much of the responsibility for the regulation and surveillance of securities markets and auxiliary supporting services. For the system to work correctly, the official regulator must have sufficient regulatory oversight to ensure that the SROs enforce securities regulations as well as their own market conduct rules, and that they act to minimize potential conflicts of interest and restraints on competition.

Third, concerns about systemic risk in capital markets do not justify prudential regulations and monitoring as intense as those in the banking sector. As a general rule, investment firms are less vulnerable than banks, on both the asset side and the liability side, to liquidity and solvency crises, and are less prone to contagion. An exception to this rule regards clearance and settlement arrangements, discussed above. However, with the increasing integration of banks and securities businesses, there is a much stronger rationale for intensifying prudential rules and oversight of the latter.

Fourth, the protection of investor's assets from loss and the insolvency of investment firms is another rationale for prudential rules and oversight of investment firms. Investment firms are often required to meet capital adequacy standards, segregate investor's assets, and meet minimum internal operational standards. In addition, the legal system should provide the basis for protecting investor's assets. Disclosure to investors of the level and type of risks to which their assets are exposed and the financial status of investment firms is essential for market discipline to play a role in reducing these risks.

Fifth, financial innovation, in particular the development of a wide variety of derivative products, is leading to some important changes in how financial firms are regulated. Although derivative trading still involves price risk, the speed with which these risks can be transformed and the opacity of the transformation process make it difficult for regulators to assess the degree of exposure of financial firms. The regulatory response to this lack of transparency has been to focus on the ability of each firm to manage these risks, and to create incentives for financial firms to put in place appropriate risk control procedures. This is a relatively new area of concern in emerging markets, since derivative products are not widely used (except in Brazil and Malaysia) or may actually be proscribed. However, as financial integration intensifies, domestic financial firms may trade in these instruments overseas.

sure that two pillars of the system—self-regulation and disclosure—result in fair and efficient markets, the structure of the securities markets is imperfect because of limited competition, and there may be short-term tensions between the regulatory and market development objectives of the authorities or the SROs. Despite these problems, however, the self-regulatory model is the best alternative, and emerging markets appear to be converging toward it.

Emerging markets have also made progress in developing their framework of law and statutory regulation. All the major emerging markets now have in place the basic building blocks of such a framework; for instance, they have enacted securities laws (Russia most recently) and established independent securities commissions.[12] Accounting standards of many emerging markets have also strengthened considerably, although accounting practices are often impeded by the lack of qualified accountants and auditors, a common problem in many emerging markets. Finally, most major emerging markets now have regulations defining disclosure standards and listing requirements.

Where the gap between developing countries and their industrial counterparts is still wide is in the more detailed, but still critical, aspects of a sound regulatory framework. For instance, about half of the emerging markets in a sample of 16 (see table 6.6, chapter 6) have not established the legal and regulatory basis for compensation funds, takeovers, and insider trading.[13] Many emerging markets have not yet instituted the legal and regulatory basis for domestic institutional investors. More broadly, there is a danger of overregulation in Asia, which may stifle market development and discourage foreign investors. In Latin America, the danger seems to be underregulation or lack of effective enforcement. In Eastern Europe and the former Soviet Union, the main task is to establish the basic legal and regulatory framework for capital market development.

The remaining agenda. Developing countries show considerable variation in the capital market attributes needed for financial integration. The most dynamic emerging markets, where progress has been particularly intense during the last five years, include most of high-growth Asia (Korea, Malaysia, and Thailand, with Indonesia and the Philippines not far behind) and two markets in Latin America (Chile and Mexico, with Brazil also ranking well). The East Asian markets stand out for their depth and liquidity, and because of efforts undertaken in the 1990s their market infrastructures are now equal to those in Latin America. The lagging emerging markets in the sample are in South Asia (India, Pakistan, and Sri Lanka) and China. Generally, these countries need to continue to improve their market infrastructures, as well as their institutional development. But even in the most advanced markets, the outstanding agenda is large. In the infrastructure area, for example, about 20 percent of all securities trades in Malaysia and Thailand do not settle on the contractual settlement date—four times more than in the United States.

To close the gap, emerging markets should pursue the following policy agenda:

- *Infrastructure.* Emerging markets should implement well-synchronized comparison, clearance and settlement, and central depository systems, with the goal of meeting G-30/ISSA guidelines, though not at the expense of reliability. Emerging markets should also pay close attention to reducing systemic risk by developing sound links with the banking and payment systems. In addition, the risk control procedures of a central clearing agency, if such an agency is required, should meet Bank for International Settlements (BIS) guidelines, and a central depository should be established early in the integration process.
- *Property rights.* The legal and regulatory framework should include two basic principles of shareholder governance: fair treatment for all shareholders and shareholder approval of key corporate decisions. In transition economies, it is essential to establish an independent registry of equity ownership so that records cannot be manipulated by management or shareholders.
- *The regulatory framework.* Emerging markets should adopt international best practice on disclosure (including accounting) and self-regulation to local conditions, and improve enforcement of these rules. Government regulatory functions (starting with oversight of trading activities) should be devolved to SROs as quickly as practicable but should take into account potential conflicts of interest and the capacity of the SROs.

Finally, emerging markets should also promote the development of domestic institutional investors, who can serve as a counterweight to foreign investors and thereby assuage fears of excessive foreign presence. Domestic institutional investors can ensure that a large pool of dedicated money will be available for bottom fishing and value picking, which will reduce the vulnerability of domestic capital markets to a rapid liquidation of assets by foreign investors. In addition, domestic institutional investors will increase the depth and liquidity of domestic capital markets, enabling the markets to absorb the benefits that integration can produce.

New Regulatory Challenges and the Need for International Cooperation

A basic problem that financial integration creates for regulators is that although financial institutions and transactions are increasingly global, their activity and authority remain mainly national in scope. Given this limited scope, regulators would not be able to insulate their domestic financial systems from overseas volatility and shocks unless they cooperated and coordinated with foreign supervisory and regulatory authorities. In other words, while the domestic policy and institutional improvements described previously are critical to prepare for financial integration, they need to be complemented by international initiatives.

The new risks and challenges. Financial integration can affect the nature and magnitude of the underlying market, counterparty, and systemic risks in domestic financial markets. In particular:

- As domestic financial firms engage in cross-border activities, they may incur new market risk from open positions in exchange- and interest-rate-sensitive foreign assets and liabilities.
- Domestic residents, including financial institutions, engaging in cross-border transactions will be exposed to new counterparty and credit risks with foreign investors and firms.
- Systemic risks also increase with financial integration, since it subjects the home country to more sources of external disturbances and increases the speed at which these disturbances are transmitted.[14] Systemic risk also rises because increasing volume and the different hours of operation among payment systems delay settlement and increase settlement risks.

These activities and associated risks are creating new and interrelated regulatory challenges in two broad areas. First, the most obvious challenge is to contain these new sources of systemic and counterparty risk at the same time that globalization is rendering the regulatory environment more complex.

Second, globalization is also magnifying the importance of regulatory issues that arise from cross-country differences in regulations and the possibility that financial intermediaries will engage in regulatory arbitrage—that is, seek to take advantage of differences in regulations and their coverage among countries.

Two other trends in international financial markets are interacting with globalization, significantly magnifying the regulatory challenge:

- First, financial firms are increasingly becoming financial conglomerates, combining traditional banking with securities operations and other nonbank financial activities.
- Second, financial innovation has resulted in a vast array of new derivative instruments that can change the risk profile of financial firms very quickly and in a very complex manner.

In summary, globalization, combined with financial innovation and conglomerates, is increasing the channels and speed of transmission of systemic shocks across borders and sectors while reducing transparency in the marketplace. This lack of transparency is undermining the ability of the market to police itself and of the authorities to regulate.

The international regulatory response. National regulatory authorities have tried to address the risks and challenges of globalization through stronger international cooperation. One clear objective of this cooperation has been to control systemic risk, since national regulatory frameworks in this area obviously have an impact across borders. Indeed, there seems to be growing concern among national authorities, heightened by the failure of Barings bank in 1995, regarding the dangers of unregulated or underregulated financial activities of global firms.[15] There has also been international cooperation in the area of investor protection, with long-standing efforts to harmonize regulations across countries and promote international cooperation in enforcement. In the securities markets, these efforts were undertaken in part to reduce transaction costs and increase market efficiency, and are motivated by pressure from institutional investors and international issuers. With regard to banks, these efforts were primarily directed at achieving a level playing field for banking institutions from different countries. And for both banks and securities markets, these efforts were also directed at addressing the fears that competition between financial centers would result in a regulatory race to the bottom, and that banks and investors would practice regulatory arbitrage.

Recent international initiatives show a gradual convergence toward regulatory systems more based on disclosure and market discipline that increase the incentives for improved internal methods of risk control.

There are several reasons for this. First, this convergence illustrates the growing global financial clout of institutional investors who strongly prefer a system based on strong disclosure. Second—and more important, as noted above, in today's sophisticated global financial markets—the risk exposure of financial firms is increasingly hard to quantify and, in any case, is changing very quickly. In addition, it is hard for regulators to keep up with the rapid evolution of financial instruments and techniques. Hence, a consensus has emerged that regulators would do better by supervising the quality of risk management (rather than the position of a firm at a particular moment in time) and by ensuring adequate disclosure for market discipline to work effectively.

The focus of international cooperation has been the Basle Committee on Banking Supervision for banking regulators, and the International Organization of Securities Commissions (IOSCO) for securities regulators. Both have played a key role in these endeavors to reduce transaction costs and systemic risk. The IMF has also played an important role, in particular in the area of ensuring adequate disclosure of macroeconomic information. The main international initiatives are described in box 1.5.

The main efforts at international collaboration in banking supervison have focused on developing prudential standards, which in early stages were designed primarily for international banks in industrial countries. The rash of severe crises in developing countries over the past 15 years has, however, recently rekindled interest in developing more comprehensive guidelines. Indeed, international supervisory and regulatory authorities are expected to issue such guidelines in the near future.

Other efforts at international collaboration in financial markets have focused on clearance, settlement, and payment systems and on regulating financial conglomerates. In the payment area, settlement and systemic risk have been reduced by harmonizing regional payment standards and increasing the overlap of hours of operation of different payment systems. With regard to financial conglomerates, securities, banking, and insurance regulators have been collaborating in developing principles for the supervision of financial conglomerates and for collaboration among the three different types of regulators.[16] Finally, the private sector itself has been the source of initiatives on best practice, as well as a key source of advice and criticism for official initiatives. The G-30 (for example, in the area of capital market infrastructure), the Institute of International Finance (in macroeconomic information standards), the International Federation of Stock Exchanges (in controlling systemic risk in equity markets), and many others have played important roles.

Policy implications for emerging markets. The above discussion suggests several implications for policymakers responsible for emerging securities markets. First, reducing information asymmetries across borders has a high payoff both for reducing systemic risk and for improving the efficiency of financial markets. At the macroeconomic level, more accurate and timely disclosure of country macroeconomic data would increase the informational content of the capital flows to developing countries and reduce the likelihood of cross-country contagion of financial shocks. More emphasis on disclosure of accurate information

Box 1.5 International Regulatory Cooperation and Coordination

THE MAIN EFFORTS OF THE BASLE COMMITTEE and IOSCO are as follows:

- Among the more successful efforts in international regulatory cooperation is the so-called Basle system for banking supervision and regulation. It consists of a series of agreements over the period 1975–92 among banking regulators from the main industrial countries. These include understandings on the allocation of regulatory responsibilities, on collaboration arrangements including information sharing and enforcement, on supervisory standards, and on the harmonization of minimum capital adequacy standards. The 1988 agreement on capital adequacy is perhaps the most important of these achievements (see annex 5.3).
- The Basle Committee has been working in the 1990s on refining capital adequacy standards so as to take into account the growing importance of market risk in bank portfolios, including the rapid increase in trading in futures and options. After extensive debate, the committee issued its final recommendations in December 1995. Two of the most important aspects of this agreement are the use of the concept of "value at risk" and permitting the more sophisticated banks to use their own internal risk management systems to determine their own capital adequacy requirements.[1] The new guidelines, however, continue to be the subject of much debate. Among the most important areas of concern are the apprehensions of securities regulators that banks and securities firms may develop models that reduce capital requirements rather than measure market risk adequately, and the impact of the guidelines on the competitive positions of international banks.
- In the securities area, to promote regulatory convergence and reduce transaction costs, IOSCO has issued many reports and resolutions on best practice, including such areas as curbing and punishing securities fraud, disclosure and accounting standards, clearance and settlement, and investor protection (which is also important in reducing systemic risk). In addition, given the strong representation of emerging markets at IOSCO, its resolutions, reports, and accompanying discussions

of the financial status and risk profile of financial intermediaries would increase the effectiveness of market discipline. And for regulators, there is a high payoff in information sharing and enforcement agreements, both between emerging and industrial country markets and among developing countries themselves. In particular, although authorities in the home country bear the main responsibility for cross-border supervision of banks' activities, authorities in host countries can help by monitoring specific aspects, such as banks' liquidity, and, most important, by removing impediments to the exchange of relevant information between supervisory authorities.

Second, as financial integration deepens, the experience of the BIS member countries suggests that it would be highly beneficial for devel-

have served as a conduit for the transfer of expertise and experience between countries.

- In the area of systemic risk, especially during the 1990s, a key focus of both the Basle Committee and IOSCO has been to contain the systemic risks arising from derivative activities. In this regard, they collaborated in several reports during 1994–95 on best practice in disclosure of both qualitative and quantitative information of derivative activities (for example, Basle Committee and IOSCO 1995a and 1995b), and in the internal management and control of risk. IOSCO is also fleshing out the recommendations made in May 1995 by the regulators of most major futures and options markets (the Windsor Declaration), including protection of customer positions and assets, and the strengthening of default procedures.
- Given that its recommendations are advisory and nonbinding to its members, IOSCO has strongly encouraged coordination among members, in particular through bilateral agreements (memoranda of understanding) regarding information sharing and enforcement.[2] While there has been a sharp increase in the number of these bilateral agreements these last few years, many of these understandings have been between industrial countries, some between industrial and developing countries, and only a few between developing countries. Recently, in response to the Windsor Declaration, both exchanges, clearinghouses, and regulators of the major global futures and option markets have signed information-sharing agreements.

1. Value at risk is an estimate of the maximum loss in the value of a portfolio, including positions in futures and options, over a certain time period and at a certain level of confidence. The confidence level refers to the probability that the loss will be lower than a presepecified maximum. See IMF (1995) for a discussion of the concept and estimation procedures.

2. These memoranda usually include all or a subset of the following: routine sharing of general information, sharing of certain information on firms operating in the two markets, access to official information held by the counterpart regulator that may help in an investigation or an enforcement action, approval of certain investigative powers of the domestic regulator in the counterpart country, and the obligation to report to the other party that a firm is experiencing financial difficulties.

Source: Dale (1996), IMF (1995 and 1996), and Goldstein (1996).

oping countries to become more active members in international arrangements regarding bank supervision. Unlike IOSCO, the Basle Committee and other international institutions in this area (for example, the European Union) include mainly Organisation for Economic Co-operation and Development (OECD) countries. It is also in the best interest of the industrial countries to extend the improvements in regulation and supervision in international financial markets to the larger and systemically important developing countries. However, there is still no clear view on the best way to achieve this extension of the multilateral framework of bank surveillance. In addition, many developing countries would have to improve significantly their prudential standards and supervisory practices to meet the minimum standards of the Basle Committee.

The Role of Official Finance

The large increase in private capital flows to developing countries raises the issue of the role that official finance plays in an age of global private capital. Although private flows now surpass official flows by a margin of five to one, the vast majority of developing countries receive relatively little private capital. Low-income countries (excluding China and India) received only 3.4 percent of total private capital flows to developing countries during the past three years, and all of Sub-Saharan Africa (excluding South Africa) received only 1.5 percent of the total. Indeed, these countries remain largely dependent on official financing (figure 1.11). The challenge for these nations, and many middle-income countries, is to establish the prerequisites for attracting private capital on a sustainable basis.

There is now compelling evidence that success in attracting private flows depends on macroeconomic fundamentals, outward orientation and a market-friendly environment, and progress on infrastructure and human resource development (box 1.2 and box 2.2). The experience of countries that have been most successful in attracting private capital suggests that official finance has played an important facilitating role in helping them establish these necessary conditions. These countries have typically relied on significant official finance during the two decades preceding the surge in private flows in the 1990s to support the buildup of physical and human capital stocks.

Perhaps even more significant, for a majority of these major recipients, the surge in private capital flows was preceded by concerted policy

Figure 1.11 Official and Private Gross Capital Flows to Low-Income Countries (excluding China and India), 1970–95

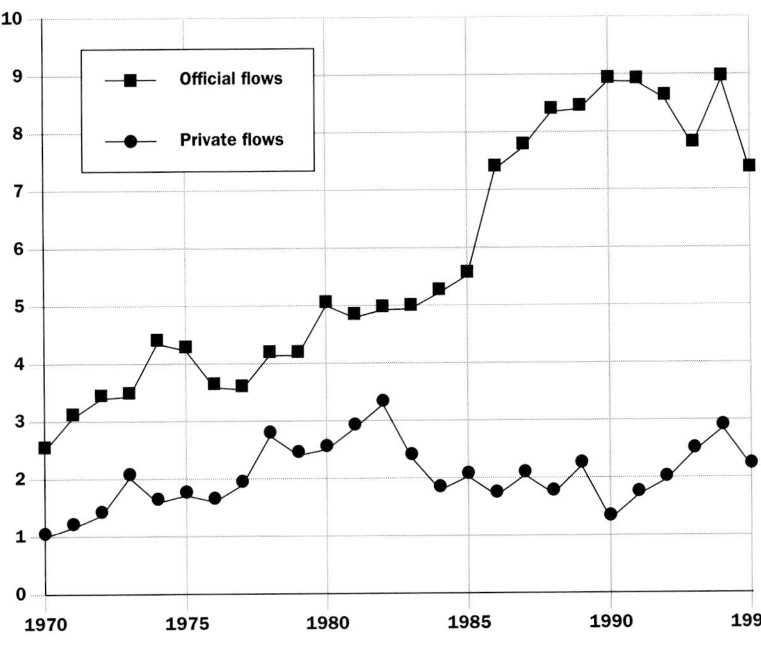

Source: World Bank data.

Except for China and India, low-income countries depend more on official financing than on private capital flows.

lending by the IMF and the World Bank, sometimes with an increase in the overall level of official assistance. For some countries, the surge was preceded by the successful completion of a Brady debt reduction operation. Policy advice and conditionality associated with this lending and the Brady operations played an important facilitating role, by helping these countries attain macroeconomic stability and adopt market-oriented policies, and by signaling these improvements to private markets. An analysis of the determinants of private capital flows for a sample of 73 developing countries shows that net lending from multilateral sources and the completion of Brady operations have both played complementary roles in facilitating private capital flows (Corbo and Hernández 1997).

The challenge for official finance in the case of the vast majority of countries that are not yet attracting private capital is to foster change that would raise private returns (through policy reforms and sound public investments) and to help countries address the two main impediments to private capital flows—high risks and limited information.

The principles that govern the role of official assistance apply as well to developing countries that are already attracting substantial amounts of private capital. Despite significant progress, most of the major developing country recipients of private capital still have limited macroeconomic track records, do not yet have robust banking systems, suffer from deficiencies in infrastructure and human resource development, and more generally lack the institutional structures needed for integrated financial markets. Accordingly, while the role of official finance has appropriately declined for this group of countries (figure 1.12), it can continue to play a valuable complementary role to private flows even in these countries for several important reasons:

- Official assistance can help sustain improvements in the policy and institutional framework. One area of particular importance is the strengthening of banking systems. Financial systems that are not performing their critical functions (resource mobilization and allocation, monitoring investments, facilitating risk management, and providing payments mechanisms) are more likely to misallocate capital and contribute to increased vulnerability in the face of growing financial integration. But strengthening the financial sector is a complex and long-term task, and the differences in countries' financial systems and the dynamic nature of financial sector development mean that no one formula will work in all systems. International agencies can be a source of knowledge of what has worked and what has failed, and why, and can also help countries with institutional development and expertise in effecting reform programs. Recognizing the important role that the financial sector plays, multilateral institutions—including the World Bank, the IMF, other multilateral development banks, the BIS, and the Group of Ten (G-10)—are expanding their efforts in this area.
- Although markets are becoming more discerning, and more countries are adopting the needed policy reforms, developing countries that are attracting private capital flows will remain vulnerable to shocks and large reversals for some time to come. The IMF, the World Bank, and other official lenders can reduce the likelihood and costs of such reversals by helping to improve the

Figure 1.12 Official and Private Gross Capital Flows to the 12 Largest Recipients of Private Capital, 1970–95

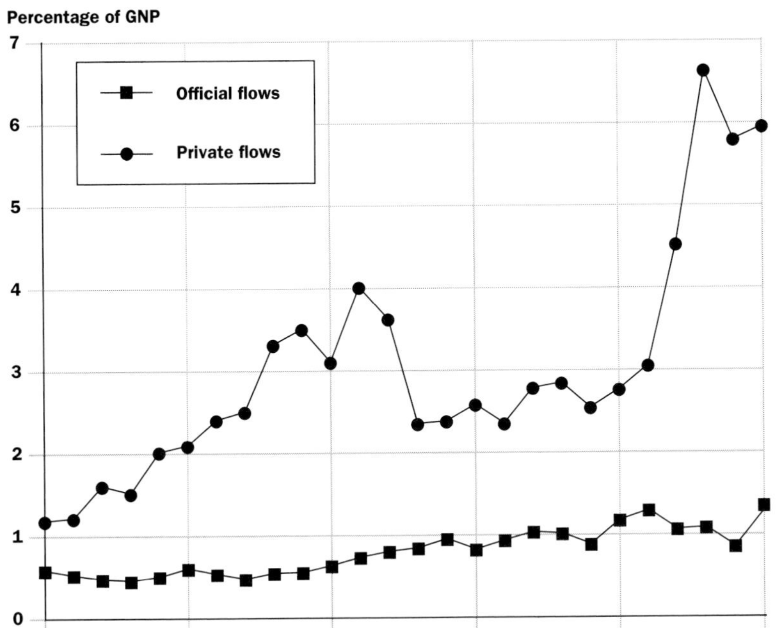

Note: The countries are Argentina, Brazil, Chile, China, India, Indonesia, Hungary, Malaysia, Mexico, Russia, Thailand, and Turkey.
Source: World Bank data.

Within the last few years, private capital has rapidly outstripped official financing in the 12 developing countries that received the largest amounts of private investment.

availability of information about these markets, and by helping countries get back on track in the face of balance-of-payments difficulties. The IMF has recently formalized the procedures used in the Mexican crisis as a mechanism for emergency financial support, and has established New Arrangements to Borrow that will make available resources of up to SDR 34 billion (special drawing rights, about US$48 billion) for such support. The IMF has also drawn up standards for the dissemination of data, and some countries have started to provide the financial markets with better information.

- Official lenders can also finance and help improve the quality of investments in human resources and infrastructure, and support adequate social and environmental protection. These are all areas where private returns will often be less than the social returns, and where public investments play a vital role in enhancing the productivity of private investment. Official assistance can also promote increased private participation in the infrastructure and human resources sectors, by supporting improvements in the policy and institutional framework and by assisting with privatization programs. In addition, support for poverty reduction and better social safety nets will not only promote human development—an important determinant of long-term growth—but reduce risks of social and political instability as well. This complementary role of official financing is being reflected in the changing composition of lending by official agencies. For instance, lending for environment, social sectors, and infrastructure now constitutes 80 percent of total World Bank investment lending, compared with 60 percent in the early 1980s.

- International financial institutions may also be able to catalyze private investment by providing selective guarantees for risks that they may be better able to mitigate—such as political risks and risks arising from shifts in the regulatory regime—or for promoting pioneering investments with large potential spillover benefits. Although third-party guarantees complicate negotiations on the cost of financing, guarantees by multilateral agencies can play a useful role in reducing the uncertainties surrounding the future policy regime. Even if the government establishes a schedule of changes for the telephone industry, for example, or commits to a formula for electricity tariffs, private lenders may still fear that such decisions will be reversed. Agencies such as the World Bank can support transactions by placing their influence and financial resources behind the government's commitment (World Bank 1997).
- Finally, official institutions can work directly with private partners to expand and improve private capital flows (de Larosière 1996).[17] In addition to the use of guarantees, the experience of the IFC and the European Bank for Recovery and Development (EBRD) shows that multilateral agencies can work directly with private companies in a number of ways. They and other multilateral agencies have helped set up joint ventures for activities such as leasing, venture capital, infrastructure development, and banking, which have not only brought benefits in terms of loan and equity financing, but have transferred know-how, encouraged financial innovation, spurred privatization, provided demonstra-

tion effects of good management and professionalism, and promoted institutional development.

The catalytic role of official finance outlined above is greater than ever before because of the increased responsiveness of private capital and the shift to market-oriented policies in developing countries. Research shows, however, that aid is not effective when the framework for good economic policies—especially sound macroeconomic policies—and governance is lacking. Indeed, increased official borrowing can have an adverse effect on private flows if the returns are not commensurate with the cost of borrowing (by reducing tax-adjusted expected rates of return) and if it sustains policy distortions and fiscal laxity. Hence policy performance is a key prerequisite and should be the driving force determining the allocation of all types of aid. Official assistance also needs to be redirected to those areas where it can be most effective and generate the greatest leverage—and this will vary according to country situations.

While official finance can continue to play a complementary role in countries that have been more successful in attracting private capital, official concessional assistance is especially important for many low-income countries. There is an urgent need for continued concessional assistance to support reform programs in these countries and address their large needs in human, social, and infrastructure development, because without such assistance they would fall even farther behind.

The infusions of private capital that financial integration is channeling to developing countries can—and will—do much to transform these nations, but whether the transformation is beneficial or detrimental depends, to a large extent, on these countries' ability to develop the institutions and implement the policies that will allow integration to succeed. Unfortunately, they must accomplish these tasks in an environment that affords restricted scope for independent action, and they must start down the road to financial integration before they are fully ready for the journey. Even so, it is within the power of these nations to realize substantial gains in the new age of global private capital.

Notes

1. Korea has been classified as a high-income country since 1996.

2. Such risks include not only sovereign risk—which is still quite high in developing countries given their relatively short policy track record—but also higher investment risks, such as legal and custodial risks, settlement and operational risks, information and regulatory risks, and nonmarket risks. Hence part of the differential in expected rates of return between industrial and developing countries reflects these higher risks in the latter.

3. Direct measures of financial integration based on the equalization of expected returns are difficult to construct for developing countries, given that forward markets or surveys of exchange rate expectations exist for only a small proportion of developing countries. Under managed exchange rates, potential "peso problem" difficulties make it hard to construct a measure of integration based on arbitrage.

4. In fact, correlations between returns in emerging markets and industrial countries would likely rise in the very process of such a massive reallocation (as emerging markets would become more integrated).

5. Technological innovations, which increase the rate of return to capital, could mitigate some of the adverse effects of an eventual decline in the labor force on the relative rate of return to capital.

6. The country episodes we analyze are Argentina 1979–82 and 1992–93, Brazil 1992–94, Chile 1978–81 and 1989–94, Colombia 1992–94, Finland 1987–94, Indonesia 1990–94, Malaysia 1980–86 and 1989–94, Mexico 1979–81 and 1989–94, Norway 1984–89, the Philippines 1978–83 and 1989–94, Sweden 1989–93, Thailand 1978–84 and 1988–94, and Venezuela 1975–80 and 1992–93.

7. Among the countries that experienced an excessively large current account deficit were Chile 1978–81, Malaysia 1980–86, Mexico 1979–81 and 1989–94, the Philippines 1978–83, and Sweden 1989–93. Country episodes in which the consumption boom was larger than expected comprise Argentina 1992–93, Brazil 1992–94, Finland 1987–94, Mexico 1989–94, Norway 1984–89, Sweden 1989–93, and Venezuela 1975–80. Finally, the country episodes in which investment was lower than expected were Argentina 1979–82, Brazil 1992–94, Chile 1978–81, Finland 1987–94, and Mexico 1989–94.

8. These banking sector reforms need to be complemented by supportive macroeconomic policies, given the importance of macroeconomic stability for sustained reforms and the possibility of increased macroeconomic swings in an open environment. In particular, the threat of large capital flow reversals and their consequent impact on the banking system (through loss of deposits, higher interest rates, and downturn in economic activity) makes macroeconomic stability an even more vital prerequisite in an integrated setting.

9. To date, foreign investors have been more attracted to emerging market debt issued in international or industrial country markets than to domestic issues in developing countries. Hence the report focuses on improvements in emerging stock markets, although many development issues in the areas of market infrastructure and the regulatory framework are common to both debt and equity markets.

10. Market infrastructure comprises the systems and institutions that facilitate the trade and custody of securities. These functions can be subdivided into matching buyers and sellers, determining price, exchanging securities for good funds, registering securities to the new owners, and collecting dividends and other custody functions.

11. Strahota (1996) describes how this model could be applied in emerging markets.

12. The latter is a relatively recent phenomenon in many Asian countries, where independent commissions replaced ministries of finance and central banks as the primary regulators of securities markets only in the early 1990s.

13. Compensation funds protect investors from losses arising from the failure of broker-dealers (not market risks), while takeover rules protect the rights of minority shareholders in a company targeted for a takeover.

14. Most directly, the effects of a collapse or the insolvency of a financial firm in another country may be transmitted to domestic markets, either directly, if the firm has established itself in the domestic market, or through the payment and settlement systems.

15. The regulatory implications of the failure of Barings are discussed in Dale (1996) and IMF (1995).

16. This includes the report of the so-called Tripartite Group and the ongoing work by the Joint Forum. See IMF (1996).

17. "The basis of MDB collaboration with the private sector is straightforward. The funds, instruments, independence, and experience of the MDBs are combined with the know-how, management capabilities, and capital of the private sector. Provided it takes account of the characteristics of the project, the market environment, and the needs of the partners, this combination is a powerful force for private sector development." (Jacques de Larosière, the Per Jacobsson Lecture, IMF, Washington, D.C., September 29, 1996.)

CHAPTER 2

The New International Environment

THE CYCLICAL DOWNTURN IN GLOBAL INTEREST rates in the early 1990s provided an important initial impetus for the resumption of private capital flows to developing countries. The fact that private capital flows to developing countries have persisted even after the upturn in interest rates in industrial countries suggests, however, that these flows have entered a new phase, reflecting structural forces that are leading to the progressive integration of developing countries in world financial markets. The two primary forces that are driving investor interest in developing countries and leading to their increased integration are the search for higher returns and opportunities for risk diversification. Although these underlying forces have always motivated investors, the responsiveness of private capital to cross-border opportunities has gained new momentum as a result of internal and external financial deregulation in both industrial and developing countries and major advances in technology and financial instruments. Figure 2.1 summarizes the process.

In industrial countries two key developments have increased the responsiveness of private capital to cross-border investment opportunities. First, competition and rising costs in domestic markets, along with falling transport and communications costs, have encouraged firms to look for opportunities to increase efficiency and returns (that is, profits) by producing abroad. This is leading to the progressive globalization of production and to the growth of "efficiency-seeking" FDI flows. Second, financial markets have been transformed over a span of two decades from relatively insulated and regulated national markets toward a more globally integrated market. This has been brought about by a mutually reinforcing process of advances in communications, in-

Figure 2.1 Structural Forces Driving Private Capital to Developing Countries

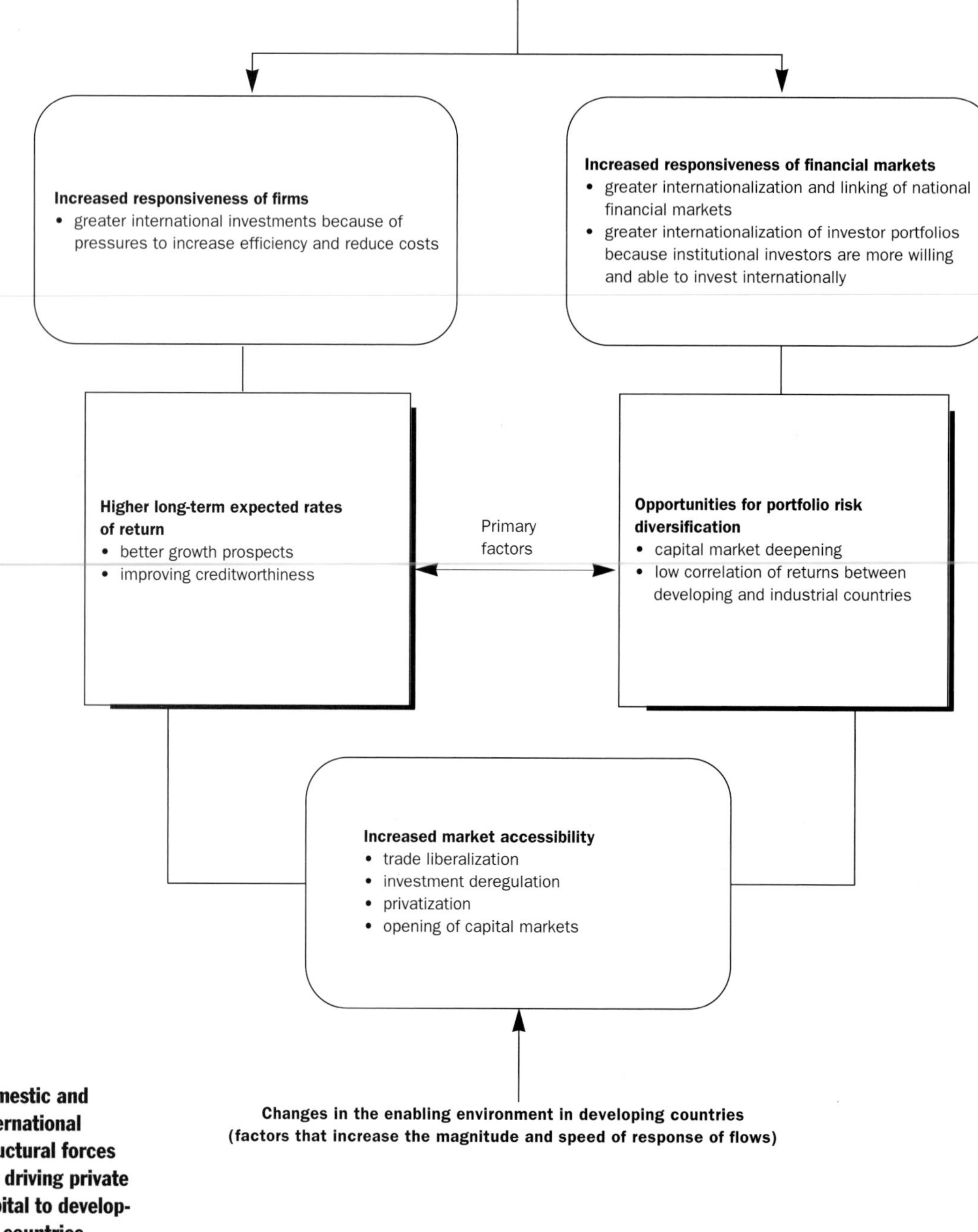

Domestic and international structural forces are driving private capital to developing countries.

formation, and financial instruments, and by progressive internal and external deregulation of financial markets. An important facet of this globalization of capital markets has been the growing importance of *institutional investors who are both willing and able to invest internationally.*

In developing countries, the environment is also changing rapidly. Since the mid-1980s, several countries have embarked on structural reform programs and have increased the openness of their markets, through the progressive lowering of barriers to trade and foreign investment, the liberalization of domestic financial markets and removal of restrictions on capital movements, and the implementation of privatization programs.

Although perceived risks of investing in emerging markets remain high, these reforms have led to improvements in country creditworthiness risks, declines in investment risk, and increases in expected rates of return. As developing countries' securities markets have broadened and deepened, and as their market accessibility has increased, these countries have also begun to offer investors significant opportunitites for risk diversification, which arise from the low correlation between rates of return in emerging markets and industrial countries. As a result, foreign investors, who initially turned to emerging markets largely because of the cyclical downturn in interest rates and stock market returns in industrial countries in 1990, have begun to consider these markets on a more long-term basis.

These changes both in the international setting and in developing countries have meant that developing countries have seen a strong surge of private capital in the 1990s. Of all the types of capital, FDI has responded most vigorously to the improving economic environment in developing countries. Commercial bank lending, which accounted for the bulk of the flows in the late 1970s and early 1980s, has also made a strong comeback. What is striking, however, is the growth of portfolio bond and equity flows. Whereas developing countries attracted barely any portfolio flows a decade ago, in the past five years they have received almost 30 percent of global equity flows. This growth was first stimulated by mutual funds, which were at the forefront of emerging market investments. More recently, pension funds have followed suit, investing either through mutual funds or directly on their own behalf. Consequently, institutional investors now form a very important part of the investor base in emerging markets, and this chapter focuses primarily on these investors and their (portfolio) investments.

Together, these developments have resulted in a wider range of investors and a broader composition of flows to developing countries, with an increasing share of these investments going to the private sector.

The process driving the financial integration of developing countries is still unfolding, but some of the implications are clear:

- Continuing deregulation of financial markets in industrial countries, and technological progress and financial innovations at the international level, will spur increased responsiveness of private capital to international investment opportunities.
- Developing countries' markets are likely to become increasingly accessible, and policy reforms are likely to deepen in countries that are already implementing such reforms and broaden to countries that are not yet embarked on the process.

As a result, the financial integration of developing countries is expected to deepen and broaden over the coming decade, against a backdrop of increasing global financial integration. Indeed, given the changes that are taking place at the international level—in particular, the rapid advances in technology, communications, and financial innovations—and the growing economic sophistication in developing countries, the progressive financial integration of the latter in world financial markets appears inevitable. Gross private capital flows may therefore be expected to rise substantially, with capital flowing not only from industrial to developing countries but, increasingly, among developing countries themselves and from developing to industrial countries.

Aggregate net private capital flows to developing countries are likely to be sustained in the short to medium term because of the continuing decline in creditworthiness risks and other investment risks, the higher expected rates of return in developing countries, and the fact that these countries are underweighted in the portfolios of institutional investors. The rate of growth, though, and eventually, the levels, will inevitably decline. There will probably also be considerable variation among countries, depending on the pace and depth of improvements in macroeconomic performance and creditworthiness. In fact, in countries where economic and policy fundamentals are quite weak, the initial manifestation of growing financial integration may take the form of net outflows of private capital.

With changes in the international financial environment, there are likely to be considerable year-to-year fluctuations in private capital flows to developing countries, even in aggregate. Emerging markets will probably continue to be more susceptible to shocks from the international environment than industrial countries are, a prospect that raises concerns in developing countries because private capital can now respond quite rapidly to actual or perceived changes.

In the international environment, three factors in particular are seen as having the potential for creating significant volatility in private capital flows to developing countries:

- Movements in international interest rates and other asset returns—especially movements in industrial country stock markets. Private capital flows to emerging markets are considered to be particularly affected by changes in these factors because investors regard these markets as marginal.[1]
- Investor herding behavior. The new investor base in developing countries—dominated by institutional investors—is widely thought to be prone to herding behavior, arising from its incentive structure and the relatively limited information available on developing country investments.
- Contagion or spillover effects, which arise when events in one emerging market cause investors to change their investment decisions in other emerging markets. The likelihood of contagion is also seen to be high in the current international environment, in part because of institutional features in the current investor base.

Emerging markets are, in fact, more susceptible to volatility emanating from the international financial environment—particularly to global interest rate and stock market movements. However, large movements in international interest rates appear unlikely, given that industrial countries are now operating in a low-inflation environment and hence are not likely to require sharp corrections in monetary stance. There is a higher likelihood of relatively large movements in industrial country stock market returns. A sizable decline in industrial country stock markets—especially in the U.S. stock market—could result in a general retrenchment, since investors would adjust to the negative wealth effect. Such a retrenchment is likely to be disproportionate with regard to investments in emerging markets, as emerging markets are more marginal in investors' portfolios. A small correction in the U.S. stock market could, however, result in a positive stimulus to emerging markets, as investors respond to the relatively higher returns in these markets. Finally, although emerging markets are more prone to potential contagion effects, the likelihood of sustained volatility arising from pure contagion is also declining, because investors are becoming more familiar with emerging markets.

At the individual country level, though, there is likely to be considerable variation. In particular, factors in the international environment could interact with domestic policies and conditions to give rise to significant differences in the volatility of private capital. Thus, the international environment could magnify and exacerbate shocks in the domestic economy. Or domestic investors can react to foreign investors' initial reactions, again leading to a magnification of the shock.

This chapter discusses these issues. The next section analyzes the factors driving private capital flows to developing countries and argues that these flows are increasingly being driven by forces that are creating permanent structural changes in international capital markets. The following section looks at the nature of these structural forces. The chapter then analyzes the effects of these forces on the growth of emerging market investments, focusing, in particular, on portfolio flows, the form of investment associated with the new investor base. Based on an understanding of the structural forces at play, the next section assesses whether private capital flows can be expected to be sustained. The chapter then analyzes the implications of the changing international environment for the volatility of private capital flows to developing countries, and it concludes with a summary of the main findings of the chapter.

The Structural Character of New Private Capital Flows

As PRIVATE CAPITAL FLOWS TO DEVELOPING COUNTRIES began to surge in the early 1990s, coinciding with declining global interest rates, it was generally assumed that these flows were being driven primarily by cyclical conditions in industrial countries. This assumption was supported by early econometric analyses (box 2.1).

The persistence of these flows in spite of global interest rate increases in 1994 and the Mexican peso crisis in 1995, however, suggests that they are being driven by more than international cyclical factors. Indeed more recent analyses (box 2.2) show several striking trends:

Box 2.1 Are Private Capital Flows a Cyclical and Temporary Phenomenon? The Early Answers

THERE HAS BEEN CONSIDERABLE DEBATE ON whether the surge in private capital flows to developing countries since the early 1990s is essentially a temporary phenomenon, driven in large part by cyclical factors in the international economy, or the result of longer-term structural changes, which would suggest that private capital flows will be sustained.

More precisely, the debate has been about the relative importance of "push" factors (factors in the global economy) and "pull" factors (factors in emerging markets) in explaining the surge in private capital flows. But since studies identified the push factor as global interest rates, and the pull factors as the improvements in countries' economic fundamentals, the arguments have also effectively been about the relative importance of cyclical factors (at the international level) versus structural factors (at the country level).

In a seminal article, Calvo, Leiderman, and Reinhart (1993) looked to see whether private capital flows to Latin America were driven primarily by cyclical factors in the international economy or by improvements in countries' economic fundamentals during the period 1988–91. Taking international reserves and the real exchange rate as proxies for private capital flows, they analyzed the degree of comovement in these variables using principal component analysis. (International reserves and the real exchange rate were used as proxies because of a lack of monthly data on aggregate private capital flows.) They found that there was a significant comovement among countries' foreign reserves and among their real exchange rates, and that the degree of co-movement increased in 1990–91 compared with 1988–89. They also found that the first principal component of both reserves and the real exchange rate exhibited a large bivariate correlation with several U.S. financial variables, including interest rates. This suggested that the main factor driving private flows to Latin America was the cyclical downturn in industrial countries and the associated decline in global interest rates.

Chuhan, Claessens, and Mamingi (1993), on the other hand, included Asian countries in their analysis. They found that improvements in countries' economic fundamentals—the country credit rating, secondary bond prices, the price-earnings ratio in domestic stock markets, and the black market premium—were as important as cyclical factors in attracting portfolio flows to Latin America. Domestic factors, moreover, were three to four times more important in explaining capital inflows to Asia.

However, since the Chuhan, Claessens, and Mamingi study considered country creditworthiness as being solely determined by improvements in the domestic economy (whereas, in reality, global interest rates also affect country creditworthiness), the study may have overstated the proportion that could be attributed to improvements in domestic fundamentals, as argued by Fernández-Arias (1994). By decomposing the improvements in creditworthiness into those arising from the decline in global interest rates and those arising from improvements in the domestic environment, he found that global interest rates accounted for around 86 percent of the increase in portfolio flows for the "average" emerging market during the period 1989–93.

On balance then, the prevailing view in the early 1990s was that cyclical factors in the international environment were the driving force of private flows to emerging markets. More recent work, however, suggests that there are some structural forces at work (see box 2.2).

Box 2.2 Are the New Private Capital Flows Cyclical or Structural? Recent Empirical Evidence

TO ASSESS THE IMPORTANCE OF INTERNATIONAL interest rates on private capital flows to developing countries, a panel regression (which uses both cross-country and time-series data) of total private long-term capital flows/GNP was run on total investment/GNP, private consumption/GNP (if private investors consider private savings to be a sign of confidence in a country's prospects, the expected sign on this coefficient is negative), the stock of total external debt minus international reserves/GNP, volatility of the real effective exchange rate, a dummy for the successful completion of a Brady deal, real export growth, the 12-month U.S. treasury bond rate, and a dummy for U.S. interest rates during 1990–93 (Hernández and Rudolph 1995).

$$\begin{aligned} F = {} & a + \underset{(1.68)^{**}}{0.097^{*}INV_{it\text{-}1}} - \underset{(1.71)^{**}}{0.087^{*}CONS_{it\text{-}1}} \\ & - \underset{(4.30)^{***}}{0.036^{*}DRES_{it\text{-}1}} - \underset{(2.24)^{**}}{0.000036^{*}VRER_{it\text{-}}} \\ & + \underset{(0.52)}{0.00355^{*}DBRAD} \\ & + \underset{(0.57)}{0.000107^{*}EXPG_{it}} + \underset{(0.34)}{0.000366^{*}IUS_{t}} \\ & - \underset{(1.24)}{0.000746^{*}IUSD_{t}} + \underset{(6.0)^{***}}{0.435^{*}F_{it\text{-}1}} \end{aligned}$$

Adjusted $R^2 = 0.48$

*Significant at the 10 percent level; **significant at the 5 percent level; ***significant at the 1 percent level.

The results show that countries with strong economic fundamentals have received the largest proportion of private flows relative to the size of their economies.

If foreign direct investment flows (FDI) are *excluded* from the regression, the following results are obtained:

$$\begin{aligned} F = {} & a + \underset{(2.43)^{***}}{0.0115^{*}INV_{it\text{-}1}} - \underset{(1.62)^{**}}{0.069^{*}CONS_{it\text{-}1}} \\ & - \underset{(4.39)^{***}}{0.031^{*}DRES_{it\text{-}1}} - \underset{(1.44)^{*}}{0.000019^{*}VRER_{it\text{-}}} \\ & + \underset{(1.01)}{0.00569^{*}DBRAD} \\ & - \underset{(0.37)}{0.000058^{*}EXPG_{it}} + \underset{(1.17)}{0.001060^{*}IUS_{t}} \\ & - \underset{(2.02)^{**}}{0.001002^{*}IUSD_{t}} + \underset{(4.94)^{***}}{0.356^{*}F_{it\text{-}1}} \end{aligned}$$

Adjusted $R^2 = 0.46$

Except for FDI, the downturn in U.S. interest rates during 1990–93 was a significant factor in explaining flows to developing countries, although domestic economic factors were also important.

To explore the influence of global interest rates on portfolio flows in particular, we analyzed the extent to which portfolio flows from the United States to 12 emerging markets in Latin America and East Asia moved together and the degree to which this co-movement was related to U.S. interest rate movements. Co-movement in flows was measured by the first principal component of the flows. The analysis was done for countries in each region separately and then in aggregate, as is shown in box table 2.2. (See Calvo, Leiderman, and Reinhart 1993 for the analysis using reserves and real exchange rates as proxies for capital flows to Latin America during 1988–93.)

- The results show that there was a high degree of co-movement in flows during 1990–93 for both regions and that this co-movement was related to movements in U.S. interest rates. This supports the hypothesis that U.S. interest rates played an important role in driving portfolio flows during 1990–93.

Box Table 2.2. Co-movement of U.S. Portfolio Flows to Emerging Markets, 1990–95

	1990–93			*1993–95*		
Region	*Principal component of flows (PC)*	*Correlation with PC of interest rate*	*Correlation with PC of interest rate and stock market returns*	*Principal component of flows (PC)*	*Correlation with PC of interest rate*	*Correlation with PC of interest rate and stock market returns*
Latin America	0.813	-0.60	-0.60	0.548	0.33	0.31
East Asia	0.675	-0.59	-0.58	0.408	0.25	0.25
Total	0.755	-0.61	-0.60	0.455	0.28	0.26

Note: Co-movement is measured by the first principal component.
Source: World Bank staff estimates.

- Since 1993, however, there has been a decline in the co-movement of portfolio flows to both regions, suggesting that country-specific factors are becoming more important.
- The decline in the co-movement of flows after 1993 is especially marked for East Asia.

Portfolio flows may also be susceptible to domestic cyclical or temporary factors. In order to assess the relative importance of cyclical factors (whether of international or domestic origin) and structural factors in driving private flows, we decomposed portfolio bond and equity flows from the United States to Latin America and Asia into their trend/cycle components. Since the structural factors that may be underlying private capital flows—such as global financial innovations or productivity improvements in recipient countries—do not occur in a predictable manner, they would be ill captured by a deterministic trend. We therefore used the Beveridge-Nelson methodology, which entails fitting a stochastic trend (the component of the flow that, in a statistical sense, is not expected to reverse), from which the temporary or cyclical components are measured.

- The results show that the cyclical component for bond flows is higher than for equity flows in both regions. On average, during 1990–95, 40 percent of portfolio bond flows to Latin America and 16 percent of bond flows to Asia were temporary or cyclical. For equity flows the proportions were 13 percent for Latin America and 5 percent for Asia.
- Portfolio flows to Latin America show a much higher degree of cyclicality.
- Despite the relatively high degree of cyclicality, there is a clear upward structural trend in portfolio flows to both regions. The structural trend in flows to Latin America begins around 1992–93. Although flows to Asia show an upward trend that began earlier, the rise in equity flows is more dramatic from 1992 onward.

(Box continues on the following page.)

Box Figure 2.2 Actual and Permanent Components of U.S. Portfolio Flows to Latin America and Asia, 1984–95

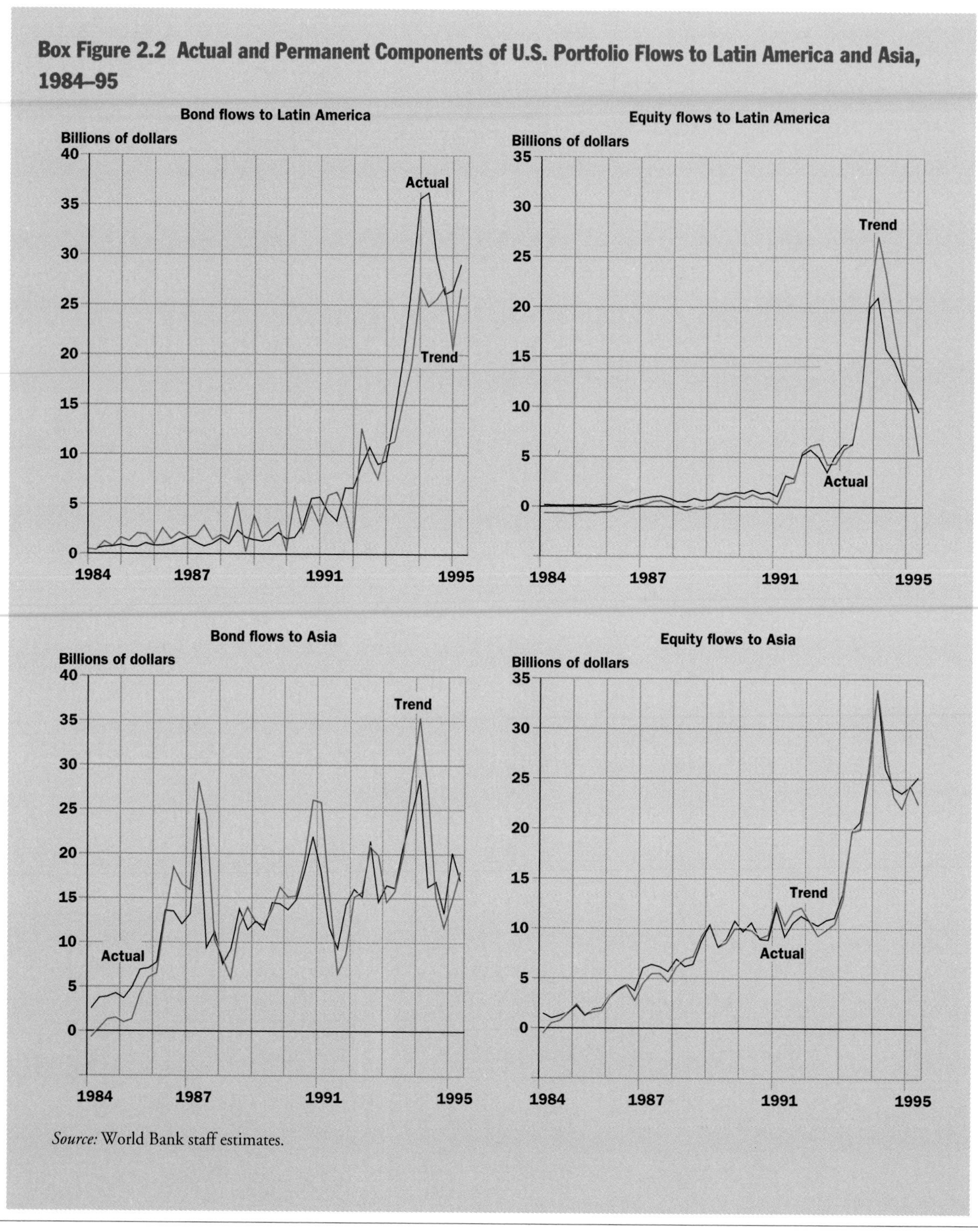

Source: World Bank staff estimates.

- Countries with the strongest economic fundamentals, such as a high investment-to-GDP ratio, low inflation, and low real exchange rate variability—factors that affect the long-term rates of return to investors—have received the largest flows as a proportion of domestic GDP. At the other end, countries with very weak fundamentals have not attracted private flows at all.
- Global interest rates are not significant in explaining FDI flows, which have been the largest component of private flows to developing countries. These flows are more sensitive to countries' macroeconomic fundamentals.
- International interest rates were an important (that is, statistically significant) factor in driving other private capital flows to developing countries during 1990–93.[2]
- More recently, the relative role of international interest rates has declined and country-specific factors have become more important. There is, moreover, a sizable difference among regions. Country-specific factors have become particularly important in East Asia.
- While there has been a relative decline in the sensitivity of portfolio flows to interest rates, portfolio flows remain quite susceptible to cyclical or temporary factors—including movements in global interest rates and changes in domestic interest rates.
- Although they are still quite cyclical, portfolio flows to both Asia and Latin America show a clear upward trend since 1992–93. Thus, even in portfolio flows, other factors are at work.

The Structural Forces Driving Private Capital Flows to Developing Countries

THE STRUCTURAL TREND NOW EVIDENT IN PRIVATE CAPITAL flows is being driven by two primary forces: higher long-term (as opposed to short-term or cyclical) expected rates of return in developing countries and the opportunity for risk diversification.

Higher Expected Rates of Return

Standard economic theory predicts that if the level of capital stock is relatively low, then, other things being equal, the marginal product of

As figure 2.2 shows, policy reforms in developing countries have strengthened economic performance and creditworthiness.

capital will be high. If not constrained by the availability of skilled labor, infrastructure, and other factors that are complements to capital in the production process, therefore, the rate of return to investment will be relatively high in countries with low levels of capital stock.[3]

For the foreign investor, country creditworthiness, or a country's ability to make resources available for external payments, is also a very important determinant of the overall rate of return to investment.[4]

With the onset of the international debt crisis, the early 1980s saw a dramatic decline in the macroeconomic performance and creditworthiness of developing countries. This was due, in part, to a deteriorating external environment, which included a sharp increase in international interest rates and recession in industrial countries.

In the mid-1980s however, the macroeconomic performance and creditworthiness of many developing countries started to improve again and this trend accelerated in the early 1990s. Developing countries that have been the major recipients of private capital have seen a decline in inflation, higher growth of output and exports, and higher and more productive investment (figure 2.2). The more stable domestic macroeconomic environment has, in turn, improved prospective rates of return to investment in general, while the growth in earning capacity (as manifested in the growth of output and exports), and reduction in the stock of external liabilities in many of the heavily indebted middle-income countries (following the implementation of the Brady Plan), has reduced country risks for the foreign investor.[5] Many of these countries have also seen a significant growth in the skilled labor force and improvements in supporting infrastructure over the past decade.

Underpinning the improvements in economic performance of developing countries has been the systematic adoption of macroeconomic stabilization programs and structural reforms by a growing number of countries and a more favorable international environment. A key element of the stabilization programs has been sustained fiscal adjustment, with fiscal deficits declining substantially from the high levels reached after the debt crisis (figure 2.2). Trade liberalization, investment deregulation, and financial sector liberalization have promoted more private sector activity and outward-oriented economies. The creditworthiness of these countries has been strengthened by the low international interest rates that have prevailed since the mid-1980s and was further boosted during the cyclical downturn in the early 1990s.[6]

Figure 2.2 Effects of Policy Reforms in Developing Countries Receiving Large Private Capital Flows

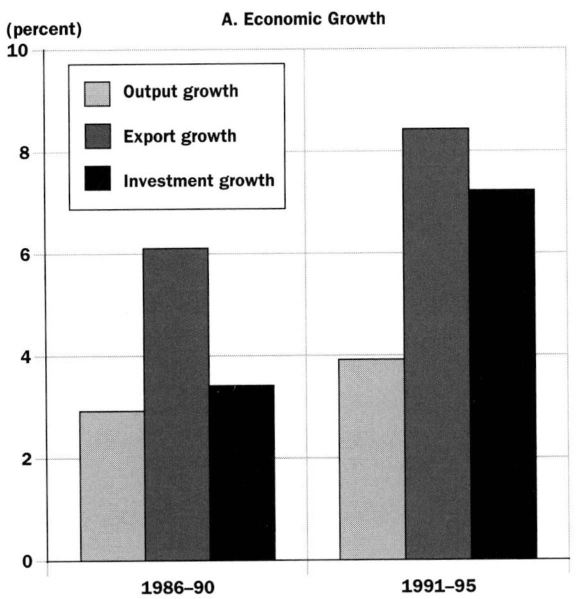

Note: This represents the average performance of major recipients of capital flows.
Source: World Bank staff estimates.

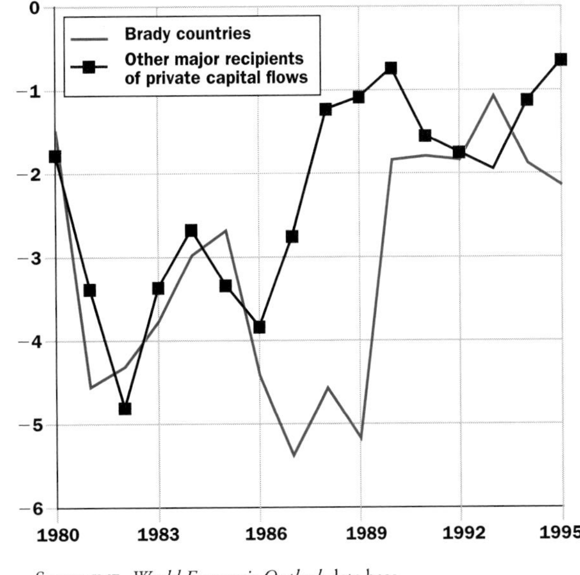

Source: IMF, *World Economic Outlook* data base.

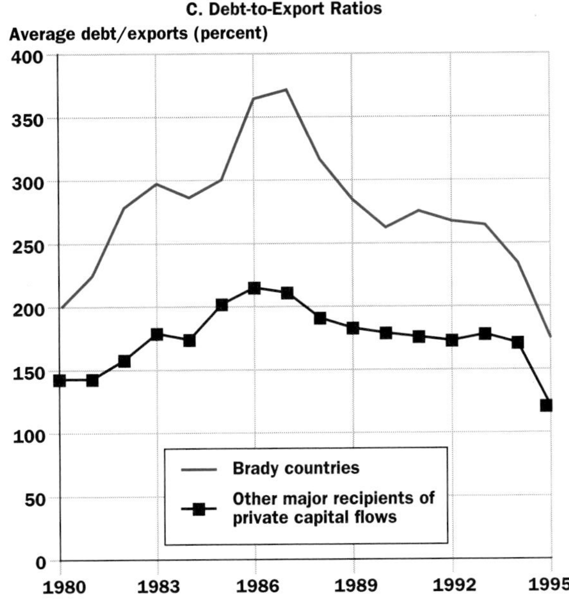

Source: World Bank data.

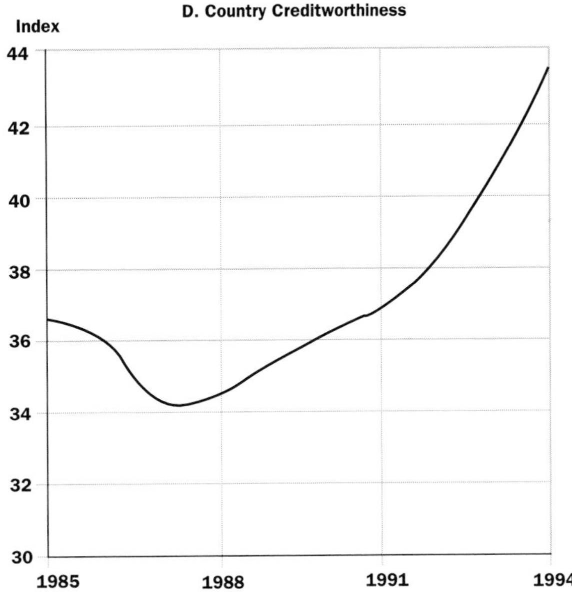

Note: This represents the average of major capital inflow recipients.
Source: Data from Institutional Investor Credit Ratings.

These reforms have meant that unlike the growth of the late 1970s, which was largely inward-oriented and led by public investment, the growth of developing countries in the 1990s is more broadly based and is led by exports. What is also noteworthy is that the improvements in economic performance and creditworthiness are being shared by a growing number of developing countries, although the process is still in its early stages in many countries (figure 2.3).

A growing number of developing countries are gaining the benefits of improved economic performance.

Although the risks of investing in emerging markets remain relatively high, the policy reforms are resulting in the progressive decline in these risks and in improvements in expected rates of return. Investors have thus begun to respond to the relatively higher expected rates of return in developing countries.[7]

Figure 2.3 Output and Export Growth, Selected Regions, 1986–90 and 1991–95
(percent)

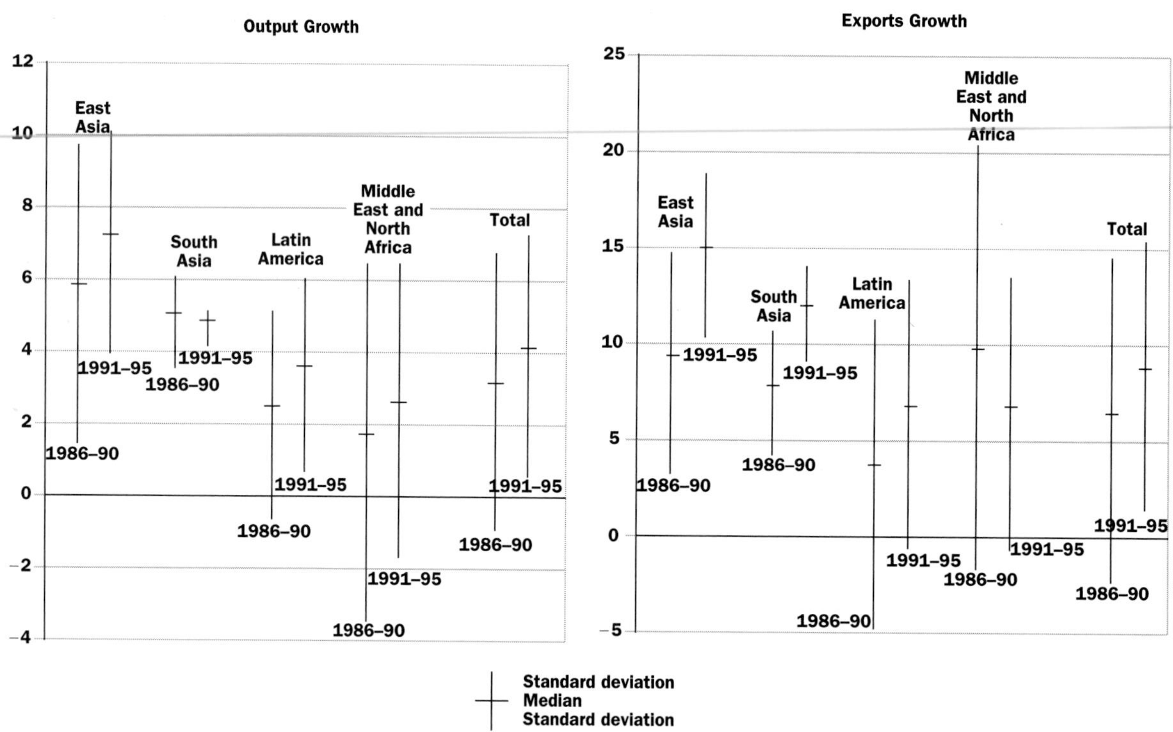

Note: As the figure shows, not only has the median growth rate of output and exports increased, but this growth has been shared more equitably across countries—that is, the dispersion around the mean has declined in several regions (particularly in export growth) in the past five years, relative to the late 1980s.

Source: World Bank staff estimates.

Opportunities for Risk Diversification

The second force behind the structural trend in private capital flows is investors' desire for portfolio risk diversification. Investors can benefit from holding emerging market equities because returns in emerging markets tend to exhibit low correlations with industrial country returns—that is, they tend not to move in tandem with those of industrial countries. In general, by holding an asset whose returns are not correlated with the returns of another asset, investors can raise the overall return on their portfolio without a commensurate increase in risk (variance).[8]

The opportunity for portfolio diversification offered by emerging markets is a relatively recent phenomenon, associated with the 1990s, that has developed as capital markets in these countries have deepened and broadened.[9] As discussed in chapter 6, by the end of 1994, the combined market capitalization of the 18 major developing countries that form the IFC Emerging Markets Index (IFCI) was, at $1.2 trillion, 13 times higher than it had been in 1985.[10] Although still much lower than that of industrial countries, the average market capitalization of these countries rose dramatically from 7 to 42 percent of GDP during the period, while turnover ratios increased approximately twofold between 1985 and 1994.[11]

As a result of this growth, financial markets in developing countries are now beginning to provide foreign investors with significant opportunities to diversify. As a hypothetical illustration, assume that investors' holdings of international assets are allocated according to the country shares implied by the MSCI-EAFE Index.[12] Given the current correlations of returns between the IFC Investible Index and the MSCI-EAFE Index, investors could both increase the expected rates of return and reduce the risks in their overall portfolio by increasing their allocations to emerging markets, according to the proportions implied by the IFCI, to 41 percent of this portfolio of international holdings (figure 2.4). This compares with current allocations of around 12 to 14 percent of investors' international portfolios to emerging markets. Moreover, given that returns among emerging markets exhibit low (and often negative) correlations with each other (figure 2.5), greater diversification within emerging markets than that implied by the overall IFCI could reduce portfolio risks even further.[13] Of course, this calculation is only hypothetical: such a large reallocation would be an upper bound of possible gains and would not even be feasible under present market conditions. In addition, correlations between developing and industrial countries are likely to rise over time as the former become more financially integrated with the global economy.[14] Nonetheless, it illustrates the potential for risk diversification that developing countries offer.

The Changing Enabling Environment in Industrial Countries

The strong response of private capital flows to the two primary forces described above has, in large part, stemmed from changes in the enabling environment in both industrial and developing countries during the 1980s and 1990s. Industrial countries have seen changes in two broad areas. First, in the real sector, increasing competition and rising

Figure 2.4 Potential Benefits from Portfolio Risk Diversification
(MSCI-EAFE and emerging markets)

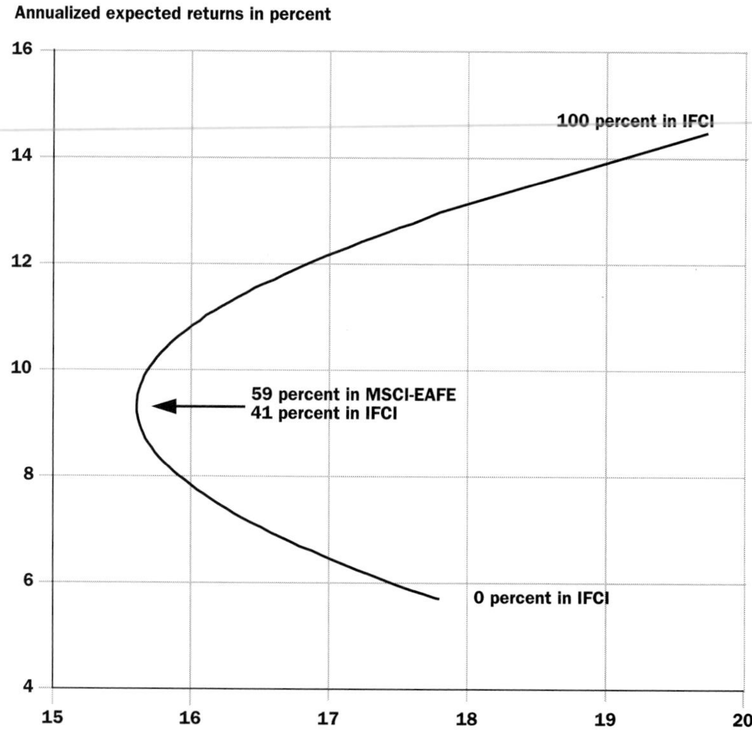

Source: World Bank staff estimates using the IFC Investable Index and the Morgan Stanley Capital International Index (MSCI-EAFE).

Emerging markets offer international investors significant potential for portfolio diversification.

Figure 2.5 Correlations of Returns among Emerging Markets

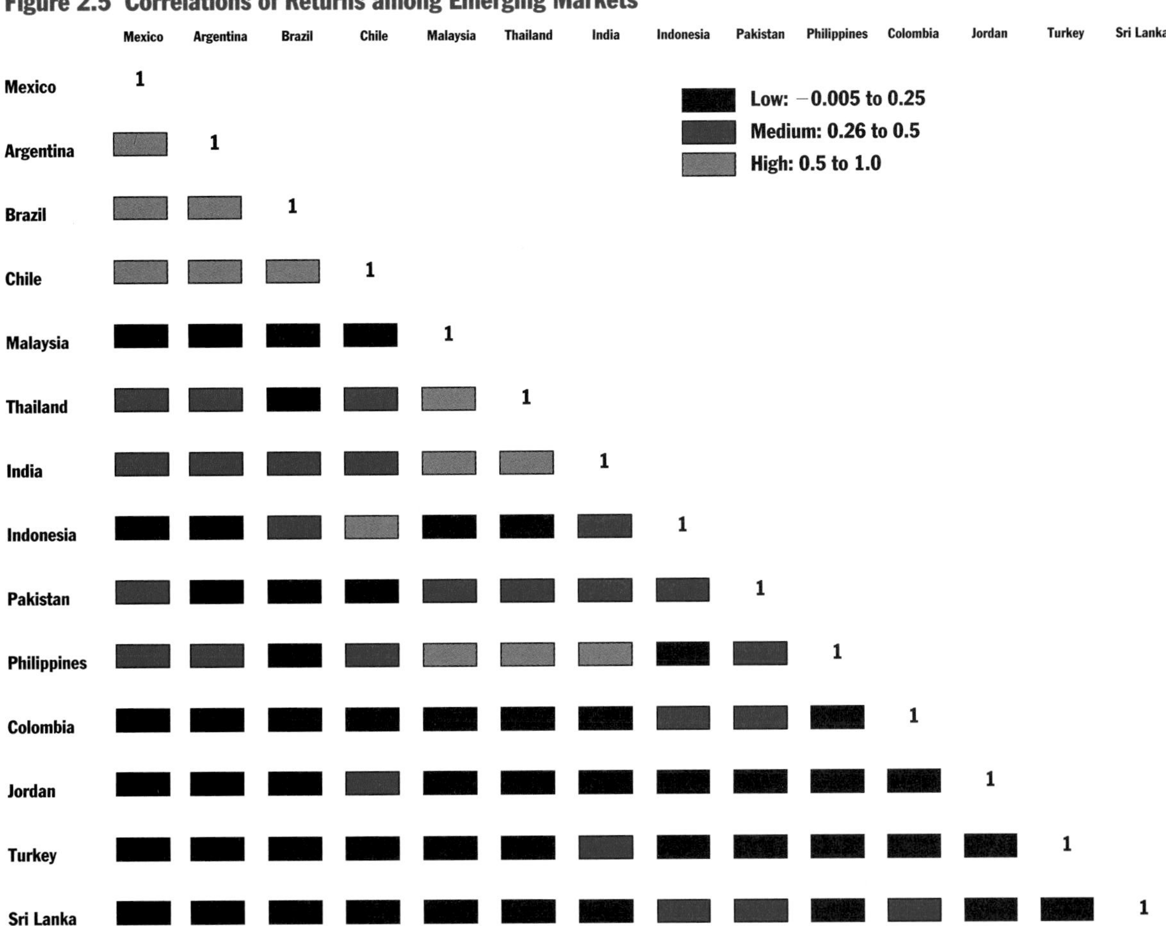

Note: Correlations computed using IFC Emerging Market Investable Index returns during January 1990–August 1996.
Source: World Bank staff estimates.

costs at home, combined with falling transport and communications costs, have heightened firms' responsiveness to opportunities to increase efficiency and reduce costs by locating investments abroad. This is leading to the progressive globalization of production and has spurred the growth of "efficiency-seeking" FDI. Second, in financial markets, a self-reinforcing process of competition, deregulation, technological advances, and financial innovations has increased the responsiveness of investors to international investment opportunities. This process is rapidly leading to the linking of domestic markets into one global market. These two forces are discussed below.

The low correlation of returns among emerging markets suggests that investors can benefit from diversification among emerging markets.

The globalization of production. The 1980s and 1990s have witnessed the progressive globalization of the production process. Competitive pressures from unilateral and successive rounds of multilateral trade liberalization, and stagnant demand combined with rising costs at home, have encouraged firms to seek new markets and increase efficiency. Initially, this involved locating the full range of production activities in a low-cost country or moving them to one. More recently, the drive for increased efficiency has involved breaking up the production process into discrete segments, each located in the best place in terms of cost and productivity considerations. This process is spurring the growth of "efficiency-driven" foreign investment flows, which encompass a wide range of corporate functions and take place in a broad number of industries with different levels of factor or skill intensity.

The globalization of production has been made possible by recent technological changes and reductions in transport and communications costs. Toyota, for example, has rationalized its production on an ASEAN-wide basis, with affiliates in each country specializing in the production of different parts that are subsequently exported to the country where final assembly takes place. Similarly, General Motors plans to establish a materials and components purchasing office in Poland for all its European affiliates.

This process is, moreover, self-perpetuating: heightened competition is driving firms to invest abroad, basing their plans on efficiency considerations, and growing FDI is making firms more competitive, thereby intensifying the competition. Consequently, *firms are becoming increasingly responsive to new opportunities that can strengthen their competitiveness;* in particular, they are looking to invest in markets that offer macroeconomic stability, supportive regulatory frameworks, well-developed infrastructure (transport and telecommunications), low costs in relation to productivity of the labor force, and more open trade regimes.

As a result, a significant proportion of current global FDI flows can be characterized as efficiency-seeking. The importance of this type of FDI is evident from the fact that the sales of foreign affiliates to the parent transnational corporation and to other affiliates of the same parent company, as a share of worldwide sales of affiliates, are high and have increased somewhat over the past decade. Moreover this increase has been more pronounced with regard to the sales of affiliates in one host country to affiliates in other host countries—corresponding with the specialization in production process implied by the more recent type of efficiency-seeking FDI.

The growing responsiveness of financial markets. The financial markets in industrial countries have also changed significantly during the 1980s and 1990s. Driven by the self-reinforcing process of competition and financial innovation, along with deregulation and technological change, they have become increasingly global in nature. Foreign exchange markets were the first to internationalize in the late 1970s, followed by bond markets in the 1980s and equity markets in the 1990s.

The internationalization of foreign exchange markets began in the late 1970s, after the collapse of the Bretton Woods system of fixed exchange rates in 1973. The internationalization of bond markets, however, gathered momentum only during the 1980s, when low inflation and positive real interest rates and yield curves made long-term bonds appealing to investors. At the same time, banks' funding costs rose for a variety of reasons. The general deflation in the 1980s and the international debt crisis placed pressures on the performance of banks' assets and resulted in a slip in their credit ratings and a rise in their funding costs. Together with their high intermediation costs associated with reserve requirements, capital, and overheads, this resulted in relatively high lending rates (Honeygold 1987). Consequently, prime borrowers such as governments and large corporations found it cheaper to raise funds directly from investors through the securities markets. The internationalization of securities markets began with the strengthening of the offshore Eurobond market. Because the Eurobond market was exempt from many of the regulations of domestic markets—especially with regard to taxation—prime issuers could usually raise funds at lower costs than in domestic markets, while investors often received higher rates of return than they did in their own regulated domestic markets.

Largely in response to market pressures, governments began to deregulate domestic financial markets by the mid-1980s. This contributed to greater convergence of issuing costs between offshore and onshore markets, thereby encouraging corporations and governments to seek capital in the major domestic securities markets while leading to the progressive internationalization of the latter. Japan, for example, relaxed regulations on the Samurai bond market in 1983, issued the first

Shogun bond in 1985, and relaxed restrictions on the holdings of domestic and Euro Yen commercial paper by nonresidents in 1988. The United States eliminated its 30 percent withholding tax on foreigners' interest income in 1984, the same year that Germany stopped taxing foreign investors' income from bonds. Germany also allowed foreigners to buy federal bonds in the primary market in 1988 and, a year later, eased restrictions on deutsche mark bonds. (Annex 2.1 lists the key domestic and international financial deregulations.)

Equity markets started to globalize much more recently, essentially in the early 1990s. They have been slower to globalize for several reasons. First, equities are much less liquid than bonds, in part because the valuation of the equity of a company is very specific to the circumstances of that company, making shares intrinsically more difficult to trade. Second, the information and infrastructure needed for investors to undertake global investments in equities (for example, comparable accounting standards and global settlement and custodial services) are only now being developed (McKinsey Global Institute 1994). What has driven the process of internationalization of equity markets is the more active stance of institutional investors, as discussed in more detail below. Neither multinational commercial banks (an important force in the internationalization of the bond markets) nor the issuers themselves (that is, multinational corporations) have played a significant role in the process.

In fact, the relative illiquidity and volatility of equities has meant that multinational commercial banks, which are highly leveraged institutions, have generally been averse to holding equities (foreign or domestic) in any significant amounts. Multinational corporate issuers have been relatively less interested in listing abroad, because the price of equities is generally driven by investors in their own countries, who hold the bulk of the company equities and know most about them (McKinsey Global Institute 1994). As discussed below, however, institutional investors, who during the 1980s concentrated on domestic equities and held the bulk of their international investments in bonds and currencies, are now rapidly increasing their holdings of foreign equities. At the same time, governments have been opening domestic stock markets to foreign investors and issuers (annex 2.1). This is providing the impetus for the internationalization of domestic stock markets.

Financial innovations during the 1980s and 1990s have also played a key role in the internationalization of financial markets. Specifically, the last two decades have seen the growth of foreign exchange and fixed income and, more recently, equity-related derivatives. These innovations can lower funding costs, enhance yields, or unbundle some of the characteristics of securities, such as their price risk, credit risk, country risk, and liquidity, to tailor portfolios to the needs of different investors to hedge price, interest rate, and exchange rate risks. As a result, these innovations have made it more attractive for borrowers to raise capital in foreign markets and for investors to make cross-border investments. For example, the use of interest rate swaps in conjunction with currency swaps has resulted in an increasingly global bond market. And, more recently, financial innovations have been promoting the internationalization of equity markets. Foreign investors are now using equity swaps, in which a domestic agent passes on the gains or losses from holding domestic equities to the foreign investor for a fee. This allows the foreign investor to avoid having to pay for high local execution costs or falling victim to insider trading practices (McKinsey Global Institute 1994). (Annex 2.1 lists the adoption of key financial innovations in securities markets.)

Technological advances have reinforced the effects of deregulation and financial innovations in internationalizing markets by increasing efficiency in gathering and disseminating information and in processing transactions. In particular, low-cost telecommunications have been instrumental in linking financial markets and have made possible 24-hour trading, which, in turn, has brought greater breadth and depth to trading. It can be argued that improved communication also encourages financial institutions to continue to develop new instruments to meet the needs of customers in previously isolated markets (Honeygold 1987).

The evolution in electronic technology has greatly enhanced the efficiency of stock markets, just as the Euroclear and Cedel standard clearing mechanisms have provided low-cost dealing and delivery in the Eurobond market. For example, NASDAQ (National Association of Securities Dealers Automated Quotation), which originated as an over-the-counter market for smaller firms unable to meet the stringent requirements and high listing costs of the major exchanges, now provides for private firms to make block sales by linking their customers together through computer terminals, at high speed and with low transaction costs. Moreover, for small-scale operations, it has been possible, since 1984, to complete instantaneous transactions of orders of up to 500 shares via the Small Order Execution System. In Japan the CORES

(Computerized Order Routing and Execution System) handles all but the largest stocks (which are still traded on the trading floor). In the United Kingdom, SEAQ International (Stock Exchange Automated Quotations System), introduced in 1985, is linked to NASDAQ in the United States and provides mutual on-screen access to the top 300 quotations in each market. Market makers can thereby display current prices around the world, improving the efficiency of trades.

The growing importance of institutional investors. The other aspect of change in the enabling environment in industrial countries has been the growth of institutional investors. These investors, both able and willing to invest abroad, have increased the magnitude of the response of private capital flows to the fundamental forces driving these flows—that is, cyclical and long-term relative rates of return and new opportunities for portfolio diversification.

The growing importance of institutional investors has been the result of the same forces—competitive pressures, deregulation, technological advances, and financial innovations—that have affected the markets on the issuing side. One type of innovation—securitization (broadly defined as the process of matching savers and creditors through financial markets as opposed to closed market credits via banks and other financial institutions)—has played a particularly important role (Gardener 1991). Specifically, securitization has meant the creation of instruments (including the conversion of loans into securities, or secondary securitization) that can be issued and traded directly on market. Because securitized assets are more cost-effective than bank loans, they have facilitated the growth of institutional investors that trade these assets at the expense of commercial banks, whose primary business remains in making loans. In particular:

- Mutual funds, which had already grown substantially in the 1950s and 1960s, attracted more savings and thereby became more important in the financial markets during the 1970s by offering money market funds. Investors found these funds an attractive alternative to the regulated deposit rates of commercial banks when market interest rates rose. In the 1980s, following the success of money market funds, mutual funds began to invest in bonds, both domestic and international, and gradually in domestic equities. This both reinforced and was reinforced by the securitization that was taking place.

- Pension funds have also become increasingly important because of broader pension coverage and—particularly since the 1970s—the rising value of contributions. The growth in pension assets was especially stimulated by changes in pension and tax laws. The United States, for example, allows companies to deduct their contributions to employee pension plans from their taxes. Moreover, employee contributions are not taxed, and interest on pension assets is not taxed until retirement. Therefore, both employers and employees have an incentive to save through a pension plan, as opposed to other forms of savings, which are taxable (Sellon 1992). Given the long-term nature of their commitments (that is, to pay retirement benefits), pension funds tend to invest in long-term instruments, including corporate equities and long-term bonds. As in the case of mutual funds, therefore—indeed, arguably more so—the growing importance of pension funds and the process of securitization have been mutually reinforcing.

There are fundamental advantages offered by institutional investors that explain their appeal to individual investors and suggest that their role will continue to expand. Pension and mutual funds provide individual investors with a low-cost method of diversifying their portfolios: pooling funds with many other investors to purchase a number of different assets. At the same time, technological advances have greatly reduced the costs of dealing with a large number of investors.

This trend away from banks and self-directed investment to institutional investors is very evident in the three countries that are major sources of funds—Japan, the United Kingdom, and the United States (figure 2.6). In the latter two, where this trend has been most pronounced, the share of household savings channeled to mutual and pension funds doubled between 1975 and 1994. However, continental Europe, with the exception of the Netherlands and Switzerland, has seen much more modest shifts to institutional investors. These varying trends largely reflect country-specific factors such as the pace of deregulation and tax policies.

The variation across countries notwithstanding, there is a clear trend toward the institutionalization of savings in industrial countries. Altogether, pension funds, insurance companies, and mutual funds in seven major industrial countries had assets close to $17 trillion in 1994, compared with $5.3 trillion in 1985.[15] Institutional investors now domi-

Figure 2.6 Institutionalization of Savings
(assets as a percentage of GDP)

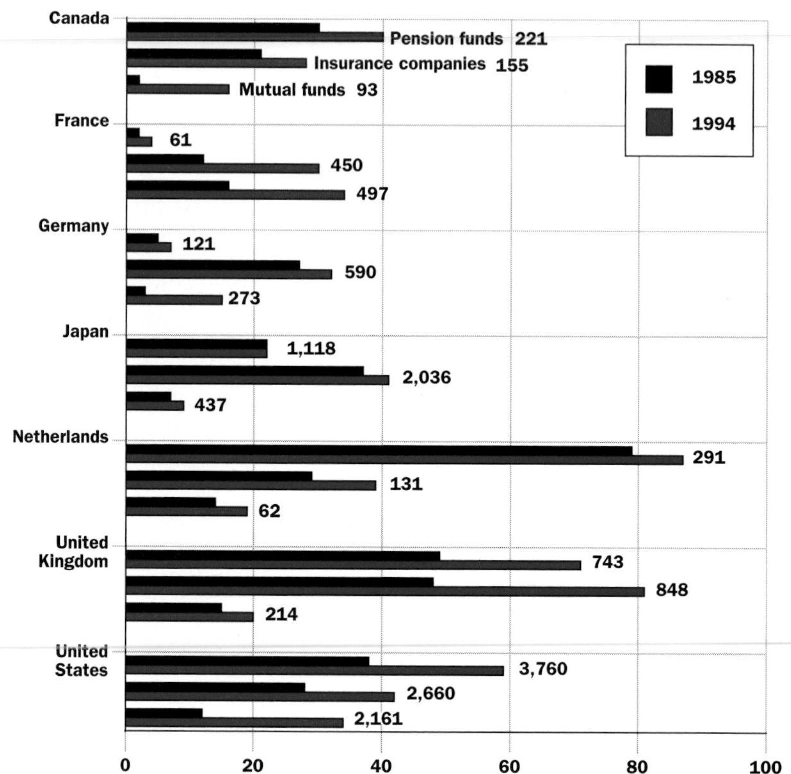

Note: Figures refer to the size of assets in billions of dollars. For the United States, assets refer to U.S. open-end mutual funds only.

Source: Data from InterSec; IMF, *International Financial Statistics* data base; the Investment Company Institute; the Investment Funds Institute of Canada; the Investment Trusts Association of Japan, the U.K. Association of Unit Trusts and Investment Funds; and the Nederlandsche Bank.

A growing proportion of household savings is being channeled through institutional investors.

nate the financial landscape, especially the capital markets. In the United States, for instance, institutional investors are now estimated to account for more than 49 percent of U.S. equities, compared with 16.5 percent three decades ago.

One reason for the success of pension and mutual funds is that individual investors are offered the benefits of professional management. Through the expertise of specialized investment advisers or fund managers, individual investors can realize higher returns from a more diversified and international portfolio than they could get by themselves, without having detailed knowledge of the countries and individual companies issuing the securities. The trend toward international diversification by institutional investors has been particularly pronounced in the United States, but it is also happening in other major industrial countries to varying degrees.

A distinction should be made between the international behavior of pension funds and of mutual funds, though. Mutual funds, driven by profits and subject to relatively few regulations, increased their international exposure much earlier and have always had a higher proportion of international assets. They have not, consequently, internationalized much more during the 1990s, except in the United States, where the international share of the mutual fund portfolio rose from 3.8 percent in 1990 to 8.9 percent in 1994.

Pension funds, on the other hand, have always been heavily regulated because of their fiduciary responsibility to deliver promised benefits. Consequently, they have tended to be more cautious in their investment strategies. Moreover, given their orientation toward long-term investments, they have tended to focus on long-term instruments. The international diversification of pension funds did not begin until the 1980s, when the long-term securities markets became internationalized and as governments began to deregulate the investment allocations of pension funds.

The trend toward greater international diversification by pension funds has been common to most industrial countries, with the exception of Germany and a few other European economies (such as Norway, Spain, and Sweden). The degree of international diversification among pension funds varies significantly, however, ranging from 24 percent of total assets in the United Kingdom to around 17 percent for Canada and the Netherlands, 9 percent for the United States, and a low of 5 to 6 percent for France and Germany (figure 2.7). Moreover, with the exception of Japan and the United States, the international exposure of pension funds remains significantly lower than that of mutual funds.

Institutional investors of the third type, insurance companies, generally have had even lower international exposure. One reason for their preference for domestic assets may be their need to match assets and liabilities—including currency composition—in the short term (Davis 1991). However, with the exception of those in Japan and the United States, even insurance companies have seen small increases in international assets.

Figure 2.7 International Diversification of Institutional Investors, Selected Countries, 1990 and 1994
(percentage of total assets)

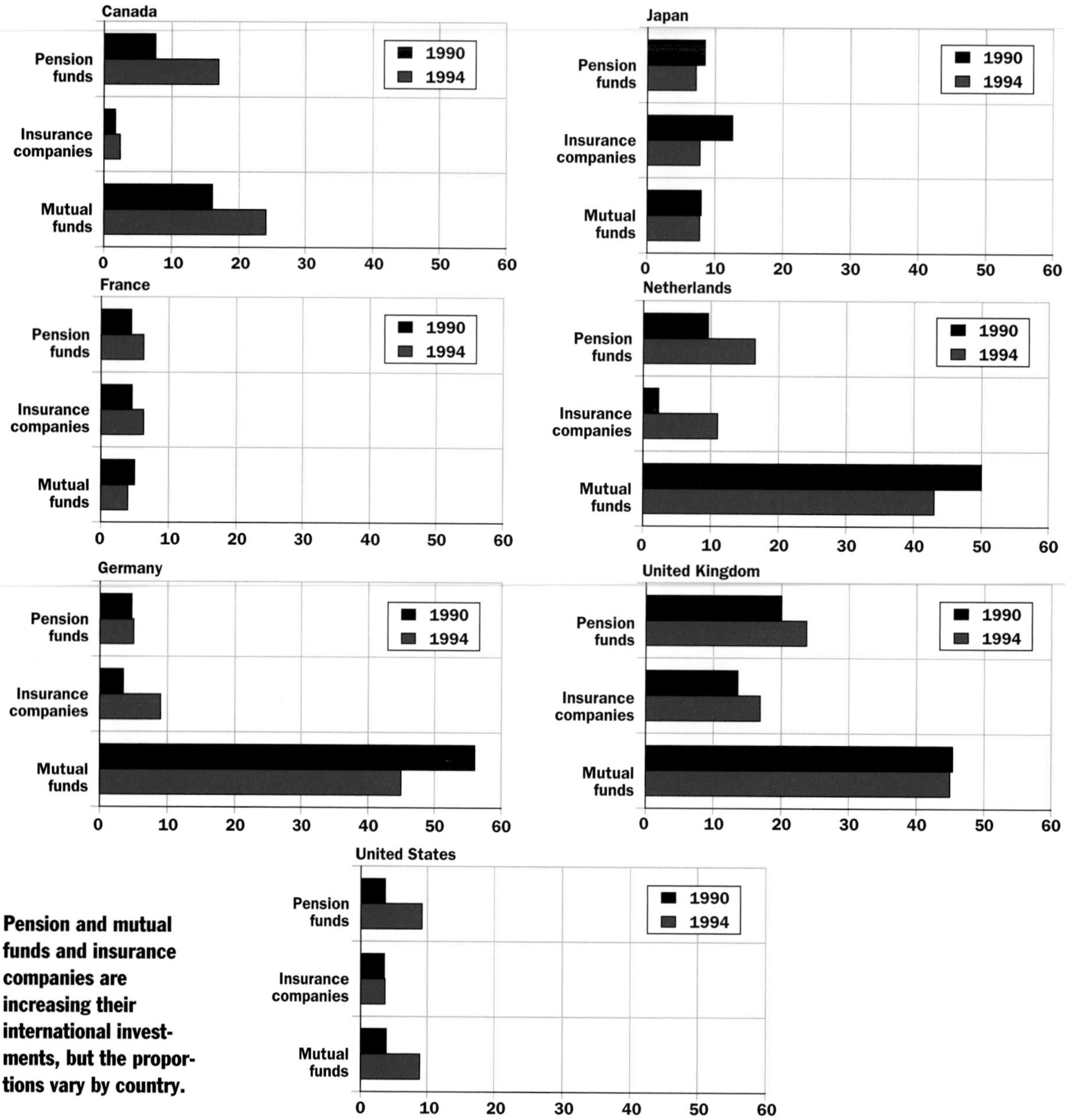

Pension and mutual funds and insurance companies are increasing their international investments, but the proportions vary by country.

Notes: For France the data on mutual funds are for 1993. Data on insurance companies for Canada and the United States are for life insurance only.

Source: World Bank staff estimates using data from InterSec, the WM Company, Nederlandsche Bank, the American Council of Life Insurance, *Bank of Canada Review,* the Investment Company Institute, the U.K. Association of Unit Trusts and Investment Funds, the Investment Funds Institute of Canada, the Investment Trusts Association of Japan.

Overall, the combination of the growth in the asset base of institutional investors and the growing internationalization of these assets has meant a rising volume of international investments by institutional investors. For example, total assets of pension funds at the global level are estimated to have increased from $4.3 trillion in 1989 to $7 trillion in 1994. At the same time, the share of international investment in their portfolios rose from around 7 percent in 1989 to 11 percent in 1994. Together, this has resulted in an increase in total international investments by pension funds from $302 billion in 1989 to $790 billion in 1994, with the growth in asset base contributing to around 40 percent of the increase in international investments, and greater international diversification contributing around 60 percent of the increase.

The Changing Enabling Environment in Developing Countries

Changes in the enabling environment of industrial countries have meant that economic agents in these countries—both firms and portfolio investors—have become more responsive to opportunities to earn higher rates of return or diversify risks through international investments. And, as discussed in the previous section, developing countries have begun to offer investment opportunities as their creditworthiness and rates of return have improved. Concomitant changes in the enabling environment of developing countries have enabled these forces to be translated into actual investments.

The most important enabling factors are simply whether private capital is permitted to flow into a country and whether the restrictions on the repatriation of profits (income) and capital are prohibitive. Along with the sharp decline in expropriation risks, the 1980s and 1990s have witnessed a progressive dismantling of barriers to capital account mobility in developing countries.[16] During 1991–93, 11 developing countries undertook full or extensive liberalization of their exchange restrictions, 23 liberalized controls on FDI flows, 15 eased controls on portfolio inflows, and 5 eased restrictions on portfolio outflows. By the end of 1995, 35 developing countries had fully open capital accounts.

Trade liberalization associated with the Uruguay Round has received much attention, somewhat eclipsing significant progress made in parallel on investment treaties, relevant for FDI. In fact, half of all investment codes and bilateral treaties have been drawn up in the 1990s, as have several important multilateral agreements.[17]

Whereas previously most national investment codes and bilateral investment treaties imposed few restrictions on the recipient countries with respect to market entry, recent laws and agreements have emphasized the free flow of investment. Many of the recent laws and agreements also contain provisions for the settlement of disputes, usually providing for several different mechanisms for their resolution—ranging from direct negotiations between the disputing parties to arbitration proceedings in which investors and host states may participate on an equal footing (World Bank 1997).

The liberalization of restrictions on portfolio capital has also translated into significant changes in the stock markets of developing countries. As recently as the beginning of 1991, only 26 percent of emerging stock markets could be categorized as having free entry for foreign investors, while 11 percent were closed to foreign investors. By the end of 1994, 58 percent of all stock markets had free entry for foreign investors, while only 2 percent remained closed (figure 2.8).

In addition to the easing of regulations pertaining to the movement of private capital, structural changes in developing countries have meant a significant expansion of areas for potential foreign investor involvement. In particular, as part of their structural reform programs, many developing countries have deregulated their investment regimes and reduced the role of the public sector in directly productive sectors, with a view to allowing greater participation of private investors. One manifestation of this has been the gradual reduction of the share of state-owned enterprise investment in total domestic investment. For the countries that have been the primary recipients of private capital flows, the average (unweighted) share of state-owned enterprises in gross domestic investment has fallen from around 25 percent in the late 1970s to 17 percent in 1991. At the same time, countries have deregulated to allow greater foreign participation in these sectors.

Foreign investor involvement in developing countries has been further boosted by the privatization of state-owned enterprises. Of the $112 billion of privatization proceeds that developing countries received during 1988–94, almost 42 percent was from foreign investors. The early privatizations were largely in the form of FDI. But there has also been a steady increase in the participation of portfolio investors. Indeed, in 1994, portfolio investors accounted for over 50 percent of the foreign participation.

Figure 2.8 Entry Restrictions for Foreign Investors in Emerging Stock Markets, 1991 and 1994
(percentage of stock markets)

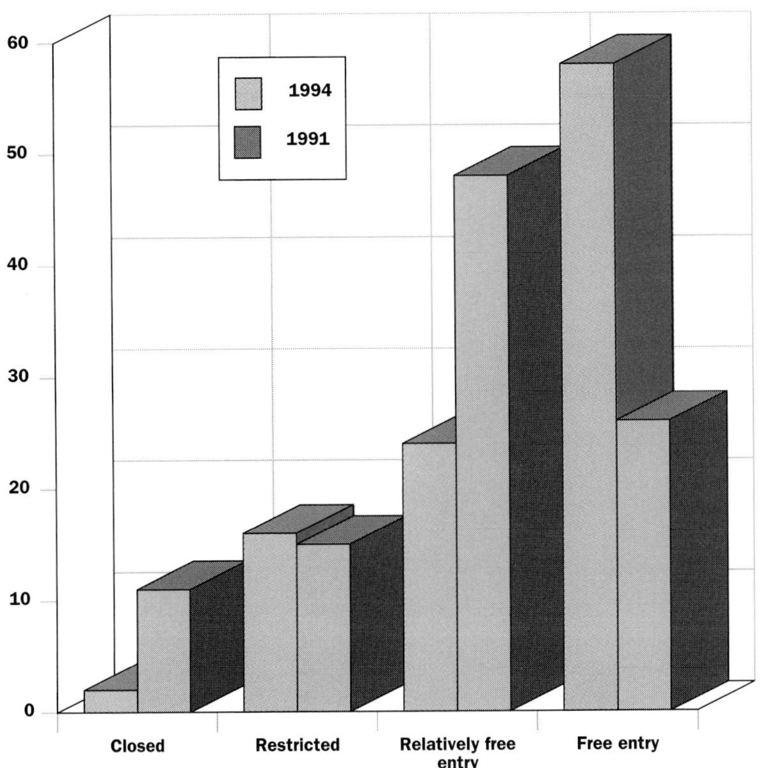

Note: Free entry—no significant restriction to purchasing stocks. Relatively free entry—some registration procedures required to ensure repatriation rights. Restricted—foreigners restricted to certain classes of stocks or only approved foreign investors may buy stocks. Closed—closed or access severely restricted.

Source: IFC, *Emerging Stock Markets Factbook 1996.*

Stock markets in emerging economies are allowing more access to foreign investors.

Finally, trade liberalizations by developing countries have provided an impetus to FDI flows in particular. As discussed earlier in this chapter, a large proportion of FDI flows is being driven by considerations of production efficiency. As a result, trade regimes in developing countries have become more important. Following unilateral and successive rounds of multilateral trade liberalizations since the mid-1980s, there has been a progressive dismantling of trade barriers in developing countries. In fact, by 1994, 42 developing countries could be categorized as having an open regime (Sachs and Warner 1995).[18]

The Outcome of Structural Changes: Growing Investment in Emerging Markets

Changes in the enabling environments of both industrial and developing countries have made private capital more responsive to underlying forces that are spurring investments in developing countries. Of all types of capital flows, FDI has responded most vigorously. The driving factor for FDI has been the sustained improvement in domestic economic fundamentals. For portfolio flows, institutional investors have been the driving force behind the surge, especially in portfolio equity. Although the initial impetus was the cyclical decline in global interest rates, as improvements in economic fundamentals and creditworthiness began to take hold and the new investor base has become more familiar with emerging market investments, the impetus has become the long-term rates of return and opportunities for portfolio risk diversification. As a result, institutional investors are the new, and increasingly important, segment of the investor base in emerging markets. Accordingly, this section focuses primarily on the new investor base and the growth of their investments in emerging markets.

Foreign Direct Investment

Developing countries have seen an almost fourfold increase in FDI flows in just five years—from $25.0 billion in 1990 to more than $95 billion in 1995. Indeed, the growth of FDI flows to developing countries has been much faster than that to industrial countries. Developing countries' share of global FDI flows has risen from 12 percent in 1990 to around 38 percent in 1995.

The nature of the FDI flows to developing countries has changed significantly. In the 1970s and early 1980s, resource extraction and import substitution were the primary motives for FDI to developing countries. In contrast, a high proportion of current FDI flows to developing countries can be characterized as efficiency-seeking investments, associated with the globalization of production. Initially directed toward basic manufacturing, these flows are now increasingly going into high-value-added and skill-intensive manufacturing sectors. Developing countries are also increasingly seeing FDI in services sectors, including the provision of infrastructure services. Opportunities for investments in services and infrastructure have expanded significantly as a result of the stronger economic growth and investment deregulation in developing countries.

The changing nature of FDI flows to developing countries is reflected in the regional destination of FDI flows and the relative selectivity in terms of country destination. East Asia has accounted for about 50 percent of FDI flows to developing countries in the 1990s. As mentioned earlier, efficiency-driven flows are sensitive not only to the strength of countries' macroeconomic fundamentals and domestic market considerations, but also to the supporting infrastructure (both regulatory and physical) and the quality and productivity of the labor force in relation to the cost. East Asian markets have therefore been primary recipients of such flows. East Asia, with its strong economic growth, is also providing growing opportunities in services and infrastructure. Latin America has been the second-largest recipient of FDI flows (accounting for 28 percent of FDI flows). In the early 1990s, a sizable proportion of these flows were the result of one-off privatizations, but countries in Latin America are also receiving efficiency-driven FDI.

Portfolio Flows

Despite a dramatic increase of portfolio flows from institutional investors into emerging markets, information on emerging market placements by such investors remains fragmentary. For mutual funds, the available information suggests the following sequence. Initially, in the mid-1980s, investment in emerging markets was in the form of closed-end funds, including country funds, which pioneered the flow of private investment to emerging stock markets. Closed-end funds are well suited to emerging market conditions, since they automatically regulate redemption risk, which can be especially large in less liquid markets. As emerging markets have become more established, more and more open-end emerging market funds have been set up. In the third stage, emerging markets have begun to figure in the allocations of international investment funds, and finally of global funds. In all three stages, however, mutual fund investments in emerging markets have remained highly skewed toward portfolio equities, with debt-oriented mutual funds accounting for less than 10 percent of mutual fund assets in emerging markets.[19]

The growth in mutual funds over the last decade has in fact been dramatic. In 1986, there were 19 emerging market country funds and 9 regional or global emerging market funds. By 1995, this had expanded to 505 country funds and 773 regional and global emerging market funds. Initially these were mainly closed-end funds, but by 1995 around 50 percent of all funds were open-end. The combined assets of all closed- and open-end emerging market funds increased from $1.9 billion in 1986 to $10.3 billion in 1989 to $132 billion in mid-1996. In addition to the dedicated emerging market funds, international funds have also increased their allocations to emerging markets. Surveys suggest that international funds based in the United States have increased their allocations to emerging markets from a bare 2 percent of their portfolios in 1989 to 12 percent in 1995 and that U.S. global funds now hold around 3 to 4 percent of their portfolios in emerging markets. International and global funds together now account for an estimated 30 to 40 percent of the emerging market assets held by U.S. mutual funds.

These trends have meant that emerging markets are accounting for a rising proportion of international investment by mutual funds—more than 30 percent of new international investments by U.S. mutual funds went to emerging markets during 1990–94. Since international investment itself has been rising, the share of emerging market assets in total mutual fund assets has risen quite sharply. In absolute terms, U.S.-based open-end mutual funds alone had around $36 billion in emerging markets by the end of 1995 (figure 2.9). Yet despite this impressive increase, the share of emerging markets in the portfolios of mutual funds remains small. Emerging markets still account for only about 2 percent of total mutual fund assets in the United States. Although emerging market exposure of U.K. mutual funds is higher—in the range of 3 to 4 percent—mutual funds in Japan and the rest of Europe still have negligible exposure to emerging markets (figure 2.10).[20]

A survey undertaken for this report confirms that pension fund investment in emerging markets is a relatively recent phenomenon (box 2.3). Almost 60 percent of the pension funds surveyed initiated exposure in emerging markets after January 1994. Interestingly, the proportion is exactly the opposite for the larger pension funds (those with assets greater than $1 billion)—that is, 60 percent had initiated exposure prior to January 1994. Larger pension funds tend to have higher exposure to emerging markets than do smaller funds, and corporate

Figure 2.9 International and Emerging Market Assets of U.S. Open-End Mutual Funds, 1990–95

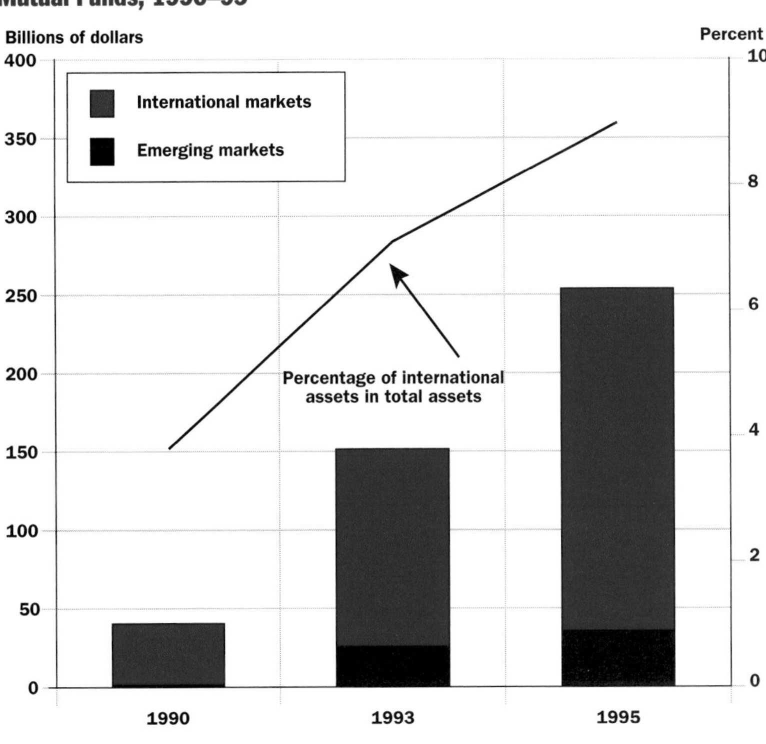

Source: Data from Micropal, Inc., and World Bank staff estimates.

U.S. mutual funds have increased their investments in international and emerging markets, although their investments are still quite low.

and endowment funds typically have much higher exposure than do government and union funds.

Although reliable data are not available, the results of two surveys suggest that U.S. pension funds currently have about 2 percent of their total assets invested in emerging markets (figure 2.11).[21] Thus, even though pension funds in the United States began to invest in emerging markets more recently than did mutual funds, their allocations are only slightly lower. Only a fraction of these funds, however, actually have a policy of allocating investment to emerging markets. Those that do generally treat all emerging markets as a single asset class and leave country allocation to the manager of the mutual fund or to an outside manager with a specific mandate.

More than half of the pension funds surveyed invest through mutual funds.[22] In fact, whereas retail investors, especially high net worth

Figure 2.10 Emerging Market Investments of Industrial Country Mutual Funds, 1993–95
(dedicated emerging market funds)

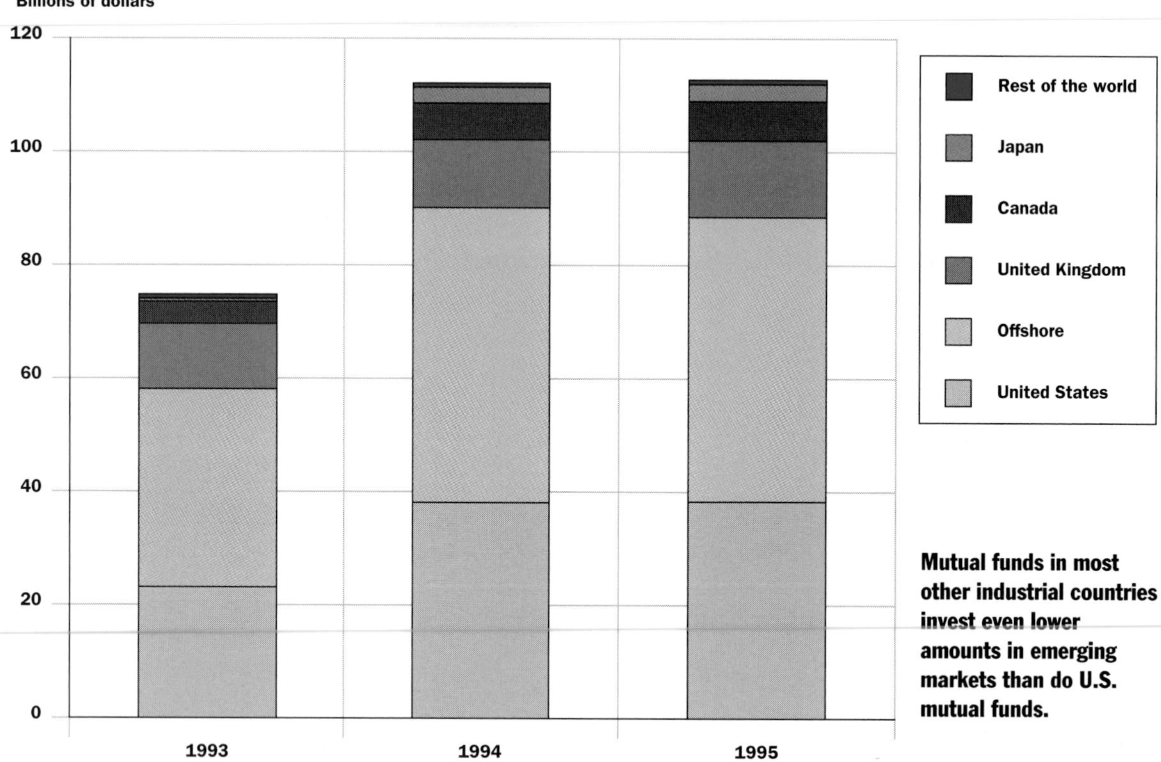

Note: Offshore denotes investment channeled through a mutual fund registered in an offshore financial center.

Source: World Bank staff estimates using data from Micropal, Inc.; the U.K. Association of Unit Trusts and Investment Funds; the Investment Funds Institute of Canada; the Investment Trusts Association of Japan.

Box 2.3 Pension Funds in Emerging Markets

Pension fund interest in emerging markets. Over 60 percent of the pension funds invested in emerging markets started investing at the beginning of 1994. Large corporate pension funds have had the longest exposure to emerging markets, with around 8 percent having invested in emerging markets since 1986–87.

Exposure in emerging markets. On average, U.S. pension funds hold around 1.5 to 2.0 percent of their portfolios in emerging market assets. This average, however, masks wide disparities among types of pension funds. The average for endowment funds is around 5 percent and that of larger corporations around 3 percent, with a few very large corporations holding up to 7 percent of their portfolios in emerging markets. On the other hand, the average for government funds is currently around 1 percent. Judging from a sample that includes data from both corporations and endowments, it seems that the larger pension funds have increased their exposure in emerging markets from an average of around 1 percent of their allocations in 1992 to just under 2 percent in 1995.

Investment motives. Around 40 percent of pension funds are interested in investing in emerging markets for the higher expected returns that these markets offer, while just under 40 percent consider both portfolio diversification and higher expected returns to be important factors. Around 13 percent—which includes the larger corporations—are investing in emerging markets primarily with a view to diversifying portfolio risks.

Investment vehicles. Over half the pension funds invest in emerging markets by buying into existing mutual funds. The remainder give specific mandates to managers. Less than 5 percent of pension funds manage emerging market investments themselves. Buying into existing funds is considered better for liquidity reasons and is also less expensive than specific mandates, given the current size of the allocations in emerging markets. The majority of the pension funds that invest through mutual funds do so by buying into global funds (over 50 percent) or regional funds (23 percent). Only 5 percent buy into country funds.

Types of investment. Almost all investments by pension funds are in the form of equity. Debt exposure is still minimal—with only the largest pension funds likely to hold emerging market debt instruments.

Policy allocation and investment strategy. Only a small proportion of pension funds treat emerging markets as a separate asset class in their policy allocations. Most invest in emerging markets as part of their international allocations. Those pension funds that do consider emerging markets as a separate asset class in their policy allocations leave the country selections to the fund managers. Annual review of policy allocations is the most common practice (over 30 percent). Less than 25 percent undertake quarterly reviews, and around 15 percent undertake monthly reviews. Changes in policy allocations, however, are a lot less frequent. Over 70 percent of pension funds undertake changes to their policy allocations every two or three years, and 13 percent every three to five years. Only 3 percent change their policy allocations annually.

Selection and evaluation of managers. Pension funds that employ outside managers generally choose them on the basis of a combination of track record and total assets under management. For emerging markets, "track record" refers as much to the length of a manager's experience as to the manager's performance. Around 40 percent of pension funds stated that the managers they selected employed a primarily "top down" approach, with another 28 percent employing managers who have a primarily "bottom up" approach to investing. Less than 3 percent of pension funds use an index alone for country allocations. The bulk of the pension funds evaluate their managers on the basis of performance relative to an index of choice as well as relative to their peers. Around 35 percent evaluate their managers relative to indices alone.

Outlook for pension fund investments in emerging markets. More than 43 percent of pension funds plan to increase their exposure to emerging markets over the next two or three years—of which the majority (60 percent) plan to increase their exposure by about 20 percent over their current levels, while the remaining 40 percent expect to increase their investments by 50 percent. Around 57 percent of pension funds expect to maintain their current levels of exposure. The rest have recently increased their allocations to emerging markets.

Source: Background survey undertaken by Kleiman International Consultants, Frank Russell Company, and World Bank staff.

Figure 2.11 International and Emerging Market Assets of U.S. Pension Funds, 1990–94

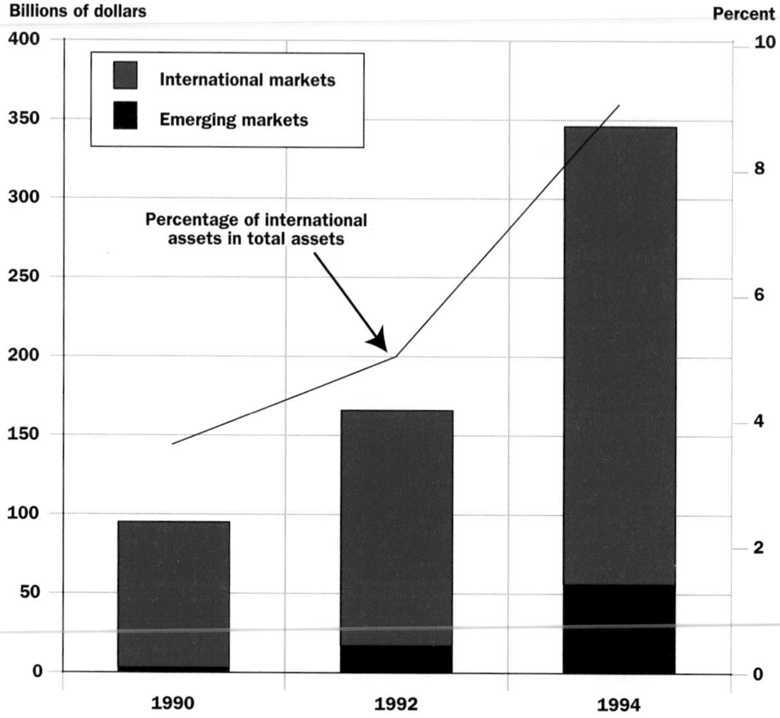

Source: Data from InterSec and World Bank staff etimates.

U.S. pension funds now invest around 2 percent of their total assets in emerging markets.

individuals, were the primary force in the early expansion of mutual funds into emerging markets, pension funds have rapidly become the dominant source of funds for mutual funds to invest in emerging markets, especially in the United States. The remainder of pension funds (around 41 percent) give the management of their assets to outside managers, who determine country allocations. Less than 5 percent of pension funds manage their emerging market investment in-house.

In absolute terms, U.S. pension funds are estimated to hold between $50 billion and $70 billion in emerging market exposure. Indeed, U.S. pension fund investments in emerging markets, including investments made on their behalf by mutual funds, have been an important factor in sustaining investment flows to emerging markets during 1994–95. As with mutual funds, most pension fund assets in emerging markets are in the form of portfolio equities.

The Prospects for Private Capital Flows

THE STRUCTURAL FACTORS UNDERLYING CAPITAL FLOWS TO developing countries are still unfolding. The changes taking place at the international level, which are increasing the responsiveness of capital flows to cross-border investment opportunities and leading to progressive global financial integration, can be expected to continue. In particular, all the forces discussed above—deregulation and breakdown of barriers, technological change, and financial innovation—continue to evolve and, as in the past, will keep reinforcing one another, creating pressures for further integration. Internal and external financial deregulation is far from complete in either industrial or developing countries. Although it is difficult to speculate on the nature of future innovation and technological change, competitive pressures and increasing integration have been stimulating investments in technology that are likely to continue to reduce transaction costs and make distant markets more accessible to small as well as large investors. Such innovations will make policy-induced barriers less effective, spurring even more deregulation and competition.

As discussed, many developing countries are still in the early stages of policy reform. The policy reforms that are being embarked upon—which focus on macroeconomic stability and the promotion of more deregulated, outward-oriented, and market-based economies—are likely to increase the productivity of investments in these countries. On the expectation that developing countries will continue to strengthen and deepen their policy reforms, and that the external environment will remain broadly favorable, developing countries are likely to grow at almost double the rate of industrial countries (figure 2.12), providing significant opportunities for productive investments.

Developing countries should provide growing opportunities for portfolio investors in particular as their share of world market capitalization, which is currently around 10 percent, rises further. As financial markets in emerging economies are not fully developed, further financial deepening—including that of capital markets—can be expected. And because developing countries are expected to grow significantly faster than industrial countries over the next decade or so, their share of world market capitalization will rise. Broadening of the base—as more developing

Figure 2.12 Developing and Industrial Countries' Growth, 1980–2005

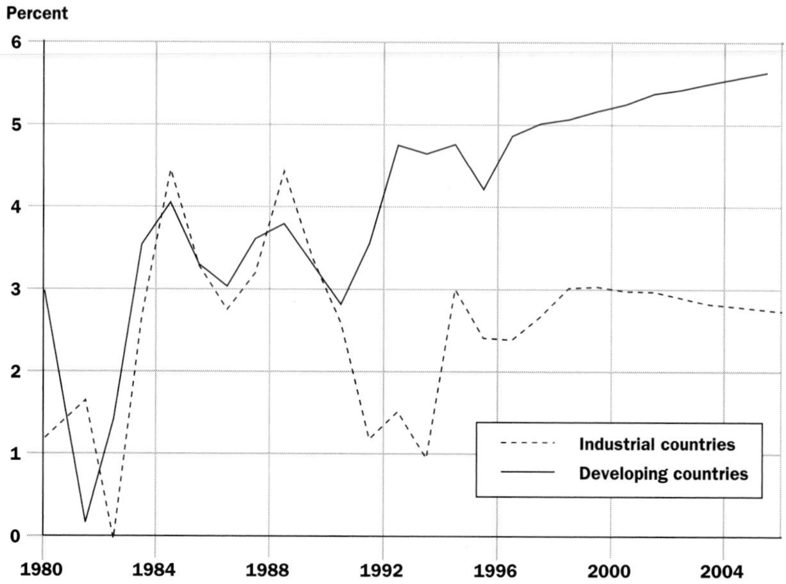

Note: This excludes the former Soviet Union and Eastern Europe.
Source: World Bank staff estimates.

Developing countries are likely to grow at nearly double the rate of industrial countries.

countries undertake reforms and liberalize—will contribute to the rising share of developing countries in world market capitalization.

Given these trends and the fact that the share of emerging markets in industrial country portfolios remains very small, there is still considerable room for an expansion of investments by institutional investors in emerging markets.[23]

As a result, the financial integration of developing countries is expected to broaden and deepen over the coming decade. As part of this process, gross private flows are likely to rise significantly, with capital flowing not only from industrial to developing countries, but, increasingly, among developing countries themselves, and from developing to industrial countries.

In the short to medium term, developing countries, in aggregate, are likely to receive net private capital flows because investment risks are declining, expected rates of return are improving, and these countries are underweighted in the portfolios of institutional investors. However, the rate of growth, and eventually the levels, will inevitably decline. Moreover, there is likely to be considerable variation among countries, depending on the pace and depth of improvements in macroeconomic performance and creditworthiness.

Aging in Industrial Countries: A New Force

An important new factor will provide further impetus to these underlying trends—the demographic shift under way in industrial countries. Industrial countries now have a pronounced bulge in their demographic structure, reflecting the aging of the baby boom generation and declining birthrates (figure 2.13). This will lead to a steady rise in the proportion of elderly to active population in all industrial countries, although the pace of this increase will be most pronounced in Japan (figure 2.14). As figure 2.13 also shows, this is in sharp contrast to the situation in developing countries, whose clearly pyramidal structure reflects a much younger population.[24]

The fact that developing countries have younger populations than industrial countries will have a positive effect on the flow of capital to emerging markets.

Figure 2.13 Demographic Structures of Developing and Industrial Countries, 1995

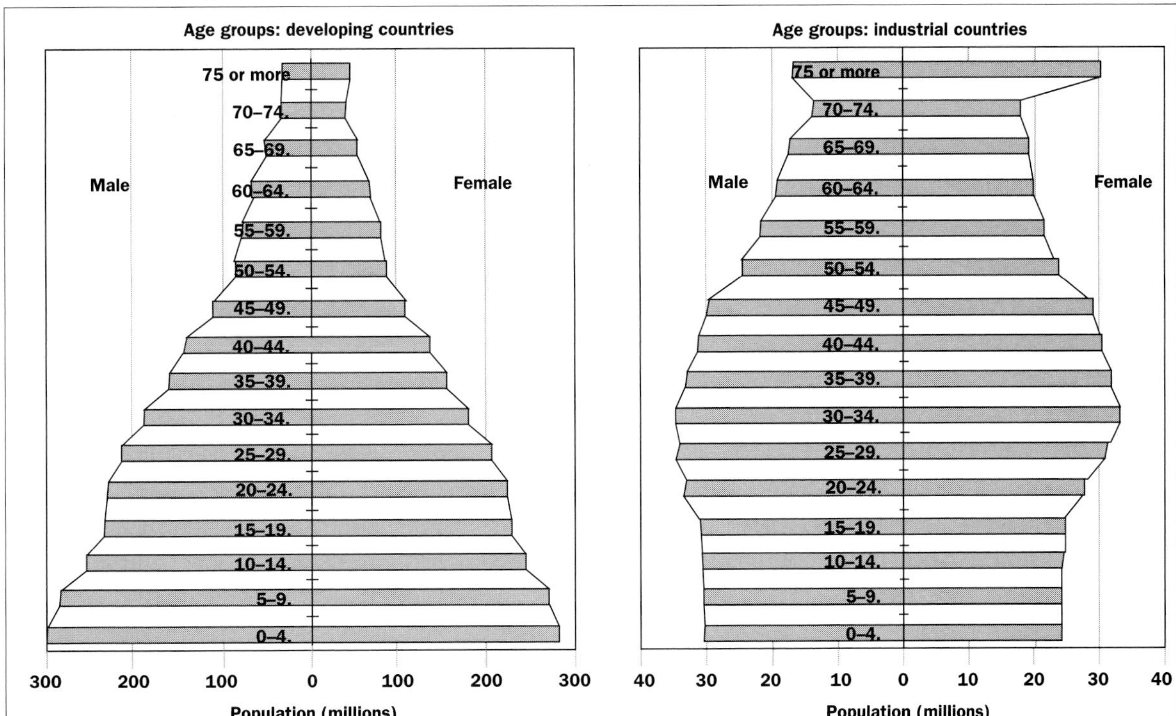

Note: Developing countries comprise low-income, lower-middle-income, and upper-middle-income countries. Industrial countries are all high-income countries.

Source: World Bank data.

Figure 2.14 Elderly Dependency Ratios, Selected Industrial Countries, 1990–2030
(ratio of population aged 65 and over to population aged 20–64)

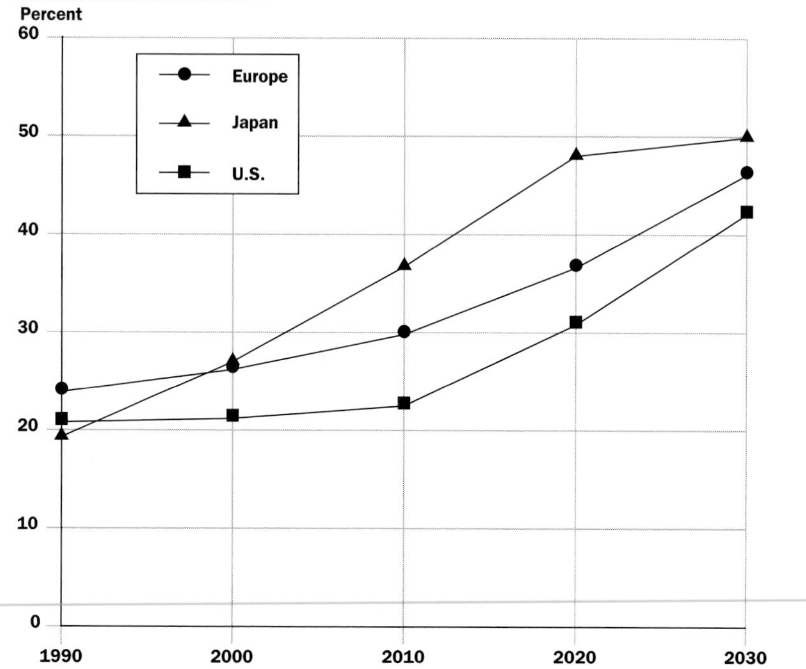

Source: World Bank (1994) and World Bank data.

The portion of the population formed by the elderly is growing in industrial countries.

There are three broad implications of this difference in demographic patterns. First, the aging of populations in industrial countries could lead to an increase in savings in the short to medium term. Second, aging and the associated slowing of labor force growth is likely to exert downward pressure on the rate of return to capital relative to that of labor in industrial countries. Given the demographic structure in developing countries, the reverse can be expected there. Thus, differences in demographics are likely to reinforce the differentials in the expected rates of return to capital between industrial and developing countries. Both of these factors should stimulate the flow of capital to emerging markets. Third, the aging of populations in industrial countries is leading to pressures for pension reform. These reforms are likely to result in greater responsiveness on the part of pension funds to investment opportunities in developing countries.

Aging, savings, and rates of return. The aging of populations in industrial countries is likely to affect the rates of return to capital in these countries through two channels. First, aging could lead to some increase in savings in industrial countries over the short to medium term. Second, aging can be expected to affect the rate of return to capital through changes in the labor market.

Effects through savings. The impact of aging on savings remains contentious, but there is reasonable basis to suggest that the demographic patterns in industrial countries are likely to lead to some increase in aggregate savings over the next 10 to 15 years, before leading to a decline.[25]

There are many channels through which aging can potentially affect savings. Since households are the primary savers in an economy, the effects of aging on private or household savings are particularly important.

- First, economic theory postulates that the savings rate varies by the age profile of economic agents and households. In particular, the standard model (that of Modigliani) postulates a hump-shaped life-cycle saving profile of households—that is, households save until retirement and then dissave. Empirically, however, the latter dissaving in the elderly is not observed: indeed the rate of savings of the elderly is positive in almost all industrial countries.
- Second, in addition to the age effect, there is a "cohort" effect. That is, different age groups differ by birth cohort, and this may cause savings behavior to vary among cohorts, based on the differences in their earnings histories and investment opportunities. A comparison of the savings rates of different cohorts reveals that later cohorts (younger generations) have recently had a higher saving rate than did earlier cohorts. In particular, the baby boom generation in the United States has had a higher savings rate at every age compared with the cohort born one generation earlier.
- Third, since savings is a product of the savings rate and income, savings are also affected by age- and cohort-specific incomes. In general, the age category at which the savings rate tends to peak, between 45 and 64, is also when incomes peak. This means that the age composition effect is reinforced by the age distribution effect. Because incomes as well as savings are highest in the 45-to-64 category, a shift of the population weight into this category will raise the annual flow of savings more than proportionately to the savings rate.

Because of these factors, the projected population structure in industrial countries can be expected to lead to an increase in private savings over the next 10 to 15 years in the OECD as a whole. First, the aging of populations will put more households into the high savings age category and fewer households into the low savings age category. Focusing on Germany, Japan, and the United States—which together account for two-thirds of OECD wealth—the following trends are expected (Börsch-Supan 1996). In the United States, over the next 10 to 15 years more households will enter the 45-to-64 age group, for which the savings rate is the highest. In Japan, the savings rate is found to be monotonically increasing with age, so an increase in the savings rate is also expected there. In Germany, however, the effect of aging on the savings rate is ambiguous: aging results in fewer households below age 37 (when savings rates are low), but it also results in a larger number of households in the saving trough after retirement. Second, the positive age effect on the savings rate is reinforced by the age-income distribution effect, particularly in the United States, where a growing number of households will fall into the 45-to-64 age group, the point at which income also peaks.[26] Third, as mentioned, there is a strong cohort effect, especially in the United States, where the baby boomers—who have had high savings rates throughout—are entering the peak savings and income age.[27]

The combination of age and cohort effects is expected to lead to a mildly decreasing aggregate savings rate in Germany and a mildly increasing aggregate savings rate in Japan. But there should be a relatively strong increase in the U.S. aggregate savings rate, from 4.7 percent in 1990 to 5.4 percent in 2000, and 5.8 per cent in 2010. Overall, the age composition effect and cohort effect are expected to lead to an increase in the volume of aggregate savings for the OECD as a whole over the next 10 to 15 years: from $1.015 billion in 1990 to $1.4 billion in 2010.[28]

While these factors could lead to an increase in the level of private savings over the next 10 to 15 years, what happens to aggregate savings in industrial countries depends on the implications of aging on public savings and on the interaction between private and public savings.[29]

The aging of populations will have significant implications for public expenditures. In particular, meeting pension fund obligations under the current pay-as-you-go systems would have significant repercussions on the fiscal deficit. Aging is also likely to increase expenditures on health. Empirical evidence from Japan and the United States shows that social expenditures on health increase very sharply with age. And while aging also means a decline in the proportion of children and hence public expenditures on schooling, such offsetting effects are not likely to be large. Since, however, there is a strong commitment to containing—and indeed reducing—fiscal deficits in industrial countries, it is increasingly being recognized that pension reforms cannot be delayed for much longer. Such reforms, including a move to a partially funded system, should result in an increase in public savings. Unless private sector behavior completely offsets this increase in public savings, aggregate savings in industrial countries should rise somewhat in the short to medium term.

Effects through the labor market. Demographic patterns, and the attendant slowdown in the growth rate of the labor force, may also affect rates of return to capital in industrial countries. More specifically, because the slower labor force growth implies fewer workers per unit of capital, other things being equal, the returns to capital relative to labor will tend to fall. (Of course, technological innovations that raise the rate of return to capital could mitigate some of the adverse effects of a slowdown in the labor force.) As the reverse is occurring in developing countries, the differences in demographics can be expected to contribute to the differential in the relative rates of return to capital between industrial and developing countries.

Both the developments in industrial country savings as well as the changes in the labor market should provide further stimulus to investments in emerging markets.

Aging and pressures for pension reform in industrial countries. The growing recognition of the burden that pension obligations under the current system will place on fiscal positions in industrial countries and the need to address the problem during the next 10 to 15 years is beginning to spur pressures to reform existing pension systems. In particular, there are pressures to move away from PAYG systems to more funded systems; to privatize pension schemes, both by increasing reliance on private employer and individual schemes—the so-called second and third pillars of old age security (World Bank 1994)—and through greater private sector management of public pension schemes; and to deregulate the investment allocations of pension funds to enable them to earn higher returns on their investments. All three factors are likely to result in greater response to investment opportunities in emerging markets (box 2.4).

The United Kingdom and the United States have been at the forefront of the shifts discussed above, but Japan and most of continental Europe are also beginning to establish market-oriented private schemes. Japan began to implement a series of reforms in recent years aimed at improving the incentives for private and individual programs and for greater international diversification.[30] Pension reform has also been high on the agenda of the European Union (EU), but it has been a contentious issue. The Pension Fund Directive, which was intended to liberalize cross-border management and investment of pension funds, was withdrawn in 1994. Shortly thereafter, however, the Euro-

Box 2.4 Pension Reforms and Their Implications for Investments in Emerging Markets

UNDER THE CURRENT PENSION STRUCTURE IN industrial countries—which is dominated by public, defined benefit schemes that are either partially funded (Japan, Sweden, United States) or financed on a pay-as you-go (PAYG) basis—the rising dependency will become a very significant fiscal burden. Under a PAYG system, the defined benefits to pensioners are not actuarially tied to contributions and are usually financed from a payroll tax. If this is the case, the benefits received by current retirees determine the taxes paid by current workers. Specifically, the payroll tax rate depends on the benefit rate (average benefit/average wage) times the dependency ratio (beneficiaries/covered workers). Meeting the defined benefit obligations in the face of a rising dependency ratio will require either further increases in the fiscal deficits or higher tax rates on the active population. (The magnitude of the overhang from unfunded pension plans is very large; net pension liabilities of public pension programs amount to some 60 percent of GDP for major industrial countries.) It is estimated that if the current system remains unchanged and is financed strictly on a pay-as-you-go basis, as opposed to moving toward partial funding, the present value of the benefits scheduled to be paid between now and the year 2150 will exceed the present value of expected contributions by two to three times the current value of GDP for most OECD countries. If this were to be financed by a payroll tax, it would mean a tax increase of about 15 to 20 percentage points (World Bank 1994). Alternatively, if there were a move towards partial funding now, with an immediate one-time increase in the contribution rate, the payroll tax increase would be lower, at around 9 to 12 percentage points in most countries (World Bank 1994). Recognition of this problem is spurring pressures for pension reform. These reforms are likely to result in a greater response on the part of pension funds to investment opportunities in emerging markets for several reasons:

- First, a move to more fully funded systems will entail a one-time hike in the current contribution to amass a temporary surplus to be used to pay the rising pension benefits. (Note that when the interest rate that capital earns is higher than the rate of wage growth—which is likely if pension funds invest greater

pean Commission issued a communication which seeks to ensure that there are no national restrictions on fund managers and to carefully define investment rules and levels of prudential control so that there are no undue restrictions on these grounds (Harrison 1995). Many European governments have started to ease investment restrictions, but this will be a slow process, in part because of strong political opposition in France, Italy, and Spain. Even if the pace of reform is uncertain, however, the direction is clear.

The magnitude of the potential increase in private pension funds and its impact on developing countries can be assessed from figure 2.15.

amounts in emerging markets—fully funded pension schemes have a cost advantage over PAYG systems. That is, the contribution rate will be lower under the former.) Increased pension payments are likely to increase total long-term savings available for investment, unless households cut back on other forms of personal savings or increase borrowing.

- Second, the privatization of pension schemes will result in more diversified institutional investments, including investments in international markets. Whereas publicly managed pension schemes are usually obliged to invest in government or government-related securities, privately managed pension schemes—in which workers or employers choose their fund managers—do not face this restriction. They have the incentive to allocate capital to investments that offer the best risk-yield combination, regardless of whether the securities are public or private. As a result, they are able to benefit from international management expertise and international diversification in investments. Indeed, it is the privately managed pension schemes that have accounted for the growth of pension fund investments in emerging markets.
- Finally, pension funds in most countries currently face some restrictions on international investments (box table 2.4). These regulations are currently not binding in countries like Canada and Switzerland (and of course the Netherlands, the United Kingdom, and the United States, where there are no major restrictions), since pension funds in these countries are allocating much smaller proportions to international investments than they are currently allowed by law. However, as the trend toward international diversification grows, these restrictions will become binding. Moreover, in places such as Germany and the Scandinavian countries, current regulations are very tight and already appear binding, since allocations to international investments are close to the maximum allowed by law. As these regulations are liberalized, we can expect to see greater international investments in these countries.

(Box continues on the following page.)

Box Table 2.4 Current Restrictions on Pension Funds' Foreign Investments

Country	*Restrictions*
Belgium	Maximum of 65 percent in equities in the OECD only.
Canada	Ceiling on foreign investment raised from 10 to 20 percent during 1990–95.
Denmark	Maximum of 40 percent in "high risk" assets, a category that includes foreign equities.
France	Maximum proportion of assets invested in shares (or mutual funds invested in shares) is 65 percent.
	Foreign investment permitted only if legal title of ownership remains in France.
	Currency matching—at least 80 percent of assets must be invested in the same currency as liabilities.
Germany	Maximum of 6 percent in non-EU bonds and maximum of 6 percent in non-EU equities.
	Eighty percent of assets must be invested in the same currency as liabilities.
Italy	Investment policies of the new private funds determined by funds' boards of directors and tend to be restricted to insurance policies, property, government bonds, and bank deposits.
Japan	Maximum of 30 percent in foreign-currency-denominated assets (part of 5:3:3:2 rule). Previously this rule applied to portfolios managed by individual asset managers, rather than to the pension fund as a whole (old requirements still apply to tax qualified pension plan assets, or TQPP). Also employees' pension fund plans considered to have sufficient management competence and experience may be exempted from the 5:3:3:2 rule on overall assets. Further deregulation planned.
Netherlands	No restrictions. "Prudent man" rule applies. Deregulation in January 1996 of ABP (the civil servants' fund and the largest pension fund in Europe).
Portugal	Maximum of 40 percent in foreign equities, listed in the European Union, New York, or Tokyo only.
Spain	No restrictions.
Sweden	Maximum of 5 to 10 percent in foreign currencies.
Switzerland	Maximum foreign equities, 25 percent.
	Maximum foreign currency bonds, 20 percent.
	Maximum Swiss franc bonds (by foreigners), 30 percent.
	Total bonds (excluding Swiss borrowers), 30 percent.
United Kingdom	No restrictions. "Prudent man" rule applies—trustees must invest assets in a prudent manner and in the most appropriate way for the membership.
United States	No restrictions (on private pension funds). "Prudent man" rule applies.

Note: The 5:3:3:2 rule in Japan is the asset allocation regulation that applies to pension fund investments. Under the new rules noted above, the pension fund as a whole must meet the following requirements:

50 percent minimum in principal guaranteed assets
30 percent maximum in domestic stocks
30 percent maximum in foreign-currency-denominated bonds
20 percent maximum in real estate.

Source: De Ryck (1996), Harrison (1995), World Bank staff interviews.

As figure 2.15 shows, private pension funds in industrial countries can significantly expand their holdings of international equities.

Figure 2.15 Pension Fund Assets and International Diversification, Selected Countries

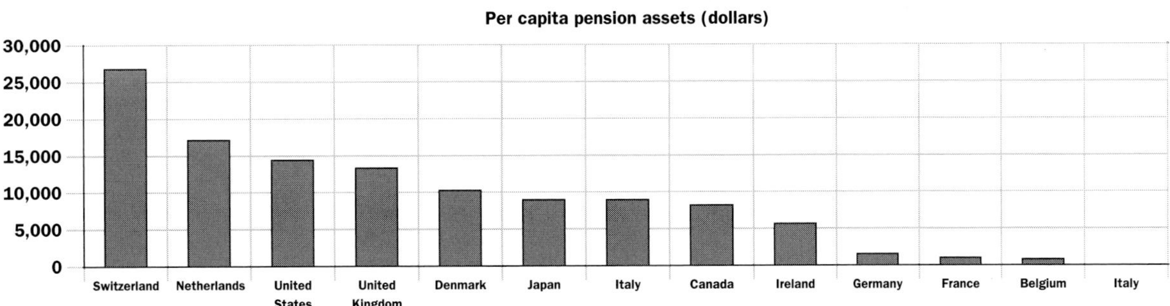

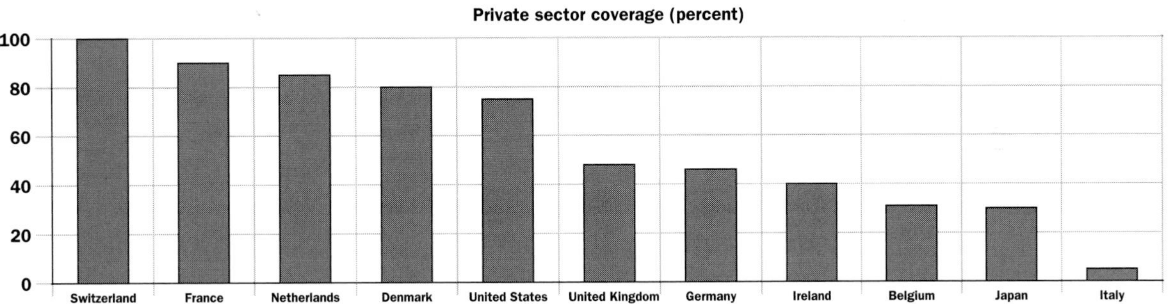

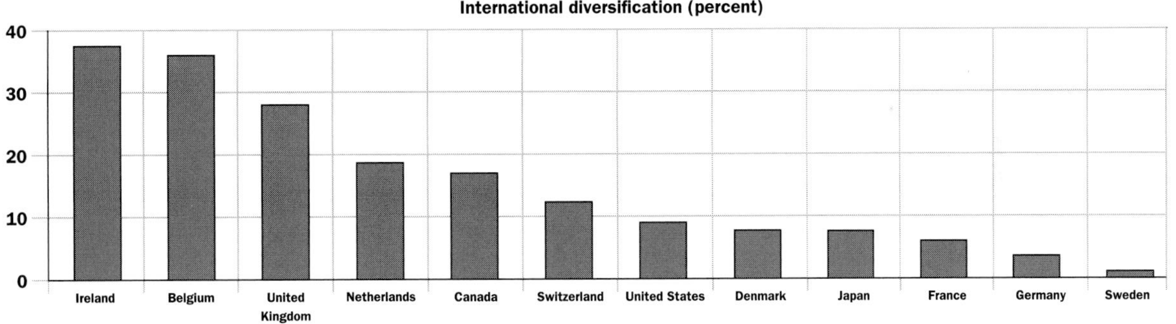

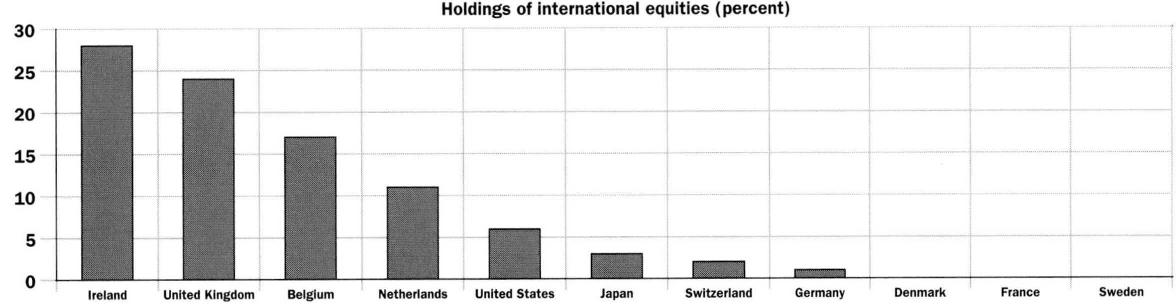

Source: World Bank staff estimates using data from InterSec, PDFM Pension Fund Indicators (1995).

Pension fund assets are extremely uneven across industrial countries and generally quite modest on a per capita basis. With aging, per capita and total pension assets will need to rise sharply. This increase can come in two ways: increases in contributions and increases in coverage. The coverage levels of private schemes, meaning the proportion of private sector employees covered by corporate pension funds, are still quite low in most industrial countries and therefore have significant potential for expansion. In fact, with pension reform, private pension fund assets are likely to increase dramatically, especially in Japan and Europe. The European Federation for Retirement Provision (De Ryck 1996) estimates that the combined EU pension fund asset base could expand ninefold over the next 25 years.

The growth of pension assets in conjunction with the trend toward international diversification should result in substantial new international investments. An increasing proportion of such new international hold-

Box 2.5 Defined Contribution Pension Plans and International Diversification

IN THE PAST 15 YEARS OR SO, DEFINED CONTRIbution corporate pension plans have grown rapidly, especially in the United States. There the share of defined contribution plans in total private pension assets is estimated to have risen from 16 percent in 1980 to 23 percent in 1995. Indeed, in 1995, 42 million people in the United States belonged to defined contribution plans with assets of $1.3 trillion, as compared with 17.5 million people and assets of $162 billion in 1980. Within the defined contribution plans, the 401(k)s—corporate pension funds in which employees contribute a percentage of their salary each year, allowing them to reduce their taxable income—in particular have seen tremendous growth. Defined contribution plans offer the employer several advantages over other plans: they are subject to fewer regulatory and administrative costs, since they need not meet an actuarial standard ensuring that a defined benefit will be provided in the future; they are more flexible, since contributions can be linked to the current performance of the employee; and the employee bears the subsequent financial risk of the pension assets.

There is a question as to whether such pension plans—where employees generally play an active role in selecting the investment medium for their pension accounts—are likely to be more conservative in their investment decisions, reducing the likelihood of significant further international investments by pension funds. In particular, it is generally presumed that these plans will tend to hold less risky assets such as domestic fixed income instruments.

ings is likely to be in the form of equities, including emerging market equities. International diversification by pension funds, and holdings of international equities in particular, is currently impeded by a number of factors. These include binding restrictions on holdings of foreign assets or international equities (as in France, Germany, Japan, and Spain); cultural biases against equity investments (as in other parts of Europe); the more conservative approach of the new pension plans (box 2.5); and restrictions on the use of international fund managers and advisers, who tend to push aggressively for international diversification (as in much of continental Europe and Japan). All of these factors are in the process of change, albeit gradually. Pension funds, therefore, are likely to be a major force in further international diversification and, in particular, in the demand for portfolio equities from developing countries. Today such pension funds hold about $70 billion of emerging market assets. This could rise very considerably over the next decade.

Evidence suggests that although such plans are more conservative in their investment allocations, with very low levels of international diversification, this situation is changing quite rapidly:

- First, a growing proportion of defined contribution programs such as the 401(k) plans, for example, is being channeled through mutual funds—which, as noted, are in a better position, relative to the individual, to invest internationally. Thus, in 1986, less than 8 percent of 401(k) assets were invested in mutual funds. By 1994, this share had risen to 30 percent.
- Second, a gradual broadening in the type of investments by these plans is under way, with the recognition that fund managers may have the specialized knowledge to undertake more risky investments. Thus, for example, in 1989, around 32 percent of the 401(k) assets invested in mutual funds were in guaranteed funds, and a further 11 percent in balanced funds, with only 9 percent in diversified equity funds. By 1995, the percentage in guaranteed funds had declined to 22 percent, while that in diversified equities had risen to 21 percent. Although equity holdings by 401(k) funds are still lower than those of traditional corporate pension funds, they are not all that low. It is estimated that 401(k) plans now have around 35 percent of their assets in equities, compared with the average proportion of traditional, defined benefit pension plans, which hold around 60 percent of their assets in equities.

Volatility Arising from the International Environment

PRIVATE CAPITAL FLOWS AND THE PROCESS OF FINANCIAL integration hold significant potential benefits (as discussed in chapter 3). Yet the volatility of these flows can have serious repercussions on the domestic economy. These concerns have been heightened in the current international environment in which new types of investors—investing in portfolio flows, which are a new form of investment for emerging markets—can and do respond more quickly to changing conditions. This section deals with factors in the international economy that can contribute to the volatility of flows and asset prices in emerging markets.

Two key questions arise with respect to volatility emanating from the international environment. First, what are the main factors that affect the volatility of flows and asset prices in emerging markets? Second, how significant are these factors in terms of their impact?

Three factors in the international environment have been identified as having an important bearing on the volatility of flows and asset prices in emerging markets. The first is movement in international interest rates and stock market returns in industrial countries. The second is potential foreign investor herding, meaning that investors follow each other in investment decisions, irrespective of whether the particular investment decision is warranted by changes in economic fundamentals. Such behavior leads to excess volatility of flows and asset prices—that is, volatility unrelated to, or in excess of, changes in economic fundamentals. The third factor is contagion, which occurs when events in one emerging market change investors' behavior in other emerging markets, regardless of whether the economic fundamentals of the latter have been affected or not.

The Role of International Interest Rates

Private capital flows to emerging markets are seen as being particularly prone to movements in international interest rates (and other asset returns). In part this is because changes in international interest rates can have sizable effects on the macroeconomic performance (through their impact on trade) and creditworthiness (through their impact on the debt burden) of developing countries. But developing countries are also seen as being more susceptible to changes in international interest rates because foreign investors still think of emerging markets as marginal investments.[31] The presumption is that because these investors consider investments in emerging markets as a means of adding higher returns to their portfolios only when their mainstream investments—in industrial countries—are underperforming, investments in emerging markets will be very sensitive to changes in industrial countries' interest rates.

The evidence suggests, however, that this presumption is true only for portfolio flows and not for FDI, which accounts for more than 50 percent of all flows to developing countries. In fact, based on the estimated relationship between private capital flows to developing countries, U.S. interest rates, and countries' macroeconomic fundamentals that is reported in box 2.2, we find that movements in U.S. interest rates account for only around 1 percent of the observed variation in total private flows—as opposed to 32 percent accounted for by changes in countries' macroeconomic fundamentals.[32]

In part, the relatively low sensitivity of aggregate flows to changes in international interest rates is due to the fact that FDI flows—especially those that occur as part of the globalization of production—are driven by firms' considerations of long-term profitability. Such flows are therefore much more responsive to changes in the investment environment of the host country than to temporary fluctuations in interest rates. Cyclical changes in interest rates may affect the start of an FDI project. It may also change the form of the financing package, but temporary movements in interest rates are unlikely to affect the magnitude of the flows associated with the project.

Portfolio flows, on the other hand, are quite sensitive to changes in interest rates. Because a portfolio investor buys bonds or shares in a company to get a rate of return, portfolio flows are highly sensitive to differentials in rates of return among countries. Moreover, should the rates of return rise elsewhere, portfolio investors, unlike FDI investors, can divest themselves of their stocks of equities or bonds relatively easily at the market price for those securities. For FDI investments, on the other hand, the value of the project is not public information, so an investor who wants to sell may not get the fair price because of problems of asymmetric information. Hence FDI investments are much more costly to reverse than are portfolio investments.[33]

Portfolio flows are also more volatile than FDI because portfolio investors consider emerging markets to be marginal investments. When international interest rates rose in the first quarter of 1994 (for the first time since 1990), portfolio flows to emerging markets declined sizably. Despite the further increases in interest rates during the year, however, portfolio flows to emerging markets recovered by the third quarter. Portfolio flows did decline sharply during the first quarter of 1995 when there was another spike in interest rates, but this period also coincided with the Mexican crisis. In fact, the recovery in portfolio flows in the second quarter of 1995 was sharper than the recovery following the interest rate increase in the first quarter of 1994, even though interest rates were around 2 percentage points higher in 1995. International interest rates rose again in early 1996, with seemingly little effect on portfolio flows to emerging markets. The effect of global interest rates on portfolio flows appears therefore to have declined somewhat (figure 2.16).[34] This is most likely because institutional investors are becoming more familiar with emerging markets and increasingly consider them to be mainstream investments.

Despite some decline in sensitivity, however, movements in international interest rates—if they are sizable—will undoubtedly continue to affect the volatility of portfolio flows to emerging markets. At the country level, if portfolio flows account for a sizable proportion of total flows, movements in global interest rates could translate into sizable volatility in flows and in domestic macroeconomic variables.

Investor herding. A second factor that has recently received a great deal of attention as a cause of volatility in portfolio flows and asset prices is herding on the part of foreign investors. Investor herding is generally attributed to problems of asymmetric information. It has been suggested that the current structure of the investor base—in which the assets of primary investors (retail investors and pension funds) are managed externally by professional fund managers—is particularly susceptible to herding behavior (box 2.6). The essence of this argument is that fund managers will follow the investment decisions of other fund managers in order to show clients that they know what they are doing. If they follow other fund managers' decisions and the investment turns out to be unprofitable, they are more likely to be thought of as unlucky than as unskilled, since other fund managers will have made the same mistake. Given that such a high percentage of household savings is now channeled through institutional investors

Figure 2.16 International Interest Rates and Portfolio Flows to Emerging Markets, 1993–96

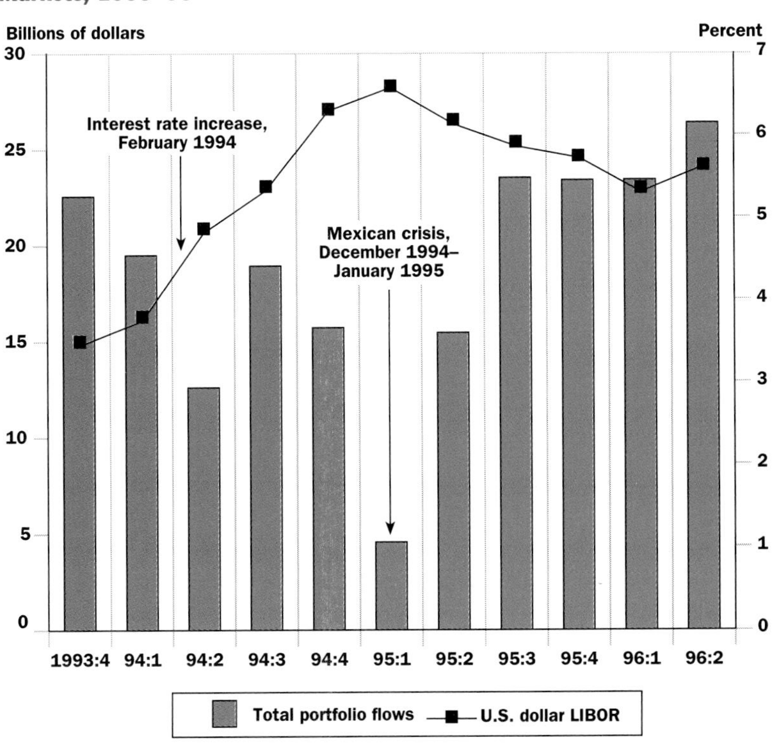

Note: LIBOR is the London interbank offered rate for six-month deposits. "Portfolio flows" refers to international issues of bonds and equities.

Source: Euromoney Bondware and World Bank staff estimates.

The effect of global interest rates on portfolio flows has declined somewhat.

that employ professional fund managers (it is estimated that 14 percent of household assets and 60 percent of pension fund assets are managed externally), the potential for such behavior clearly exists.

Much also depends on how the mandates of fund managers are set: some mandates could reinforce these incentives to herd. Mandates of external fund managers of pension funds in the United Kingdom, for example, often stipulate that the fund manager perform at least as well as the median fund. Consequently, underperformance relative to the median is penalized, while overperformance is not rewarded proportionately. This could arguably provide more of an incentive to herd than if fund managers are evaluated against an index as well as against peers, as is often the case in the United States, or asked to achieve a minimum yield, as in Japan (Griffith-Jones 1996b).

Box 2.6 Is the Current Investor Base Prone to Herding?

HERDING ON THE PART OF INVESTORS IS GENERally explained by a variety of asymmetric information problems. For example, it has been argued that asymmetric information between fund managers and the primary investors (retail investors or pension fund managers) can give rise to "principal-agent" problems and result in herding behavior by fund managers (see Scharfstein and Stein 1990). The reasoning is as follows. Fund managers can be either highly skilled or of low abilities. Highly skilled managers will tend to receive informative signals about the value of an investment, while those of low ability will receive purely random signals. Since the ability of fund managers (the agents) cannot be determined with certainty, they need to signal the quality of their abilities to the primary investor (the principal). And as the investment decisions of highly skilled managers will tend to be correlated (because they are all observing the same piece of "truth"), whereas the decisions of low-ability managers will not (their signals will be random), it pays for an individual fund manager to make the same investment decision as other fund managers in order to signal that he is a manager of high skill. Even if the investment turns out to be unprofitable, an unprofitable decision is not as bad for the reputation of a fund manager when others make the same mistake—in a world in which there are systematically unpredictable components of investment value, they can all share in the blame.

Thus, even if a fund manager's own information suggests that an investment has negative expected value, he may choose to pursue it if other fund managers have done so. Conversely, he may choose not to undertake an investment even if he believes it to have a positive expected value if other fund managers have chosen not to make the investment.

Clearly, to the extent that household and pension fund assets are managed externally by professional fund managers (that is, to the extent that a principal-agent setup exists)—and to the extent that the performance of a fund manager is evaluated relative to that of other fund managers—incentives to herd out of reputational concerns can exist. It is estimated that 14 percent of the assets of individuals and about 60 percent of pension fund assets in the major industrial countries are managed through fund managers, including bank managers, insurance managers, and mutual fund managers (InterSec). In general, though, the performance of a fund manager tends to be evaluated both in relation to the performance of other fund managers and in relation to an appropriate index. (Thus, if the fund manager specializes in emerging markets, his performance may be evaluated relative to the performance of the IFC Emerging Market Index, for example.) The fact that managers are also evaluated relative to an index may somewhat dampen the incentives to herd out of concerns for reputation (although, of course, if foreign investors account for a significant proportion of a country's market capitalization, their herding actions could influence the index as well). In addition, since fund managers' salaries depend on the returns they achieve, they will clearly also attach weight to the profitability of their investment decisions. Their salaries are usually a percentage of the assets under their management, which, in turn, is a function of their performance over the preceding two years or so. Third, there may be a "superstar" effect (see Rosen 1981), in which the top-ranked fund managers earn disproportionately higher wages. For managers ranked in or near the top 100, the incentives to herd will also be much lower.

Herding behavior may also be stronger in emerging markets because the investors are less familiar with these markets and will thus be reluctant to rely solely on their own assessment of the fundamental value of an investment. Under these circumstances, investors will at least partly adjust their investment decisions according to those of other investors, behavior that could lead to herding or trend chasing. A factor that will have some dampening effect on such behavior, however, is the high transaction costs associated with equity investments, which constitute the bulk of institutional investors' investments in emerging markets. Because of high transaction costs, turnover ratios of equity investments are generally less than one-third that of bonds.

It has been argued that pension funds are less prone to short-term trend chasing and volatile behavior than are mutual funds (Griffith-Jones 1996b). In particular, the argument has been that retail investors have shorter investment horizons and are hence more prone to responding to short-term trends than are pension funds, and that since retail investors are the primary investors in mutual funds, mutual funds are more likely to respond to short-term trends. An important factor in this regard is the frequency with which fund managers' performance is reviewed. Pension funds tend to review their external managers' performance and policy allocations every two or three years, although monitoring generally takes place annually (box 2.3). The performance of mutual fund managers who serve retail investors as well, on the other hand, does tend to be evaluated by the market over a much shorter horizon.[35] However, over 50 percent of pension fund investments are undertaken through the purchase of shares in mutual funds, so the distinction between mutual funds and pension funds is, in practice, more blurred.

While the theory of investor herding is plausible, it is difficult to demonstrate empirically. Studies have tested for investor herding and positive feedback trading (buying stocks whose prices are rising and selling those whose prices are falling) in the United States (Lakonishok, Shleifer, and Vishny 1992). In particular, they have looked at the extent of correlation across fund managers' buying and selling of individual stocks. There is little evidence from these studies to support the notion that there is investor herding in the United States.[36]

For emerging markets, it is difficult to test for investor herding by looking directly at the buying and selling patterns of fund managers for individual stocks—given the paucity of data. An indirect way of assessing whether foreign investors herd in emerging markets, though, is to look at the behavior of stock market prices and returns. If investors herd, changes in stock market prices and returns in one period will tend to be accentuated in the next period, so prices will tend to exhibit periods of upward or downward swings (that is, prices will tend to be somewhat predictable), which eventually reverse, leading to excess volatility. Since there are other reasons why stock prices and returns may exhibit such patterns, however, price swings could suggest investor herding only if they are accentuated when foreign investors become important in an emerging market.[37] Moreover, such herding could be on the part of foreign and domestic investors—who could be overreacting to the decision and actions of foreign investors, thereby contributing to excess volatility.

Figure 2.17 illustrates the behavior of asset returns in a sample of emerging markets as institutional investors have become important. A ratio greater than one indicates positive autocorrelation in returns—that is, it shows that returns exhibit successive periods of increases (or decreases). As figure 2.17 shows, the degree to which these markets were prone to such periods of upward or downward swings increased in the period in which foreign investors first became important in these markets—which could suggest foreign investor herding or domestic investors' overreaction to the actions of foreign investors. What is noteworthy, however, is that all the markets in the sample (with the exception of Mexico) saw a decline in excess volatility as the duration of foreign investor presence increased.[38] This finding is consistent with the hypothesis, discussed below, that the potential for foreign investor herding at the country level diminishes as these investors become more familiar with markets and as these markets become more financially integrated. As discussed in chapter 6, foreign investor presence in emerging markets can also promote, among other things, better information disclosure, which in turn can reduce problems of asymmetric information and the potential for investor herding—whether by foreign or domestic investors. Again, this is consistent with the finding that excess volatility declines as the length of foreign investor presence increases.

The possibility that emerging markets may be subject to investor herding was also analyzed by testing whether Brady bond prices have spillover effects on local stock market returns over and above what is justified by changes in a country's economic fundamentals. If so, this would be consistent with less informed investors (foreign or domestic)

Figure 2.17 Excess Volatility in Emerging Markets, Selected Countries and Years
(measured by the variance ratio test)

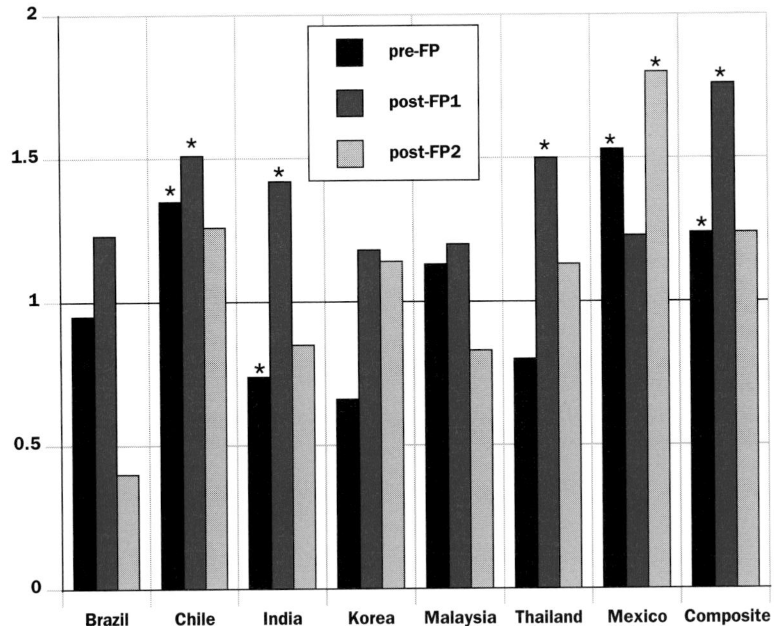

* Statistically significant at the 10 percent level.

Note: FP denotes foreign presence. FP1 indicates the first period of increased foreign presence, which differs across countries. This threshold date was taken to be the period in which total assets of open- and closed-end dedicated emerging market funds reached $500 million or more. FP2 is the following period, up to 1996. For example, mutual fund assets in Thailand passed $500 million in 1988. Thus the period prior to foreign participation (pre-FP) is taken to be from early 1986 to the end of 1987, the initial period of foreign participation (FP1) is from early 1988 to the end of 1990, and the later period of foreign participation (FP2) runs from early 1991 to the end of 1996. Cross-country comparisons are not meaningful because other factors can affect the variance ratio (see note 37).

Source: World Bank staff estimates using the IFC Investable Return Index.

Countries are more susceptible to investor herding in the early stages of integration, but such herding tends to decline the longer foreign investors are active in a market.

overreacting to Brady bond price movements in making their investment decisions in local stock markets—in the belief that those investing in Brady bonds (primarily foreign traders, commercial and investment banks, and hedge funds) have more information about changes in the economic conditions of the country and in the value of the investments than they do. As box 2.7 shows, there is in fact some evidence to suggest that such spillover effects exist.

Box 2.7 Do Investors Overreact to Changes in Brady Bond Prices?

ONE POSSIBLE FACTOR THAT HAS BEEN WIDELY cited as a cause for market inefficiency and excess volatility in emerging markets is herding by investors, particularly international investors, whose access to information may be limited.

When such information does become available, investors may overreact, so stock price movements in emerging markets are greater than would be justified by the subsequent impact of the news on dividends. One such example is the discount on Brady bonds. It has been suggested that investors in emerging markets often watch changes in Brady bond prices to infer information about changes in countries' economic fundamentals and that they tend to overreact to these changes in prices.

This proposition was tested by examining whether there was excess volatility in stock markets and whether this excess volatility was correlated with movements in Brady bond discounts (prices).[1] Efficient market hypothesis suggests that stock prices should be equal to the discounted present value of future dividends. The extent to which the volatility of actual stock prices exceeds the volatility of the theoretical stock prices is the measure of excess volatility.

In seven out of the eight emerging markets we examined, stock market prices were found to exhibit excess volatility that was correlated with movements in Brady bond prices. This suggests that investors may indeed overreact, or herd, in response to movements in the price of Brady bonds.

Coefficient Measuring Effect of Brady Bond Prices on Excess Volatility

Country	*Coefficient*
Argentina	0.59*
Brazil	0.37*
Chile	0.30
Jordan	0.03*
Mexico	0.59*
Nigeria	0.47*
Philippines	0.47*
Venezuela	0.20*

* Significant at the 5 percent level.

1. Using the methodology developed by Campbell and Shiller (1987), we examined the relationship between the actual dividend/price ratio p, and the theoretical dividend/price ratio p^*, equal to the present discounted value of the growth of dividends Dd. According to this methodology, all information relevant to forecasting Dd is included in p^*. Therefore divergences between the actual price/dividend ratio and the theoretical price/dividend ratio, which is correlated with movements in Brady bond prices, is evidence of overreaction in equity prices to movements in Brady bond prices. A significant positive coefficient indicates that stock market prices p rise above the theoretical prices p^* when there is good news in Brady bond prices.

Source: World Bank staff estimates.

The key question, though, is whether such herding behavior results in significant volatility in asset prices and returns in emerging markets. Studies that have compared the behavior of asset returns in emerging markets with those in industrial countries have found that emerging markets do exhibit greater volatility. These studies have found evidence of return reversals at long horizons—that is, periods of overperformance are followed by periods of underperformance—evidence that, again, could be consistent with investor herding. However, these reversals are not much different from those in industrial countries (Richards 1996). Furthermore, data on the short-term volatility of returns do not suggest that there has been a generalized increase in the overall volatility of returns following liberalization of emerging markets (Richards 1996, Bekaert and Harvey 1995).

Several factors also suggest that emerging markets should become less susceptible to volatility related to foreign investor participation as these markets become more integrated:

- The conditions under which emerging market investments are undertaken are changing rapidly. In particular, institutional investors are becoming more familiar with emerging markets—as evidenced by the significant increase in both the volume and quality of broker research into emerging markets over the past four to five years. The potential for herding should diminish as better macroeconomic, industry, and company information becomes available to foreign investors—a result of financial integration and capital market development.
- The form of investor participation changes and broadens as countries become more integrated (box 2.8). In the initial, or "pre-emerging," stage of integration, the likelihood of herding is low because investors are specialized and dedicated. Countries in the newly emerging stage are more vulnerable to herding because investments are in a less dedicated form and investors are investing in an environment of possible asymmetric and incomplete information. Finally, as markets become more mature and integrated, the investor base tends to become more heterogeneous and better informed, dampening the potential for excess volatility at the country level.
- As markets become more integrated, another factor comes into play: inefficiencies at the country level will have been exploited, so that excess returns are made not at the country level but at the level of individual stocks. Accordingly, fund managers' investment strategies will tend to move away from top-down allocation and active management at the country level to bottom-up allocation and active management at the stock level. That is, their strategies will combine more passive, indexed-based investment at the country level with the active selection of stocks. The potential for herding at the country level should therefore di-

Box 2.8 The Form in Which Foreign Investors Participate in Emerging Markets Will Vary with the Extent of Financial Integration

IN THE VERY EARLY STAGES OF FINANCIAL INTEGRATION, foreign participation tends to be in the form of boutique investment funds. These funds are usually not very large, and their investment objectives are generally quite narrowly defined; they are looking for selective opportunities in specialized markets. The investments of these funds tend to be based on detailed country, sector, and company knowledge. At this stage, therefore, the likelihood of herding is low.

As countries reach the newly emerging stage, investor participation broadens. For most emerging countries, the process is one of first having country funds—which are relatively dedicated money—and then entering regional funds and global emerging market funds (box figure 2.8). In the latter cases, investments are made across a region or across several emerging market regions, and the funds are correspondingly less dedicated at the country level. At this stage, moreover, investments tend to be based on an active discretionary allocation strategy at the country level. With less dedicated flows and the possible problem of asymmetric and incomplete information among fund managers (particularly since there are less specialized managers participating), there is a greater potential of herding behavior.

Finally, as markets become more mature, more integrated, and better known to investors, there appear to be two opposing forces at work. First, the investor base broadens further, with global fund managers also investing in these countries. These fund managers are, other things being equal, less likely to have detailed knowledge at the country and stock levels than are specialized emerging market managers. On the other hand, as mentioned above, at this stage the level and quality of information available to investors in general is much greater at the country, sector, and stock levels. This dampens the tendency toward excess volatility.

minish, even if it remains at the level of individual stocks. Investors at this stage of integration are also likely to be more tactical in the timing of their investments (selecting national markets according to current levels of key benchmark asset returns relative to their long-run equilibrium value). They act, from the country's perspective, in a countercyclical manner.

In general, therefore, the potential for volatility arising from foreign investor participation can be expected to follow an inverted U-shaped curve, as countries move from the pre-emerging stage of financial integration to the mature emerging stage. It is likely to be highest when countries are in the newly emerging stage of financial integration. The factors underlying this process are summarized in table 2.1 below. What is more, the experience of countries that have begun the process of integration earlier suggests that the peak of herding behavior and the

Box Figure 2.8 Changes in the Form of Investor Participation as Countries Become More Integrated

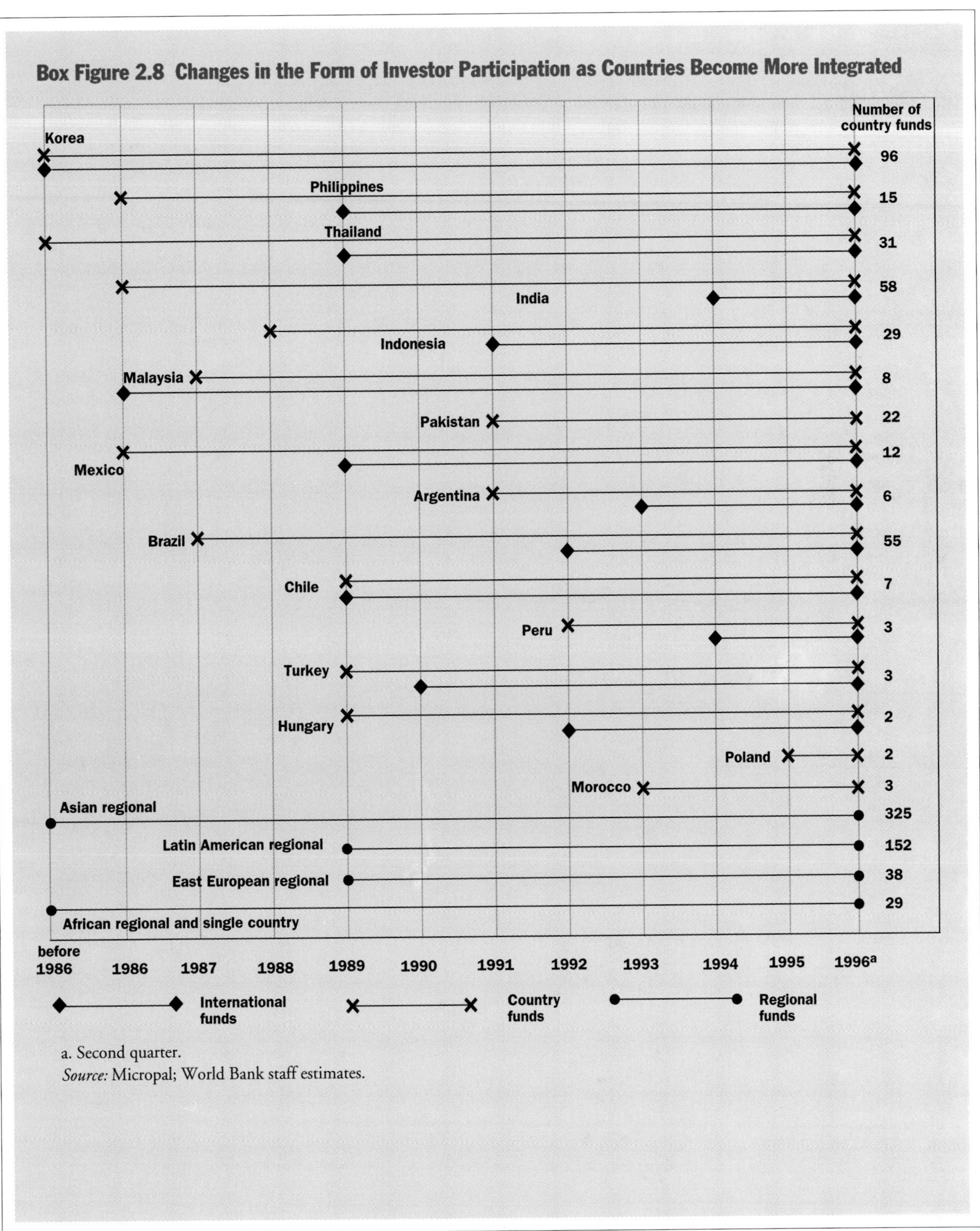

a. Second quarter.

Source: Micropal; World Bank staff estimates.

Table 2.1 Volatility in Various Stages of Financial Integration

	Investor Market Structure and Conditions		
	Pre-emerging	*Newly emerging*	*Mature emerging*
Factors that can increase volatility		Countries begin to have regional and emerging market funds that are less dedicated at the country level. Also, most investors in these emerging markets, while perhaps using an index as a benchmark, are likely to have a discretionary allocation strategy. This will typically involve looking at macroeconomic conditions in countries (a top-down approach), but also include considerations of market liquidity and what other investors are doing. This strategy may result in herding behavior.	In addition to managers of country, regional, and emerging market funds (and managers with these specialized mandates), there will also be global fund managers, who, unlike the specialized managers, may be operating with relatively little information at the country level.
Factors that can dampen volatility	Boutique investors undertake careful stock analysis for a select group of countries, which have such low market capitalization that they are not in any international index.	In the early stages of the newly emerging markets, there are dedicated (country) funds. Although in later stages there will be less dedicated money and higher risks of herding, in practice active managers undertaking discretionary allocations typically tend to take only small bets off the index. Therefore, even if there is a risk of herding, the absolute magnitudes of flows are not likely to be large.	As markets become better known to investors and more information is available, the specialist or knowledgeable managers are in a better position to undertake tactical asset allocations (which involve selecting national markets according to current levels of key benchmark asset returns relative to their long-run equilibrium). This is likely to have some countercyclicality and dampen volatility. As markets become large enough to enter the global index and inefficiencies at the country level have been exploited, investors are more likely to use the index to allocate over countries (that is, to undertake passive investing) and use stock picking as a means of adding to the value within country allocations. This is likely to reduce the risk of herding at the country level.

associated increase in excess volatility appear to last for a relatively short period, as discussed above (figure 2.17).

Cross-Country Contagion

The Mexican crisis highlighted the issue of contagion—spillover effects from one country to another—which can be another source of volatility for emerging markets. Conceptually, two types of contagion can be distinguished. The first is fundamentals contagion, in which a shock in one country can affect investments in other countries because the countries share similar fundamentals or are exposed to common external shocks. Or it is possible that the shocks in one country are transmitted through trade or financial channels and thereby affect the economic fundamentals of other countries.[39]

The second type of contagion occurs when shocks in one country affect investments in other countries, even if the economic fundamentals of the latter have not changed. This could be termed "pure" contagion. From the country's perspective, such changes in investments would constitute excess volatility. Investors' initial reactions in the wake of the Mexican crisis, which erupted in the last quarter of 1994, were an example of pure contagion. Because investors were not sufficiently discriminating among emerging markets, portfolio flows to almost all emerging markets declined very sharply in the first quarter of 1995. Indeed, international equity and bond issues by emerging markets declined by around 86 percent in the first quarter of 1995 over the previous quarter. Moreover, all regions were hit significantly—although Latin America was the most affected. In fact, the only countries that issued international bonds of any significant magnitude in the first quarter of 1995 were Korea and Portugal.

By the second quarter of 1995, however, many emerging markets had returned to the international financial markets, and there was a much greater differentiation in the terms of borrowing. This initial contagion was also reflected in equity prices in emerging markets. Almost all emerging markets saw declines in domestic equity prices during the first quarter of 1995. By the end of May, however, countries whose macroeconomic fundamentals were relatively strong saw a recovery in prices. In fact, there is evidence to suggest that the magnitude and duration of the decline in stock market prices was clearly related to some key macroeconomic fundamentals—average inflation rate and

Although stock prices in emerging markets declined after the Mexican crisis, the reaction was relatively mild and transitory for countries with good macroeconomic fundamentals.

growth of output and exports—before the onset of the crisis (figure 2.18).[40] In sum, there is evidence of contagion arising from investors' behavior. However, evidence also suggests that international markets have discriminated among countries relatively quickly after the initial reaction.

Figure 2.18 Impact of the Mexican Crisis on Stock Prices in Emerging Markets, 1994–95

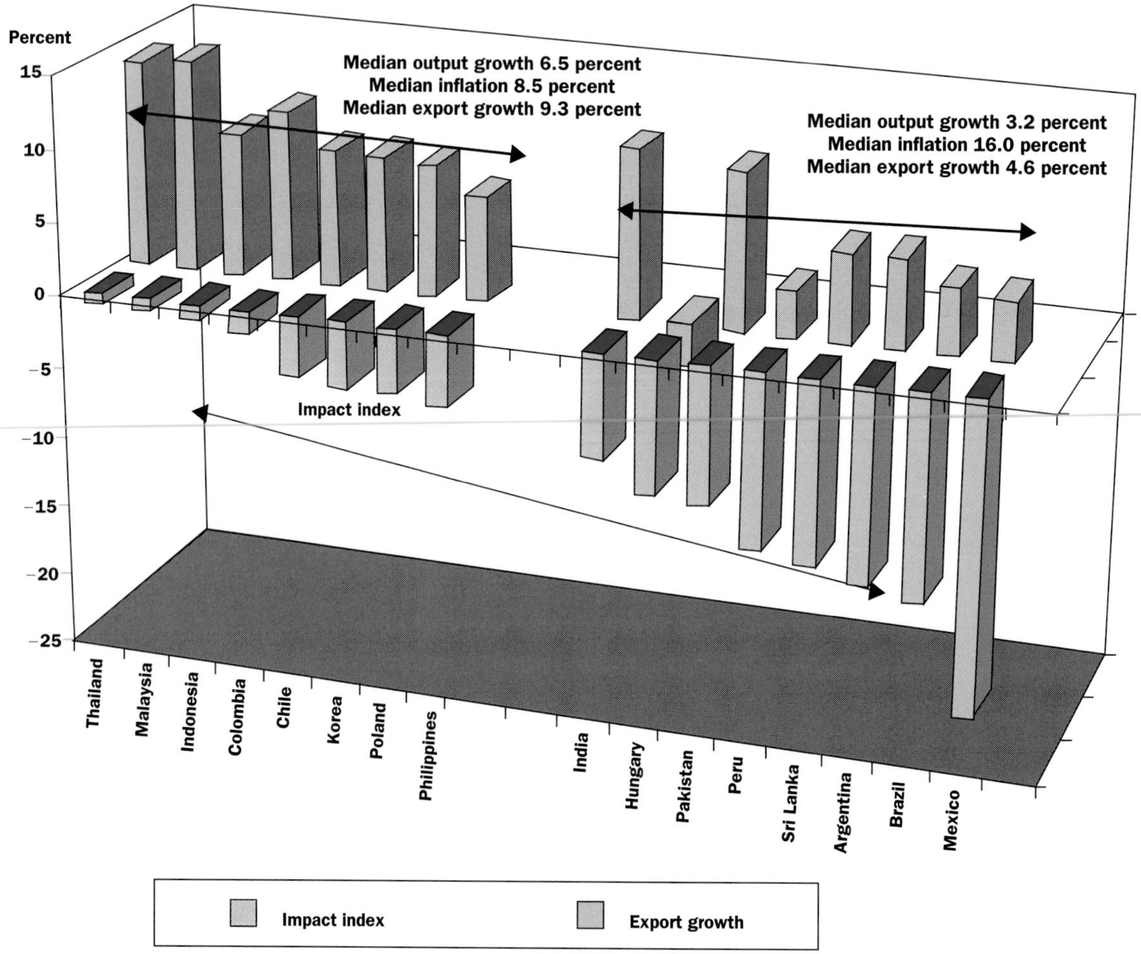

Percent
15
10
5
0
-5
-10
-15
-20
-25

Median output growth 6.5 percent
Median inflation 8.5 percent
Median export growth 9.3 percent

Median output growth 3.2 percent
Median inflation 16.0 percent
Median export growth 4.6 percent

Impact index

Thailand
Malaysia
Indonesia
Colombia
Chile
Korea
Poland
Philippines
India
Hungary
Pakistan
Peru
Sri Lanka
Argentina
Brazil
Mexico

Impact index
Export growth

Note: The impact is measured both in terms of the magnitude and the duration of the decline in stock market prices from December 16, 1994, to the end of May 1995. As the impact is measured as an index, it is a negative number, as shown on the bottom half of the graph. The top half shows the average export growth in percent per year in each country, as well as the median output and export growth and rates of inflation of the two groups of countries—the group in which the Mexican crisis had a relatively small impact (an impact index of −1.0 to −5.0) and the group in which the impact was relatively large (an impact index of −5.0 to −20.0). As the graph shows, the group of countries in which the impact was relatively small had stronger economic fundamentals.

Source: World Bank staff estimates.

Even if investors are becoming more discriminating, however, two factors, related to the investment strategy (rather than behavior) of institutional investors and to the structure of the current investor base, have the potential to contribute to contagion.

- Institutional investors appear to invest in emerging markets using a two-step allocation process in which they first allocate a proportion of their portfolio to emerging markets as an asset class, and then allocate among individual emerging markets within this. Asset returns in one emerging market are therefore evaluated on the basis of returns to both the world portfolio and a broad emerging market portfolio. Under these circumstances, shocks that lead to any changes in asset returns in one emerging market will lead to changes in investment allocations to other emerging markets (Buckberg 1996). However, the magnitude of contagion arising from this process is likely to be relatively small, since it involves portfolio rebalancing within the overall allocation to emerging markets as an asset class, which itself is still quite small.[41]
- A high likelihood of contagion also derives from the fact that a sizable proportion of mutual funds that invest in emerging markets are open-end funds. Unlike closed-end funds, open-end funds are required to redeem claims on demand. Since managers are particularly averse to large losses, redemptions—or the fear of redemptions—will tend to affect the portfolio decisions of open-end mutual funds. (In fact redemption risk is an important reason why open-end mutual funds tend to have much higher turnover ratios, averaging around 100 percent, compared with those of closed-end funds, at 50 percent or less.) Such funds may be forced, by capital losses in one country, to sell holdings in other countries, either in order to keep their country shares in the correct proportions or to meet investor redemptions.[42] Evidence shows, for example, that following the Mexican crisis, U.S. mutual funds sold shares in all emerging regions—including Asia. In the longer run, though, fund managers were able to substitute between regions, reallocating a bigger share of their portfolios to the assets of the regions where macroeconomic fundamentals were perceived to be strong. Thus, contagion arising from the purely institutional nature of mutual funds appears to be short-lived.[43]

In sum, a shock in one emerging market may well lead to some volatility in flows and asset prices in other emerging markets. However, experience suggests that such contagion will be short-lived—lasting only until investors have reevaluated the prospects in individual emerging markets.

Conclusion

PRIVATE CAPITAL FLOWS TO DEVELOPING COUNTRIES HAVE continued to grow despite the increase in U.S. interest rates in 1994 and the Mexican crisis in 1994–95—albeit at a slower rate. Aggregate private flows have shown resilience because a significant proportion has been in the form of FDI , which is less susceptible to cyclical and other short-term shocks than other types of flows. While portfolio flows initially declined by substantial amounts in response to these shocks, their recovery has also been impressive. Despite the large drop in the first half of 1995, portfolio flows recorded only a small decline for the year as a whole: it is estimated that in 1996 they rose to levels comparable to the peak reached in 1993.

This chapter has argued that the sustained increase in private capital flows reflects the fact that these flows have now reached a new phase, one driven by increased financial integration, although low interest rates in industrial countries provided the initial impetus. The two fundamental forces driving the growing investor interest in and integration of developing countries are:

- higher long-term expected rates of return, as a result of policy reforms and improved creditworthiness
- the opportunities that developing countries provide for risk diversification because of low correlation between returns in developing and industrial countries.

The chapter has also argued that the magnitude and speed of response of private capital flows to investment opportunities is much higher than it was in the late 1970s and early 1980s, because of significant changes that have taken place in the enabling environment of both industrial and developing countries.

As a result of these changes, emerging markets have seen growing investment by institutional investors. Whereas in 1986 there were only

19 emerging market country funds and 9 regional and global funds, in 1995 there were 505 country funds and 773 regional and global emerging market funds. And although pension funds have started to invest in emerging markets only recently, in the United States the average share of emerging markets in pension fund portfolios is comparable to that in mutual funds' portfolios. In the case of some of the larger U.S. pension funds, the share of emerging markets in total assets is considerably higher.

The factors that are driving financial integration of developing countries are still unfolding:

- At the international level, the factors that are increasing the responsiveness of private capital to cross-border investment opportunities—deregulation, competition, financial innovations, technological advances, and reductions in communications costs—are still far from complete, and are likely to continue to reinforce one another.
- This process will receive added impetus from the aging of populations in industrial countries. The most important element with regard to the demographics in industrial countries is the pressure for pension reform and the deregulation of pension fund investments it is likely to exert.
- In developing countries, market accessibility can be expected to increase, and policy reforms are likely to deepen—in countries that are already implementing such reforms—and broaden, as more countries embark on the process of integration.

As a result, the financial integration of developing countries is expected to deepen and broaden over the coming decade, against a backdrop of increasing financial integration at the global level. Indeed, given the changes that are taking place at the international level—in particular, the rapid advances in technology, communications, and financial innovations—and the growing economic sophistication in developing countries, the progressive financial integration of developing countries appears to be inevitable. Gross private capital flows may therefore be expected to rise substantially, with capital flowing not only from industrial to developing countries but, increasingly, among developing countries themselves and from developing to industrial countries.

As noted above, net private capital flows to developing countries can expected to be sustained, even though the rate of growth, and eventually the levels, will inevitably decline. Moreover, there is likely to be considerable variation among countries, depending on the pace and depth of improvements in macroeconomic performance and creditworthiness. Indeed, in countries where economic and policy fundamentals are very weak, the initial manifestation of growing financial integration may take the form of net outflows of private capital.

Private flows to developing countries are also likely to be subject to fluctuations from year to year, even in aggregate. International investors tend to be very responsive to changes in the international environment, including interest rates, and to events in other countries, since they see each country as one of many options. Although the degree to which international interest rate movements affect portfolio flows to emerging markets is declining, emerging markets are still quite marginal in foreign investors' portfolios. These markets therefore remain quite susceptible to cyclical conditions in industrial countries. However, since large increases in international interest rates are unlikely—industrial countries are now operating in a low inflation environment and hence are unlikely to require sharp corrections in monetary stance—the volatility in aggregate flows to developing countries arising from international interest rate movements is not likely to be very large.

Foreign investors are still relatively unfamiliar with emerging markets, so there remains a potential for volatility arising from investor herding. However, there is a learning process involved, and the peak of the volatility arising from investor herding in a market does not appear to be sustained for very long. Foreign investors are also beginning to differentiate among emerging markets. This fact suggests that while a shock in an individual emerging market is still likely to result in some volatility in other emerging markets as investors reevaluate the prospects in the latter, such pure contagion is likely to be relatively short-lived.

The main risks of volatility and large reversals lie at the individual country level. As argued above and elaborated in subsequent chapters, while some of the major recipients have relatively well established policy and performance track records, most developing countries lack strong macroeconomic, banking sector, and institutional underpinnings, and hence remain vulnerable to potential instability and reversals of flows. While international investors are becoming more discerning, market discipline tends to be much more stringent when investor confidence is lost—triggering large outflows—than during the buildup to a potential problem. Financial integration can therefore magnify shocks or the costs of policy mistakes, leading to greater instability.

Annex 2.1

Table 2.2 Key Deregulations, Financial Innovations, and Technological Advances

Year/ country	*Domestic financial liberalization*	*External financial liberalization*	*Financial innovations*	*Technological advances*
1970–80 United States	Public ownership of members of the stock market. Deregulation of securities firms' commissions (May Day). Beginning of phasing out of deposit price controls. International Banking Act for national treatment of U.S. and foreign banks.		Warrants. Options introduced on CBOE. Money market funds certificate. Treasury bond futures on CBOT. Futures on IMM.	NASDAQ computer quotation. DOT computer quotation. ITS.
United Kingdom		Relaxation of foreign exchange controls.	Options market.	TALISMAN centralized clearing (1979–93).
Japan	Securities firms offer medium-term government bond funds.	Overseas stock listing. New Foreign Exchange and Foreign Trade Control Law. Foreign exchange banks established. First Samurai bond issued and listed. Interbank foreign exchange trading begins in Tokyo. Foreign stock listing on TSE. Ban on issuance of Japanese corporate bonds overseas lifted. First issue of Euro yen bonds by a nonresident. First issue in Japan of unsecured yen bonds by a foreign private company. Gensaki bonds offered to nonresidents. Domestic DC market begins, open to nonresidents. Law on foreign securities firms.	Negotiable certificates. New bond funds.	

Year/ country	*Domestic financial liberalization*	*External financial liberalization*	*Financial innovations*	*Technological advances*
1981–90 United States	Banks allowed to affiliate with securities firms for underwriting. Security Pacific is the first bank to set up a limited securities firm subsidiary. Federal Reserve approves limited securities underwriting. CFTC approves GLOBEX. Federal Reserve approves limited debt-equity underwriting by commercial banks.	30 percent withholding tax on interest income paid to foreigners repealed. NYSE, AMEX, NASD allow foreign issuers if they comply with home country laws. Primary Dealer Act requires reciprocity before foreign financial institutions can become dealers in the U.S. securities market. Rule 144a exempts from registration privately placed debt and equity offered to qualified institutional buyers.	NYSE composite index future. NYSE composite index option. NYSE composite index future option. S&P index option. Treasury bond futures on NYFE. Currency options introduced. NYSE trading of instruments linked to foreign equities.	AMEX and Toronto line. ITS and NASDAQ link. Coordinated circuit breakers installed. CBOT begins evening trading.
United Kingdom	Financial Services Act. Deregulation of commissions.	Foreign membership of stock markets.	LIFFE futures market. Treasury bond futures. Negotiable bankers' acceptances. Commercial paper. Gilt warrants.	ITS, SEAQ International. SEAQ automated quotation.
Japan	Japanese bank allowed to lend long-term Euro yen to borrower of their choice. New Bank Law and Securities Exchange Law. Securities firms allowed to sell foreign exchange CDs and CPs in the domestic market. Banks allowed to deal in government bonds. Interest rate deregulation begins. Taxes on bond transactions reduced. Commissions for large transactions lowered. Foreign banks open trust subsidiaries.	Commercial paper of foreign issue. Foreign membership of stock market. Samurai bond regulations relaxed. Foreign exchange trading no longer tied to commercial trade, hedging and swaps allowed. Yen-foreign exchange conversion limits for foreign banks abolished. Withholding tax on Euro yen bonds issued by Japanese residents removed. Medium- and long-term Euro yen loans liberalized. First Shogun bond issued. First Euro yen straight bond issued.	Warrants. Treasury bond futures. Money market funds certificates. Negotiable bankers' acceptances. Stock futures 50. TOPIX stock index future. Nikkei stock index future. Introduction of government bond future. Euro yen floating rate notes, zero-coupon bonds, DCs, warrants.	CORES, automated quotation, second section. Centralized depository and clearing. JASDAQ introduced. TIFFE opens.

(Table continues on the following page.)

Table 2.2 (continued)

Year/ country	*Domestic financial liberalization*	*External financial liberalization*	*Financial innovations*	*Technological advances*
Japan (cont.)		Japan Offshore Banking Market opened. Japanese firms make markets on SEAQI. Restrictions on Japanese purchases of foreign securities removed. Insurance company and pension fund trust accounts allowed to increase foreign exchange assets. Japanese financial institutions allowed to trade in overseas futures markets. Four Japanese securities firms become primary dealers in U.S. government securities markets. Restrictions on domestic and Euro yen CP issues by nonresidents relaxed. All financial institutions allowed to trade as brokers in overseas financial futures.	Domestic and Euro yen CP markets introduced. Stock index futures traded on Osaka exchange	
1991–96 United States	Restrictions on U.S. banks are eased to allow them to compete with securities houses.			After-hours trading on NASDAQ International.
United Kingdom				Alternative Investment Market for small firms (AIM); Tradepoint.
Japan	Commercial banks allowed to establish securities subsidiaries. Securities houses allowed to establish trust bank subsidiaries. Securities houses allowed to offer money market funds.	Ministry of Finance authorizes trading of non-Japanese financial futures through GLOBEX. Domestic bond market further deregulated, easing the criteria for issuance on the Samurai market. Issuers no longer have to have investment-grade rating.		

Year/ country	*Domestic financial liberalization*	*External financial liberalization*	*Financial innovations*	*Technological advances*
Japan (cont.)	Deregulation of commissions. Securities and Exchange Council proposes that banks and other financial institutions be allowed to own securities subsidiaries. Diet eliminates separation of commercial and investment banking. Deregulation of time deposits; other savings deregulation to follow. Across-the-board deregulation of financial markets planned by 2001: easing restrictions on portfolio allocations of pension funds, removal of restrictions on foreign exchange transactions, and further liberalization of domestic financial markets, including liberalization of fixed commissions of securities transactions.	Valuation method for foreign bonds held by institutional investors is changed. Previously had to be valued at cost; now can be valued at market value or cost—the same treatment that is accorded to Japanese government bonds. Law requiring companies to mark to market their foreign currency assets whenever the yen moved by over 15 percent is eliminated. Regulations on foreign exchange positions of foreign exchange banks is eased, to promote investments in foreign-currency-denominated bonds.		

Note: AMEX, American Stock Exchange; CBOE, Chicago Board Options Exchange; CBOT Chicago Board of Trade; CFTC, Commodity Futures Trading Commission; CORES, Computer-Assisted Order, Routing, and Execution System; DC, deep discount bonds; DOT, Designated Order Turnaround System; IMM, Chicago International Money Market; ITS, Intermarket Trading System; JASDAQ, Japanese Association of Securities Dealers Automated Quotation; LIFFE, London International Financial Futures Exchanges; NASDAQ, National Association of Securities Dealers Automated Quotation; NYFE, New York Futures Exchange; NYSE, New York Stock Exchange; SEAQ, Stock Exchange Automated Quotation; SIPC, Securities Investors Protection Corporation; TIFFE, Tokyo Financial Futures Exchanges; TOPIX, Tokyo Price index; TSE, Tokyo Stock Exchange.

Sources: Sobel (1994); McKinsey Global Institute (1994); Goldstein and Mussa (1993).

Notes

1. Developing countries are also more susceptible than industrial countries to real sector shocks resulting from, for example, terms-of-trade changes or a slowdown in industrial country activity. Their greater susceptibility arises from the fact that their economies tend to be less diversified and because their stock of outstanding debt is generally higher. However, the susceptibility of developing countries to such shocks is declining because these economies are becoming more diversified.

2. The analysis suggests that the decline in global interest rates in 1990 provided a strong impetus to private flows (especially portfolio flows) to developing countries; allocation was determined largely by economic fundamentals. This is corroborated by the second piece of analysis which shows that there was large co-movement of U.S. portfolio flows to developing countries and that this co-movement was correlated with U.S. interest rates. In other words, U.S. interest rates appear to have had an important bearing on portfolio capital movements to developing countries during 1990–93.

3. Since savings tend to be a function of per capita income, savings are lower in developing countries (under financial autarky) than in industrial countries, and therefore so is the stock of capital.

4. A high default risk increases the likelihood of noncompliance with contractual payments—either explicitly or implicitly through, for example, discriminatory taxes against the foreign investor. Declining creditworthiness therefore increases the variability and reduces the expected rates of return to the foreign investor (Fernández-Arias 1994). In contrast, domestic investors are concerned only about returns to the individual project.

5. Macroeconomic stability has been found to be a very important determinant of investment. Macroeconomic volatility is estimated to have reduced developing country growth between 1960 and 1990 by as much as 0.9 percentage points per year (Schmidt-Hebbel 1995).

6. In principle, international interest rates can affect country creditworthiness through two main channels. First, since creditworthiness reflects the present value of the resources available for external payments, it is directly sensitive to the investor's discount rate—that is, to international interest rates (Fernández-Arias 1994). A decline in international interest rates increases the present value of resources available for external payments and therefore country creditworthiness. Second, international interest rates can affect a country's debt burden if debt is held at variable interest rates. Hence a decline in international interest rates can reduce a country's external debt burden.

7. Such risks include not only sovereign risk, which is still quite high in developing countries, given their relatively short policy track record, but also higher investment risks, such as legal and custodial risks, settlement and operational risks, information and regulatory risks, and nonmarket risks.

8. According to the Capital Asset Pricing Model (CAPM), the optimal portfolio allocation in a fully efficient and integrated capital market is the world market portfolio. Therefore, an investor with a portfolio that is underinvested in foreign assets (as a percentage of world market capitalization) can, by increasing his holdings of foreign assets, either lower risk without sacrificing expected return or increase the expected rate of return for a given level of risk. The benefits of such diversification arise from undertaking investments that are relatively uncorrelated with each other. Because domestic securities have a common exposure to country-specific shocks, domestic securities are likely to exhibit stronger correlation with each other, so that international diversification may reduce risks more quickly than domestic diversification (see Reisen forthcoming).

9. That private capital flows in the 1990s are being driven by portfolio diversification motives as well as expectations of higher returns is reflected in the fact that developing countries have now become recipients of portfolio equity flows—the form of investment for which risk diversification is most important—and the fact that gross flows are sizably larger than net flows.

10. The growth and development of stock markets is, in general, very dependent on the availability and disclosure of high-quality information. This may explain why

stock markets tend to become more important in the financial structure of economies as these economies develop: companies become larger and countries develop the requisite accounting and disclosure standards. Mishkin (1996) for example, discusses how securities markets are more prone to problems of asymmetric information and adverse selection than are commercial banks—so the development of the securities markets is likely to evolve after that of the banking sector. Demirgüç-Kunt and Levine (1996b) provide evidence on how financial structures differ across countries and change as countries develop.

11. As argued in chapter 6, foreign investors themselves have made a significant contribution to this development—and the process has been self-reinforcing. As these investors have entered the markets, they have contributed to their deepening, which in turn has increased their attractiveness as markets.

12. The MSCI-EAFE is the Morgan Stanley Capital International Index, including Europe, Australia, and the Far East. The IFCI is the IFC Emerging Markets Index, which takes into account restrictions on foreign investors.

13. In fact, portfolio diversification benefits can be reaped as long as the correlation among returns is less than one.

14. Even based on the current rates of return and correlations among these returns, the above example would be an upper limit, since any large shift in the portfolio mix of institutional investors would likely raise prices—in the short to medium term—and could also result in an increase of their volatility, given the relative thinness of developing country stock markets.

15. Canada, France, Germany, Japan, the Netherlands, the United Kingdom, and the United States. There is some double counting entailed, since pension funds typically make a significant proportion of their investments through intermediaries, including other institutional investors. For instance, in Europe and the United States, pension funds account for about half of mutual fund assets. In Japan, pension funds make most of their investments through insurance companies and trust banks.

16. Expropriations by governments, which were substantial in the 1960s and 1970s, have virtually ceased since the mid-1980s.

17. These include the General Agreement on Trade in Services (GATS), which sets standards for market entry and for the uniform treatment of firms—whether domestic or foreign; the Agreement on Trade Related Investment Measures (TRIMS), which imposes equal treatment of all firms (excluding services); and the Agreement on Trade Related Aspects of Intellectual Property Rights (TRIPS), which is beginning to address the protection of intellectual property rights—a concern that is particularly important for many high technology transnational companies (World Bank 1997).

18. An open trade regime is one that fulfills the following criteria: nontariff barriers covering less than 40 percent of trade, average tariff rates of less than 40 percent, a black market exchange rate that is depreciated by less than 20 percent relative to the official rate, the lack of a state monopoly on exports, and a nonsocialist economic system.

19. The main holders of emerging market debt (Brady bonds, Eurobonds, global bonds, and Yankee bonds) are commercial and investment banks, hedge funds, and a few of the larger insurance companies and pension funds.

20. Other than those in the United Kingdom and the United States, most emerging market funds or international funds with emerging market exposure are, for tax reasons, domiciled in offshore centers.

21. One survey was undertaken for this study; the other is based on emerging market allocations of the Frank Russell universe. This figure is much higher than had been previously estimated—that is, IMF (1995) put the figure at 0.5 percent and Chuhan (1994) at 0.2 percent.

22. Even the 401(k) plans (the most popular type of defined contribution corporate pension plan) have seen a growing trend of investing through mutual funds, rising from around 8 percent in 1986 to 30 percent in 1994.

23. The existence of "home bias"—or a preference for home assets—may mean that investors will continue to hold smaller shares of emerging market assets than that

implied by the latter's share of world market capitalization. Many reasons have been put forward for the existence of home bias, such as the fact that optimal portfolio calculations do not take into account factors like the importance of nontraded goods, the role of human capital, transaction costs, and the ability to achieve quasi-international diversification by holding shares in domestic multinationals. These factors may explain part of home bias, but by no means all of it. To the extent that home bias exists because investors are not sufficiently familiar with emerging markets, it can be expected to diminish over time. At a minimum, the share of emerging market assets in investors' holdings of international assets should rise.

24. The demographic shift is more advanced, however, in China and some Latin American countries.

25. According to the findings of some studies, such as Gokhale, Kotlikoff, and Sebelhaus (1996), aggregate savings in industrial countries have already peaked and can be expected to show continued declines. Also, it should be noted that aging is only one factor to affect savings rates and the aggregate level of savings.

26. The age effect on the savings rate is slightly negative in Germany, because of the early retirement age.

27. In 1990, the vanguard of the U.S. baby boom generation was 44 years old, while the youngest baby boomers were 27. In the year 2010, therefore, the baby boomers will be between ages 45 and 64.

28. These effects were channeled through age-and cohort-specific household rates, savings rates and disposable household incomes. They also allow for population growth.

29. Aging could also affect the demand for private investment, and hence net private savings. However, there is little empirical basis on which to assess the direction and magnitude of these effects. One channel is through the labor market and the effects on the relative rate of return to capital. As discussed below, the slowdown in labor force growth is likely to place downward pressure on rates of return to capital in industrial countries. In a closed economy, this could have feedback effects, reducing the savings rate. However, in an open economy—with the possibility of investing in regions with higher rates of return to capital, such as emerging markets—feedback effects are less likely.

30. The two main changes are liberalization of the rules that apply to Japanese corporate pension funds on the use of foreign fund managers, and relaxation of the restriction on investment, including foreign investment, on all fund managers.

31. If interest rates affected the volatility of flows to emerging markets purely through their effects on developing country creditworthiness, much of differences in the volatility of flows *among* emerging markets would be explained by the differential impact of international interest rates on countries' debt burdens. However, a very small proportion of the difference in volatility of flows among emerging markets appears to explained by differences in the (floating interest rate) debt burden.

32. A variance decomposition shows that domestic macroeconomic factors as a block account for 32 percent of the variation in total private flows (including FDI) in the short run and 66 percent in the long run, while U.S. interest rates account for 1 percent in the short run and 2 percent in the long run.

33. The distinction between FDI and portfolio flows should not however, be exaggerated. It has been argued, for example, that an FDI investor who wants to get out of a country can borrow on the domestic market against his investment and then take his money out. And sustained shocks, such as deterioration of a country's longer-term economic fundamentals, can lead to a reduction in reinvested earnings and a faster repatriation of earnings as a means of divesting.

34. As noted in box table 2.2 , the strong negative correlation between (the first principal component of) private capital flows and (the first principal component of) global interest rates, which was clearly evident during 1990–93, is not seen in the more recent period.

35. There is evidence to suggest that mutual fund managers alter the riskiness of their portfolios at the end of the year, presumably because their performance on an annual basis is critical (Chevalier and Ellison 1995).

36. There is slight evidence of investor herding in small cap stocks only.

37. The variance ratio test is used to assess the presence of investor herding (see Aitken 1996). A variance ratio greater than one indicates positive autocorrelation in asset returns. This means that price increases (or decreases) in one period are followed by price increases (or price decreases) in the following period. (A variance ratio of less than one indicates negative autocorrelation—price increases followed by price decreases, or price decreases followed by price increases.) It should be noted, however, that deviations from a variance ratio of one do not necessarily indicate stock market inefficiency. Other reasons include market microstructure-related factors such as infrequent trading or time-varying risk premiums. Evidence of price predictability therefore should not necessarily be taken as evidence against stock market efficiency. Significant increases in price predictability that coincide with increased foreign investor participation, though, may suggest foreign investor herding (or domestic investors overreacting to foreign investors' actions).

38. Note that the Mexican crisis is included in the sample period.

39. Goldfajn and Valdés (1996) discusses how shocks can be propagated to other countries through the channel of financial intermediation.

40. The impact index was constructed by multiplying the percentage of decline in prices from December 16, 1994, to the period of the maximum fall in prices and the duration of the decline up to the end of May 1995. A regression of the impact index on export growth and a dummy (which took the value of one if either inflation was below 10 percent or if output growth was over 6.5 percent when inflation was above 10 percent, and zero otherwise) yielded the following result:

$$ind = 14.7 - 4.96^{*}DUM - 0.61^{*}EXPGR$$
$$(-1.79)^{*} \qquad (-2.03)$$
$$\text{Adjusted } R^2 = 0.48.$$

* Statistically significant at the 10 percent level.

41. Buckberg (1996) finds that emerging market returns are determined by both world market returns (which include industrial countries) and by other emerging market returns. In fact, evidence suggests that emerging markets are more sensitive to returns in other emerging markets than to returns on the world portfolio for 12 of the 13 countries. Note that contagion arising from portfolio rebalancing implies a positive shock to other emerging markets when one emerging market is hit negatively.

42. An open-end mutual fund, unlike a closed-end fund, must sell its underlying shares to meet investor redemptions.

43. See Frankel and Schmukler (1996).

CHAPTER 3

The Benefits of Financial Integration

MUCH OF THIS REPORT IS DEVOTED TO UNDERstanding and avoiding the pitfalls on the road to financial integration. In this chapter, we focus on the goal itself, the long-term benefits obtainable from a well-managed integration, concentrating deliberately on the best-case scenario.

Fundamentally, the benefits of integration fall into two main categories. On the production side, integration permits greater international specialization and facilitates the allocation of scarce resources to their most productive uses independent of location, thereby accelerating growth. On the consumption side, integration allows individuals (both in the newly integrating and, to a lesser extent, in the already integrated economies) to insure themselves against adverse developments in their home economy both through international portfolio diversification and by tapping global capital markets to smooth temporary declines in income. We look at both benefits in turn. While, from a purist standpoint, the gain to financial integration is quite narrowly defined, we also touch upon many of the accompanying benefits of integration (such as the development of good accounting standards or improvements in settlement systems), which could, strictly speaking, be attained without integration but in practice are part of the overall benefits package.

Integration and Growth

TWO ENGINES DRIVE ECONOMIC GROWTH: CHANGES IN THE *quantity* of inputs—in particular, labor and capital, broadly defined—and changes in their *quality*.

Investment

In a financially closed economy, investment must be funded by domestic savings. The two are matched by movements in the real interest rate—the cost of borrowing and the return to savings. Without international capital flows, there can be no presumption that the returns to investment are equal across countries, resulting in resource misallocation: on the margin, highly profitable investment projects in some countries may not be undertaken for lack of financing, although lower-return projects are funded elsewhere. Financial integration, whether on the national or the international level, severs the link between local savings and local investment, allowing savings to "run as surely and instantly where it is most wanted, and where there is most to be made of it, as water runs to find its level" (Bagehot 1924, p. 12). Investors are able to borrow and savers are able to lend internationally, thus the global rather than the national interest rate becomes the relevant cost of capital and return to savings. Of course, savings and investment must still match, but they now do so on a global rather than a national scale. Following integration, investment is, under ideal circumstances, reallocated toward the most rewarding projects (on a risk-adjusted basis), regardless of their location, financed by corresponding capital flows seeking the highest risk-adjusted returns. World production increases, a gain partly accruing to savers in the less productive economies, who now receive higher returns, and partly accruing to firms in the more productive economies, who now enjoy a reduced cost of capital.

The new pattern of capital flows depends on the relative return to investment across countries. Extensive research over the last decade has established a by-now-familiar set of characteristics of successful economies, including (most important) sound macroeconomic policies and good microeconomic fundamentals. The point is important: it is the relative *return* rather than the relative development level that drives capital flows; in consequence, as we saw in the previous chapter, financial integration has primarily resulted in capital flows to countries already enjoying high domestic investment levels. Integration thus raises the payoff for establishing good fundamentals; it does not substitute for fundamentals. In consequence, the trend toward integration may, at least temporarily, widen the gap between the high- and the low-growth developing economies, although in the long term this very widening raises the benefits of improving fundamentals in the low-growth group.

For the growing subgroup of developing countries already offering attractive investment opportunities, integration permits an acceleration of investment by augmenting domestic savings with foreign savings. The potential gains vary from country to country, depending on the relative profitability of investment opportunities and on the difference between the domestic cost and the world cost of capital before integration. If capital inflows reach 3 to 4 percent of GDP (a typical figure for current large capital importers), the growth rate, based on typical capital shares and capital output ratios, would increase by about half a percentage point (Reisen 1996). This temporary growth effect is by no means negligible yet it is dwarfed by the range of growth rates among developing economies, again illustrating that the successful tapping of foreign capital markets is only one of many ingredients in a successful growth strategy.

Can integration permanently raise growth rates in the opening economy, or even in the world economy? Any permanent growth effect must come through an increase in world saving rates or faster productivity growth. There is little reason to believe that integration boosts world saving rates. Indeed, a decline is more likely, since diversification of income risk and access to world capital markets to smooth out temporary income fluctuations reduce the need for precautionary savings.[1] Any permanent gains from integration are thus more likely to come through the *quality* rather than the *quantity* of investment.

Productivity

Integration may boost productivity growth by shifting the investment mix toward projects with higher expected returns, a shift brought about by an improved ability to reduce and to diversify the higher risk typically entailed in higher-return projects. The risk of any particular investment can conceptually be divided into four parts: a global component (for instance, a world recession), a national component (for instance, higher profit taxes or political instability), a sector component (for instance, a technological advance), and a component specific to the particular investment. The sector- and the project-specific risks can be diversified domestically, resulting in sizable benefits from the national financial integration typically preceding international integration. Global risks by their nature cannot be diversified away. This leaves national risk, which cannot be diversified within a country but can be diversified internationally.

If national shocks are a quantitatively important part of the overall risk of investment projects, the diversification benefits obtained by adding another domestic investment project to a portfolio of other domestic projects are lower than the benefits of adding the same project to a portfolio of internationally diversified projects. In consequence, a foreign investor can pursue projects with higher *project* risks and returns while keeping *portfolio* risk to an acceptable level. A move from a system of closed national economies to an integrated world economy thus permits a global switch toward projects with higher expected returns, thereby increasing the average world growth rate (Obstfeld 1995). The effect is reinforced if integration also permits a reduction in *project risk.* For instance, if opening is associated with an expansion of the market for domestic production, susceptibility to domestic demand changes declines, enabling a shift to more specialized—and more productive—capital (Saint-Paul 1992).

The quantitative significance of a switch to higher-return investments in the wake of integration depends on three factors: the technological lag of a particular country, risk aversion, and the speed with which existing capital can be reallocated. Simulation studies suggest that the gains are of a very large magnitude. The size of gains reflects the magic of compound interest: even small increases in growth rates have first-order level effects over time. For the economies lagging farthest behind current best practice, the gains comprise both catch-up and the global efficiency gain, while the leading economies benefit from only the latter change. Yet even for these economies the benefits of higher output, and hence consumption growth rates, are very significant: a well-managed integration is a win-win situation.

The equalization of returns across countries and the higher growth rate resulting from a globally more productive capital stock provide the long-term benefits of integration proper. In addition, integration provides more immediate benefits through knowledge spillovers, particularly in financial markets and via FDI. While these benefits are not strictly dependent on financial integration, integration tends at least to accelerate the knowledge transfer.

Financial System Spillovers

The cost of capital to the end borrower consists of four components: the real interest rate on minimum-risk liquid assets, the risk premium imposed by the financial intermediary for financing particular ventures, the cost structure of the financial system, and the profit margin charged. Integration affects all four components. We have discussed the effect of integration on the real interest rate and the risk premium above: integration replaces the local with the world interest rate and reduces the risk premium to the extent that foreign lenders can better diversify the country risk. The other two components—the cost structure of the financial system and the profit margin—are also affected if integration enhances the depth of the financial system (allowing fixed costs to be spread over a broader base) or its competitiveness.

Beyond the effect on the cost of capital, a deepening of the domestic financial system in the wake of integration also aids growth through a more efficient allocation of resources, in turn leading to further financial deepening. This positive feedback loop between financial and real development is well established. International integration is likely to augment the feedback. Foreign financial institutions will introduce or create access to new financial instruments, while participation of foreigners in domestic securities markets enhances liquidity, in turn facilitating long-term maturity transformation.

The empirical evidence is quite firm: domestic financial deepening is strongly associated with both higher investment and faster productivity growth (figure 3.1).[2] Indeed, there is increasing evidence that external financial markets are more important in less developed economies than in more developed ones. For example, analyzing data on the 100 largest corporations listed in the stock market in 10 developing countries during the 1980s, Singh (1994) finds that these corporations relied strongly on external sources for financing, and in particular on equity markets.[3]

Equally unambiguously, financial integration is associated with an increase in financial system depth (and hence, indirectly, growth) both in terms of bank lending and in terms of asset market liquidity and turnover (box 3.1). Figure 3.2 shows that stock market capitalization and turnover in countries that have received the highest levels of portfolio equity inflows have increased more than in countries receiving lower levels of flows. The figure correlates, for a group of selected emerging stock markets, aggregate portfolio equity inflows with the change in market capitalization and trading value during their respective inflow episodes (as defined in chapter 4), all as a ratio to GDP. The data also suggest significant spillovers to domestic activity during these episodes. This can be seen in table 3.1, which compares the ratio of

Figure 3.1 Initial Financial Depth and Future Growth

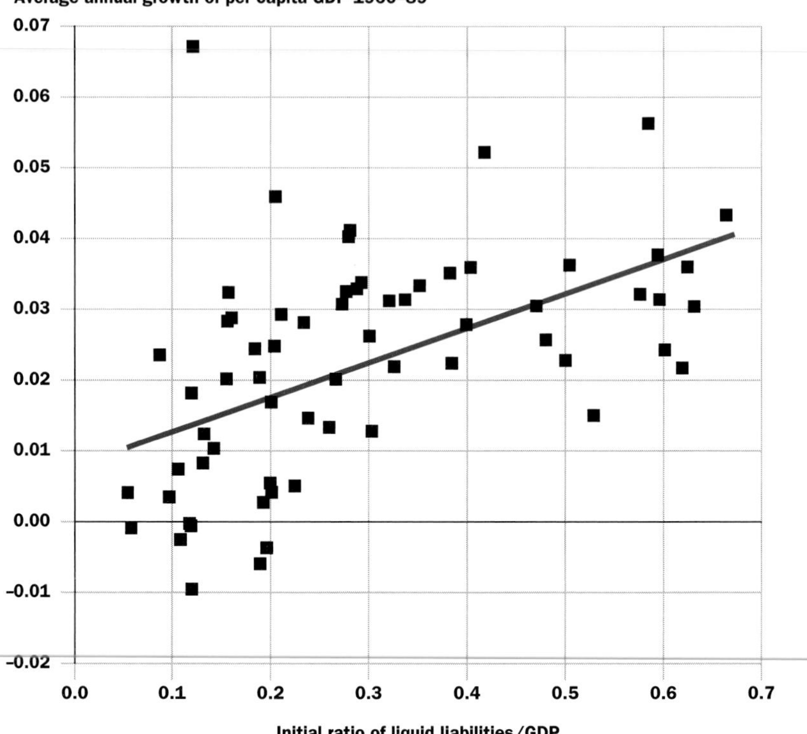

Source: Levine (1991).

Domestic financial deepening is strongly associated with increased investment and faster productivity growth.

trading value to GDP in the year immediately preceding the inflow episode with the value of trading activity in the last year of the episode, adjusted for the proportion accounted for by foreign investors and normalized by GDP.[4] Table 3.1 also shows that the number of new listings on the stock exchanges rose during the inflow period in 10 out of the 13 countries. As shown in figure 3.2, the increase in both market capitalization and trading volume has been associated with an increase in foreign portfolio flows. Most convincingly, figure 3.3 shows that those countries that received the largest portfolio equity flows were also those that saw the largest increase in the volume of domestic trading as a ratio to GDP during the inflow period. The table, of course, establishes only correlation, not causation. Disentangling the causal effect of international integration is quite difficult, since most episodes of external financial liberalization are accompanied by domestic financial

As figure 3.2 shows, market capitalization and trading volume increased more in countries that received the largest portfolio equity inflows than in countries that received smaller amounts.

Figure 3.2 Portfolio Equity and Capital Market Development, Selected Countries

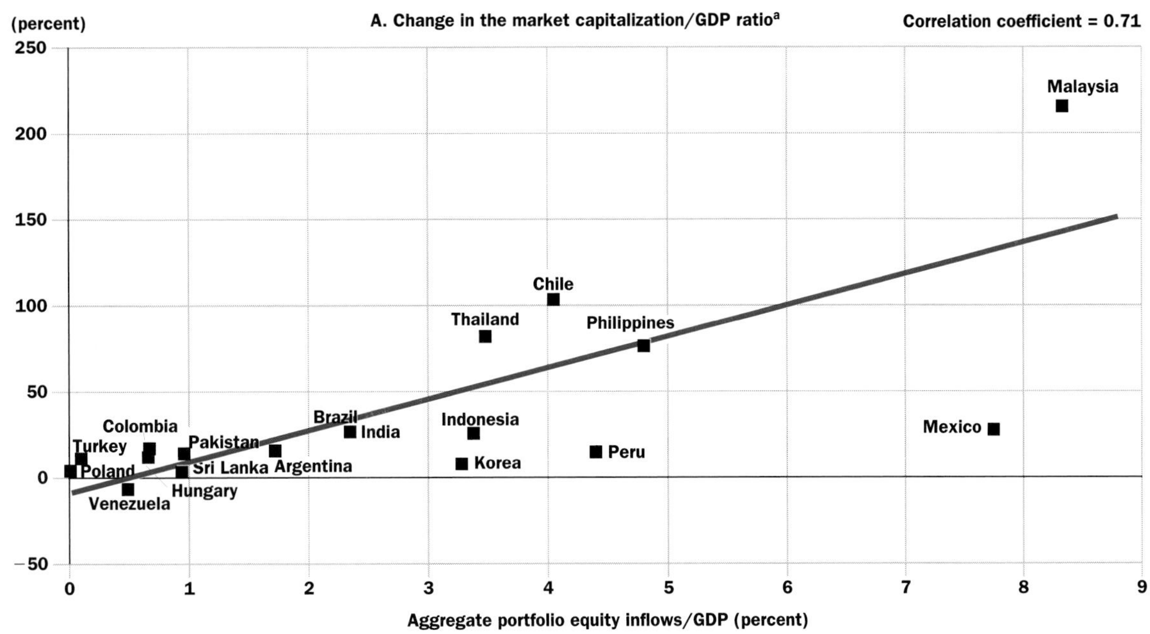

a. Change in market capitalization as a percentage of GDP between the start of the inflow period and 1994.

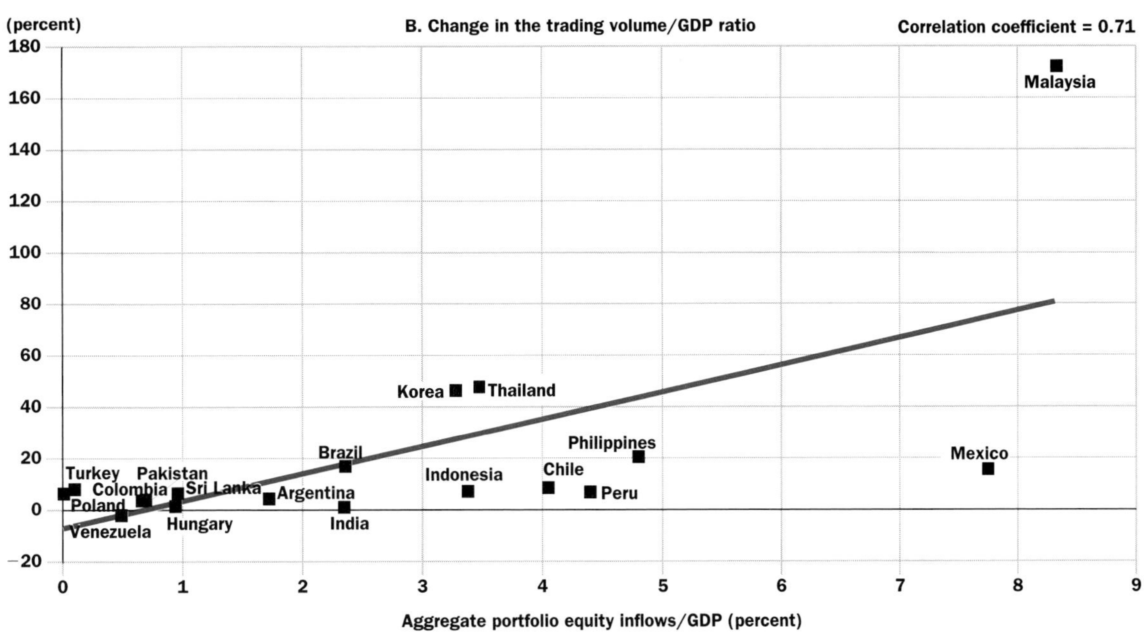

Note: Aggregate portfolio equity inflows/GDP is equal to the sum of portfolio equity inflows during the inflow episode divided by the 1994 GDP.
Source: IFC, *Emerging Stock Markets Factbook 1996*; World Bank data.

Box 3.1 The Empirical Link between Integration and Deepening

THE LINK BETWEEN FINANCIAL INTEGRATION and financial deepening can be assessed by regressing indicators of financial system development on indicators of integration and a set of other determinants, including the development stage (proxied by per capita GDP), the rate of inflation, and economic openness (proxied by the trade-to-GDP ratio). We base our analysis on regressions performed both for a composite measure of financial integration (Montiel 1994) taking into account observed capital flows, excess consumption volatility, interest parity violations, and the extent to which investment is funded by domestic savings, and for a second measure based on the size of excess returns (Levine and Zervos 1995a). For both measures, a higher value denotes a greater degree of integration. The regression was performed for two measures of financial sector depth: the ratio of banking sector loans to the private sector to GDP, and stock market turnover as a fraction of GDP. The coefficients on the financial integration measures, reported below, were positive and, for the excess returns measure, significant at the 5 percent level. The regressions also confirmed the familiar negative relation between inflation and financial sector development, again illustrating the role of good fundamentals as prerequisites for a country to benefit fully from financial integration. The results are thus quite suggestive of a positive link between integration and financial deepening. It stands to reason that the linkage is at least partly causal, though the causality pattern is difficult to establish empirically, since financial integration is frequently accompanied by additional liberalization steps for domestic financial markets.

	Financial development	
Financial integration	*Bank loans*	*Turnover*
Aggregate index	0.093*	0.003
Excess returns	0.033**	0.029**

* Statistically significant at 10 percent.

** Statistically significant at 5 percent.

Since financial deepening is strongly and at least in part causally associated with growth, the positive effect of financial integration on financial deepening provides an indirect link between integration and growth. To examine whether there is also a direct link, we estimate a standard growth regression (Barro and Sala-i-Martin 1995) for a group of 24 developing countries for which the financial integration measures were available. Including only the two financial integration measures reveals a positive and, for the excess returns measure a significant, link between integration and economic growth. Adding the financial development indicators reveals that, looking backward, the major benefits of integration have come through enhanced financial development. Given the typical lags involved in both investment and saving responses, not too much should be read into the absence of a significant direct link between integration and growth; since significant improvements in financial integration have been achieved only in the last few years, a full assessment of the longer-term growth effects cannot yet be undertaken.

liberalization efforts. However, indirect evidence suggests that international financial integration deserves at least partial credit for domestic financial market deepening.

The quantitative benefits of deepening are likely to be augmented by improvements in the *quality* of financial intermediation. Part of the improvement will come through prerequisites for successful integration,

Table 3.1 Change in Domestic Activity in Selected Emerging Equity Markets

	Domestic trading activity/ GDP[a] *(percent)*		*New listings*	
Country	*Pre-episode*[b]	*1994*	*Pre-episode phase*[c]	*During episode*
Argentina	0.60	—	−27	1
Brazil	3.74	12.79	70	−48
Chile	2.53	—	−7	74
India	9.33	7.06	261	460
Indonesia	0.53	1.68	33	159
Korea	29.94	70.83	314	30
Malaysia	7.56	89.36	44	240
Mexico	3.34	—	−3	3
Pakistan	0.49	1.78	78	213
Peru	0.31	2.46	117	−76
Philippines	2.31	10.88	−59	48
Poland	0.04	4.13	9	35
Thailand	9.17	36.36	48	264

— Not available.

a. Based on the value of shares traded accounted for by foreign investors in 1995, as detailed in table 6.2, chapter 6.

b. Pre-episode refers to the year preceding the beginning of the inflow episode, as detailed in chapter 4.

c. Number of newly listed companies during the period of equal length preceding the inflow episode for each country.

Source: IFC, *Emerging Stock Markets Factbook 1996.*

such as improvements in domestic accounting and supervision standards. Another part will come through learning about better practice coupled with the pressures created by greater competition. Most important, however, will be the momentum for additional reforms and development unleashed even by limited first steps toward integration. For example, an initial deepening of the banking system will raise the return to introducing an efficient payment system; the development of domestic equity markets will motivate efforts to improve settlement systems; the potential for issuing securities in foreign markets will enhance incentives to improve domestic accounting standards; and so forth. Once begun, integration is thus likely to trigger reinforcing dynamics, creating a virtuous cycle of further institutional development that makes possible even more complete integration. Of course, the dynamics thus unleashed also carry significant risks and need to be well managed, as discussed in detail in subsequent chapters.

Developing countries that received the largest portfolio equity flows saw the largest increase in the value of domestic trading as a ratio to GDP during the inflow period.

Figure 3.3 Growth in Domestic Trading in Selected Emerging Equity Markets

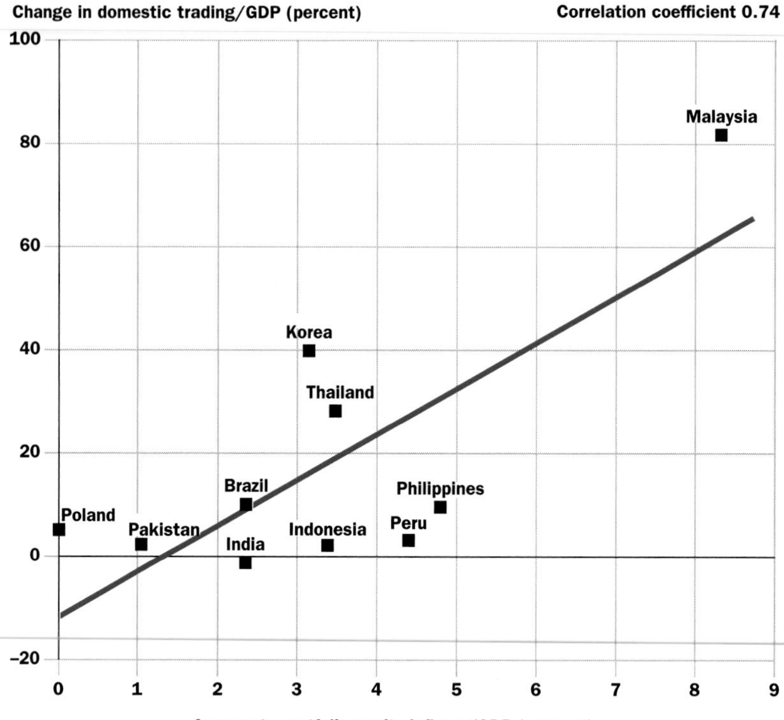

Note: Aggregate portfolio equity inflows/GDP is equal to the sum of portfolio equity inflows during the inflow episode divided by the 1994 GDP.
Source: IFC, *Emerging Stock Markets Factbook 1996;* World Bank data.

The evidence on the ancillary benefits of integration is necessarily anecdotal, but it is suggestive. For example, as shown in table 3.2, average bank profits and average costs in the 1980s were higher for those OECD economies that prohibited entry of foreign banks (closed) than

Table 3.2 Bank Operating Ratios, OECD Economies, 1980s

Indicator	*Open*	*Closed*
Gross earnings margin/volume	3.21	4.48
Pretax profits/volume	0.58	0.78
Operating costs/volume	2.27	3.25

Note: "Open" denotes economies that permitted entry of foreign banks; "closed" denotes economies that prohibited entries.
Source: Terell (1986).

for those permitting entry (open), suggesting that the increased competition in integrated economies led to efficiency gains.

Table 3.3 shows that even the fairly efficient and integrated European Union members stand to reap sizable benefits from adopting best-practice methods, suggesting even larger gains for less efficient and integrated economies.

Another indirect effect of integration, the impact of enhanced competition on interest rates, is shown in table 3.4, reporting, for France, Germany, and Spain, the spread between the short-term interest rate and the deposit rate before and after a period of significant financial integration.

In sum, integration promises significant indirect benefits through improved *efficiency* of the financial system, including the liquidity effects of enhanced deepening, knowledge spillovers, enhanced competition, and improved accounting and supervision standards. The

Table 3.3 Potential Savings from Adopting Best Practice, Selected EU Countries

(percentage of current cost)

Sector	*France*	*Germany*	*Italy*	*Spain*
Banking				
Consumer credits	105	136	0	39
Credit cards	0	60	89	26
Mortgages	78	57	0	118
Foreign exchange	56	31	23	196
Commercial loans	0	6	9	19
Insurance				
Life	33	5	83	37
Home	39	3	81	0
Public liability	117	47	77	24
Securities				
Institutional equity	0	69	47	153
Institutional gilt	57	0	92	60
Overall potential reductions				
Banking	25	33	18	34
Insurance	24	10	51	32
Securities	23	11	33	44
Total	24	25	29	34

Note: An entry of zero implies a cost at or below the average of the four lowest-cost providers. Best practice is measured as the average of the four lowest-cost providers.

Source: Dermine (1993).

Table 3.4 Spread between Short-Term and Deposit Rates: France, Germany, and Spain, 1980–89

	France	*Germany*	*Spain*
1980–85	11.7	6.5	14.5
1986–89	8.8	5.5	9.3

Source: Dermine (1993).

improved ability to allocate scarce resources in turn raises the quality of investment, increasing growth and hence further stimulating financial sector development, giving rise to a positive feedback loop. The available evidence suggests sizable potential gains even for highly developed economies, raising the prospect of significant gains for less integrated countries.

FDI Spillovers

International financial integration also opens the door to both inward and outward FDI, which may influence growth through three channels. First, FDI may increase the total volume of investment in the recipient economy. Second, even if it substitutes for rather than augments domestic investment, it may be more productive than the capital it replaces. Third, it may generate spillover effects that raise the productivity of existing domestic capital.

Although it is difficult to determine the extent to which FDI adds to the total volume of investment, the majority of studies conclude that net inward FDI tends to raise total domestic investment. Indeed, more tentative evidence suggests that the value of domestic investment replaced by FDI is often less than the additional domestic investment triggered by FDI (for instance, follow-up investment by domestic suppliers), so that a dollar of FDI raises the sum of domestic and foreign investment by *more* than a dollar (Borenzstein, de Gregorio, and Lee 1995).

The second benefit of FDI—higher productivity of foreign, compared with domestic, investment—is fairly noncontroversial.[5] Domestic firms benefit from better knowledge of local markets; to compete, foreign firms must offer a compensating advantage, notably greater efficiency. The third potential benefit of FDI consists of spillover effects through a variety of channels, including learning by doing, introduction of new techniques in upstream and downstream collaborators, pressures to improve the efficiency of domestic institutions, and so on. Privately financed additions to total infrastructure investments—an emerging trend—will likewise enhance the productivity of existing enterprises. Significant spillover effects have been established in a number of illuminating case studies, though the precise nature of benefits is specific to the particular circumstances of the recipient and source countries. Strong indirect evidence of the importance of spillover effects is provided by the stylized fact of a sizable increase in exports following inward FDI—an increase not solely attributable to reexporting by the new foreign enterprises.

FDI thus affects growth in two ways: by contributing to the volume of investment and by helping to improve efficiency. The empirical evidence suggests that the primary growth impact comes through improved efficiency rather than an increased quantity of investment. In interpreting these results, however, three caveats must be kept in mind. First, the quality effects are self-eliminating: as domestic practices are adjusted, the scope for additional spillover benefits decreases. Second, the evidence strongly suggests that FDI follows rather than initiates growth. The benefits from FDI, much like the financial market benefits of integration, are thus more likely to buttress existing virtuous cycles than to originate new ones; integration magnifies the benefits of good fundamentals, it does not substitute for them. Third, the net effect of FDI on growth will differ across recipients. In highly distorted economies, FDI may primarily exploit domestic rent-extracting opportunities; in economies with functioning markets, relative returns are more likely to channel FDI to bottlenecks, with substantially greater benefits.

Summary

International financial integration promises substantial growth benefits that can come through a number of channels. First, integration severs the link between domestic savings and investment, enabling increased investment in the more productive economies while raising the returns to savers in less productive ones. Second, integration permits an improved global pooling of risks, making possible a shift of the investment mix toward projects with higher expected returns. Third, integration enhances the depth and efficiency of the domestic financial system, with important positive feedback effects to investment and growth. And fourth, integration allows for important spillover effects through FDI, enhancing the efficiency of the domestic capital stock. The composition and magnitude of these benefits will differ by country and will depend crucially on the presence of promising fundamentals and sound economic policies.

Diversification Benefits

THE PRODUCTION-SIDE BENEFITS OF INTEGRATION DISCUSSED above find a mirror image on the consumption side. Individuals in the newly integrated economies can stabilize their income and consumption by holding foreign assets (augmenting labor income depending on the domestic economy with capital income depending on foreign economies) and by using international capital markets to buffer consumption against temporary swings in the domestic economy. Integration thus allows individuals to reduce the dependence of their consumption on the fortunes of the domestic economy, which is likely to be the source of most of their labor income.

While residents of already integrated economies benefit from continuing integration by gaining another outlet for their savings, and hence additional diversification, the benefits accrue primarily to the residents of the newly integrating developing economies, for three reasons. First, the starting degree of diversification is likely to be very limited. Second, terms of trade and other shocks tend to have a particularly large impact on poorer economies with less diversified production structures and less effective automatic stabilizers. Third, the welfare cost of reducing consumption in the face of adverse developments is largest for countries with low per capita incomes, and hence so are the gains from reducing consumption volatility through integration.

How large the gains from risk reduction will be depends on how much the volatility of consumption can be reduced, and on the value individuals place on this reduction. A sizable literature on the composition of portfolios (partly reviewed in the previous chapter) suggests that consumers in both mature and developing economies do not reap the full benefits possible from diversification. The same conclusion is suggested by a look at consumption volatility. If individuals effectively used capital markets to stabilize consumption, income volatility would significantly exceed consumption volatility. Furthermore, the growth of consumption would be more highly correlated across countries than the growth of income, since consumers in all countries would hold claims on—and hence base their consumption choices on—global rather than national production. Neither prediction is supported by the data: for most low- and middle-income countries, the standard deviation of consumption growth exceeds the standard deviation of GDP growth, while the correlation of domestic GDP growth with world GDP growth exceeds the correlation of domestic consumption growth with world consumption growth.

Table 3.5 illustrates these stylized facts, reporting, for eight regions, the mean and standard deviation of consumption growth, as well as their correlation structure. For the four developing regions in the column headings—South America, Central America, Africa, and Asia except East Asia—the standard deviation of consumption growth (the second figure in parentheses) exceeds the average consumption growth rate (the first figure in parentheses), suggesting substantial scope for stabilizing consumption. The ranking is reversed for the four more highly developed regions, yet again volatility of consumption growth is sizable and differs substantially across regions, indicating unexploited diversification benefits, which are also suggested by the low correlations of consumption growth rates across regions.

Table 3.5 Cross-correlation of Consumption Growth, Selected Regions, 1960–87

Region	*South America (3.11–4.57)*	*Central America (1.68–2.96)*	*Africa (1.31–3.59)*	*Asia (except East Asia) (0.91–3.02)*
North America (2.35–1.76)	–0.24	–0.11	–0.41	0.11
Northern Europe (2.87–1.31)	0.44	0.28	–0.03	–0.29
Southern Europe (3.13–3.03)	0.39	0.11	0.32	–0.16
East Asia (3.64–2.12)	0.13	0.36	0.07	–0.29

Note: The first figure in parentheses is the average consumption growth between 1960 and 1987; the second figure is the standard deviation of consumption growth for the same period.

Source: Obstfeld (1995).

The evidence thus quite strongly suggests that substantial reductions in the volatility of consumption could be obtained by enhanced use of international financial markets to smooth out temporary domestic income disturbances and to diversify national risks. Whether this potential reduction is a significant benefit depends on the value individuals place on reducing the variability of consumption. While the quantification of these gains remains an active area of research, the preponderance of evidence suggests sizable, although not very large, gains from reducing risk. For developed markets, upper bounds on gains are on the order of a 5 percent increase in permanent consumption, with somewhat larger benefits likely for developing countries with higher consumption volatility (Tesar 1995, van Wincoop 1994).

To summarize, the gains from integration on the consumption side come in two ways: the scope for reduced risk through improved diversification and the ability to employ international financial markets to offset temporary income movements, and the ability to shift toward a portfolio with higher expected returns, the mirror image of the shift toward investment projects with higher expected returns discussed above. The empirical evidence suggests that while there is substantial scope for risk diversification, the primary gains do not come through the reduction of risk per se, but rather through the ability to raise average portfolio returns (and hence consumption growth rates) as a consequence of diversification.

Conclusion

WELL-MANAGED INTERNATIONAL FINANCIAL INTEGRATION promises substantial benefits. The benefits accrue on both the production and the consumption side. Integration promises to boost growth rates, partly because better diversification allows a shift to riskier but more productive investments, and partly because of spillovers in the financial sector and via FDI. Integration also promises to reduce the volatility of consumption by allowing a better diversification of portfolios and by permitting international borrowing and lending to offset the effect of temporary swings in national fortunes. Empirical studies suggest that the primary benefits will come not through the first round of diversification effects (that is, through the change in the geographic ownership pattern of *existing* assets), but rather through the more gradual change in new investments toward higher-return projects made possible by the scope for risk reduction and international equalization of returns.

It bears emphasizing again that our focus in this chapter has been on the best-case scenario. If the integrating economy suffers from distortions outside the financial markets, the welfare effects of integration may differ quite significantly, and at the margin might even lead to impoverishing inflows. The following chapters are devoted to this challenge of managing the transition to full financial integration.

Notes

1. The overall effect of integration on savings is ambiguous. While precautionary savings will likely decline, a higher return may stimulate savings, depending on the familiar tradeoff between income and substitution effects.

2. The literature is quite voluminous. See Levine and Zervos (1995a) and De Gregorio and Guidotti (1995) for recent work. The 1989 *World Development Report* (World Bank 1989) provides an in-depth assessment of the linkages between financial sector and overall development.

3. Demirgüç-Kunt and Maksimovic (1994) and Glen and Pinto (1994) present additional evidence.

4. This makes the conservative assumption that all trading activity in that year was of domestic origin. Also, we assume that the proportion of trading activity accounted for by foreign investors during the last year of the inflow episode was that shown in table 6.2, which actually refers to 1995. It is unclear to what extent and in what direction this assumption distorts the results. However, for countries for which time-series data are available, (for example, Thailand), the share of foreign investors in trading was lower in 1994 than in 1995. This suggests that domestic trading was larger than shown in the table.

5. An exception occurs if FDI is motivated by the avoidance of tariffs on imports. The importance of "tariff jumping" as a major cause of FDI is, however, widely viewed as on the wane (World Bank 1997).

CHAPTER 4

Challenges of Macroeconomic Management

WHILE INCREASED FINANCIAL INTEGRATION may provide substantial macroeconomic benefits for developing countries, the integration process also carries with it some difficult macroeconomic challenges. Policymakers in these countries have been concerned with three types of problems:

- The potential for macroeconomic *overheating*, in the form of an excessive expansion of aggregate demand as a consequence of capital inflows.
- The potential *vulnerability* to large, abrupt reversals of capital flows because of changes in creditor perceptions.
- The more general, long-term implications of financial integration for the conduct of macroeconomic policy. As integration advances, policymakers will have to manage the enhanced macroeconomic volatility that may prevail when the economy becomes more exposed to external shocks. In addition, policymakers will need to face these and other shocks with reduced policy autonomy.

This chapter will examine how macroeconomic management can cope with all these challenges.

As explained in chapter 2, two forces are driving the growing investor interest in and integration of developing countries: improvements in long-term expected rates of return, following policy reforms and strengthening creditworthiness, and the opportunities offered by developing countries for risk diversification. These two forces are being abetted by favorable changes that have taken place in the enabling environments of both industrial and developing countries—that is, in the economic, regulatory, and technological conditions that influence production, and govern and underpin the operation of capital markets. As a result of these factors, the initial manifestation of increased integration has been one-way net flows of capital into the newly integrated countries that are quite large relative to the size of the recipient economies. Thus the danger of macroeconomic overheating has been very real.

Countries have a broad menu of macroeconomic policies at their disposal to address this problem. This chapter describes the choices that have been made from this menu in a large group of countries, as well as the macroeconomic implications of such choices. A broad finding is that countries have generally succeeded in avoiding overheating but have done so by bringing to bear nearly the full array of policies at their disposal. Cross-country comparisons reveal both similarities and differences among policy approaches. All the countries examined tended to maintain officially determined exchange rates, and almost all relied heavily on sterilized intervention in the foreign exchange market. Capital controls were used by those countries that received the largest inflows of capital relative to the size of their economies in order to reduce up front the potential for overheating. While the available evidence is not strong and covers only some of these countries, it does indicate that capital controls were effective in the short run in reducing the overall magnitude of capital inflows as well as influencing their composition. Cross-country differences also emerged in the area of nominal exchange rate management (with some countries resisting real appreciation more than others) and the magnitude of fiscal tightening. These differences in approach reflected the relative magnitude of the capital inflow and initial macroeconomic conditions as well as broad development strategy. There are indications that the differences in strategy produce different macroeconomic outcomes, with countries that were able to avoid substantial real appreciation and that tightened fiscal policy tending on average to have lower current account deficits, a mix of absorption more oriented toward investment, and faster economic growth.

A particularly important aspect of macroeconomic management during the inflow period concerns the potential link between postinflow macroeconomic performance and vulnerability—that is, susceptibility to changed perceptions of creditworthiness. The chapter uses the Mexican crisis to examine the relationship between macroeconomic performance and vulnerability by assessing how the incidence and severity of the so-called tequila effect emanating from Mexico were linked to macroeconomic performance in other developing countries. Our key findings are that certain initial interpretations of the crisis, which attributed it to the role of short-term capital and the size of the current account deficit in Mexico, are not well supported by the cross-country evidence. Instead, countries that were less vulnerable to the Mexican crisis tended to be those that had avoided real appreciation and imposed a tight fiscal policy during the inflow period, thereby absorbing a larger share of investment and achieving more rapid growth than they would have done under different policies. Thus the policy mix employed in the effort to combat overheating seems to matter from the perspective of vulnerability as well.

The two macroeconomic challenges of overheating and vulnerability are likely to be particularly important during the transition to financial integration, when international investors are adjusting their portfolios and when policy credibility is not yet well established in the capital-importing countries. As indicated above, however, new macroeconomic challenges will continue to arise even when the process of integration is well advanced. In particular, financially integrated developing countries will find themselves operating in a very different macroeconomic environment, one in which capital movements are highly sensitive to changes in prospective foreign and domestic rates of return. In that context, the macroeconomic consequences of domestic macroeconomic shocks (including changes in policies) will be altered, and the country will also be faced with new types of shocks arising in international financial markets. This new environment may thus be characterized by enhanced volatility, which poses an ongoing challenge for macroeconomic management. In this chapter we consider the role of four types of policy instruments in this new context: fiscal policy, exchange rate policy, monetary policy, and policies regarding the free movement of capital. The picture that emerges from this discussion is consistent with the lessons from experience mentioned above: in a financially integrated environment, both fiscal responsibility and flexibility are very important, and although nominal exchange rate management is not precluded, the scope for allowing the real exchange rate to deviate from its equilibrium value is much reduced. Sterilized intervention, while having the advantage of flexibility, is likely to become less effective as integration increases. The same is true of restrictions on capital movements. The best case for such restrictions on macroeconomic grounds is that they can act as transitional devices to preserve monetary autonomy while other policy reforms are implemented.

In the next section we will review how countries have responded to the problem of overheating associated with the recent surge in capital inflows. We will then look at the vulnerability of different countries in the aftermath of the Mexican crisis to assess the role of policies as determinants of vulnerability. Next we will examine the long-term implications of increased financial integration for macroeconomic management. The final section will summarize the key implications for macroeconomic policy.

Capital Inflows and Overheating: The Country Experience

OUR DISCUSSION OF THE PROBLEM OF OVERHEATING AND the elements of a successful response is divided into four parts. First, we briefly describe the transmission mechanism through which a surge in capital inflows can trigger overheating of the domestic macroeconomy and the range of options available to policymakers to prevent overheating. We then describe the policies that were adopted by developing countries in response to the most recent surge in capital inflows. With this background, we next examine the macroeconomic performances of these countries and evaluate their success in avoiding overheating. We then summarize the main policy conclusions that can be drawn from this country experience.

The Macroeconomic Consequences of Capital Inflows

To examine how individual developing countries have fared in coping with the macroeconomic consequences of capital inflows, we have compiled data on capital flows to a sample of 21 developing and transition economies as shown in table 4.1. These countries together accounted for 95 percent of the total FDI and portfolio flows to economies of these types during 1988–95. This table tells a now-familiar story. Substantial inflows began in 1988–89 in several East Asian economies that had weathered the international debt crisis of the 1980s relatively well and made significant domestic policy adjustments in

Table 4.1 Net Private Capital Inflows to 21 Developing Countries, 1988–95
(percentage of GDP)

Country	*Inflow episode*[a]	*1988*	*1989*	*1990*	*1991*	*1992*	*1993*	*1994*	*1995*	*Cumulative flows/ GDP at end of episode*	*Mean ratio*	*Coefficient of variation*
Argentina	1991–94				1.3	3.8	2.9	3.1		9.7	2.8	0.38
Brazil	1992–95					2.8	2.3	1.9	4.8	9.4	3.0	0.44
Chile	1989–95		3.3	8.6	3.1	7.4	6.3	7.7	4.0	25.8	5.8	0.39
Colombia	1992–95					1.8	5.6	5.6	6.2	16.2	4.8	0.42
Costa Rica	1988–95	10.6	12.0	4.4	4.7	9.2	9.1	2.5	5.3	44.0	7.3	0.44
Hungary	1993–95						17.5	8.5	18.4	41.5	14.8	0.37
India	1992–95					1.2	1.7	2.7	1.7	6.4	1.8	0.35
Indonesia	1990–95			2.5	1.9	1.3	0.2	1.1	3.6	8.3	1.8	0.66
Korea	1991–95				2.6	2.5	0.6	2.4	3.5	9.3	2.3	0.45
Malaysia	1989–95		2.9	5.7	11.1	15.3	23.2	1.2	6.6	45.8	9.4	0.82
Mexico	1989–94		2.6	2.2	7.5	7.6	8.5	3.3		27.1	5.3	0.54
Morocco	1990–95			4.6	2.9	2.5	3.0	5.0	3.2	18.3	3.5	0.29
Pakistan	1992–95					2.5	4.9	3.8	3.3	13.0	3.6	0.28
Peru	1990–95			3.9	5.4	5.3	4.6	10.8	8.2	30.4	6.4	0.41
Philippines	1989–95		2.1	3.9	4.4	2.3	4.4	7.9	5.2	23.1	4.3	0.45
Poland	1992–95					4.1	6.8	3.1	12.0	22.3	6.5	0.61
Sri Lanka	1991–95				3.9	5.3	8.2	6.5	3.5	22.6	5.5	0.36
Thailand	1988–95	7.4	10.4	12.3	12.3	8.6	7.7	8.3	12.1	51.5	9.9	0.21
Tunisia	1992–95					4.1	7.1	5.1	4.1	17.6	5.1	0.28
Turkey	1992–93					1.9	4.1			5.7	3.0	0.53
Venezuela	1992–93					3.3	2.0			5.4	2.7	0.34

a. The period during which the country experienced a significant surge in net private capital inflows.
Source: World Bank data; IMF, *World Economic Outlook* data base; IMF, *International Financial Statistics* data base.

mid-decade. Outside East Asia, large inflows started to appear after the inception of the Brady Plan, with Chile and Mexico leading the way in 1989 and other Latin American countries following.[1] By 1991, several more countries in both East Asia and Latin America were participating in the episode, as were Morocco and Sri Lanka. One year later, private capital was flowing to all regions represented in this sample, although flows were far from uniform across countries. During this period, annual inflows of 4 to 5 percent of GDP were not unusual, and several countries experienced one or more years in which net private inflows exceeded 8 percent of GDP, compared with near-zero or negative values during the debt crisis period. Cumulative flows have varied substantially, from extreme values of over 40 percent of 1995 GDP in several countries in the sample (Hungary, Malaysia, and Thailand), which received very large flows for an extended period, to a low of about 6 percent of GDP in India, Turkey, and Venezuela. Overall, then, financial integration has been associated with levels of capital inflows that have been both large and persistent for many of these countries, resulting in cumulative net inflows that in several cases are bound to carry enormous challenges for domestic stabilization policy.

The transmission mechanism. The key short-run macroeconomic concern associated with a surge in capital inflows is that of an excessive expansion of aggregate demand—that is, macroeconomic overheating. This outcome can be produced through the following transmission mechanism:

- If a country maintains an officially determined exchange rate, the commitment to defend the parity causes the central bank to intervene in the foreign exchange market to purchase the foreign exchange generated by the capital inflow. To do so, the central bank creates high-powered domestic money.
- This expansion of the monetary base creates a corresponding expansion in broader measures of the money supply, lowering domestic interest rates and raising domestic asset prices.
- This action in turn triggers an expansion of aggregate demand. If the economy possesses excess capacity, the short-run implications may be to increase domestic economic activity and cause the current account of the balance of payments to deteriorate. Eventually, however (and perhaps rather quickly if domestic excess capacity is limited), excess capacity will be absorbed and the expansion in demand will trigger an acceleration in domestic inflation.
- If the exchange rate peg is maintained, rising domestic prices will cause the real exchange rate to appreciate, abetting the current account deterioration associated with the expansion in aggregate demand.

Policies to Control Overheating

To avoid potential overheating, developing countries can and have intervened at every step in this transmission process. Policy can attempt to reduce the required scale of intervention in the foreign exchange market, restrict the monetary expansion associated with a given magnitude of intervention, and offset through other means the effects on aggregate demand of a given magnitude of monetary expansion. These policies are not exclusive, and most countries have brought a wide variety of these instruments into play. An overview of the specific policy choices made by individual countries in a subsample of 13 countries for which detailed information is available is provided in table 4.2. The specific forms that some of these policies have taken are discussed below.

Reducing net inflows of foreign exchange. Some policies have restricted the required scale of intervention in the foreign exchange market, either through reducing the capital account surplus of the balance of payments or through an offsetting increase in the current account deficit. The main instruments available to the authorities are the following:

- The magnitude of gross capital inflows can be reduced by imposing a variety of direct or indirect *controls on inflows.*
- Even if gross inflows are freely allowed, the *liberalization of capital outflows* or the *accelerated repayment of public debt* can be undertaken to attempt to reduce net inflows.
- The implications of a net capital account surplus on the foreign exchange market can be counteracted by accelerating *trade liberalization* to increase the current account deficit.
- The most extreme option in this category would be to eliminate all foreign exchange market intervention by *floating the exchange rate.* The resulting appreciation of the domestic currency would both reduce net inflows through the capital account and create a current account offset.

Except for floating the exchange rate, all of these instruments were used by policymakers in recipient developing countries. Capital controls were adopted in several countries, in particular those that received the largest amounts of private capital flows (Chile, Malaysia, Mexico, and Thailand) or those that were constrained in their ability to use other policy instruments to reduce potential overheating and vulnerability (Brazil, Colombia, and Indonesia). In most of these countries, capital controls took the form of new restrictions. Brazil, for instance, enacted financial transaction taxes on foreign purchases of domestic bonds in 1993, and on purchases of domestic stocks in 1994. Mexico in 1992 imposed restrictions on the foreign exchange liabilities of banks. Indonesia in 1991 took several measures to discourage swaps

Table 4.2 Main Policy Responses to Surges in Capital Inflows, 1988–95

Country	*New restrictions on inflows*	*Liberalization of outflows*	*Trade liberalization*	*Nominal appreciation*	*Sterilized intervention*	*Higher reserve requirements*	*Tighter fiscal policy*	*Other*
East Asia								
Indonesia	1991		1990-ongoing		1990–93		1990–94	Repayment of public external debt, 1994; widening of exchange rate band, 1994–95
Korea		1989–94	1992–94	1989	1989, 1992–93	1990	1992–94	
Malaysia	1992, 1994	1988–94	1988–94		1992–93	1989–92, '94	1988–94	
Philippines		1992, 1994–95	ongoing	1992 (small)	1990–93	1990	1990–95	Accelerated debt repayment, 1994–95
Thailand	1995	1990–94	1990		1988–95		1988–91	Accelerated debt repayment, 1988–90
Latin America								
Argentina							1991–93	
Brazil	1993–95				1994–95			
Chile	1991–93	1990–94	1991	slight, 1991–92 large, 1994	1990, 1992–93	1992	1989–95	Widening of exchange rate band, 1992
Colombia	1993–95	1991–94	1991	slight, 1991 large, 1994	1992–95	1991		Exchange rate band adopted, 1994
Mexico	1992	1991	1989–93		1990–93		1989–93	Exchange rate band adopted, 1991
South Asia								
India	1992–95	ongoing	ongoing		1993–94	1993–94	1992	
Pakistan		ongoing	ongoing		1993–94			
Sri Lanka	1993	1993	1992–95		1991–93	1991–93		

and offshore borrowing by state-owned enterprises and tightened the limits on net open foreign exchange positions of commercial banks. The most concerted and sustained efforts at constraining capital inflows, however, were made by Chile and Colombia, and, in 1994, by Malaysia, as described in box 4.1. In other cases, countries reacted to the surge in capital inflows by not eliminating existing controls. Thailand, for instance, has not eliminated restrictions on the net foreign exchange and foreign liability positions of commercial banks and finance companies, and on holdings of deposits in foreign exchange by domestic residents. But in 1995 and 1996, Thailand, too, imposed new con-

Box 4.1 Capital Controls in Chile, Colombia, and Malaysia

CHILE INTRODUCED CONTROLS ON CAPITAL INflows in June of 1991. These took the form of minimum nonremunerated reserve requirements of 20 percent on new foreign credits (except credits granted to exporters) with maturities of less than one year. The requirement was extended to all external credits regardless of maturity one month later. These deposits, although applied uniformly across maturities, were required to be maintained only for one year, whatever the maturity of the loan. This implied a tax rate that varied inversely with the maturity of the loan. In 1992, the 20 percent reserve requirement on foreign loans was extended to foreign currency bank deposits. In May the required reserve ratio was increased to 30 percent, except for foreign credits with maturity of more than one year that were registered with the central bank under Article 14 of the foreign exchange regulation. The latter also became subject to the 30 percent reserve requirement in August 1992. Finally, in July of 1995 reserve requirements were extended to all types of foreign investments in Chile, including the issue of secondary American depository receipts (ADRs).

In Colombia, capital controls were introduced in September of 1993. These took the form of nonremunerated reserve requirements on direct external borrowing by firms, with the reserve ratio set at 47 percent. Unlike in Chile, the requirement was to remain in place for the duration of the loan, but it applied only to loans with a maturity of 18 months or less, except for trade credits. The control regime was tightened in 1994. In March the maturity of loans subject to reserve requirements was extended to three years, and in August to five years. In addition, the required rate was set on a graduated scale, with higher rates for shorter maturities. The range was from 140 percent for loans with maturities of 30 days or less to 42.8 percent for those with 5-year maturities.

In Malaysia, the experience with capital controls was quite different. Controls were imposed at the beginning of 1994, in response to a sharp acceleration of capital inflows in 1993. Measures included the imposition of limits on the foreign exchange liabilities of banks, the extension of reserve requirements to such liabilities, a ban on the sale of short-term securities to foreigners by residents, and the imposition of a regulation requiring that domestic currency deposits of foreign institutions be non-interest-bearing. This was followed in February by a halt to trade-related swaps and the imposition of fees on non-interest-bearing foreign deposits. Controls were gradually removed over the course of 1994, and by January 1995 only the reserve requirement for the foreign currency liabilities of banks remained in place.

trols in the form of nonremunerated reserve requirements on a variety of offshore borrowing by banks and finance companies.

A decline in net official capital inflows has offset, at least partially, the surge in private flows in several countries. This offset was significant in Chile, India, Indonesia, Morocco, the Philippines, Sri Lanka, Thailand, and Tunisia (table 4.3).[2] In Chile, Indonesia, and Thailand, the offset was the result of a deliberate policy decision to accelerate the repayment of public external debt in order to reduce the surplus on the capital account of the balance of payments and thus the extent of re-

Table 4.3 Disposition of Private Capital Inflows during Inflow Episodes
(change)

	As a percentage of GDP[a]					
Country	*Net private inflows* (1)	*Net official inflows* (2)	*Current account deficit*[b] (3)	*Reserve accumulation*[c] (4)	*Change in current account (percent)*[d]	*Change in reserve accumulation (percent)*[e]
Argentina	2.30	0.02	1.79	0.53	77	23
Brazil	2.75	−0.17	0.64	1.94	25	75
Chile	1.83	−2.06	−4.86	4.62	2,070	−1,970
Colombia	4.91	−0.90	4.90	−0.89	122	−22
Costa Rica	−0.26	−3.26	−4.52	0.99	128	−28
Hungary	15.50	−1.75	9.78	3.97	71	29
India	0.63	−0.56	−1.21	1.28	−1,720	1,820
Indonesia	1.42	−0.65	0.15	0.61	20	80
Korea	4.20	0.26	4.97	−0.51	111	−11
Malaysia	5.95	−0.31	2.86	2.78	51	49
Mexico	7.17	−0.14	7.05	−0.02	100	0
Morocco	3.74	−2.25	0.11	1.39	7	93
Pakistan	2.51	−0.26	0.92	1.33	41	59
Peru	4.43	−0.27	1.38	2.79	33	67
Philippines	3.78	−0.65	0.66	2.47	21	79
Poland	5.93	0.41	3.89	2.44	61	39
Sri Lanka	4.81	−1.26	−0.19	3.74	−5	105
Thailand	6.83	−1.21	2.31	3.31	41	59
Tunisia	4.38	−1.47	3.73	−0.82	128	−28
Turkey	2.57	−0.58	1.38	0.61	69	31
Venezuela	9.03	−1.15	14.59	−6.71	185	−85

a. Columns 1–4 show the change in the main components of the balance of payments during the respective inflow periods as compared with the immediately preceding period of equal length.
b. A minus sign means an improvement in the current account balance.
c. A minus sign means a decline in reserve accumulation.
d. Column 3/(columns 1 + 2).
e. Column 4/(columns 1 + 2).
Source: World Bank data; IMF, *International Financial Statistics* data base.

serve accumulation required by the central bank. As shown in table 4.2, most countries have continued to liberalize private capital outflows during their inflow episodes, partly as an aspect of ongoing financial liberalization. In some cases, however—Korea being a notable example—the pace of outflow liberalization has been varied in response to the strength of inflows.

Finally, free-floating exchange rates were not adopted by any of the countries in the sample, but Chile, Colombia, and Mexico adopted exchange rate bands, providing added flexibility for exchange-rate movements. In Chile and Colombia, the exchange rate proved to be fairly flexible within the band, accommodating significant nominal appreciation in response to inflows, while in Mexico the band was designed to accommodate a small amount of nominal depreciation. The floor of the band was fixed at the peso price of the U.S. dollar in November 1991, when the band was adopted, and the ceiling was set according to a system of minidevaluations. By way of contrast, in most East Asian countries (Indonesia, Korea, Malaysia, and Thailand) nominal exchange rate policy continued to be directed to the preservation of external competitiveness (that is, to prevent excessive appreciation of the real exchange rate) in the face of capital inflows.

Offsetting the impact of capital inflows on domestic monetary aggregates. There are two policies that restrict the magnitude of the monetary expansion associated with a given amount of intervention in the foreign exchange market:

- Expansion of base money associated with a given amount of intervention can be restricted by *sterilizing* the effects of intervention on the monetary base—that is, by contracting domestic credit to offset the expansion of the net foreign assets of the central bank, through mechanisms such as open market operations or transferring public sector deposits from commercial banks to the central bank.
- *Increasing reserve requirements* on domestic financial institutions reduces the impact of the expansion of the monetary base on the growth of broader monetary aggregates.

Sterilized intervention was the most widely and intensively used policy response to the arrival of capital inflows among the countries in our sample. The extent of sterilized intervention in a country can be estimated by examining the composition of the change in its monetary base. Changes in net foreign assets and in domestic credit in opposite directions are suggestive of sterilization operations. This decomposition of the annual change in the monetary base for the countries in the sample, provided in annex 4.1, suggests that most of the countries sterilized heavily for at least some portion of their inflow episode, and some (Indonesia, Korea, Mexico, the Philippines, Sri Lanka, and Thailand) did so fairly continuously over the entire episode.[3] The intensity of sterilization tended to vary countercyclically in many cases, with the degree of sterilization increasing when domestic economic conditions were strong and decreasing when they were weak. For example, in Latin America, Brazil sterilized heavily when inflation accelerated in 1992, Chile did so following an acceleration of inflation in 1991, and Colombia did so when inflation accelerated in 1992–93. In East Asia, Indonesia sterilized heavily in response to excess demand pressures through 1992, but eased monetary policy when the economy weakened in early 1993. Sterilization was intensified in association with economic recovery in 1994. The evidence suggests that sterilization proved to be effective in these cases in restraining the expansion of the monetary base.[4]

Sterilization took the form of open market bond sales, central bank borrowing from commercial banks, shifting government deposits from commercial banks to the central bank, raising interest rates on central bank assets and liabilities, and curtailing access to rediscounts. Chile, Colombia, and Indonesia all pursued sterilization through open market operations very early and aggressively, seeking to offset all effects of capital inflows on the monetary base, while Korea, Mexico, the Philippines, and Thailand were not so ambitious, seeking only to ameliorate the effects on the base. Transfers of government or public enterprise deposits to the central bank took place in Indonesia, Malaysia, and Thailand, while Mexico sterilized by placing its privatization proceeds in the central bank, in effect selling real assets to absorb the monetary base. India sterilized almost entirely by altering required reserve ratios. In contrast to these countries, Argentina did not rely on sterilized intervention, permitting capital inflows to influence its money supply.

Changes in reserve requirements have taken various forms, ranging from altering required reserve ratios on all domestic currency deposits to raising marginal reserve requirements on only a subset of bank liabilities. Chile, Colombia, Malaysia, the Philippines, and Sri Lanka, in particular, relied on repeated increases in average or marginal reserve requirements. In most of these countries, the increases in reserve requirements show up as decreases in the broad money multiplier in annex 4.1. Some countries, such as Thailand in 1995, imposed quantitative credit ceilings on banks.

Offsetting the impact of monetary expansion on aggregate demand. If the arrival of capital inflows is permitted to result in the expansion of broad monetary aggregates, the expansionary effects on aggregate demand can be neutralized through *fiscal contraction.*

Fiscal adjustment was a key component of the stabilization and market-oriented reform programs that many countries undertook prior to receiving capital inflows. Consequently, it is difficult to interpret a tight fiscal stance, or a further tightening of that stance, as a policy response to capital inflows rather than as a continuation of an ongoing adjustment process. Whatever the reason, a tighter fiscal stance during the inflow episode does help reduce aggregate demand pressures. In almost all the countries in the sample, the central government's annual fiscal balance as a ratio to GDP improved relative to its average value during the pre-inflow period. As shown in annex 4.1, Brazil, and Sri Lanka were the exceptions.

In summary, it is evident that the sample countries reacted rather vigorously to the arrival of capital inflows and that they employed virtually the entire arsenal of macroeconomic policy to combat overheating. All of these policy options are available not just to respond to the possibility of overheating, but also to offset the destabilizing effects of external financial volatility on the domestic economy when integration is well established, as will be discussed later in the chapter.

The Results of Policies to Prevent Overheating

How successful were these policies in preventing the overheating associated with a surge in capital inflows? Once again, macroeconomic performance can be understood in terms of the transmission mechanism that operates during the inflow episodes. According to this mechanism, two conditions are necessary for capital inflows to have an expansionary impact on aggregate demand. First, a change in the net private capital inflow must represent an addition to the country's capital account surplus, rather than merely a change in the identity, whether private or public, of the country's external creditors. Second, the central bank must intervene actively in the foreign exchange market, purchasing the additional foreign exchange generated by the capital inflow. To check whether these conditions were present in the sample countries during the inflow periods, table 4.3 decomposes the balance of payments in each of the countries, to account for the disposition of the change in the private capital account surplus among changes in net inflows from official sources, the current account deficit, and reserve accumulation.

The table shows that, as noted above, a reduction in flows from official creditors indeed provided an important offset to the increase in private inflows in several countries. In particular, Costa Rica did not register a net increase in the capital account surplus during the 1980s and 1990s. Indeed, both net private and official inflows declined during the period, and thus Costa Rica did not face an overheating problem of the type described above. Hence, Costa Rica will be excluded from the sample from now on. The table also confirms that recipient countries did not prevent overheating by allowing their currencies to float. For the majority of countries, reserve accumulation absorbed a significant portion of the change in the capital account surplus—more than half in nine countries.[5] Thus, in reaction to the arrival of capital inflows, central banks intervened heavily to prevent the nominal appreciation of the domestic currency. In the absence of foreign exchange intervention, of course, the current account deficit would have completely offset the capital account surplus. This implies that the arrival of capital inflows, together with central bank intervention, resulted in substantial upward pressure on the money supplies of the vast majority of recipient countries—the traditional channel for the generation of overheating.

Symptoms of overheating. To see whether these countries actually experienced macroeconomic overheating, we can examine the behavior of four variables during the periods when the countries began to receive large private capital inflows. These variables are: acceleration of economic growth, large current account deficits, accelerating inflation, and an appreciation of the real exchange rate.

The countries in the sample showed no systematic pattern of accelerating inflation, deteriorating current account, and appreciating real exchange rates. For each of these variables, approximately half the countries experienced the outcome associated with overheating and half did not. Moreover, in each country the four variables seldom moved consistently in the direction associated with overheating (for example, many countries in the sample experienced faster growth but lower inflation, other countries experienced higher inflation but lower current account deficits, and so on). Moreover, none of the variables provided a stronger signal of overheating in countries that received the largest cumulative capital inflows. Finally, even when a variable moved in a direction consistent with the emergence of overheating, it was often fairly easy to identify factors other than the capital inflow that could have accounted for its performance. For example, among the sharpest accelerations of growth in the sample were those registered by Argentina, Hungary, Peru, and Poland—two transition economies and two that had undergone discontinuous changes in their macroeconomic regimes. Clearly in these cases both economic growth acceleration and capital inflows were responding to a third factor—the change in policy regime. This is confirmed by the fact that all four of these countries underwent a sharp deceleration of inflation at this time. Indeed, the experience suggests that an acceleration of inflation, perhaps the single most direct symptom of overheating (both because it is undesirable in itself and because it contributes to an increase in the current account deficit through real exchange rate appreciation), is by no means unavoidable during a surge in capital inflows. Thirteen of the countries in the sample reduced their inflation rates during their inflow episodes, and five of the 13 saw large decelerations.[6] The macroeconomic outcomes for these countries are summarized in table 4.4.

The surge in capital inflows also did not necessarily result in an appreciation of the real exchange rate, since only 12 of the countries in the sample registered a real appreciation during the inflow period. Moreover, none of the five East Asian countries in the sample experienced a large real appreciation during their inflow periods: four had large real depreciations, while the other kept its real exchange rate approximately stable. By contrast, six of the seven Latin American countries in the sample registered real appreciation, and in most cases the magnitude was substantial. Argentina, Colombia, Mexico, and Peru registered by far the largest real appreciations in the sample. In addition, at least for most of the countries affected, the mechanism generating the real appreciation was clearly not an acceleration of inflation, as posited at the beginning of this section, because of the 12 countries that registered a real appreciation, 10 did so with *reduced* domestic inflation. This was true, for example, in Argentina, Mexico, and Peru.

In contrast to the inflation experience, a stylized fact emerging from this sample is that such inflows are often associated with upward pressure on the current account deficit. The current account deficit fell

Table 4.4 Macroeconomic Performance during Inflow Episodes
(change from immediately preceding period of equal length)

Country	*Inflow episode*	*Average annual GDP growth (percent)*	*Average annual inflation (percent)*	*Average current account*[a]	*Average REER*[b]
Argentina	1991–94	9.1	-801.1	1.8	91.7
Brazil	1992–95	3.1	-93.5	0.6	7.4
Chile	1989–95	5.7	-4.1	-4.9	-25.5
Colombia	1992–95	1.6	-4.8	4.9	14.7
Hungary	1993–95	7.5	-5.5	9.8	18.9
India	1992–95	-0.7	0.1	-1.2	-30.8
Indonesia	1990–95	2.2	1.3	0.2	-29.4
Korea	1991–95	-2.5	0.8	5.0	4.4
Malaysia	1989–95	4.0	1.4	2.9	-24.5
Mexico	1989–94	2.9	-74.4	7.1	20.0
Morocco	1990–95	-3.3	0.1	0.1	-6.5
Pakistan	1992–95	-2.3	1.7	0.9	-9.0
Peru	1990–95	3.3	-79.1	1.4	120.9
Philippines	1989–95	2.2	-3.1	0.7	-10.7
Poland	1992–95	8.5	-146.7	3.9	37.9
Sri Lanka	1991–95	2.0	-2.2	-0.2	0.6
Thailand	1988–95	3.9	-1.1	2.3	-18.9
Tunisia	1992–95	0.5	-2.2	3.7	0.6
Turkey	1992–93	1.4	5.0	1.4	1.0
Venezuela	1992–93	-5.0	-2.7	14.6	9.8

a. As a percentage of GDP. A minus sign indicates an improvement in the current account balance.
b. Percentage change in the real effective exchange rate. A positive number indicates an appreciation.
Source: IMF, *World Economic Outlook* data base; IMF, *International Financial Statistics* data base.

during the inflow period in only three of the 20 countries, and increases in current account deficits tended to be much larger than decreases. Only Chile managed to achieve significant reduction in its current account deficit during the period when capital inflows increased.

The real exchange rate and current account outcomes have been associated, even if only weakly, with each other. As figure 4.1 suggests, countries with the largest real appreciations have also tended to exhibit the largest increases in current account deficits. Omitting Argentina and Peru, whose enormous real appreciations are clearly an exception, the simple cross-country correlation between real appreciation and increases in the current account deficit in the sample is 0.60.

Figure 4.1 Change in the Current Account Deficit and the Real Effective Exchange Rate during Inflow Episodes, Selected Countries

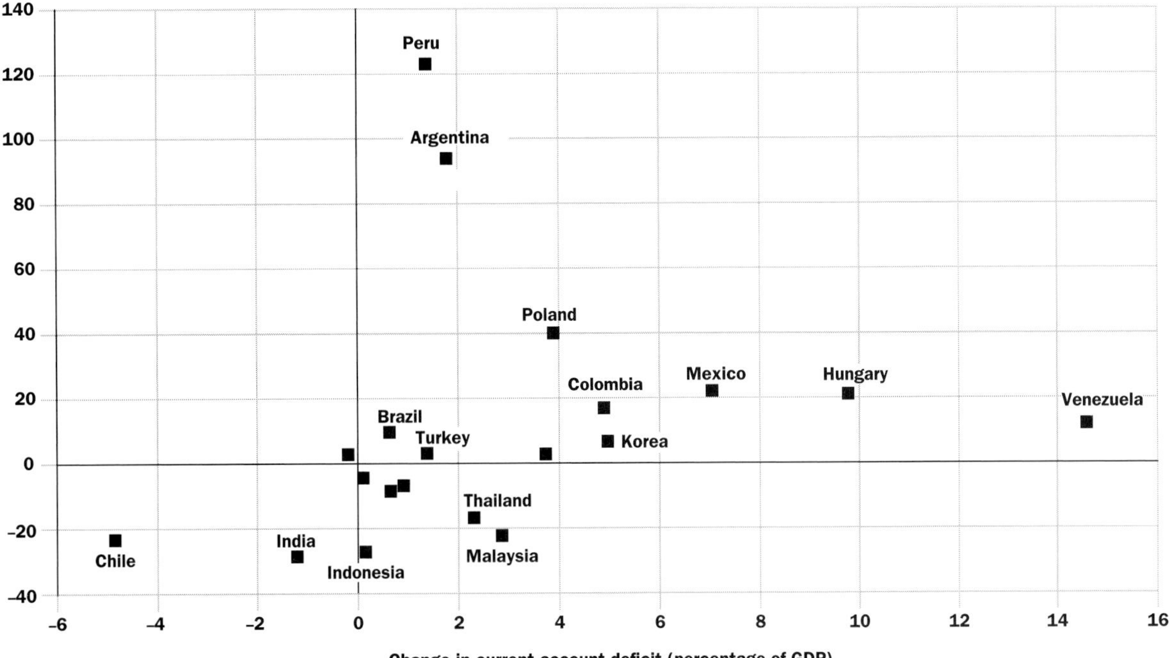

Note: Inflow episodes are compared with the immediately preceding period of equal length.
Source: IMF, *International Financial Statistics* data base.

In summary, the countries in the sample have avoided the overt symptoms of macroeconomic overheating, except for pressures on the current account. While four of the countries have exhibited large spurts of economic growth and one country (Brazil) underwent a burst of near hyperinflation, the factors behind these experiences were unusual, easily identifiable, and not attributable to the arrival of capital inflows. Substantial accelerations of inflation—the factor most directly indicative of overheating—have been almost completely absent in this group of countries, although inflationary pressures may recently have increased in those countries that received the most flows in East Asia. While several countries did have a large appreciation of the real exchange rate, regional differences suggest these may have been related to country-specific nominal exchange rate policies rather than to a generalized phenomenon such as the arrival of capital inflows. This interpre-

Larger current account deficits are associated with real exchange rate appreciation during capital inflow episodes.

tation is supported by the observation that real appreciation has tended to be associated with a deceleration, rather than an acceleration, of inflation. However, consistent with concerns about overheating, increases in the current account deficit were much more common and larger than decreases, and tended to be correlated with the real exchange rate outcome. Although, unlike countries in the previous lending boom, most countries have not absorbed all the private capital flows through a rise in the current account deficit and have increased reserves, the size of the current account deficits is of concern in certain countries, especially some of those that received the largest amounts of flows.

The composition of absorption. To the extent that capital inflows have altered the current account–to-GDP ratio in these countries, the level of absorption relative to income will have changed. The composition of this change—that is, its allocation between consumption and investment—may in turn influence the effects of the inflow on the real exchange rate as well as on the economy's growth rate. Thus the next step in analyzing the macroeconomic consequences of the inflows is to examine changes in the composition of absorption.

For 15 of the 20 countries in the sample, as shown in table 4.5, the arrival of capital inflows was associated with an increase in the ratio of investment to GDP. In some cases the increase was dramatic. In Thailand, for example, the ratio of investment to GDP increased by 13 percentage points. Only in Peru and Poland did the ratio decline sharply. The increase in the investment ratio in the large majority of countries implies that the consumption-to-GDP ratio would have to decline for the current account to improve.[7] By and large, however, this did not happen: while three-quarters of the countries had increases in the investment ratio, few of them financed these increases through reductions in the consumption ratio, thus resulting in the higher current account deficits described above.

How are these changes in the composition of absorption related to symptoms of overheating described previously? First, figure 4.2 suggests that the behavior of economic growth in the sample countries is related to changes in the composition of absorption. Countries that increased the share of investment in GDP also tended to register larger increases in the rate of economic growth during the inflow period. Leaving aside the outliers in growth performance identified earlier (Argentina, Hungary, Peru, and Poland), the simple correlation between changes in the investment ratio and in the growth rate among the

Table 4.5 Composition of Absorption during Inflow Episodes
(change from immediately preceding period of equal length)

Country	Inflow episode	As a percentage of GDP		
		Current account deficit[a]	Total investment	Total consumption
Argentina	1991–94	1.8	0.6	4.4
Brazil	1992–95	0.6	-2.0	3.6
Chile	1989–95	-4.9	10.2	-8.5
Colombia	1992–95	4.9	0.9	4.1
Hungary	1993–95	9.8	1.6	6.4
India	1992–95	-1.2	-1.3	-1.7
Indonesia	1990–95	0.2	5.7	-5.2
Korea	1991–95	5.0	4.7	1.1
Malaysia	1989–95	2.9	4.8	-1.8
Mexico	1989–94	7.1	2.4	6.7
Morocco	1990–95	0.1	-1.1	0.8
Pakistan	1992–95	0.9	1.0	-2.0
Peru	1990–95	1.4	-4.0	3.1
Philippines	1989–95	0.7	1.7	6.1
Poland	1992–95	3.9	-11.1	11.3
Sri Lanka	1991–95	-0.2	2.2	-1.9
Thailand	1988–95	2.3	13.4	-11.2
Tunisia	1992–95	3.7	2.6	-1.4
Turkey	1992–93	1.4	1.3	-0.5
Venezuela	1992–93	14.6	6.8	6.8

a. A minus sign indicates an improvement in the current account balance.
Source: IMF, *World Economic Outlook* data base; IMF, *International Financial Statistics* data base.

countries in the sample is weakly positive, amounting to 0.32.[8] Second, as shown in figure 4.3, changes in the composition of absorption also appear to be correlated with changes in the real exchange rate. In particular, an increase in the consumption-to-GDP ratio is associated with real appreciation, the simple cross-country correlation (excluding the two outliers, Argentina and Peru) being 0.74.

While this positive correlation may reflect causation running from consumption to the real exchange rate (for example, reflecting a greater intensity of nontraded goods in consumption than in investment) or the reverse (reflecting higher domestic real interest rates when the real exchange rate appreciates), the underlying stance of fiscal policy appears to have played a role. Several countries that significantly tightened fiscal policy (as indicated in annex 4.1)—including Chile, Indonesia, Malaysia, and Thailand—also reduced their share of consumption in GDP during the inflow period. Moreover, all of these coun-

Figure 4.2 Change in Growth and the Composition of Absorption during Inflow Episodes, Selected Countries

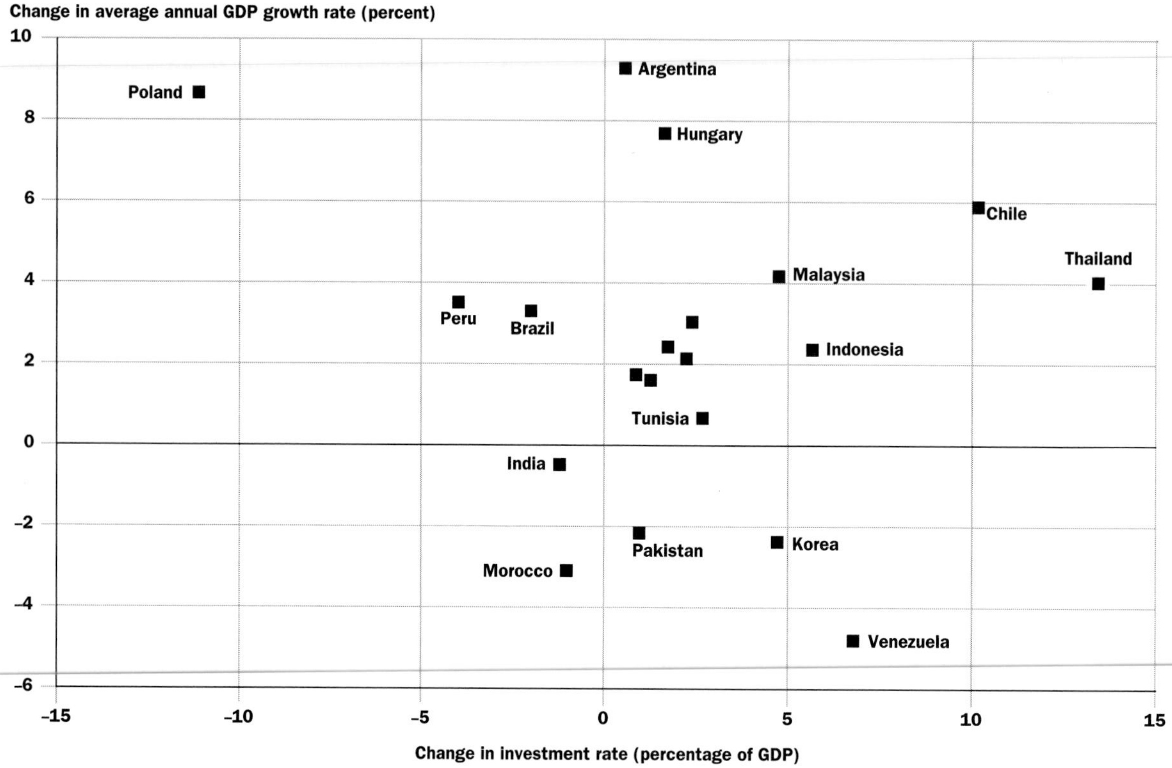

Note: Inflow episodes are compared with the immediately preceding period of equal length.
Source: IMF, *World Economic Outlook* data base.

Improvements in growth performance are associated with increases in investment rates during capital inflow episodes.

tries also achieved a substantial real exchange rate depreciation during the inflow period. Among these countries, Chile also reduced its current account deficit during the inflow period. While the current account deficit increased in Malaysia and Thailand, these two countries also experienced very substantial rises in the share of investment in GDP, as well as in their rates of economic growth, in association with the arrival of capital inflows.

Policy Conclusions

Four main conclusions can be drawn from this country experience:

- The majority of countries attempting to cope with the effects of integration eschewed direct intervention to restrict capital in-

Figure 4.3 Change in the Composition of Absorption and the Real Effective Exchange Rate during Inflow Episodes, Selected Countries

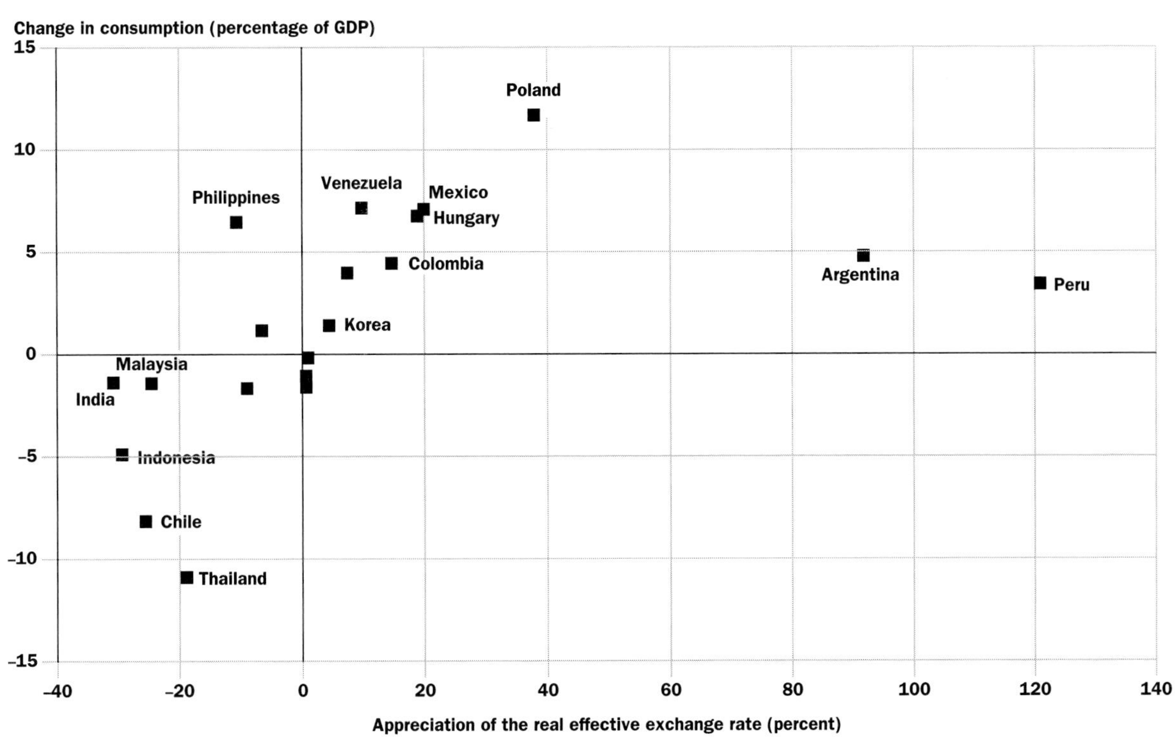

Note: Inflow episodes are compared with the immediately preceding period of equal length.
Source: IMF, *International Financial Statistics* data base; IMF, *World Economic Outlook* data base.

Real exchange rate appreciation is associated with increases in consumption rates during capital inflow episodes.

flows. However, capital controls were adopted by seven of the countries in the sample, in particular those that received the largest amounts of private capital flows or those that were constrained in their ability to use other policy instruments to contain overheating.

- Countries did not make wholesale changes in their foreign exchange regimes. Bands were introduced by Chile, Colombia, and Mexico, but only those of Chile and Colombia seemed designed to accommodate some nominal appreciation in response to capital inflows. In the context of adherence to predetermined exchange rates, outcomes with respect to the real exchange rate generally depend in the short run on how the nominal exchange rate is managed. In this respect, the experience of the recipient countries was diverse. Several countries indeed experienced real appreciation, but this was typically associated with a *decline* in the inflation rate. Thus, the emergence of real appreciation in these countries did not reflect overheating but rather the use of the exchange rate as a nominal anchor in the context of price stabilization. Where the nominal rate was managed with the goal of increasing competitiveness, as in the several East Asian countries in our sample, real appreciation either failed to materialize or was minimal.

- Tight monetary and fiscal policies were the key weapons in the fight against overheating. Tight monetary policy generally took the form of sterilized intervention in the foreign exchange market. This tool was effective in restricting expansion of the monetary base (suggesting that financial integration had not proceeded to the point of removing short-run monetary autonomy from these countries). Sterilization also proved to be a flexible tool, with several countries varying the intensity of sterilization in response to domestic economic conditions. Similarly, the majority of countries appear to have tightened fiscal policy in response to inflows, albeit to very different degrees.
- These differences in fiscal performance appear to be closely related to outcomes with regard to the composition of absorption and the real exchange rate. A particular reliance on tight fiscal policy appears to have been conducive to avoiding the symptoms of overheating while producing more limited real appreciation, lower current account deficits, and a higher share of investment in absorption.

Policy Regimes and Vulnerability

IN THE CONTEXT OF FINANCIAL INTEGRATION, VULNERABILITY refers to the possibility that a country may find itself confronted with a sudden, large, and relatively long-lasting reduction in net capital inflows. The macroeconomic dislocations produced by such an event can be extreme, as experienced by many developing countries in the context of the international debt crisis of the 1980s, and more recently by Mexico. In addition to avoiding overheating, therefore, newly integrated developing countries that are importing large quantities of capital need to set the avoidance of such vulnerability as an important policy objective. The challenge to policymakers is to identify and implement policies that can minimize (or at least do not magnify) vulnerability to external financial shocks.

One way to identify such policies is to examine the experience of capital-importing countries in the aftermath of the Mexican crisis. Macroeconomic characteristics of countries that were successful in weathering the accompanying financial storm (the tequila effect) can be credited with reducing their vulnerability. The severity of the tequila effect for a developing country is measured in terms of two criteria: the ability of the country to sustain private capital flows in 1995 at a level approaching those of earlier periods and the behavior of equity prices in the country during the first half of the year. These indicators were chosen because portfolio flows and equity prices were relatively volatile in the wake of the Mexican crisis, and thus were highly sensitive to changes in cross-country investor sentiment. These criteria are used below to separate countries into two groups—those heavily affected by the Mexican crisis and those not so affected.

The sorting of countries into those heavily influenced by the tequila effect and those not so affected is shown in table 4.6. The tequila effect proved to be important for Argentina, Brazil, India, Pakistan, Turkey, and Venezuela, in addition to Mexico itself.[9] Countries that weathered the storm well, according to our criteria, include Chile, Colombia, Indonesia, Korea, Malaysia, and Thailand. Only three countries did not clearly fall into one or the other category—Chile, Colombia, and Turkey. Although Chile and Colombia were somewhat affected by the Mexican crisis, they were classified as less affected on the basis of their stock market performance, which remained somewhat stable despite their having undergone reductions in portfolio flows. The stock market measure is more reliable for Latin American countries because it is less likely to be contaminated by regional contagion among international investors. Turkey is also an ambiguous case because stock market prices remained strong despite a sharp drop in capital flows. But because of this drop, Turkey has been placed in the "strongly affected" category.

What distinguishes these two groups of countries? Table 4.6 provides a list of potential discriminating characteristics. It may be useful to begin our discussion with the size of the current account deficit. While Mexico's current account deficit was the largest among the countries in the crisis group for several years before the crisis, four of the six countries in the noncrisis group had current account deficits in 1993

Table 4.6 Vulnerability to the Mexican Crisis, Selected Countries, 1988–93
(percent)

	Impact of shock		Country fundamentals										
						As a percentage of GDP							
						1993		Average			Average		
Group and Country	Change in portfolio equity flows, 1994–95	Change in stock prices, 12/94–3/95	Av. FDI/ total private inflows	Av. GDI/ GDP	Av. inflation	Central gov't. balance	CA balance	Central gov't. balance	CA balance	DOD/ XGS 1993	GDP growth rate	Export growth rate	Change in REER
Strongly affected													
Argentina	−75.6	−25.7	65.9	16.3	990.9	1.7	−3.1	−2.9	−0.4	408.5	2.6	6.5	121.0
Brazil	−41.4	−36.1	28.0	22.3	1,375.4	−0.1	−0.2	−0.9	0.3	312.3	0.7	9.3	16.6
India	−73.1	−18.3	4.9	21.9	9.5	−7.1	−0.4	−7.4	−2.1	290.6	5.3	7.6	−41.5
Mexico	−64.2	−58.7	39.5	19.6	34.8	0.4	−6.5	−2.6	−4.2	195.1	2.7	3.6	40.7
Pakistan	−45.3	−21.0	58.5	18.0	8.5	−7.7	−7.7	−7.9	−4.1	271.5	4.8	7.1	−15.1
Turkey	−52.8	16.7	16.7	22.8	66.6	−6.7	−3.5	−4.3	−0.5	226.9	4.2	7.2	30.1
Venezuela	−31.0	−14.1	64.8	18.7	43.1	−2.5	−3.3	−2.5	1.3	211.9	3.3	7.1	−11.6
Average	−54.8	−22.5	39.8	20.0	361.2	−3.1	−3.5	−4.1	−1.4	273.8	3.4	6.9	20.0
Less affected													
Chile	−77.3	−8.7	55.4	23.2	17.9	2.2	−4.5	3.6	−1.8	167.8	7.5	11.0	9.6
Colombia	−59.1	0.6	35.8	17.1	27.2	−0.3	−3.8	−0.8	0.6	172.4	3.8	9.3	0.9
Indonesia	−9.4	−6.0	18.9	27.2	8.2	0.0	−1.7	−0.3	−2.2	211.7	8.2	9.7	−3.4
Korea	−10.5	−5.2	16.3	33.2	7.0	0.3	0.1	−0.2	0.8	48.9	7.9	7.8	2.8
Malaysia	60.5	2.8	60.5	31.3	3.5	0.2	−4.6	−2.1	−2.3	53.0	8.7	13.6	−3.4
Thailand	−378.4	−4.5	30.8	37.6	4.8	2.0	−4.9	3.3	−5.4	86.9	10.3	16.8	2.3
Average	−79.0	−3.5	36.3	28.2	11.4	0.7	−3.2	0.6	−1.7	123.5	7.7	11.4	1.5

Note: CA, current account; GDI, gross domestic investment; DOD/XGS, debt outstanding disbursed/exports of goods and services; REER, real effective exchange rate. All averages and differences are for 1988–93 unless otherwise noted.

Source: IMF, *World Economic Outlook* data base; World Bank data.

that, relative to the size of their economies, exceeded those of all countries in the crisis group except Mexico itself and Pakistan.

The factors that seem most important in discriminating between the two groups can loosely be associated with either macroeconomic outcomes or macroeconomic policies:

- *Macroeconomic outcomes.* The two groups differ with respect to the precrisis rate of real output growth, the composition of absorption, and the rate of inflation. Of the six noncrisis countries, all except Colombia exhibited growth rates faster than the fastest-growing crisis country. Overall, these countries averaged 7.7 percent annual real growth; the country with the lowest share of investment in GDP among the noncrisis countries had a higher ratio than any of the crisis countries. The noncrisis countries averaged a 40 percent higher share of investment in GDP than the crisis countries. As mentioned earlier in this chapter, changes in growth and in the share of investment in absorption are positively correlated in the broader country sample from which this subsample was drawn. Finally, the inflation outcomes of the two groups were also quite different. Countries in the crisis group had much higher average inflation during 1988–93 than those in the noncrisis group, even after excluding Argentina and Brazil from the former.
- *Macroeconomic policies.* Real exchange rate outcomes were quite different in the two groups of countries. Four of the seven countries in the crisis group experienced very substantial real appreciation prior to the crisis. In contrast, only Chile in the noncrisis group experienced real appreciation, and Chile's total real appreciation was much less than that of any of the appreciating countries in the crisis group.[10] Overall, the crisis countries registered a 20 percent real appreciation, on average, during 1988–93, compared with 1.5 percent for the noncrisis countries. Fiscal policy also proved to be very different for the two groups for the five years preceding the Mexican crisis. On average, the central government budget in the noncrisis countries had a surplus of 0.6 percent of GDP during 1988–93, while the crisis countries had an average deficit of 4 percent of GDP over the same period. In 1993, the central government balance still registered an average surplus (of 0.7 percent of GDP) in the noncrisis countries while the crisis

countries remained in deficit. The third difference between the two groups was the debt-export ratio, with all but one of the crisis countries exhibiting a ratio larger than the largest value registered among any of the noncrisis countries.[11]

How do we make sense of these results? The most important lesson for policymakers is that since creditors (both domestic and foreign) can be expected to take their capital out of a country when they think that a policy change could impair the value of their investment, then vulnerability will arise when the perception is created that a devaluation, nonpayment of public sector debt, or the imposition of restrictions on capital outflows is about to occur. Such expectations are likely to arise when the real exchange rate is perceived to be out of line, the government's debt obligations are large, fiscal adjustment is perceived as politically or administratively infeasible, or the country's growth prospects are bleak. From the perspective of creditors, therefore, a high share of investment in absorption and a strong record of growth, a low stock of government obligations coupled with demonstrated fiscal flexibility (in the form of small deficits and low inflation), and a real exchange rate broadly perceived to be in line with fundamentals all augur well for future debt service. The evidence suggests that these characteristics are most directly associated with a country's ability to avoid vulnerability. From a policy perspective, countries need to have an active exchange rate policy that avoids substantial appreciation of the real exchange rate and responsible fiscal policies. Evidence from the previous section suggests that this policy mix, in turn, is associated with stable real exchange rates, a relatively larger share of investment in GDP, and faster economic growth.

Macroeconomic Management with Growing Financial Integration

SHORT OF THE CRISIS SITUATION ASSOCIATED WITH VULNERAbility, cross-border capital flows may exhibit substantial volatility—that is, temporary shocks to either capital inflows or outflows caused by changes in world economic conditions or by less extreme changes in portfolio managers' perceptions of domestic creditworthiness. This increased volatility may well be a fact of life for developing countries as they become more integrated with international financial markets, even after stock adjustment inflows associated with the transition have tapered off, and even if severe crises are avoided. This section examines general principles of macroeconomic management for newly integrated countries facing relatively brief and frequent fluctuations in cross-border capital flows. The question for policymakers is how to frame macroeconomic policies in the presence of such volatility, and in particular, what broad principles should guide policy in several key areas of macroeconomic management.[12]

Earlier in this chapter we listed the tools available to domestic policymakers for coping with financial volatility. In broad terms, they consist of policies regarding the free movement of capital, exchange rate policy, monetary policy, and fiscal policy. This section will consider the role of each of these policies in macroeconomic management and how they may be linked.

Restricting the Free Movement of Capital

The most direct response to external financial volatility is to contain its impact by restricting the movement of capital—that is, imposing capital controls. However, economists have long questioned both the effectiveness and the desirability of such restrictions. We take up each of these issues in turn.

Capital controls are of questionable effectiveness. Although economists tend to have strong views about the effectiveness or ineffectiveness of capital controls, empirical evidence on the issue is ambiguous. Assessing the effectiveness of controls is complicated by a host of factors, including the definition of effectiveness itself (that is, what is the objective to be achieved) and the conditions that determine the effectiveness of different types of controls (see box 4.2).

Are Capital Controls Desirable?

Even if capital controls can be effective, that does not mean they should be used. Since effective controls distort private economic decisions, the benefits of imposing them should outweigh the costs. This section evaluates four arguments for restricting capital movements as a way to control volatility and achieve macroeconomic stabilization under a high degree of financial integration.

Box 4.2 Objectives of Capital Controls and Conditions for Effectiveness

Objectives. The effectiveness of capital controls can only be measured relative to the objective they are designed to achieve. There are three basic types of objectives: to preserve some degree of domestic monetary autonomy over a period of time, to restrict the magnitude of net capital flows into or out of the country, and to affect the composition of capital flows. However, because monetary autonomy cannot be achieved unless the magnitude of net flows is restricted, these three objectives boil down to two: restricting the size of net capital flows and affecting their composition.

Conditions for effectiveness of different types of controls. The effectiveness of controls may depend on a variety of factors that not only differ across countries but also change over time as the process of financial integration proceeds.[1] These factors include:

- *The state of technology.* This affects transaction costs in conducting arbitrage among different financial centers. The lower the costs, the more difficult it will be to implement effective controls.
- *The extent of international cooperation in reporting cross-border claims.* In the case of controls on outflows, for example, host countries may be unwilling to declare the assets of residents from capital-exporting countries, whether or not these residents try to circumvent foreign exchange regulations.
- *The size of the misalignment motivating inflows or outflows.* If effecting a capital inflow or outflow for an arbitrage operation involves a fixed cost imposed by the control regime, then the deterrent effect of this cost may be nullified if the arbitrage gains promise to exceed the cost.[2]
- *The design of the controls themselves, in particular their comprehensiveness.* Controls that are not comprehensive—for example, those that apply to only certain types of flows—can be evaded by changing the composition of flows. While such controls would be ineffective in preserving monetary autonomy (or limiting the total magnitude of flows), they may, how-

- *"Incredible" reform.* The first argument is that controls may be effective in coping with distortions that arise when the government implements an incredible stabilization or trade liberalization (one that observers do not believe it can carry out). Lack of confidence in the government's ability to sustain its announced exchange rate or tariff policies may make external borrowing appear temporarily cheap, with potentially destabilizing effects on the domestic economy.[13] The best solution to this problem is for the government to take steps to achieve credibility—most commonly, by getting its fiscal accounts into order—since fiscal problems are often the cause of policy reversal. If this is not feasible, controls on capital movements may be a second-best policy.
- *Insulation from shocks arising in the international financial market.* The second argument for capital controls on both inflows and outflows is that they can insulate the domestic economy from identifi-

ever, still be able to alter the composition of flows.

- *The structure of the domestic financial system.* This may determine the effectiveness of partial controls that leave room for evasion by channeling flows through alternative domestic intermediaries.
- *The size of trade flows.* This would determine the scope for under- and overinvoicing, as well as for altering leads and for lags on trade credit.
- *The types of cross-border flows targeted by the controls*—that is, controls on capital outflows may differ in effectiveness from controls on inflows, all other things (that is, potential arbitrage margins) being equal. One argument is that the residence of the capital-importing or -exporting agent may matter. Domestic residents may be more prepared than foreign agents to evade restrictions, making controls on outflows less effective than controls on inflows.
- *The efficiency of the controlling bureaucracy.*

In practice, restrictions on capital movements have taken many forms, ranging from the outright prohibition of a wide array of capital account transactions (such as those that have given rise to parallel foreign exchange markets in both industrial and developing countries) to prudential restrictions on the acquisition of foreign assets by domestic pension funds or of foreign liabilities by domestic banks. Different restrictions designed to achieve different objectives can be expected to vary in effectiveness, both in achieving their stated purposes and in the wider sense of financially insulating the domestic economy from external shocks.

1. Some analysts have argued that controls of any type can be effective under any arbitrary set of circumstances, while others have argued that controls of any type can never be effective. Neither argument is valid.

2. This means, in particular, that the size of capital flows in the presence of controls is not a reliable indicator of the effectiveness of controls, since large flows may simply indicate large arbitrage opportunities.

able external financial shocks—that is, they can limit the incidence of volatility by preserving some degree of financial autarky. Since controls directly address the source of the shock, they may, it is argued, succeed in stabilizing the economy without introducing new distortions. This argument for quantitative controls, however, is less persuasive than the first. From the country perspective, fluctuations in world interest rates are just an intertemporal dimension of what terms of trade fluctuations are intratemporally. If intratemporal price fluctuations do not require insulation, it is not clear why intertemporal fluctuations should do so.

- *Preservation of short-run monetary autonomy.* Under perfect capital mobility, the effectiveness of monetary policy can be preserved only if exchange rate policy is flexible. In this case, however, unpleasant tradeoffs may arise between internal (inflation) and external (current account) balance targets. Tight monetary policy adopted to combat inflation, for example, would increase the domestic real interest rate while causing the real exchange rate to appreciate, possibly resulting in a deterioration of the trade balance. Capital controls would enable the monetary authorities to avoid this tradeoff between targets by making it possible to preserve monetary autonomy with an officially determined exchange rate. Thus controls would, in effect, provide a second independent macroeconomic instrument—either monetary policy or the exchange rate—to simultaneously address the two targets of inflation and the external balance of payments. The benefits for macroeconomic management are large, however, only if other stabilization instruments are not available. If fiscal policy is sufficiently flexible to be used for stabilization purposes, for example, then price stability and satisfactory current account performance can be pursued through the combined use of fiscal and exchange rate policy.[14]

- *Changing the composition of inflows.* Finally, there is the argument that controls can be used to alter the composition of capital inflows. Even if controls can be used for this purpose, whether or not they should be depends on whether the composition of inflows matters. Unfortunately, there is currently no consensus on this issue. While researchers have provided some support for the idea that reliance on short-term flows is associated with enhanced vulnerability and volatility, the evidence is mixed.
- A separate argument for being concerned with the composition of flows is that certain types of inflows may be driven by implicit government guarantees (for example, external borrowing by domestic financial institutions) and thus may not be welfare enhancing. But even if such flows could be discouraged by capital controls, it is not clear that the same implicit guarantees do not also apply to other types of flows (such as direct lending to domestic firms) through less direct means (Dooley 1996). If they do, then the case for altering the composition of flows would have to rely on the differential welfare effects of direct government guarantees extended to financial institutions for different types of flows. This case seems plausible a priori.

Summary and conclusion. Empirical assessment of the effectiveness of capital controls is an inexact science (box 4.3). Although many devel-

Box 4.3 Effectiveness of Capital Controls in Chile, Colombia, and Malaysia

THE NATURE OF THE CAPITAL CONTROLS THAT were imposed in each of these three countries was described in box 4.1. Since these controls were imposed relatively recently, evidence on their effectiveness is limited and somewhat contradictory. Net private capital inflows contracted in Chile in 1991 and (rather drastically) in Malaysia in 1994, the years in which the controls were implemented. Inflows accelerated in Colombia in 1994, however, despite the imposition of controls in September of the previous year.

The problem with such before-after assessments, of course, is that other factors could have accounted for these outcomes in all three countries. Unfortunately, there is no more systematic evidence available for Malaysia. (The consensus among observers, however, is that the Malaysian controls were quite effective in stemming short-term capital inflows; see, for instance, Quirk and Evans 1995.) The Chilean and Colombian experiences have been studied in more detail.

One insight from these studies is that the effectiveness of capital controls in altering the magnitude of total capital flows, or of particular types of flows, can be measured by capital flow equations in which the interest rate differential is adjusted by adding an estimate of the implicit tax rate imposed by measures such as unremunerated reserve requirements. Cardenas and Barreras (1996) followed this procedure for Colombia and found no statistically significant impact for the tax term. At the same time, however, they found that the tax term affected domestic interest rates (suggesting an enhanced degree of monetary autonomy) and the black market premium. They also found a substantial change in the term structure of external borrowing at the time that regulations were changed. They interpret this evidence as suggesting that controls did not affect the total magnitude of capital inflows into Colombia but altered their composition toward longer maturities. This conclusion is supported by Quirk and Evans (1995), who based their judgment on an analysis of changes in flow composition following the implementation of controls.

For Chile, analysts have examined the change in the composition of flows and have estimated capital flow equations. Le Fort and Budnevich (1996) and Quirk and Evans (1995) all conclude, from their analyses of changes in the composition of Chile's external financing after the imposition of the unremunerated reserve requirement, that the composition of flows was altered in the direction of longer maturities. On the other hand, Valdés-Prieto and Soto (1996) estimated capital flow equations for short-term capital and found that the tax variable did not have a statistically significant effect on aggregate flows of short-term capital, although a negative and statistically significant effect appeared for at least one important component.

oping countries that maintained controls during the initial period of financial integration seem to have preserved a meaningful degree of monetary autonomy, the effectiveness of controls is likely to decrease as the countries become more integrated. As conditions change in these countries, the evidence from industrial countries may become more relevant for them, and controls will be able to preserve a degree of monetary autonomy for only a limited period of time. In addition, controls have not been able to prevent large capital outflows and inflows in response to large prospective arbitrage profits. Finally, the available evidence suggests that controls can be effective in altering the composition of flows.

With regard to the desirability of implementing controls, we can conclude that:

- Prudential restrictions on external borrowing and lending by domestic financial institutions may plausibly be warranted. These restrictions on capital movements have a clear second-best rationale, since they are directed at a specific distortion: the inability of the government to credibly commit to removing certain implicit guarantees.
- Temporary restrictions on capital movements designed to address "incredible liberalization" or "incredible stabilization" problems are also warranted if credibility is not achievable, again on second-best grounds. Such restrictions may be of limited effectiveness, however, if the size of the perceived arbitrage margin is large.
- Restrictions on capital inflows for more general macroeconomic stabilization purposes may be motivated by the desire to insulate the domestic economy from "pure" external financial shocks or to preserve monetary autonomy in an effort to free up an additional policy instrument. The first goal is questionable, since it is based on the premise that the government is better informed about the duration of shocks than the private sector. With regard to the second objective, the best solution to this problem may be to increase the flexibility of fiscal policy rather than adopt capital controls. At best, this objective provides an argument for retaining restrictions as a transitory device, until the fiscal system can be reformed to make fiscal policy an effective stabilization tool.

Exchange Rate Policy

Exchange rate regimes. Different exchange rate systems can be and have been used by countries while becoming integrated with the rest of the world—in particular, pure floating; managed, or dirty, floating; fixed exchange rate; or a currency (or quasi-currency) board. Each system has consequences for the effectiveness of monetary and fiscal policy. Thus, while in a pure floating system fiscal policy is less effective and monetary policy more effective, in a fixed exchange rate system the opposite results (Mundell 1968). Therefore, the advantages or disadvantages of each system vary from country to country depending on the nature—nominal versus real—of the shocks affecting each country and the ability of the authorities to have a flexible fiscal policy. Countries in which fiscal policy cannot be modified effectively in the short run should not relinquish monetary policy completely by adopting a fixed exchange rate system.

In recent years an increasing number of economies have adopted "flexibly managed" exchange rate systems, which give them the option of effectively using monetary policy at the cost of eroding their credibility regarding inflation targets. The few exceptions have been economies where the credibility of the government was extremely low—Hong Kong during the 1980s and Argentina and Estonia during the 1990s—all of whom adopted currency boards because of the need to regain market confidence.[15] The major difficulty facing these economies, however, is to maintain a flexible enough fiscal policy and build cushions—such as a large stock of international reserves—to improve the resilience of the economy to shocks.

In the aftermath of the Mexican crisis, many thought that the days of managed exchange rate systems were over. However, most countries were able to go through the Mexican crisis without modifying their exchange rate systems. The evidence to date shows that international capital markets have been selective since the Mexican episode and that fundamentals matter (Sachs, Tornell, and Velasco 1996). Thus, there are indications that officially determined exchange rates can be managed successfully within a consistent macroeconomic policy framework. In particular, the success of flexibly managed systems depends on two things:

- whether policymakers can actually succeed in tracking the equilibrium real exchange rate, so that fundamentals-driven speculative attacks can be avoided
- whether governments can achieve enough credibility to cause market expectations to coalesce around the "good" equilibrium in a multiple-equilibrium situation, thereby avoiding speculative attacks driven by self-fulfilling expectations.

These are the two most important sources of volatility associated with a managed exchange rate regime. The experiences of Chile,

Colombia, and the four East Asian countries that were not affected by the Mexican crisis suggest that both of these objectives are within the reach of policymakers in developing countries.

Exchange rate management. Since managing the exchange rate indeed seems to be the preference of most developing countries, the issue of how to manage the rate in a financially integrated world becomes an important one. One way to approach this problem is to consider the exchange rate regime as consisting of a band around a moving central

Box 4.4 Recent Country Experience with Exchange Rate Bands

THE BANDS THAT HAVE BEEN ADOPTED IN developing countries to date typically have been implemented on the heels of exchange rate–based stabilization programs. They thus represent the "flexibilization" stage of such programs. While the bands share this common background, the choices that individual countries made in their implementation have been rather different. All of these countries have adopted a *crawling central parity*, a key feature of the developing-country bands that distinguishes them from the European ERM, but the rules governing the behavior of the central parity have differed across countries. In Chile, the central parity has been adjusted continuously, with announced daily depreciations for the coming month, based on a forecast of foreign and domestic inflation over the coming month. Periodic revaluations reflecting perceived changes in "fundamentals" (associated with capital inflows) have been superimposed on this gradual nominal depreciation. In Israel, by contrast, the central parity was initially fixed relative to a basket of currencies in January of 1989, and then in December 1991 it was allowed to crawl at an annual rate determined by the difference between the government's *targeted* rate of inflation over the coming year and a forecast of foreign inflation. Mexico announced no central parity but fixed the lower bound of the band and announced a predetermined rate of daily depreciation for the upper bound, implying a gradually increasing band width. The daily change in the peso-dollar parity was initially set at 20 cents per day, when the band was adopted in November 1991, and was later increased to 40 cents per day in October 1992, allowing for an accelerated annual rate of depreciation of the peso. By the time of the Mexican crisis, in December 1994, the width of the band had increased to 14 percent. Colombia formally introduced a crawling band in January 1994, although a de facto band existed under the *certificados de cambio* system that was adopted in the attempt to reduce the cost of sterilizing capital inflows.[1] The initial rate of crawl was set at 11 percent and was increased to 11.5 percent at the end of 1994.

Band widths tended to increase over time in each of these cases. As already indicated, the Mexican band widened automatically over time, since its upper bound was depreciated continuously, while its lower bound was fixed. Band widths also increased over time in Chile and Israel, but in discrete fashion and relative to an announced parity. The width of the Chilean band started out at 2 percent around the central parity in 1985 and had increased to 10 percent by 1992. Similarly, the width of the Israeli band was increased from 3 percent to 5 percent around the central parity in March 1990. Colombia began with a total band width of 12.5 percent under the certificados de cambio system parity. The decisions that need to be made then consist of how to adjust the parity, how wide to make the band, and how to intervene within the band.

The experiences of Chile, Colombia, and the East Asian countries (box 4.4) suggest that the objective of setting the central parity should be to maintain competitiveness—that is, the central parity should track the long-run equilibrium real exchange rate—to prevent expectations of discrete realignments. This means adjusting the parity not only in

but widened the band to plus or minus 7 percent when a crawling peg was formally adopted at the beginning of 1994. Concerning intervention inside the band, only Chile appears to have made use of the full band width, with the exchange rate regularly approaching the upper and lower bounds. Israel and Mexico were much more active to restrict fluctuations to a narrower zone inside the band.

The relevant lessons from experience with exchange rate bands in developing countries can be summarized as follows (see Helpman, Leiderman, and Bufman 1994). First, moving to a band from a fixed rate, or to a band with a crawling central parity from one with a fixed parity, has not obviously been associated with a loss of price stability. Second, bands have been associated with a variety of real exchange rate experiences. In Chile, the real exchange rate depreciated during the early years of the band, and it appreciated after capital inflows began to arrive in 1989. In Mexico and Colombia, by contrast, the exchange rate was associated with fairly continuous real appreciation. Israel's real exchange rate has been relatively stable since the adoption of the band. These differences reflect different weights attached to competitiveness and price stability by the authorities in the management of the central parity and suggest that the crawling nature of the central parity—which allows this variety of real exchange rate outcomes and which distinguishes these bands from their European counterparts—is an important clue to their survival up to the present in three of the four countries that have adopted them.

Finally, the adoption of a band does not represent a magic solution to credibility problems. The Chilean, Israeli, and Mexican bands were all characterized by periods in which expectations of realignment—associated with the behavior of "fundamentals"—emerged, even before the Mexican crisis. The long cycles in interest rate differentials associated in timing with the renewal of the Pacto agreements in Mexico, as well as the behavior of interest rate differentials in Israel around the time of realignments, suggest that markets identify episodes of misalignment and act quickly on expectations of devaluation. In Colombia, revaluations occurred twice (at the beginning and end of 1994), when market pressures were strong and the exchange rate was at the lower end of the band. Similar events occurred in Chile during 1991–94.

1. Under this system, sellers of foreign exchange received dollar-denominated claims on the central bank, denoted certificados de cambio. These could be redeemed at maturity (initially three months, but extended to one year in August of 1991) for the full face value at the then-prevailing exchange rate, redeemed before maturity at 87.5 percent of face value, or sold freely in the market.

accordance with the domestic-foreign inflation differential but also in accordance with changes in the underlying equilibrium real exchange rates, which are driven by permanent changes in fundamental factors such as the terms of trade, commercial policy, fiscal policy, and conditions in external financial markets.[16] Recent evidence indeed suggests that five East Asian economies—Indonesia, Malaysia, the Philippines, Singapore, and Thailand—have all tracked their long-run equilibrium values fairly closely during recent periods of substantial capital inflows in those countries (Montiel 1996).

On the assumption that the central parity seeks to track the long-run equilibrium real exchange rate, the next issues are how wide the band should be and how much intervention should take place within it. The desirable width of the band depends on the value to the domestic economy of an independent domestic monetary policy. The larger the scope for the exchange rate to deviate from its central parity—that is, the wider the band—the greater the scope for an independent domestic monetary policy. In turn, the usefulness of an independent monetary policy for reducing volatility depends on the availability of alternative stabilization instruments (a flexible fiscal policy) and on the sources of shocks to the economy. The traditional analysis of this issue focuses on the implications of shocks in the domestic money (nominal) and goods (real) markets, the standard prescription being that, holding fiscal policy constant, domestic real shocks call for exchange rate flexibility, while domestic nominal shocks call for fixed exchange rates. This suggests that if fiscal policy is not available (or is costly to use) as a stabilization instrument, countries in which domestic real shocks predominate should adopt fairly wide bands, while those in which domestic nominal shocks are dominant should keep the exchange rate close to its central parity. With a flexible fiscal policy, however, domestic real shocks can be countered through fiscal adjustments, thereby diminishing the value of independent monetary policy as a stabilization instrument. Thus the adoption of a fairly narrow band is more likely to be consistent with the stabilization objective if fiscal policy is available as a stabilization instrument.

Regarding intervention within the band, the logic of this analysis suggests that for a given band width, active intervention should accompany nominal shocks, whereas real shocks instead call for some combination of exchange rate and fiscal adjustment. Consider, however, an alternative source of shocks—that is, "pure" external financial shocks, say, in the form of fluctuations in world interest rates. In this case, exchange market intervention policy determines the form in which the shock is transmitted to the domestic economy. If world interest rates fall, for example, and active (unsterilized) intervention keeps the exchange rate fixed at its central parity, domestic monetary expansion and lower domestic interest rates will ensue—an expansionary shock. If, on the other hand, the central bank refrains from intervention, the domestic currency will appreciate in real terms and the domestic real interest rate will rise—a contractionary shock. Purely from the perspective of stabilizing domestic aggregate demand, the appropriate intervention policy within the band in this case depends on the direction in which it is feasible or desirable to move fiscal policy. If fiscal policy is literally inflexible, then the choice confronting monetary authorities is between real appreciation (under no intervention) or overheating (under full unsterilized intervention). To avoid both overheating and real appreciation requires a mix of fiscal contraction and intervention to keep the nominal exchange rate close to its central parity.

Conclusions. Experience suggests that crawling pegs remain a viable exchange rate option for developing countries that become integrated into world capital markets. However, the scope for deviating from fundamentals, as well as from commitment to the announced regime, is much reduced under these circumstances. Managed rates are certainly capable of generating macroeconomic volatility in this environment, but they have not generally done so.

The following conclusions can be drawn with regard to exchange rate management:

- The central parity should be managed so as to track, to the extent possible, the underlying long-run equilibrium real exchange rate. This means not just offsetting inflation differentials but also adjusting the real exchange rate target to reflect permanent changes in fundamentals. Large and persistent temporary misalignments should be avoided, primarily because they threaten the sustainability of the regime and make speculative attacks more likely.
- Small temporary deviations from the central parity can play a useful stabilizing role when fiscal policy is inflexible and either real domestic shocks dominate or exchange rate flexibility is required to ensure that external shocks affect domestic demand in the right direction.
- In general, fiscal flexibility can substitute for exchange rate flexibility as a stabilizing device.

Monetary Policy

Fixing an exchange rate target in the face of capital movements implies central bank intervention in the foreign exchange market, which has the effect of altering the stock of base money. Sterilized intervention is the indicated policy for a government attempting to simultaneously run an independent monetary policy (targeting either some monetary aggregate or some domestic interest rate) and fix the nominal exchange rate. As already indicated, however, if capital mobility is high, such an attempt may not be successful in the absence of capital controls.

The purpose of sterilized (as opposed to unsterilized) intervention is to prevent a change in the demand for domestic interest-bearing assets from causing too large a change in the price of those assets, essentially by meeting the demand shift with a supply response. Thus, sterilization in response to capital inflows involves an increase in the supply of domestic debt in one form or another. As in the case of capital controls, the general issues that arise in this context are not only whether sterilized intervention can work to stabilize domestic aggregate demand but also, if it can, whether it is desirable. As shown in annex 4.2, even if sterilization remains possible for financially integrating developing countries, its effectiveness in insulating domestic demand from external financial shocks is questionable. Sterilization is most effective when domestic interest-bearing assets are close substitutes among themselves but are poor substitutes for foreign interest-bearing assets. Under these circumstances, sterilized intervention can insulate domestic aggregate demand from transitory portfolio shocks. However, the conditions necessary for sterilized intervention to be effective imply that its effectiveness may depend on how it is attempted. Because bank borrowers may not have access to securities markets, for example, sterilizing by raising reserve requirements on banks is likely to be less effective in insulating the domestic economy from portfolio disturbances than is sterilizing through open market bond sales.

If sterilization is possible, when is it beneficial? The answer is that sterilization is beneficial whenever the prices of domestic assets need to be insulated from shocks; that is, whenever the economy experiences transitory shocks to portfolio preferences—domestic nominal shocks or external financial shocks—or when the authorities seek to accommodate a permanent change in portfolio preferences in a gradual fashion. When this happens, domestic aggregate demand can be stabilized by preventing changes in portfolio preferences from being transmitted to the real sector through changes in exchange rates and asset prices. On the other hand, domestic real shocks do not call for sterilized intervention, since in this case the asset price adjustments triggered by the shock are likely to prove stabilizing.

Conclusions. The point for policymakers is that sterilized intervention may be indicated when an economy experiences shocks to portfolio preferences. Even when it is desirable for stabilization purposes, however, sterilization may carry a fiscal cost, particularly for governments whose claimed intentions not to devalue or default on debt are not fully credible, resulting in high domestic interest rates.[17] Thus, the use of this tool without impairing the government's solvency requires fiscal flexibility. Countries that lack such flexibility may be tempted to sterilize through changes in reserve requirements, despite the likelihood that the use of this tool will result in imperfect insulation, because the fiscal implications of doing so are less adverse than those of open market operations. This advantage, however, is at the cost of implicit taxation of banks and their customers.

Fiscal Policy

From the standpoint of reducing volatility, the key characteristics of fiscal policy are short-run flexibility, the perceived solvency of the public sector, and its vulnerability to liquidity crises.

Short-run fiscal flexibility plays an important role in neutralizing shocks. The importance of short-run fiscal flexibility was emphasized earlier in this chapter. Recall, for example, the reference case of a "pure" external financial shock for a country with well-integrated financial markets. In this case, sterilized intervention is not an option, and thus the country has only one independent monetary policy instrument. Faced with an external financial shock, the domestic monetary authorities can choose a value for either the exchange rate or the domestic money supply (and thus the domestic interest rate), but not for both. Therefore, when both the level and the composition of aggregate demand are important, the authorities will find themselves one instrument short and may face an unpleasant choice between, say, stabilizing domestic demand and safeguarding the competitiveness of exports.

This tradeoff suggests an important role for short-run fiscal flexibility. If fiscal policy can be counted upon to sustain the *level* of aggregate demand at its preshock value (by adopting a more or less expansionary stance as needed), then the choice of monetary response can be based on the *desired composition* of aggregate demand. In the absence of short-run fiscal flexibility, however, the nature of the monetary response may depend on tradeoffs between the level and composition of demand.

How can fiscal flexibility be achieved? There are at least two important constraints tending to limit the flexibility of fiscal policy. The first concerns inflexibility of fiscal *instruments,* arising from inefficient tax systems that associate large excess burdens with policy-induced changes in tax revenues, as well as from political imperatives that tend to drive up the level of public expenditures. Structural measures that remove rigidities on either the expenditure or revenue side of the government's budget—such as privatization of state enterprises and tax reform designed to widen the tax base and remove egregious distortions in marginal tax rates, as well as to improve the efficiency of tax administration—can thus make an important contribution to enhancing fiscal flexibility. The second restriction on fiscal flexibility arises from the behavior of creditors. If fiscal profligacy during good times causes creditors to question fiscal solvency during bad times, then countercyclical fiscal measures will be ruled out by an inability to finance deficits during downturns. The upshot is that overly expansionary fiscal policy in response to positive shocks is likely to make fiscal policy procyclical in *both* directions by constraining fiscal flexibility when the economy is hit by adverse shocks (Gavin and others 1996).[18] Thus a key step in achieving symmetric fiscal flexibility is the implementation of mechanisms that permit the fiscal authorities to restrain spending when times appear to be good. Recent research suggests that institutional aspects of the budget process may play important roles in restraining the growth of expenditures during such times. Transparency in the budget process, as well as a hierarchical, rather than collegial, process of budget formulation that permits the finance ministry to restrict the growth of spending by line ministries when budget constraints appear to be eased, have been associated empirically with a more restrained fiscal stance, on average. Thus, broader institutional reforms designed to safeguard the perceived solvency of the public sector may be needed in some cases to complement more conventional structural reforms if fiscal policy is to achieve the desired degree of flexibility.

Public sector solvency is important to creditors. Beyond the role of short-run stabilization in response to external financial shocks, fiscal policy plays a more fundamental role in the context of increased financial integration, when both the direction and the magnitude of capital flows are likely to become very sensitive to perceptions of domestic public sector solvency. Potential insolvency can generate large capital outflows and large interest rate premiums, as creditors try to avoid taxation of domestic assets while demanding compensation for exposing themselves to the risk of taxation they face by continuing to lend in the domestic economy. This situation is aggravated when the government makes explicit guarantees to creditors, however, since the value of the guarantees will fluctuate with the government's perceived financial ability to back them. The key point is that in the context of high financial integration, the stock dimension of fiscal policy, in the form of changes in the government's perceived net worth, may itself represent an important source of shocks to the domestic economy, transmitted through the terms on which both domestic and foreign creditors are willing to hold claims on the domestic economy.

The stock and flow dimensions of fiscal policy are not independent. A critical link between them is created by the fact that what matters for creditors is the *perceived* solvency of the public sector. For a government whose long-run fiscal stance is uncertain, short-run policy changes will be scrutinized for information about the government's longer-run intentions. Knowing this, governments may be reluctant to act in ways that may be perceived as sending the wrong signal to creditors, and this reluctance may limit the government's short-run policy flexibility. Thus, achieving a reputation for fiscal responsibility may maximize the government's short-run policy flexibility.

Debt management policies will determine the likelihood of a debt run. Public sector solvency requires that the public sector's comprehensive net worth be positive. However, the need to preserve macroeconomic stability in a financially integrated environment may impose stricter conditions on the public sector's balance sheet than simply maintaining a positive value of comprehensive net worth. The composition of assets and liabilities may matter as well. In particular, a public sector that is solvent (that is, one that can credibly honor its obligations over a sufficiently long horizon) may nevertheless be vulnerable to short-run liquidity crises. If the public sector is perceived as unlikely to honor its short-term obligations, then creditors will be reluctant to take on the government's short-term liabilities, and in a vicious cycle, the government may then be unable to meet its short-run obligations. The likelihood of such a debt run depends on the maturity and currency composition of the public sector's liabilities relative to that of its assets—that is, on the government's debt management policies.

In managing the composition of its debt, the government faces a difficult tradeoff between enhancing its credibility, on the one hand, and exposing itself to liquidity crises, on the other. The existence of long-term (fixed-interest) domestic-currency-denominated (nominal) debt provides the government with some financing options that it does not have if its debt is short-term and denominated in foreign currency—that is, it can effectively repudiate the long-term debt by inflating or devaluing, thereby reducing the debt's real value. Given the nominal interest rate on this debt, it may indeed be sensible for a welfare-maximizing government to do so, since by acting in this way it would have the option of sustaining productive expenditures or reducing distortionary taxes. However, the prospect of the government exercising this option would raise domestic nominal interest rates, making it expensive for the government to borrow long-term in nominal terms. And even if the government never intends to behave in this fashion, the time inconsistency problem involved may make it very difficult for the government to convince its creditors of its honorable intentions. To reduce its borrowing costs, the government may therefore be induced to borrow short-term and in foreign currency. By doing so, it eschews the option of gaining from devaluation or inflation at the expense of its creditors, and thus enhances the credibility of its promise to do neither. The problem is, of course, that in doing so it incurs liquid foreign-currency-denominated liabilities, thereby making itself vulnerable to debt runs, as happened in the Mexican crisis, described in box 4.5.

The way out of this dilemma is to note when it arises in acute form—that is, when the government actually retains the discretion to act as creditors fear, when it lacks credibility on other grounds (for example, when it has a reputation for acting in a discretionary fashion), and when the government's revenue needs are high and conventional taxation is highly distortionary. In other words, the existence of long-term nominal debt is only one factor in the government's decision to devalue or inflate, and creditors can rationally expect the government to forgo the option of inflating away the real value of their assets if it is institutionally unable to do so, if it is perceived as placing a high value on the credibility of its policy announcements, or if inflating creates few net benefits from the government's perspective. Thus, the govern-

Box 4.5 The Mexican Tesobono Crisis

THROUGH A COMBINATION OF DEBT RESTRUCTURING, privatization, and a succession of overall fiscal surpluses, the Mexican government achieved a drastic reduction in its total stock of outstanding debt over the period from 1988 to 1994. By the beginning of 1994, the stock of Mexico's outstanding public sector amounted to about 30 percent of GDP, most of it in long-term, domestic-currency-denominated instruments. However, events during the first four months of 1994 (the Chiapas rebellion in January, the increase in U.S. interest rates beginning in February, and the assassination of presidential candidate Luis Donaldo Colosio in March), coupled with an ongoing and substantial real appreciation of the peso, created expectations of devaluation that dried up capital inflows and built a substantial devaluation premium into domestic interest rates. Since the current account deficit was quite large, the central bank incurred substantial reserve losses. The government responded by sterilizing the monetary impact of the reserve losses and reducing the cost of refinancing maturing government debt by issuing short-term dollar-denominated instruments (Tesobonos). The share of Tesobonos in Mexican government debt increased from 5 percent in January 1994 to almost 55 percent by January 1995. By the end of 1994, when the balance of payments crisis hit, the Mexican government faced payment obligations on the stock of Tesobonos amounting to $17 billion for the first six months of 1995.

This stock of obligations exceeded Mexico's foreign exchange reserves—$6 billion at the end of 1994—as well as credit lines of $8 billion available to the country under NAFTA (North American Free Trade Agreement) arrangements. Consequently, there was no prospect of repayment in the event of a debt run unless exceptional arrangements were made with official creditors. The events surrounding the balance of payments crisis in December, as well as the government's failure to put in place adequate exceptional arrangements until February of 1995, coordinated the expectations of creditors around the debt run equilibrium, and in the early weeks of 1995 the Mexican government proved unable to roll over its Tesobono debt. The effect was to transform a currency crisis into a broader crisis of confidence in macroeconomic policy, which required much stricter and more costly adjustment policies than most observers would have predicted as a result of the currency devaluation alone.

ment can avoid making its borrowing costs overly sensitive to the composition of its debt by creating institutions that limit its discretion (for example, by increasing the independence of the central bank), by establishing a reputation for nondiscretionary behavior, and by choosing levels of expenditure and mobilizing sources of taxation that minimize distortions.[19] Under these circumstances, the option to borrow long term in domestic currency terms may be retained, and the likelihood that macroeconomic stability will be impaired by runs on government debt would be minimized.

In sum, when financial integration is high, short-run fiscal flexibility is very important, since it provides an additional instrument for stabilizing domestic aggregate demand in response to external financial shocks, thereby freeing monetary or exchange rate policy to address other macroeconomic objectives. Moreover, a stable perception of fiscal solvency becomes crucial for preventing the domestic public sector itself from becoming an important source of macroeconomic shocks, transmitted through the terms on which creditors are willing to hold claims on the domestic economy. Indeed, the perception of public sector solvency may itself be the most important component in freeing up fiscal policy to play a short-run stabilizing role. Finally, under high financial integration, institutional arrangements that limit the government's ability to act in a discretionary fashion, or that enhance its incentives to avoid doing so, may preserve the government's access to low-cost long-term finance, thereby preventing the emergence of debt runs that could introduce an important source of macroeconomic instability even when the public sector is solvent.

Lessons for Macroeconomic Management

INCREASED FINANCIAL INTEGRATION IN DEVELOPING COUNTRIES has been driven in part by improvements in macroeconomic management. Continued good performance in this area will be crucial for many of these countries to retain the strong ties to world capital markets that they have forged over the last several years. In spite of the progress that has been made, however, integration continues to pose important macroeconomic challenges. In this chapter, we have considered three of these challenges: the possibility of overheating, particularly in the initial stock adjustment phase of financial opening up; the potential vulnerability of financially open economies to sharp reversals in capital flows; and the need to cope with new sources of macroeconomic volatility. To address these challenges, policymakers have four types of broad policy instruments at their disposal: controls on the free movement of capital, exchange rate policy, monetary policy, and fiscal policy. On the basis of experience, a successful strategy for addressing all three of these issues, using a combination of these tools, can be summarized as follows:

- The central component of good macroeconomic management under increased financial integration is the same as under financial autarky: responsible and flexible *fiscal management*. However, fiscal policy management becomes even more important under financial integration. Fiscal policy can be critical to avoiding overheating when capital inflows materialize, it can help to address the primary causes of vulnerability, and it can provide a valuable instrument to cope with volatility.

- While the avoidance of *overheating* implies relying on tight monetary policy as well as on fiscal policy if a country adheres to officially determined exchange rates, the monetary-fiscal mix seems to matter. Countries that rely more heavily on tight fiscal policy tend to generate a mix of absorption in response to capital inflows that favors investment over consumption and to generate both less real appreciation and smaller current account deficits. In the sample of countries examined in this chapter, the orientation toward investment was associated with faster economic growth.[20]
- This mix of macroeconomic outcomes was also associated with reduced *vulnerability* to the tequila effect that accompanied the Mexican crisis. Thus, an active fiscal policy may play an important role not only in securing the growth benefits of financial integration but also in reducing one of the dangers to which financially integrated countries can become exposed: vulnerability to external financial crisis.
- Finally, fiscal policy has an important analytical role to play in managing *volatility* more generally, for several reasons:
    - (a) Flexible fiscal policy provides a short-run stabilization instrument that reduces the incentive to restrict capital movements to stabilize the economy while using exchange rate policy to maintain competitiveness.
    - (b) Fiscal flexibility and solvency are likely to reduce the incidence of "incredible" reforms, which create distortion-induced cross-border capital flows.
    - (c) Fiscal flexibility is necessary to ensure that the equilibrium real exchange rate tracks the actual rate under exchange-rate-based stabilization in a world of high capital mobility.
    - (d) Under managed exchange rates, the availability of fiscal policy as a stabilization instrument determines the desirability of exchange-market intervention in response to domestic real shocks. It also determines the feasibility of simultaneously adjusting the level and composition of aggregate demand in response to "pure" external financial shocks.

(e) Because sterilized intervention has fiscal effects, the feasibility of this policy under imperfect capital mobility depends on whether these effects can be accommodated by fiscal policy.
(f) Sterilized intervention may also, through its effects on the stock of public sector debt, affect the perceived incentives facing the fiscal authorities. The consequences of this for domestic macroeconomic stability depend on the credibility of the authorities' announced fiscal stance.
(g) Perhaps most significant of all, fiscal policy affects the perception of public sector solvency. This may be the most important determinant of country risk, and thus of cross-border capital movements.
(h) Finally, even a solvent government may be vulnerable to debt runs if it issues a large stock of short-term foreign-currency-denominated debt. Retaining the option to borrow long-term in domestic currency requires that the government establish a reputation for nondiscretionary behavior and structure its expenditures and revenues so as to limit its perceived incentives for debt repudiation through devaluation or inflation.

- Another important policy lesson is that *exchange rate management* appears to remain possible under the degree of financial integration that developing countries have achieved up to this point. However, as in the case of fiscal policy, appropriate exchange rate management is particularly important when there is a high degree of financial integration. In particular, an active exchange rate policy that prevents the emergence of misalignment becomes crucial, particularly in avoiding vulnerability to external financial crises. This does not imply a loss of control over the domestic price level. The countries in our sample that have managed their exchange rate with the objective of maintaining competitiveness, thereby achieving a stable or depreciating real exchange rate, did not exhibit deteriorating inflation performance in the context of capital inflows. In short, a policy mix that relies on nominal exchange rate management to maintain competitiveness while placing significant weight on fiscal policy to achieve internal balance is fairly effective in both avoiding overheating and reducing vulnerability.
- If the nominal exchange rate is to be officially determined, then *monetary policy* will have a role in macroeconomic management

only if natural or policy-imposed barriers to capital movements remain strong enough to preserve some degree of monetary autonomy. The evidence to date suggests that they do, despite increased financial integration. Sterilized intervention therefore continues to be a feasible policy to preserve macroeconomic stability in response to cross-border capital flows. The flexibility of this policy has made it the instrument of choice for the majority of developing countries receiving capital inflows. These countries have sterilized aggressively and in a variety of ways, in a largely successful effort to prevent inflows from generating macroeconomic overheating. Use of this policy to control the economy is subject to many caveats, however. When potential arbitrage margins are large, for example, the sterilization of inflows may turn out to be so expensive that it impairs fiscal credibility, thus proving counterproductive, while the sterilization of outflows may provoke Mexican-style balance-of-payments crises. Even in less extreme circumstances, the domestic asset substitutability conditions necessary for sterilization to effectively stabilize aggregate demand are unlikely to be met, whatever form of sterilization is adopted. Thus, sterilization is, at best, an imperfect instrument for stabilizing domestic demand. And in the specific case of capital inflows, the evidence suggests that a policy mix which restrains demand with less weight on sterilization and more on restrictive fiscal policy has been more beneficial than one which does the opposite.

- Finally, the role of *restrictions on capital movements* as a tool for integrating countries to achieve stabilization needs to be carefully circumscribed. While capital controls have not been able to prevent large outflows or inflows in response to large prospective arbitrage profits, they have been found to be effective in the short term in reducing the magnitude and altering the composition of net capital inflows. The most compelling macroeconomic arguments for the use of controls are that they are second-best prudential regulations on the behavior of financial intermediaries, as discussed in the next chapter, and they are a transitional device to preserve an enhanced degree of monetary autonomy pending the reforms required to permit the use of fiscal policy as a stabilization instrument. However, in the longer term, both the effectiveness and the desirability of capital controls are questionable.

Regarding desirability, the central problem, of course, is that by restricting the degree of financial integration, controls limit the gains that can be derived from integration—if for no other reason than they create perceptions of an unfriendly environment. And as developing countries become more financially integrated, the evidence from industrial countries suggests that controls will lose effectiveness.

Annex 4.1

Table 4.7 Monetary and Fiscal Policies during Capital Inflow Episodes

(percent)

Country and indicator	*Inflow episode*	*Pre-inflow period*[a]	*Year during episode* 1	2	3	4	5	6	7	8
Argentina										
Growth of M2	1991–94	988.6	141.3	62.5	46.5	17.6				
Growth of monetary base		2,135.7	116.3	40.7	36.1	8.5				
Change in net foreign assets		—	18.0	121.3	30.7	0.2				
Change in domestic credit		—	98.3	-80.5	5.5	8.3				
Change in multiplier		12.0	11.6	15.5	7.6	8.4				
Central government balance		-5.6	-1.2	0.4	1.7	-0.5				
Inflation		1,467.0	171.7	24.9	10.6	4.2				
Brazil										
Growth of M2	1992–95	1,224.2	1,606.6	2,936.6	1,146.3	38.9				
Growth of monetary base		1,263.8	1,148.2	2,424.4	2,241.7	11.9				
Change in net foreign assets		726.7	1,763.0	5,017.1	2,019.9	57.4				
Change in domestic credit		537.1	-614.8	-2592.7	221.8	-45.5				
Change in multiplier		62.9	36.7	20.3	-46.8	24.1				
Central government balance		-1.1	-0.9	-0.1	1.6	-1.7				
Inflation		1,337.0	1,008.7	2,148.4	2,668.5	84.4				
Chile										
Growth of M2	1989–95	30.5	31.2	23.5	28.1	23.3	23.4	11.3	25.8	
Growth of monetary base		65.2	-3.3	58.3	22.6	16.2	14.6	21.9	15.8	
Change in net foreign assets		6.9	8.7	45.5	17.8	27.7	13.7	21.9	8.1	
Change in domestic credit		58.4	-12.0	12.8	4.8	-11.5	0.9	-0.1	7.6	
Change in multiplier		-12.0	35.6	-22.0	4.4	6.1	7.7	-8.6	8.7	
Central government balance		-1.4	6.1	3.5	2.5	3.0	2.2	2.2	3.9	
Inflation		20.3	17.0	26.0	21.8	15.4	12.7	11.4	8.2	
Colombia										
Growth of M2	1992–95	—	45.0	37.5	34.6	21.5				
Growth of monetary base		34.1	36.7	25.2	26.3	10.1				
Change in net foreign assets		43.8	63.4	17.5	5.6	27.9				
Change in domestic credit		-9.7	-26.7	7.7	20.7	-17.8				
Change in multiplier		—	6.1	9.8	6.6	10.3				
Central government balance		-0.9	-1.3	-0.3	-0.2	0.0				
Inflation		28.4	27.0	22.6	23.8	21.0				

(Table continues on the following page.)

Table 4.7 (continued)

Country and indicator	Inflow episode	Pre-inflow period[a]	Year during episode 1	2	3	4	5	6	7	8
Indonesia										
Growth of M2	1990–95	26.1	44.6	17.5	19.8	—	—	—		
Growth of monetary base		13.7	16.3	3.3	19.7	—	—	—		
Change in net foreign assets		16.1	58.1	62.3	76.6	—	—	—		
Change in domestic credit		-2.3	-41.8	-59.0	-56.9	—	—	—		
Change in multiplier		11.8	24.3	13.7	0.1	—	—	—		
Central government balance		-1.1	1.3	0.0	-1.2	-0.7	0.0	0.8		
Inflation		7.5	7.8	9.4	7.5	9.7	8.5	9.4		
Korea										
Growth of M2	1991–95	18.6	21.9	14.9	16.6	18.7	15.6			
Growth of monetary base		22.7	18.2	10.9	27.5	9.2	16.3			
Change in net foreign assets		22.4	-0.9	18.2	16.5	18.2	17.7			
Change in domestic credit		0.4	19.0	-7.3	11.0	-9.0	-1.5			
Change in multiplier		-1.9	3.1	3.6	-8.5	8.7	-0.6			
Central government balance		0.0	-1.6	-0.7	0.3	0.5	0.4			
Inflation		4.9	9.3	6.2	4.8	6.3	4.5			
Malaysia										
Growth of M2	1989–95	9.3	15.2	10.6	16.9	29.2	26.6	12.7	20.0	
Growth of monetary base		7.6	24.3	22.7	14.5	21.8	11.6	36.2	24.7	
Change in net foreign assets		13.3	27.9	36.3	18.9	80.7	115.5	-29.3	-11.5	
Change in domestic credit		-5.7	-3.6	-13.6	-4.4	-58.9	-103.9	65.5	36.1	
Change in multiplier		1.7	-7.3	-9.9	2.1	6.0	13.4	-17.3	-3.8	
Central government balance		-7.3	-3.2	-3.0	-2.5	-0.9	0.2	2.8	1.2	
Inflation		2.5	2.8	2.6	4.4	4.8	3.5	3.7	5.3	
Mexico										
Growth of M2	1989–94	63.6	115.9	75.8	49.3	22.8	14.5	21.7		
Growth of monetary base		47.9	10.2	35.3	27.8	14.4	10.4	21.2		
Change in net foreign assets		25.3	-0.3	30.2	75.8	16.6	49.3	-103.0		
Change in domestic credit		22.7	10.5	5.1	-48.0	-2.2	-38.9	124.2		
Change in multiplier		10.0	95.9	30.0	16.8	7.4	3.7	0.5		
Central government balance		-9.5	-5.0	-2.8	-0.2	1.6	0.4	-0.8		
Inflation		92.9	20.0	26.7	22.7	15.5	9.8	7.0		

Country and indicator	Inflow episode	Pre-inflow period[a]	Year during episode 1	2	3	4	5	6	7	8
Morocco										
Growth of M2	1990–95	12.9	21.5	16.8	9.3	7.9	10.2	7.0		
Growth of monetary base		13.6	24.3	24.8	-8.0	8.6	6.2	5.2		
Change in net foreign assets		3.1	43.8	23.9	16.3	15.1	11.0	-14.8		
Change in domestic credit		10.5	-19.5	0.9	-24.3	-6.5	-4.9	20.0		
Change in multiplier		-0.4	-2.3	-6.4	18.7	-0.6	3.8	1.8		
Central government balance		-6.6	-0.6	-1.0	-2.2	-2.1	-2.9	-5.0		
Inflation		6.2	6.9	8.0	5.7	5.2	5.1	6.1		
Philippines										
Growth of M2	1989–95	15.0	30.1	22.5	17.3	13.6	27.1	24.4	24.2	
Growth of monetary base		21.2	38.9	17.7	20.1	13.0	18.9	5.1	17.2	
Change in net foreign assets		-67.7	19.3	-33.7	63.7	44.8	42.1	19.2	13.9	
Change in domestic credit		88.9	19.6	51.3	-43.6	-31.8	-23.2	-14.1	3.3	
Change in multiplier		-4.1	-6.3	4.1	-2.3	0.5	6.9	18.4	6.0	
Central government balance		-3.2	-2.1	-3.5	-2.1	-1.2	-1.6	-1.6	-1.4	
Inflation		15.3	12.2	14.1	18.7	8.9	7.6	9.1	8.1	
Sri Lanka										
Growth of M2	1991–95	12.8	22.4	16.4	23.1	19.2	19.4			
Growth of monetary base		15.4	27.9	8.5	25.2	19.1	16.1			
Change in net foreign assets		-11.2	37.3	24.4	54.8	23.9	8.3			
Change in domestic credit		26.6	-9.5	-15.9	-29.7	-4.8	7.8			
Change in multiplier		-1.9	-4.2	7.3	-1.6	0.1	2.9			
Central government balance		-9.6	-9.8	-6.1	-7.1	-9.1	-8.8			
Inflation		10.7	12.2	11.4	11.7	8.4	7.7			
Thailand										
Growth of M2	1988–95	18.8	18.2	26.2	26.7	19.8	15.6	18.4	12.9	17.0
Growth of monetary base		11.2	14.9	16.9	18.6	13.3	17.9	16.1	14.5	22.6
Change in net foreign assets		5.6	48.4	74.6	62.5	56.2	35.1	44.3	38.1	51.8
Change in domestic credit		5.6	-33.6	-57.7	-43.9	-43.0	-17.3	-28.2	-23.6	-29.2
Change in multiplier		6.9	2.9	8.0	6.8	5.8	-1.9	1.9	-1.5	-4.5
Central government balance		-3.7	2.6	4.2	4.6	4.1	2.5	2.0	2.0	2.6
Inflation		6.1	3.8	5.4	6.0	5.7	4.1	3.4	5.2	5.7

(Table continues on the following page.)

Table 4.7 (continued)

Country and indicator	Inflow episode	Pre-inflow period[a]	Year during episode 1	2	3	4	5	6	7	8
Tunisia										
Growth of M2	1992–95	11.6	8.3	6.1	8.1	6.6				
Growth of monetary base		12.0	7.2	4.8	7.2	9.4				
Change in net foreign assets		9.4	10.6	2.5	37.4	6.3				
Change in domestic credit		2.5	−3.4	2.3	−30.1	3.1				
Change in multiplier		−0.2	1.1	1.3	0.8	−2.6				
Central government balance		−4.5	−2.4	−2.9	−2.7	−4.2				
Inflation		7.4	5.8	4.0	4.7	6.2				

— Not available.

Note: M2 refers to the sum of currency, demand deposits, time deposits, savings deposits, and foreign currency deposits (IFS, line 35). Domestic credit is calculated as the difference of the monetary base (IFS, line 14) and the central bank's net foreign assets (IFS, line 11 minus line 16c). Changes in net foreign assets and domestic credit are expressed as a percentage of the monetary base. The multiplier is defined as the ratio of M2 and the monetary base. Central government balance is expressed as a percentage of GDP. Inflation is based on consumer prices (IFS, line 64).

a. Denotes the period of equal length immediately preceding the capital inflow stage. Figures are averages of annual figures.

Source: IMF, *World Economic Outlook* data base; IMF, *International Financial Statistics* data base.

Annex 4.2 Can Sterilization Be Effective?

WHETHER STERILIZATION CAN WORK essentially depends on relative substitutability among assets, both between domestic and foreign interest-bearing assets and among different types of domestic assets. If domestic interest-bearing assets are perfect substitutes among themselves, then the issue of whether sterilization can work amounts to whether it is possible to prevent a change in demand for domestic interest-bearing assets from causing a change in their price through a suitable quantity response. Clearly, this will depend on the degree of substitutability between domestic and foreign interest-bearing assets. If they are close to perfect substitutes, then the quantity response would have to approach infinity to prevent a price response. This is what is typically meant by the impossibility of sterilization.

However, it is also possible for sterilization to be ineffective in preventing a change in the price of domestic assets even if foreign and domestic interest-bearing assets are imperfect substitutes. This is the case when domestic assets are imperfect substitutes among themselves and a capital inflow represents an increased demand for a particular type of domestic asset that the central bank cannot provide, either directly or indirectly. In this case, sterilized intervention that keeps the monetary base constant, by issuing an asset other than that demanded by the agents generating the capital inflow, could not prevent relative price adjustments among domestic assets as portfolio equilibrium is restored. If such price adjustments cannot be avoided, then it may not be feasible to insulate aggregate demand. For example, aggressive sterilization in Mexico did not prevent the arrival of capital inflows from being associated with a stock market boom. One interpretation of this experience is that external creditors wished to acquire equity in Mexican firms, while the sterilization instrument issued by the central bank consisted of claims on the Mexican government. In this case, the maintenance of portfolio equilibrium in the face of increased external demand for Mexican equities would have required higher equity prices in Mexico, even if the sterilization of capital inflows had been complete.

Because sterilization involves the issuance of additional domestic debt, and because its effectiveness depends on substitutability among domestic assets, the form that it takes may matter for both its effectiveness and its desirability. Capital-importing countries have used three alternative sterilization techniques:

- transferring public sector deposits out of the commercial banking system and into the central bank
- selling public sector bonds in secondary bond markets
- increasing the reserve requirements on domestic banks.

While these techniques share the common objective of stabilizing the domestic money supply, the analysis below suggests that their macroeconomic effects may be quite different.

Sterilization through transfers of public sector deposits. Consider the effect of a capital inflow triggered by a shift in private sector (domestic or foreign) preferences from foreign to domestic interest-bearing assets. To effect this portfolio reallocation, the private sector has to sell foreign exchange to the domestic central bank. When the public sector offsets a purchase of foreign exchange by transferring public sector deposits from commercial banks to the central bank, it leaves the stock of base money unchanged but exchanges a claim on the domestic banking system for an external claim. At the same time, the private sector changes its portfolio in the opposite direction.

There are two ways that the macroeconomic equilibrium can be affected by this transaction, even if the monetary base is unchanged. First, if interest-bearing deposits in the domestic banking system are imperfect substitutes in private portfolios for other domestic interest-bearing assets, then private portfolio equilibrium will be disturbed unless the domestic asset for which there is increased demand happens to be deposits in the domestic banking system. If that is the case, then the private sector and the government simply exchange claims on the banking system and there are no price implications to the transaction. But if it is not the case, then relative domestic asset prices will have to change to maintain portfolio equilibrium. If the initial asset shift was toward domestic securities, for instance, the yield on such securities would presumably have to fall and interest rates on bank assets and liabilities would have to rise.

The second effect is a fiscal one. To the extent that the yield on domestic deposits differs from the yield on foreign exchange reserves, the solvency of the domestic public sector will be affected by the transaction. In the particular case of sterilization through shifts in public sector deposits, the liquidity services provided by such deposits suggest that the public sector's net interest receipts could rise or fall as a result of the sterilization operation.

Sterilization through open market operations. Open market sterilized intervention requires the central bank to sell enough domestic bonds to purchase the foreign exchange associated with the inflow, thereby leaving the monetary base unchanged but increasing the stock of outstanding domestic public sector debt. The amount of new debt is therefore equal to the increase in demand for interest-bearing claims on the domestic economy. The effect of the transaction on the central bank's balance sheet is to leave its liabilities (the base) unchanged, but to change the composition of its assets, reducing its claims on the domestic government and increasing its international reserves. From the standpoint of the nonfinancial public sector as a whole, sterilized intervention amounts to a portfolio transaction in which the domestic nonfinancial public sector issues interest-bearing debt denominated in domestic currency in order to acquire a foreign interest-bearing claim.

Sterilized intervention through open market operations is not likely to be costless, however. The portfolio reallocation implied for the public sector involves issuing a high-yielding liability (domestic currency debt) in exchange for a lower-yielding asset (international reserves). This interest differential leaves the public sector in a weakened financial position.[21] The net adverse effect of such transactions on the public sector's solvency is overstated by the interest differential, however, because this differential presumably exists in part to compensate creditors for the currency and country risk associated with holding domestic public debt. By issuing such debt in exchange for reserves, the public sector is receiving a benefit that partly offsets the interest penalty—that is, the option to reduce the real value of its obligations by devaluing or defaulting. Nonetheless, these benefits may be worthless to a government that never intends to exercise these options (but is unable to convince its creditors of this fact). In this case, sterilized intervention carries a fiscal burden, the cost of which depends on the ease with which an offsetting fiscal adjustment can be effected.

As in the previous case, the conditions required for sterilization through open market operations to be effective in insulating the domestic economy are that domestic interest-bearing assets must be perfect substitutes among themselves or, if they are not, that sterilization operations must be capable of supplying precisely those assets that are in increased demand.

Sterilization through restrictions on domestic credit growth. Sterilized intervention through transfers of public sector deposits and open market bond sales operates by fixing the size of the monetary base. An alternative is to allow the base to expand as a result of central bank intervention in the foreign exchange market, but to restrict expansion of the money supply by raising reserve requirements on banks, thus causing the money multiplier to contract.

Again, the objective is to fix the price of domestic interest-bearing assets in the face of an increase in the demand for such assets. From a portfolio allocation perspective, this policy works, in principle, by having the private sector rather than the central bank issue the domestic interest-bearing assets that are in increased demand. When commercial banks face higher reserve requirements, they are forced to absorb the additional monetary base emitted by the central bank in the course of its foreign exchange operations, rather than acquire domestic interest-bearing assets in the form of credit extended to domestic agents. The contraction of credit on the part of commercial banks causes domestic agents who would otherwise have borrowed from these banks to instead issue securities. Since these securities are precisely the assets that are in increased demand by the nonbank public, the supply of domestic interest-bearing assets expands to meet demand, so there is no change in the price of such assets.

However, bank borrowers squeezed out of credit markets by higher reserve requirements may not have access to securities markets and thus may be unable to supply the assets that are in higher demand. An extensive literature on precisely this problem for the United States claims that because of asymmetric information, borrowers with low net worth who lack other forms of collateral are able to obtain credit only from institutions that are highly specialized in evaluating and monitoring loans (banks). Such borrowers cannot securitize their liabilities. If this is the case, then there is a prima facie case for imperfect substitutability among the relevant domestic assets when sterilization is pursued through a policy of altering reserve requirements, suggesting that insulation of the domestic economy is less likely to be achieved under this policy than through open market operations.[22]

An additional difference between sterilization through restrictions on domestic credit and through open market operations is fiscal cost. In the case of domestic credit restriction, the public sector still acquires interest-bearing foreign assets but does so by emitting noninterest-bearing liabilities (that is, the monetary base). Thus, the public sector's fiscal situation actually improves when sterilization is effected by increasing reserve requirements. This approach, however, implicitly taxes private agents. The requirement that banks hold a larger stock of noninterest-bearing reserves imposes an explicit tax on them, which must be apportioned in some way among bank depositors, borrowers, and shareholders. The incidence of the tax will depend on the elasticity of supply of bank deposits, as well as on the demand for bank loans.

Notes

1. Costa Rica has been receiving large amounts of capital relative to the size of its economy at least since the mid-1970s.

2. In principle, causation can run both ways between private and official flows.

3. Econometric tests conducted for Chile and Indonesia as part of this study are consistent with essentially full sterilization of changes in net foreign assets during the recent capital inflow episodes in these countries.

4. Several countries exhibit a pattern in which growth of the base accelerates sharply when inflows begin to arrive, then decelerates as sterilization is implemented. Examples are Chile in 1990–92, Indonesia in 1990–91, Korea in 1991–92, and the Philippines in 1991–92.

5. In Chile, while the increase in net private inflows was offset on average by a decline in official flows, improvement in the current account balance led to a large overall balance-of-payments surplus and hence upward pressure on the money supply.

6. More recently, there may have been some buildup of inflationary pressures in those countries that received the most flows in East Asia: Indonesia, Malaysia, and Thailand.

7. This abstracts from changes in net factor income and net current transfers.

8. While it may be natural to interpret causation as running from investment to growth, the two other logical alternatives (from growth to investment and both reflecting the influence of a third variable) are also plausible.

9. While it may seem odd to include Mexico, recall that the objective is to identify the fundamentals associated with vulnerability, not to determine spillover effects.

10. While Chile experienced real appreciation during 1988–93, its real exchange rate during 1989–94 was more depreciated than during the preceding six-year period, as indicated in table 4.4.

11. The debt-export ratio can be interpreted as an indicator of past fiscal policies as well as of future fiscal constraints.

12. In contrast to the issues of overheating and vulnerability, the management of capital account volatility cannot readily be analyzed by reviewing country experience—at least not the experience of developing countries, which has been dominated by one-way flows associated with the process of integration itself (inflows) and the recent Mexican crisis (outflows). Thus this section relies heavily on analytical principles and related empirical work.

13. Strictly speaking, this is a domestic rather than an external financial shock, but it has an important external dimension.

14. The lack of fiscal flexibility has been cited as an important motivation for the adoption of capital controls in Chile, whose central bank has simultaneously pursued inflation and real exchange rate targets since 1985.

15. The main advantage of a currency board is its positive effect on the credibility of the government's commitment to low inflation (for a more detailed discussion see annex 5.4 in chapter 5).

16. This does not rule out using the exchange rate as a nominal anchor for stabilization purposes in a world of high capital mobility. Doing so without restricting capital movements, however, requires that fiscal policy be capable of adjusting the fundamentals that determine the equilibrium real exchange rate in such a way as to cause the equilibrium real exchange rate to track the actual rate implied by the nominal exchange rate rule and any remaining inertial inflation.

17. The fiscal cost of sterilization arises from the gap between the interest rate on domestic public sector (government or central bank) liabilities and that on reserve assets. This has been estimated at about 1 percent of GDP for

Chile, Colombia, and Indonesia during periods of heavy sterilization. (Peak costs of sterilization have also approached this value in Malaysia.)

18. Instances of procyclical fiscal policy are most evident in countries subject to long terms-of-trade shocks. Nigeria and Venezuela, two countries in which oil revenues loom large in public sector budgets, provide vivid illustration of the problem.

19. When credibility problems become extreme, the government's financing problems may become severe enough to warrant the adoption of institutional devices that will improve credibility but may greatly circumscribe the government's freedom of action—that is, adopting a currency board or joining a currency union. The position taken previously in this chapter that such arrangements are not necessarily mandated in a highly financially integrated environment reflects the judgment that most countries have not faced such severe credibility problems in recent years.

20. While the possibility is not explicitly examined here, it is also likely that a policy mix emphasizing tight fiscal policy would have exerted feedback effects that would moderate the pace of capital inflows by keeping domestic interest rates lower than they would have been otherwise.

21. Calvo (1990) has argued that the weakening of the government's financial position creates an incentive for it to inflate. The extent to which this is so depends on the currency denomination of the debt as well as on the properties of the government's loss function.

22. For evidence on similar segmentation in Latin American credit markets, see Rodríguez (1994). Chinn and Dooley (1995) provide similar evidence of segmentation in the bank credit markets of East Asian developing countries.

CHAPTER 5

The Effects of Integration on Domestic Financial Systems

THE BANKING SYSTEM PLAYS A LEADING ROLE IN THE process of financial integration and is one of the main channels through which the benefits of integration materialize. This is so because banks dominate financial intermediation in developing countries (table 5.1) and therefore they end up directly or indirectly intermediating a large proportion of private flows. Since an increasing share of private flows is being used by the private—as opposed to the public—sector in recipient countries, banks are increasingly responsible for its allocation. In addition, as discussed in chapter 3, in the medium and long term, banks in developing countries can benefit from financial integration by adopting more advanced financial technologies, achieving greater diversification in their portfolios, having access to a larger supply of funds, and realizing efficiency gains derived from economies of scale and scope and a higher degree of market competition.

However, the transition toward greater financial integration also involves risks for the economy in general (chapter 1) and the banking sector in particular. During the process of financial integration banks will be adversely affected by increased macroeconomic volatility and by structural changes in banking. The main structural changes affecting the banking sector that result from integration are an increase in competition, which can erode banks' worth, and exposure to new sources of risk that banks may not be prepared to manage properly.[1] Because conditions can change more swiftly and markets can react faster and with increased amounts of funds, the room for maneuver available to policymakers is significantly reduced in an integrated environment. The weaker the initial conditions in the banking sector—and in the macro-

Table 5.1 Indicators of Financial Intermediation, Selected Countries

	Percentage of GDP				*Bank intermediation ratio, 1994*[b]
	Securities outstanding[a]		*Deposit money bank assets*		
	1990	*1994*	*1990*	*1994*	
Asia					
India	35.0	93.4	41.7	45.3	80
Indonesia	13.5	32.6	62.3	64.9	91
Korea	91.4	105.4	64.6	72.3	38
Malaysia	196.5	352.6	95.8	104.6	64
Taiwan (China)	83.2	134.7	148.5	196.0	80
Thailand	37.8	113.8	78.3	106.8	75
Latin America					
Argentina	9.4	30.4[c]	29.3	26.1	98
Brazil	11.9	66.6	68.2	64.0	97
Chile	54.5	155.8	52.2	52.8	62
Colombia	22.8	34.4	23.7	27.8	86
Mexico	44.6	73.9	30.8	47.1	87
Venezuela	22.4	18.2	29.3	27.0	92
Industrial nations					
Germany[d]	88.9	132.7	149.1	152.0	77
Japan	189.5	178.2	164.1	156.8	47
United States	203.7	244.5	87.0	74.4	23

a. This includes, where available, short-term money market instruments, government bonds, corporate bonds, and equities at market value.

b. This is the ratio of the banking sector's assets to the assets of all financial institutions. Nonbank financial institutions are broadly defined to include insurance companies, investment funds, finance companies, and so on. The definitions, however, tend to vary somewhat from country to country.

c. This figure is for 1993.

d. The banking sector in Germany is larger than in other countries because of the universal banking system adopted in this country.

Source: BIS (1996); IMF, *International Financial Statistics* data base; World Bank data.

economy—are in integrating economies, the greater the challenge for policymakers. One of these challenges arises because during integration banks are given easier access to funds and are therefore able to expand lending much more quickly, so they can finance a longer-lasting boom in expenditures and asset prices. If initial conditions in the banking sector are weak, banks are likely to extend credit in excess and to more risky sectors.

The process of financial integration is usually accompanied in its early stages by a surge in private flows that may increase bank lending and exacerbate macroeconomic and financial sector vulnerability. The surge in private inflows is partly due to improved economic prospects in the recipient country, which, in turn, will increase economic agents' expectations. The inflows also often finance a rapid expansion in bank lending and aggregate expenditures, accelerating economic growth and validating agents' expectations, and cause an increase in asset prices. These effects can reinforce one another, leading to additional borrowing, higher expectations and output growth, and increased levels of expenditures and asset prices (chapter 1). In developing countries with weak infrastructure and regulatory institutions in banking—a common condition in many emerging economies—the surge in bank lending and the rise in asset prices will be associated with a deterioration in banks' portfolios. Poorly managed and supervised banks will tend to invest in highly profitable although risky activities. For example, poorly regulated banks may finance consumption booms and speculative activities, such as a boom in construction and real estate, that increase macroeconomic vulnerability. Also, because of poorly diversified portfolios and lack of adequate provisioning, the surge in bank lending usually exacerbates financial sector vulnerabilities. This chain of events is potentially costly not only because of resource misallocation but also because in the extreme it can lead to financial distress and crisis.

An integrating economy is more likely than an autarkic one to experience a boom-bust cycle in bank lending, and the potential cost associated with such a course is higher. This is so because, as argued earlier, in an integrated environment banks can expand lending more quickly and in larger amounts, circumstances can change more swiftly, and markets react faster. All these factors can lead to swift changes in market sentiment and cause large reversals of flows, creating significant macroeconomic and financial sector distress and carrying high economic and social costs. In addition to the direct costs of bailing out failed banks, the sudden loss of liquidity in the banking sector, which is more difficult to contain in an integrated environment, can amplify economic downturns. Such distress can set back economic reforms severely, as was the case with several Latin American countries following the debt crisis of 1982.

An important challenge, therefore, is for a country to maintain or improve the health of its banking system. Doing so will determine to a large extent whether it is able to realize the benefits of financial integration and avoid its pitfalls.

To distill lessons for financial sector reform in the face of growing integration, this chapter looks at the role that banking systems have played in the process of financial integration, and how they have, in turn, been affected by this process. It draws on the experience of a wide range of country episodes during the 1980s and 1990s, periods when these countries received substantial capital inflows as a result of integration. The episodes studied here are historical and do not reflect current country conditions. The sample analyzed here differs from that used in chapter 4 in that it includes both industrial and developing countries, and in the case of some developing countries more than one episode is studied.[2] The purpose of using this sample is to highlight the role of the banking sector in the process of financial integration. A detailed description of the sample of country episodes is provided in annex 5.1.

A number of important conclusions emerge from this wide-ranging country experience:

- First, countries that received substantial capital inflows as part of the process of financial integration also typically experienced a lending boom, reflecting higher levels of direct and indirect intermediation of capital flows by the banking system.
- Second, countries in which the lending booms were greater and in which no compensatory macroeconomic policies were implemented typically experienced a significant increase in macroeconomic vulnerability, as indicated by a widening of the current account deficit above what one would expect on the basis of the size of the inflows, relatively large consumption booms, and relatively small investment booms—relative to the size of the inflows.
- Third, lending booms were often associated with an increase in financial sector vulnerability despite the fact that booms tended to improve bank profitability in the short term.
- Fourth, countries in which lending booms were associated with an increase in *both* macroeconomic and financial sector vulnerabilities typically experienced banking crises.
- Fifth, countries that took actions to restrain the lending boom, or pursued prudent macroeconomic policies, fared well and avoided major crises.

Based on these findings, the chapter draws the following main policy conclusions:

- Extremely weak initial conditions in both the macroeconomy and the financial sector may warrant a cautious approach toward external financial liberalization.

- Financial integration makes it imperative for countries to move aggressively to create a prudent incentive and institutional framework for their banking systems. Given the larger volume of funds that is intermediated during the early stages of financial integration, and the greater risks of vulnerability from the increased magnitude and speed of market reaction, countries should move forward in implementing policies aimed at strengthening the supervision and prudential regulation of banks.
- A strong macroeconomic stance, and especially a strong fiscal position, can help prevent or postpone financial sector distress.
- Because of the high costs of a banking crisis (box 5.1), and the time needed to improve the macroeconomic position and strengthen the banking system, a strong case can be made for containing lending booms associated with the early stages of financial integration. This would help mitigate an increase in macroeconomic and financial sector vulnerabilities associated with large lending booms, especially when macroeconomic and financial sector conditions are weak.
- Finally, given the increased susceptibility to banking crises, countries should put in place mechanisms that enable policymakers to deal with such crises promptly and effectively. Delaying the actions necessary to contain a crisis will only increase its costs.

The rest of the chapter is organized in three sections. We first examine the extent to which the surge in private capital flows following the opening of the capital account causes an increase in bank lending, and how the lending boom exacerbates macroeconomic vulnerability. We then analyze the reasons for increased vulnerability of the banking sector following a surge in capital flows and the subsequent lending boom. Next, we integrate the analysis of the two previous sections by comparing the changes in macroeconomic and financial sector vulnerabilities in countries that have experienced banking crises with those that have not, and summarize the major policy lessons relevant for countries undergoing financial sector reforms along with integration. These lessons extend previous work on financial sector reform by adding the factor of integration, which makes financial sector reform significantly more complicated. The discussion ends with an analysis of the most effective measures for managing a banking crisis in an integrated environment.

Box 5.1 The Costs of Banking Crises

POLICYMAKERS MUST BE CONCERNED ABOUT banking crises because these crises are costly in terms of lower economic growth, and the political consequences of allocating losses among bank stockholders, creditors, depositors, and taxpayers can be significant. It is important to note, however, that the direct economic cost of a banking crisis derives from the decrease in economic activity and growth that results from a reduction in the total volume—or a more inefficient intermediation—of loanable funds, while the allocation of losses has primarily distribution effects (usually very important) but on its own does not imply an economic (deadweight) loss. Nevertheless, the allocation of losses is important because it changes the incentives of the different groups of economic agents and, through this, can lead to lower investment and growth. For example, forcing the corporate sector to repay its past-due loans, although it may be fair practice (depending on the primary cause of the sector's financial difficulties), may be counterproductive for the purpose of facilitating the economic recovery.[1] Indeed, in the presence of a debt overhang problem entrepreneurs may decide not to start new—or to discontinue old—investment projects, because from a private point of view it may not be worth investing in projects whose profits will benefit the firm's creditors (banks). Similarly, allowing banks to recover their losses by increasing spreads—thereby taxing depositors and debtors in good standing—will reduce the volume of funds intermediated through the banking system and may lead to lower investment and growth.

Quantifying the economic losses associated with a banking crisis is a cumbersome task, mainly because it is not clear how to separate the decrease in economic activity due to the banking crisis per se from that which is due to other exogenous factors (such as a terms of trade shock). In fact, a banking crisis may result from a decrease in economic activity caused by other factors, with the banking sector playing a key role in amplifying the effect of the exogenous shock on aggregate output. Figure A shows the average output growth for the precrisis, crisis, and postcrisis years for country episodes where a banking crisis occurred. Although the decline in economic growth overstates the cost of banking crises, the magnitude of the decline suggests that these costs are significant.[2] The country episodes shown in the figure experienced, on average, a positive growth of about 5 percent a year in the precrisis period, and slightly negative economic growth in the crisis and postcrisis years, implying a decrease in output growth of about 5.2 percent per year.

The allocation of losses, often used as a measure of the cost of banking crises, is also quite significant. Figure B shows the cost of restructuring banking systems after the crisis, measured by loans from the central bank to commercial banks and other rescuing measures, for some of the countries in our sample. The average cost for the episodes shown is about 10 percent of GDP and 23 percent of total loans. These figures appear strikingly high when compared with the cost of the savings and loan restructuring program in the United States, which by 1991 had reached 5.1 and 7.8 percent of GDP and total loans, respectively (Rojas-Suárez and Weisbrod 1996; see also Goldstein and Turner 1996).

1. If the ultimate cause of the banking crisis is the implementation of "wrong" economic policies by the authorities, then it can be argued that the corporate sector is not fully responsible for defaulting on its debt.

2. In addition to overstating the cost of crises because of the difficulty in separating other exogenous factors that reduce output growth, the figure overstates these costs by implicitly assuming that growth in the precrisis (boom) period is normal.

Box Figure 5.1 Costs of Banking Crises

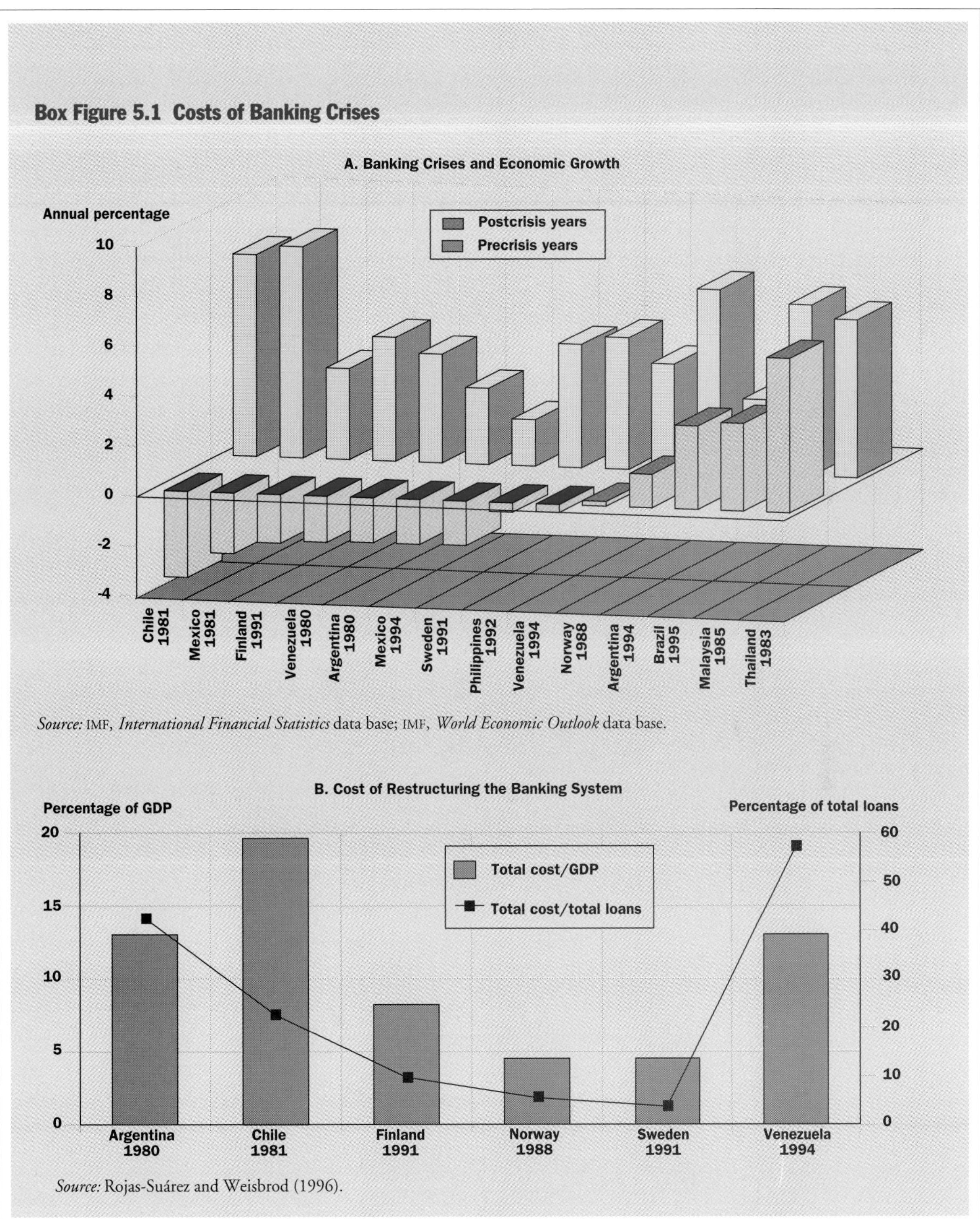

Source: IMF, *International Financial Statistics* data base; IMF, *World Economic Outlook* data base.

Source: Rojas-Suárez and Weisbrod (1996).

Bank Lending and Macroeconomic Vulnerability

THIS SECTION FOCUSES ON THE INTERACTION BETWEEN capital flows and bank lending. We explore the role of bank lending in propagating and amplifying the effects of international financial integration on macroeconomic variables. In particular, we focus on how bank lending can make the economy vulnerable to shocks that can affect market sentiment toward a country and ultimately trigger a banking—and sometimes a balance-of-payments—crisis. We begin with a general discussion of the role of banks in the macroeconomy in which we highlight the interaction between bank credit and capital flows. Next, the section looks at the problems a number of countries have experienced as they become more financially integrated.

The Role of Banks in the Macroeconomy

Financial intermediaries play a crucial role in the process of economic development and growth by channeling savers' money to more productive uses in an economy; they do this by screening and selecting investment projects and transforming assets, usually from short-term deposits to long-term investments, but more generally from illiquid to liquid assets.[3] The fact that banks overcome informational problems between lenders and borrowers and facilitate the creation of liquidity makes them vulnerable to confidence crises and, therefore, susceptible to runs and liquidity crises (Diamond 1984, Diamond and Dybvig 1983, Ramakrishnan and Thakor 1984).

There has been extensive research on the role of the banking sector in the macroeconomy and its importance in propagating and amplifying business cycles; it has led to the conclusion that bank credit, and not just monetary balances, affects macroeconomic performance—far beyond what standard macroeconomic models suggest.[4]

Past studies have asserted that the banking sector amplifies the magnitude of the business cycle because bank credit behaves procyclically. For example, a positive development in the real sector that raises expectations about the future will increase firms' willingness to invest, induce them to borrow more, and cause an expansion in bank credit. This process, if accommodated by the monetary authorities, will lead to a lending boom, which, in turn, will enable market participants to increase their level of expenditure and will accelerate economic growth. The increase in economic growth reinforces the expansion of lending and spending by validating economic agents' expectations about the future. The state of euphoria triggered by the initial increase in spending also leads to an increase in asset prices and financial wealth, which raises the value of loan collateral, increases households' aggregate consumption, and further reinforces the process. At the same time, however, the economy as a whole becomes more vulnerable because of the increase in indebtedness of firms and households and the risk of a collapse in asset prices. A plunge in asset prices would reduce borrowers' financial wealth and thereby affect the financial health of banks. A shock that reduces economic growth, or that leads agents to believe that the current conditions are no longer sustainable, will induce agents to cut their spending on consumption and investment and thereby will slow economic growth. Firms and households will then have difficulty servicing their debts, banks will start calling loans back in and liquidating the assets used as collateral, and asset prices will plunge, all of which will deepen the slowdown in economic activity. Because the banking system is vulnerable to confidence crises, this sequence of events may lead to a bank run, further reducing total credit and liquidity and aggravating the slowdown in economic activity.[5]

In addition to amplifying the magnitude of the business cycle, a poorly regulated and supervised banking industry will tend to misallocate resources, increasing the economic cost of the boom-bust cycle in bank lending. Poorly capitalized and regulated banks may, for instance, invest excessively in risky projects, such as real estate, or in other sectors prone to suffer boom-bust cycles. Also, poorly managed banks operating under distorted incentives will not diversify their portfolios adequately, thus exacerbating financial sector vulnerability. These banks will suffer greater losses during the contractionary phase of the cycle. The weaker initial conditions in the banking sector are, the more vulnerable countries will be to large downturns and costly banking crises.

In an integrated environment these effects can become even more pronounced (for a review of recent developments in the literature see box 5.2). This is so for several reasons. First, integration gives banks access to a larger supply of funds to intermediate, either directly or indirectly, which allows them to increase credit rapidly.[6] Second, financial integration usually occurs with the implementation of economic re-

Box 5.2 International Financial Integration and Boom-Bust Cycles

DESPITE THE EXTENSIVE LITERATURE DOCUMENTING BOOM-bust cycles in bank lending and the associated fluctuations in economic activity, these issues have only recently been investigated in the context of the financial integration process. In general, the conclusions that emerge from reviewing this literature appear to be straightforward. First, although the presence of foreign credit may result in larger cyclical fluctuations than could otherwise occur, it is the domestic banking sector that amplifies the magnitude of the macroeconomic cycle. And second, the domestic banking sector exacerbates the vulnerabilities in the emerging economies.

For example, in a recent paper Sachs, Tornell, and Velasco (1996) conclude that the impact of the Mexican peso crisis of December 1994 on other emerging economies—the so-called tequila effect—can be partly explained by the level of private sector debt held by the countries' banking systems. In other words, developing countries in which bank credit was growing rapidly during the surge in private flows in the early 1990s were more vulnerable to the shocks of the Mexican crisis. Similarly, recent work by Kaminsky and Reinhart (1996) and Hausmann and Gavin (1995) provides empirical evidence that the boom-bust cycles in domestic bank credit, asset prices, and economic activity resemble and precede those in the external accounts. This confirms that in financially integrated economies the domestic banking sector plays an important role in amplifying cyclical swings. Finally, Goldfajn and Valdés (1996) use a theoretical model to show that in a financially integrated economy the existence of a domestic banking system exacerbates capital movements from abroad and, therefore, amplifies the magnitude of external shocks.

forms—in the financial sector, the real economy (trade, fiscal), or both—that improve the country's economic prospects and raise agents' expectations. Third, integration increases the sources of risk and the speed of market reaction.

The first two reasons above, the implementation of economic reforms and the easier access to funds, create the necessary conditions for a lending boom to start. In particular, the surge in private flows that usually accompanies financial integration provides the additional resources needed to finance an increase in aggregate demand and output, validating agents' expectations. Given the size of the capital inflows for the average recipient country observed in recent years, the potential for experiencing a large increase in asset prices and a lending boom—one lasting several years—is faster in an integrated environment.

The third reason above, the increased sources of risk and speed of market reaction, makes it more likely that a banking industry operating under suboptimal conditions—a common occurrence among developing countries—will misallocate resources, exacerbating the country's macroeconomic and financial sector vulnerabilities. In particular, if an increasing amount of funds flowing into a country is intermediated by an undercapitalized and poorly regulated banking sector, one that is too prone to risk taking, the economy is likely to end up investing either insufficiently or in risky projects. This could be the case if the banking sector finances a consumption and imports boom, which in turn will make the economy more vulnerable to shocks. Because of the additional sources of risks and faster market response, the likelihood and the cost of a banking crisis increase with integration.

Capital Inflows, Bank Credit, and Macroeconomic Vulnerability: Country Experiences

A lending boom has usually accompanied a surge in private capital flows in countries that have recently undergone financial integration. Figure 5.1 shows the ratio of bank lending to the private sector as a share of GDP, in the years prior to and during the surge in capital inflows for a number of countries in the 1980s and 1990s. In all except two episodes in the sample (Chile and Venezuela in the 1990s), the share of bank lending to GDP was higher in the inflow periods than in the years prior to the inflow. For all countries and all episodes taken together, the average lending-to-GDP ratio during the years prior to the inflow surge was 29.4 percent. During the inflow periods, the average lending-to-GDP ratio was 40.9 percent.

As the analysis in the previous section suggests, countries in which the banking sector intermediates proportionately larger inflows will probably become more vulnerable to macroeconomic shocks. To illustrate this issue, we can look at the experience of countries that in recent years have received significant capital inflows while becoming more integrated. For all the countries in our sample the evidence suggests that the current account deficit, on average, increased during periods of

Figure 5.1 Bank Lending to the Private Sector during Inflow and Pre-inflow Periods, Selected Countries and Years
(as a percentage of GDP)

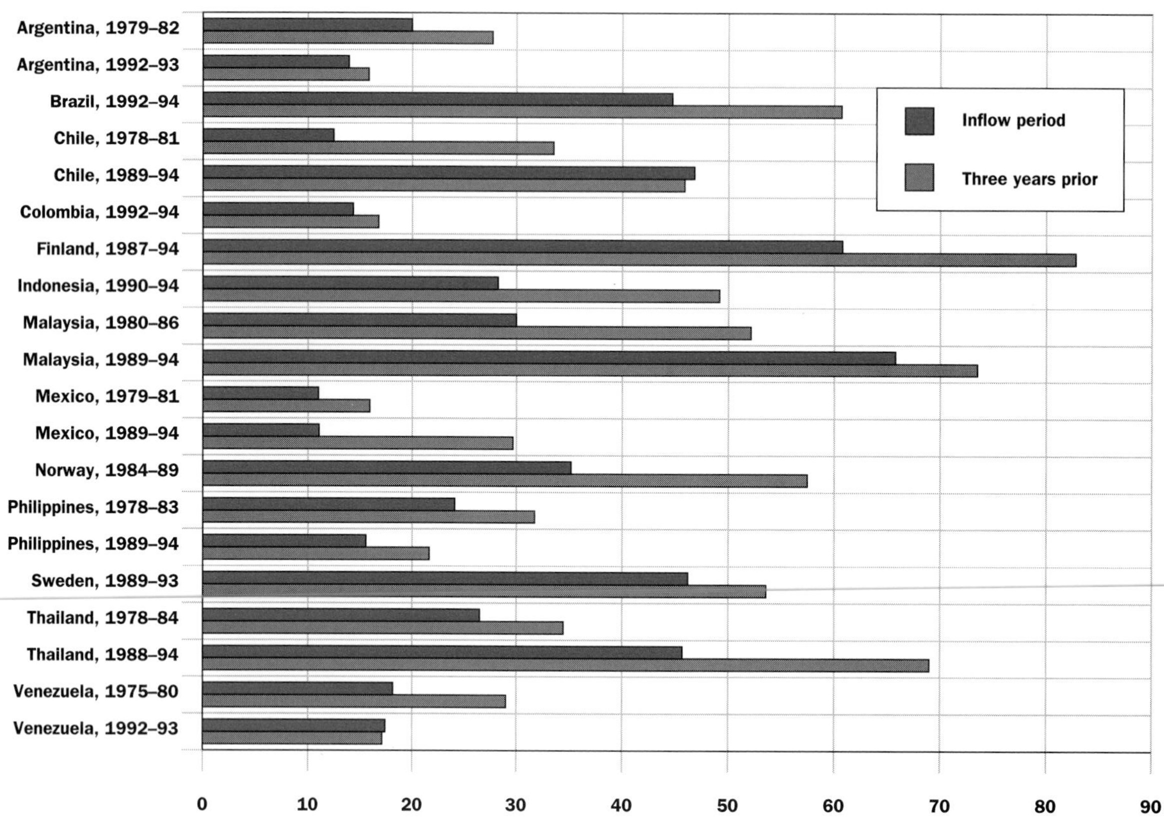

Source: IMF, *International Financial Statistics* data base.

During periods of large capital inflows, bank lending to the private sector has surged.

high capital inflows, and that the increase was, in general, proportionally larger in those country episodes where bank and nonbank credit to the private sector grew more during the inflow period. Conversely, the current account deficit was proportionally smaller, given the size of the capital inflow, in those country episodes that saw a smaller expansion in bank and nonbank credit (box 5.3). While several policies can affect the level of the real exchange rate (chapter 4), the country episodes in our sample that show the greatest real exchange rate appreciation are also, in general, the ones in which bank credit grew more.[7]

The banking sector plays a leading role in the allocation of loanable funds among economic sectors, and is partly responsible for the overheating and increased macroeconomic vulnerability that may result from the surge in private capital flows. The challenge for policymakers, then, is to control the effects of private capital inflows, which can finance an increase in either aggregate investment or consumption, or both. Although an increase in investment does not guarantee a higher rate of economic growth, it is certainly preferable to an increase in aggregate consumption, which is more likely to lead to an overheating of the economy and, in the extreme, can affect the market sentiment toward the country.

In countries that have recently become more financially integrated, inflows of foreign capital have been used to finance an increase in both investment and private consumption. There was a positive association between investment and capital inflows, and in a number of the episodes in our sample, the increase in investment was smaller than that predicted by the size of the inflows. This result usually occurred in those episodes where the increase in bank and nonbank lending was among the largest. Similarly, the increase in private consumption was also proportionally larger, given the size of the capital inflow, among the episodes that had the largest increase in bank and nonbank lending (box 5.4). It is important to note that the majority of the episodes where bank and nonbank lending grew the most ended in banking crises. The conclusion to be drawn here is that one of the ways in which a poor bank intermediation process can exacerbate macroeconomic vulnerability, in the context of increased financial integration, is by biasing the increase in aggregate expenditures that would result from an increase in capital inflows toward consumption instead of investment.

The discussion above suggests several things:

- First, countries experiencing a surge in private capital inflows often also experience a lending boom, but the magnitude of the boom varies significantly among them.
- Second, countries experiencing the highest increase in bank and nonbank lending are usually those in which macroeconomic vulnerabilities—measured by the increase in the current account deficit, excess consumption, and underinvestment—are exacerbated the most.
- Third, countries with the largest lending booms during an inflow episode usually later experience a banking crisis.[8] This implies that a rapid growth in bank lending should be avoided, or at least watched closely by the economic authorities in emerging countries, especially when conditions in the banking sector are weak.

Box 5.3 Excessive Bank Lending Tends to Increase the Current Account Deficit

THE EXPERIENCE OF THE COUNTRY EPISODES IN our sample shows that, as expected, the current account deficit, on average, increased during periods of high capital inflows (figure A). More important, figure B below shows that, in general, the increase in the current account deficit was proportionally larger, given the size of the capital inflow, in those country episodes where bank and nonbank credit to the private sector grew more during the inflow period (the measure of "proportionality" is indicated by the solid line in figure B). Countries such as Chile (1978–81), Malaysia (1980–86), Mexico (1979–81 and 1989–94), the Philippines (1978–83 and 1989–94), and Sweden (1989–93) exhibited larger current account deficits than expected, given the size of the inflows they received. These countries also experienced a larger increase in bank lending than the remaining country episodes in the sample. The average excess deficit ratio (that is, the ratio of the actual current account deficit to that predicted by the size of the inflows) for the country episodes mentioned above was about 1.3, and the average growth in bank lending was more than four times the growth in GDP. For the rest of the country episodes shown in figure B the average deficit ratio was 0.74, while the average lending growth was only two and a half times the growth in GDP.

To summarize, figure B seems to indicate that the countries that exhibited the largest current account deficits following the surge in inflows were those that experienced the largest increases in bank lending proportional to GDP. In particular, for the sample of country episodes shown in the figures it follows that an increase in private capital flows of, say, 10 percentage points of GDP leads to a worsening in the current account balance of about 3.2 percentage points of GDP, on average. Nevertheless, the latter increases to about 4.9 percentage points of GDP (an increase of about 50 percent) for those countries that experienced an increase in bank lending above the sample average. This result follows from the following regression:

$$\underset{}{cad} = \underset{(2.95)}{1.91} + \underset{(2.43)}{0.324}{}^{*}\,kaflow + \underset{(1.46)}{0.17}{}^{*}(kaflow^{*}dbank)$$

where *cad* is the current account deficit (as a share of GDP), *kaflow* is the share of private flows to GDP, *dbank* is a dummy that equals 1 for those country inflow episodes where the increase in bank lending exceeded the sample average (*t*-statistics are in parentheses; note that the coefficient on the interactive term is significant at 10 percent using a one-tail test).

Box Figure 5.3 Capital Inflows and the Current Account

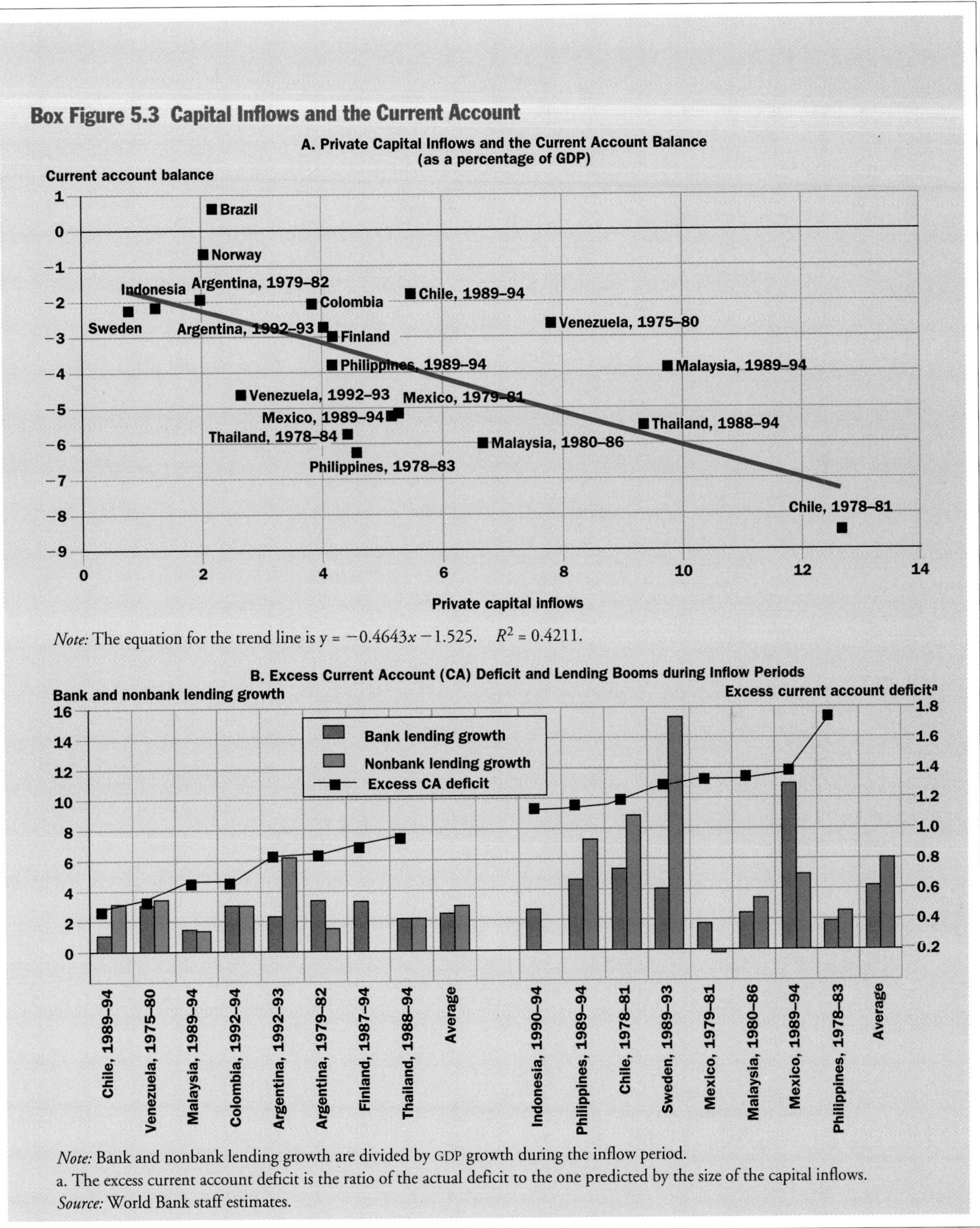

Note: The equation for the trend line is $y = -0.4643x - 1.525$. $R^2 = 0.4211$.

Note: Bank and nonbank lending growth are divided by GDP growth during the inflow period.

a. The excess current account deficit is the ratio of the actual deficit to the one predicted by the size of the capital inflows.

Source: World Bank staff estimates.

Box 5.4 Excessive Bank Lending Can Lead to Underinvestment and Overconsumption

THE EPISODES IN OUR SAMPLE SHOW THAT PRIvate capital inflows have been used to finance an increase in both investment and private consumption as illustrated by the positive slope of the regression lines in figures A and C below. Although the correlation between investment and inflows was positive, however, the increase in investment was smaller than that predicted by the size of the inflows in a number of countries: Argentina (1979–82), Brazil (1992–94), Chile (1978–81), Finland (1987–94), and Mexico (1989–94). Furthermore, the increase in investment appears to have been lower than it could have been, given the size of the inflows, in precisely those countries where the increase in bank and nonbank lending was among the largest. Underinvestment, measured as the difference between the predicted and the actual investment in a regression of the change of investment against inflow size, is shown in figure B. For the episodes with the largest increase in bank lending, the underinvestment averaged 2.7 percentage points of GDP, while the increase in bank lending averaged about six times that of GDP. For the remaining countries and episodes in our sample, these variables averaged –2.2 percent and 2.3 times, respectively. Moreover, for the episodes in our sample, regression analysis indicates that an increase in private capital inflows of, say, 10 percentage points of GDP leads to an increase in gross investment by almost the same amount. However, the increase in investment drops to about half this figure (the magnitude of this increase is reduced by 4.6 percent of GDP) in those episodes where the increase in bank lending has been higher than average.

An increase in bank lending following a capital inflow surge can exacerbate macroeconomic vulnerability by reducing potential investment and financing a consumption boom. This was, in fact, observed in the inflow episodes studied in this chapter. Figures C and D show that the increase in private consumption was proportionally larger, given the size of the inflows, in the group of countries that had the largest increase in bank and nonbank lending. Excess consumption is defined as the difference between actual consumption (as a share of GDP) and the consumption share predicted on the basis of the inflows received by each country. Argentina (1992–93), Brazil (1992–94), Finland (1987–94), Mexico (1989–94), Norway (1984–89), Sweden (1989–93), and Venezuela (1975–80)—all episodes that ended in a banking crisis—exhibited increases in consumption larger than those predicted by the size of their inflows. At the same time, the average increase in bank lending in these countries (adjusted by GDP growth) was more than three times that observed in the remaining countries combined. Thus for the episodes in the sample, the empirical evidence verifies that increases in bank lending amplify the positive effect of inflows on private consumption and, therefore, increase the vulnerability of the economy.

Box Figure 5.4 Effects of Capital Inflows on Investment and Consumption

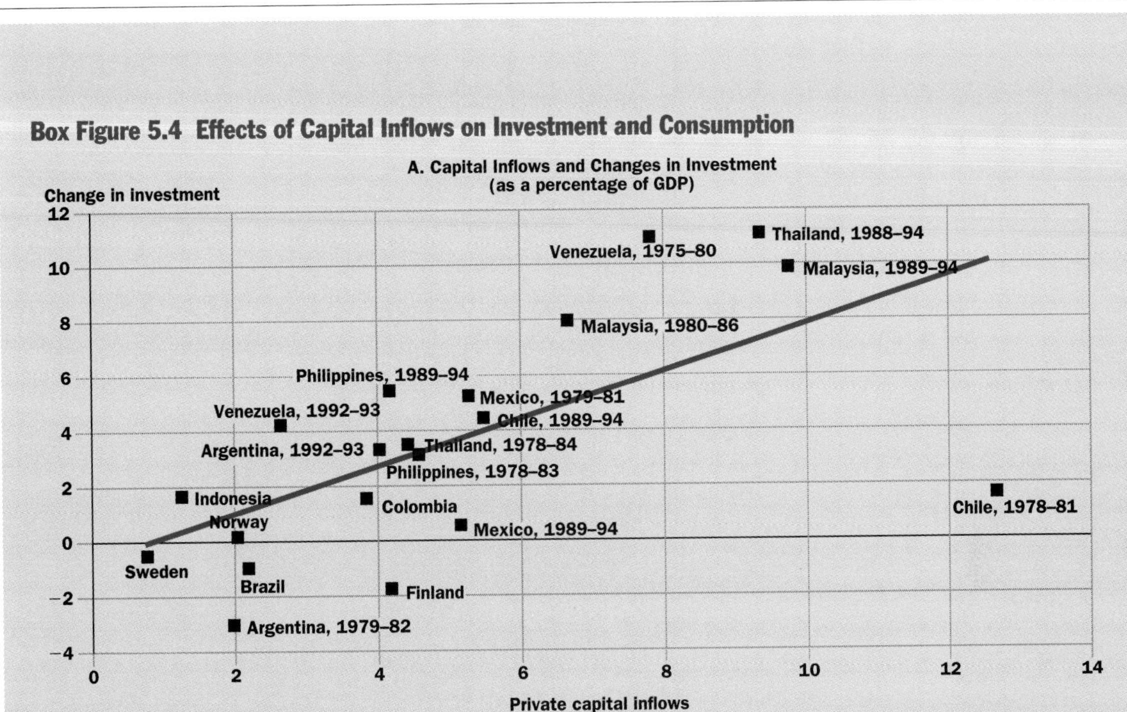

Note: The equation for the trend line is $y = 0.8132x - 0.7138$. $R^2 = 0.3762$.

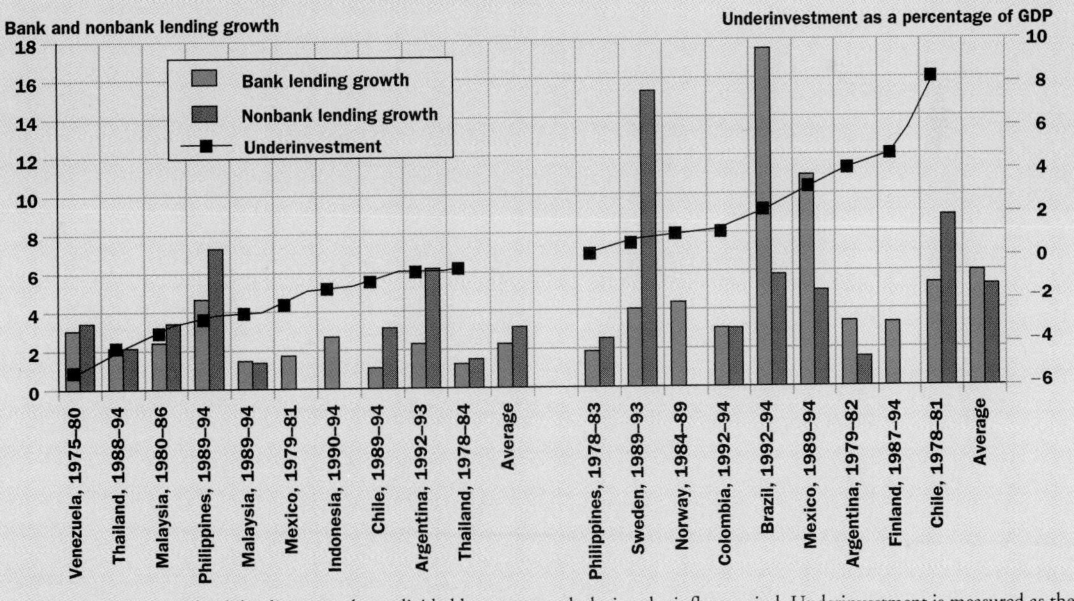

Note: Bank and nonbank lending growth are divided by GDP growth during the inflow period. Underinvestment is measured as the difference between the investment predicted by the size of the inflows and actual investment.

Box Figure 5.4 (continued)

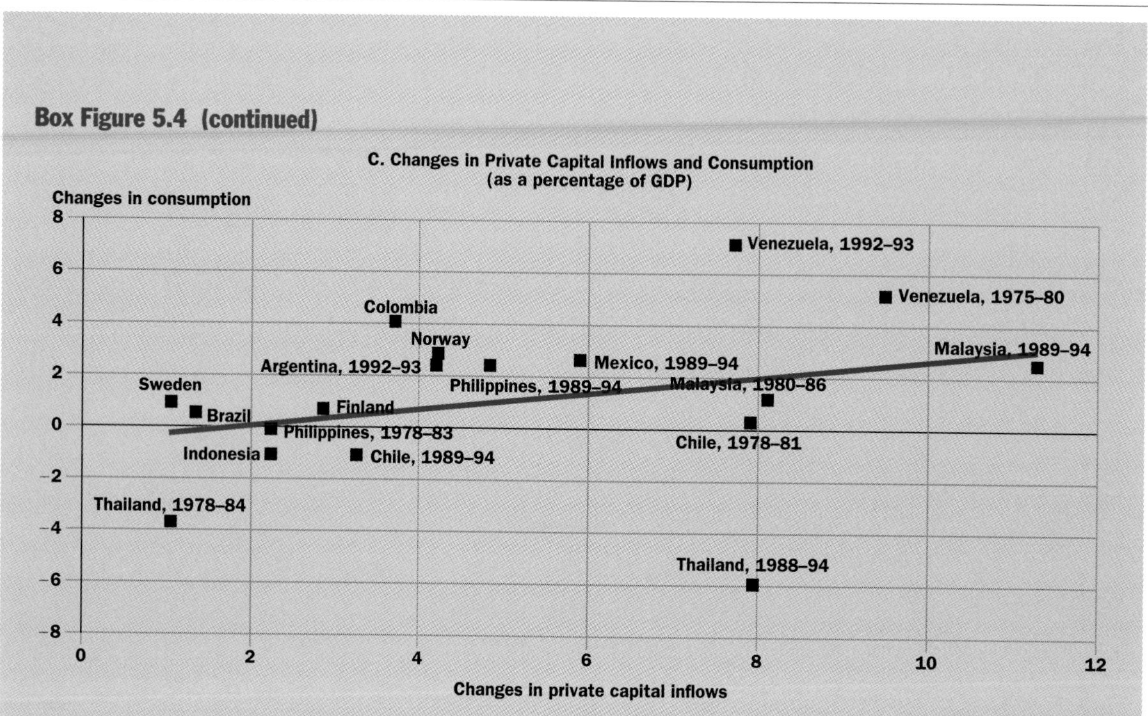

Note: The equation for the trend line is $y = 0.3136x - 0.5616$. $R^2 = 0.103$.

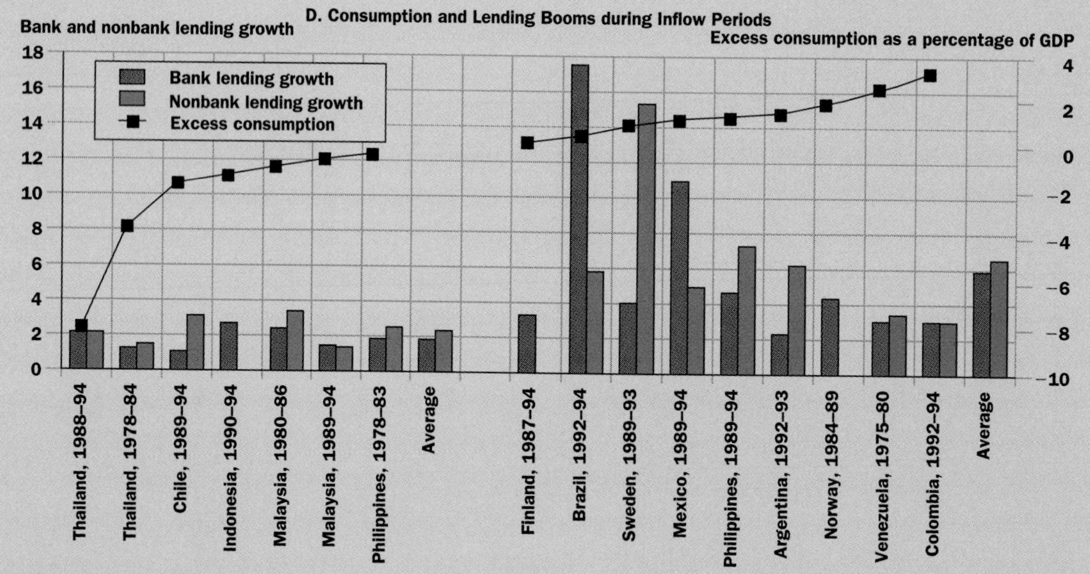

Note: Bank and nonbank lending growth are divided by GDP growth during the inflow period. Excess consumption is the difference between actual consumption and that predicted by the size of the inflows.

Source: World Bank staff estimates.

Two exceptions to these rules in our sample were Indonesia and Thailand during the early 1990s; these countries went into their inflow episodes with a relatively low degree of initial monetization, have experienced high economic growth, and have pursued prudent macroeconomic management. Thus they were able to avoid or delay difficulties in the financial sector (box 5.5).

Capital inflows and lending booms may also exacerbate economic vulnerabilities and ultimately lead to crisis by inducing an excessive and unsustainable increase in asset prices. This is a common outcome in most country episodes, especially when the domestic and external financial sectors have been rapidly liberalized, and its most clear mani-

Box 5.5 Bank Lending Booms and Overheating: The Importance of Fiscal Policy

TWO EXCEPTIONS TO THE BOOM-BUST CYCLE WERE INDONESIA (1990–94) and Thailand (1988–94). These two countries experienced a significant increase—20 percent or more of GDP—in bank and nonbank lending during the inflow period. Neither country has, however, suffered a deterioration in macroeconomic fundamentals or, until 1994, seen an overt banking crisis.[1] This can be attributed to at least three factors. First, both countries had a relatively low degree of monetization and shallow financial markets at the beginning of the inflow episode—private bank lending to GDP was below 30 percent prior to the inflows in Indonesia and about 45 percent in Thailand, while in Malaysia, for example, it was above 60 percent. Second, both countries grew at 7 percent or a higher rate on an annual basis during the inflow period. Third, these countries have had careful macroeconomic management over time. A low degree of initial monetization implies that financial assets may increase proportionally more than aggregate output without necessarily causing an increase in aggregate spending. Similarly, careful macroeconomic management and rapid growth imply that bank credit can expand without creating the standard symptoms of overheating. In fact, both countries had a significant improvement in their fiscal stance during the inflow period, as measured by the government surplus, which increased by more than 2 and 6 percent of GDP between the pre-inflow and inflow periods in Indonesia and Thailand, respectively.

1. As discussed elsewhere, Indonesia (1990–94)—and more recently Thailand (1995–96)—have seen a worsening in financial sector vulnerability.

festation is through the prices of stocks and real estate. The rise in asset prices, which corresponds to a drop in the cost of funds, tends to exacerbate vulnerabilities because it increases financial wealth and can thereby raise the level of households' indebtedness and consumption. Indeed, households often use their newly appreciated assets as collateral for new loans. Furthermore, the increase in asset prices can trigger borrowing for speculative purposes such as buying stocks and real estate. If the surge in prices proves to be unsustainable, which will be the case if asset prices rise excessively—and as shown in figure 5.2 this has been a common outcome toward the end of several inflow periods—then the economy will need to adjust to a lower level of aggregate spending later on. Most important, the bursting of the asset price bubble will lead to a decline in the financial situation of banks as the stock of nonperforming assets rises. This is so because the increase in interest rates that accompanies the drop in asset prices will cause overindebted households and speculators to start defaulting on their debts. In addition, the value of assets used as collateral will be insufficient to cover the banks' losses. In sum, the plunge in asset prices will leave banks in a weaker fi-

Figure 5.2 Stock Prices during Inflow Periods, Selected Countries
(stocks' real price index)

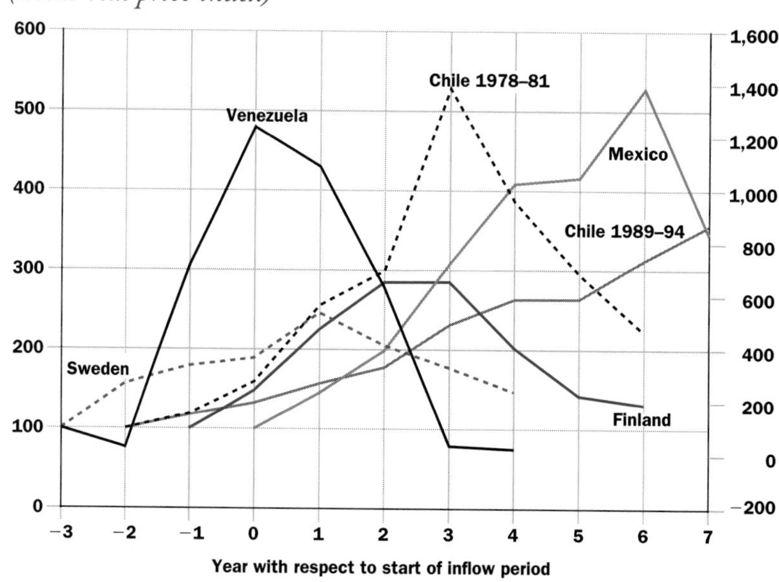

Note: The index for Finland, Mexico, and Sweden is shown on the left; the index for Chile during the 1980s and 1990s and for Venezuela is shown at the right.
Source: IMF, *International Financial Statistics* data base.

The surge in asset prices associated with inflow periods often proves to be unsustainable.

nancial situation and may even lead to crisis.[9] Capital inflows can also weaken the banking sector in other ways. These are discussed next.

Bank Lending and Financial Sector Vulnerability

THE SURGE IN PRIVATE CAPITAL FLOWS THAT ACCOMPANIES financial integration in developing countries usually leads to an increase in monetization and to banks intermediating a larger volume of funds. The increased financial intermediation, especially when it occurs over a short period of time, not only can exacerbate macroeconomic vulnerability, as discussed in the previous section, but may also exacerbate microeconomic problems, especially when the banking system suffers from initial distortions and weaknesses. These microeconomic problems are important for two reasons. First, banks could face financial distress and eventually a crisis, which in turn could mean the derailment of the entire macroeconomic and fiscal stabilization program (Velasco 1987). Second, financial fragilities may impose constraints on the implementation of other economic policies. For example, the weak financial conditions in the banking industry in Mexico during 1993–94 restrained the government from increasing domestic interest rates, a policy needed to prevent the loss of international reserves. Similarly, in 1994 the central bank in Venezuela had to expand liquidity to assist domestic banks despite rapid inflation and large foreign exchange losses.

In this section we discuss the ways in which international financial integration has affected the banking industry in countries that have liberalized their capital accounts. First we present the conceptual framework for thinking about this issue and discuss the indicators used to evaluate the performance of the banking sector in countries receiving capital inflows. We then describe the different country episodes and finally present our major conclusions from these country experiences.

Lending Booms and Banking Sector Vulnerabilities

A fast-growing banking industry will become more vulnerable if it is unable to evaluate the risks of increased lending (because of lack of trained personnel), and if its greater risk exposure is not accompanied by an improved ability to absorb negative economic shocks. Two common indicators of banks' ability to absorb shocks are their capitalization rates, measured as the stock of capital relative to the stock of bank assets, and their level of provisioning, measured as the provisions made for future losses as a share of the stock of total loans. An increase in provisions against future losses reduces the probability that banks could go under if borrowers default on their loans. An increase in the capital-asset ratio reduces the likelihood that banks could default on their own borrowing if investment projects turn out to be unsuccessful. (In addition, because shareholders' potential losses increase with the size of capital-asset ratios, well-capitalized banks are usually better monitored by their shareholders and therefore hold safer portfolios than do poorly capitalized banks.) Two other indicators, related to banks' ability to withstand short-term shocks, are the liquidity of their assets and relative maturity of their assets compared with their liabilities. A lower degree of asset liquidity and a shorter maturity of liabilities relative to assets make banks more vulnerable to liquidity crises.

A booming banking industry is likely to appear profitable and strong. While increased profitability may indicate improved operating conditions, however, in many instances it may simply be a consequence of the fact that banks are investing in riskier projects. A fast-growing banking industry has the opportunity to prevent or limit increased financial vulnerability if banks use these additional profits to increase their capitalization rates and provision against future losses.

Based on the above, this section analyzes the impact of increased financial integration on the banking sectors in a number of country episodes. The analysis consists of studying the behavior of several financial indicators obtained from the banks' balance sheets during the years surrounding the inflow episode. In particular, we look at profitability indices, capitalization ratios, the level of provisions and nonperforming loans, and the magnitude of exposure to foreign exchange risk. We use these indicators, in addition to indicators of banks' portfolio composition, when available, to assess the financial health, risk exposure, and resilience to shocks of these banking sectors.

Country Experiences

Countries can be classified according to the way they behaved during inflow periods and lending booms: some of them strengthened their banks, some experienced a deterioration in the health of their banking sector, and some of them experienced an improvement in some indicators and a worsening in others.

Countries that strengthened their banks. Chile, Colombia, and Malaysia all used their most recent capital inflow and lending boom periods to strengthen their banking systems.

- In Chile between 1990 and 1995, commercial banks were able to improve the quality of their assets by reducing more than half the stock of nonperforming loans (as a share of the total) while at the same time increasing their liquidity by about 40 percent (figure 5.3). Similarly, commercial banks reduced their foreign exchange exposure by about 30 to 40 percent between 1988 and 1994 (figure 5.4). It is important to note that the improvement in the financial indicators of Chile's commercial banks was achieved despite the fact that asset profitability in this period—measured by net interest margins—fell by about 25 percent (figure 5.5).
- Colombian banks, however, exhibited an increase of about 50 percent in net interest margins (figure 5.5), an improvement in capitalization (figure 5.6), a rise in loan loss provisions of about 70 percent (figure 5.7)—along with a worsening in asset quality, as measured by nonperforming loans, of about 40 percent (figure 5.3)—and a 50 percent decrease in the return on equity (calculated after provisions). The Colombian case is a clear example of how authorities can use a lending boom period to tighten regulations and make banks more resilient by forcing them to use the additional profits to increase their capitalization and provisioning.
- Malaysia also took the most recent capital inflow episode as an opportunity to strengthen its financial sector. Malaysian banks steadily increased their rate of capitalization after 1989, almost doubling it during 1989–95 despite the lack of a significant increase in profitability during the same period (figures 5.6 and 5.5).

Countries whose banks became weaker. By contrast, a number of countries saw a worsening in their banking systems' ability to withstand shocks during capital inflows and lending booms—in particular Argentina, Brazil, Mexico, and Venezuela during the early 1990s; Sweden during the mid- to late 1980s; and Chile in an episode during the early 1980s.

- Venezuela, for example, shows a fall in loan loss provisions in the years prior to its banking crisis, in 1994, despite the fact that asset quality was deteriorating, as became evident after the crisis began (figures 5.3 and 5.7). Furthermore, banks' profitability (measured by net interest margin) increased in the years preceding the crisis (figure 5.5).
- Capitalization rates in Brazil also fell by about 21 percent between 1991 and 1995 (figure 5.6), even though during the same period banks' profitability increased by about 35 percent and asset quality deteriorated significantly (figures 5.3 and 5.5). Banks in Mexico, however, although experiencing an important deterioration in asset quality (figure 5.3), along with a rise in profitability (figure 5.5) in the years preceding the 1994 crisis, increased their loan loss provisions only marginally between 1992 and mid-1994—the index rose 20 percent during this period (figure 5.7). In addition, Mexican banks suffered from a significant increase in their exposure to foreign exchange and real estate risks. Indeed, foreign exchange exposure grew about 40 percent between 1988 and 1994 (figure 5.4), while the share of banks' portfolios invested in real estate increased by about 80 percent (figure 5.8) between 1991 and 1995.
- At the beginning of the capital inflow episode in Argentina, banks had relatively high levels of reserves and capital, which provided important cushions for managing the crisis later on (annex 5.4), although they were playing a minor role in intermediation.[10] As domestic inflation declined and inflows surged, the banking sector started to intermediate larger volumes of funds and the authorities began to implement reforms aimed at strengthening the supervision and monitoring of banks. The increase in bank lending during 1992–93 occurred along with an increase in banks' profitability, a decrease in capitalization (an expected outcome, given the initial conditions), a fall in loan loss provisions, and a deterioration in asset quality (figures 5.5 and 5.7).
- The cases of Chile and Sweden during the 1980s are similar to those discussed above in many respects. Capital ratios of Chilean banks fell by about 50 percent between 1977 and 1980, despite the fact that banks' profitability was high in the years preceding the 1981–83 crisis (figure 5.6). Moreover, during the same period Chilean banks experienced a decline in the maturity of liabilities

and an increase in foreign exchange exposure (figure 5.4). Conversely, Swedish banks saw a fall in their capitalization rates of about 31 percent between 1988 and 1991, and increased their foreign exchange exposure by about 50 percent between 1986 and 1990 (figures 5.4 and 5.6).

Countries where banking sectors strengthened in some aspects and weakened in others. The countries in the last group analyzed here were able to strengthen some aspects of their banking industries during the inflow and lending boom episodes while at the same time allowing a deterioration in other indicators of banking sector health. These countries include Indonesia during the 1990s, Malaysia during the early 1980s, and Thailand in both the 1980s and the 1990s.

- In Malaysia, during the first capital inflow episode in the late 1970s and early 1980s, banks steadily increased their capitalization by about 80 percent, from an equity-over-total-assets ratio of about 3 percent in 1980 to a new high of about 5.5 percent in 1984 (figure 5.6). This increase, however, could not prevent the banking crisis that occurred in 1985–87, largely because during the inflow period banks aggravated their vulnerabilities by overinvesting in real estate. Indeed, between 1980 and 1985 the share of Malaysian banks' portfolios represented by loans and advances to the real estate and housing sectors rose from 25 to 35 percent and increased further, to almost 37 percent, in 1987.
- As in Malaysia, banks in Thailand increased their capitalization by about 35 percent between 1989 and 1995, while during 1988–94 their profitability increased by about 49 percent and the provisioning against future loan losses rose by about 24 percent (figures 5.5, 5.6, and 5.7). However, between 1989 and 1995 Thai banks also increased their exposure to foreign exchange risk by a factor of four (figure 5.4) and further increased their exposure to real estate risk, which had been on the rise since 1985. Indeed, the share of real estate and construction loans in the portfolios of Thai banks, which increased by about 20 percent between 1984 and 1988, rose by about 41 percent (figure 5.8) between 1988 and 1995.

The case of Thailand during the 1990s differs from its capital inflow episode in the 1980s in several ways. First, there was only a minor increase in Thai banks' exposure to the real estate business during the first inflow period. Second, Thai banks decreased their exposure to foreign exchange risk between 1980 (or earlier) and 1985 (figure 5.4). And finally the capitalization of Thai banks steadily decreased between 1978–79 and 1983, the first year of its 1980s banking crisis (figure 5.6).

Indonesia's banking sector during its most recent capital inflow episode (1990–94) exhibits several of the symptoms of a weakening banking system, except that banks significantly increased their provisioning against future loan losses (figure 5.7). While bank provisioning increased between 1989 and 1994, however, bank capitalization decreased by about 30 percent during the same period, and foreign exchange exposure rose by 275 percent (figures 5.4 and 5.6). As in Thailand and other countries, banks in Indonesia increased their exposure to sectoral risk during its inflow episode by raising the share of loans to the service sector by more than 7 percentage points during 1989–94. More worrisome, however, is the fact that the increase in the share of loans to the service sector, typically considered to be a nontradable sector, had a negative effect on lending to the trade sector, a result that could make the overall banking system more vulnerable to variations in the value of the nominal and real exchange rate (figure 5.8).

Conclusions

Our analysis has shown that while some countries have used surges in capital flows and lending booms to strengthen their banking systems, other countries, or even the same countries in different periods, have not. By using the increased profits that often accompany a lending surge to improve banks' health and shock resistance, some countries not only mitigated the microeconomic vulnerabilities that normally surface in a fast-growing industry but, more important, may also have prevented painful banking crises. In other words, while fortifying banks' ability to react to shocks, these countries may have managed to limit the size of the lending boom. Conversely, countries that did not improve the conditions in their banking sectors during inflow periods, but rather allowed bank lending to increase without addressing microfinancial vulnerabilities, generally saw a banking crisis later on.

This conclusion is clearly illustrated by comparing Chile's two attempts during the past two decades to become more financially integrated with the rest of the world. The first attempt, in 1979, ended in

Figure 5.3 Change in Nonperforming Loans
(as a percentage of total loans)

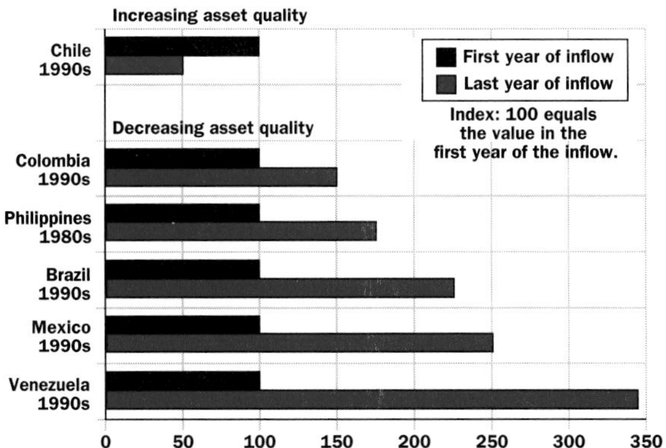

Figure 5.4 Change in Foreign Currency Exposure

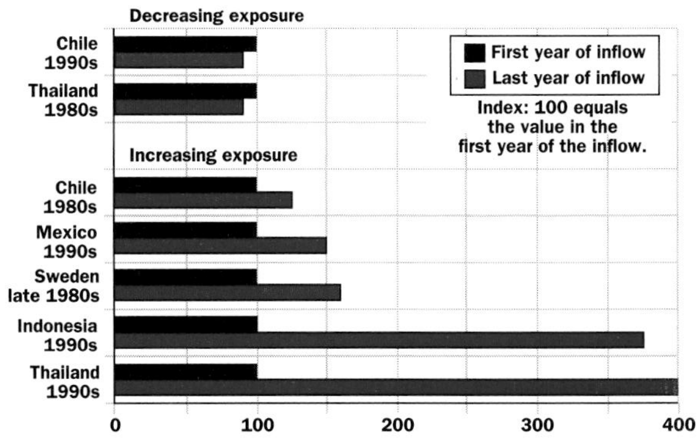

Figure 5.5 Change in Net Interest Margin
(profitability index: net interest margin)

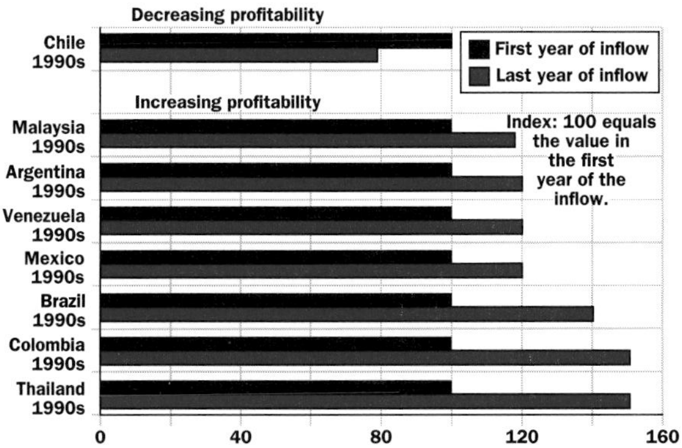

Figure 5.6 Change in Capital-Asset Ratios

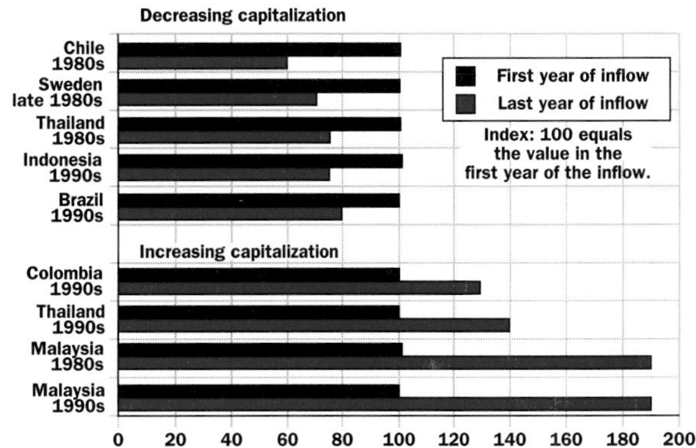

Figure 5.7 Change in Loan Loss Provisions
(as a percentage of total loans)

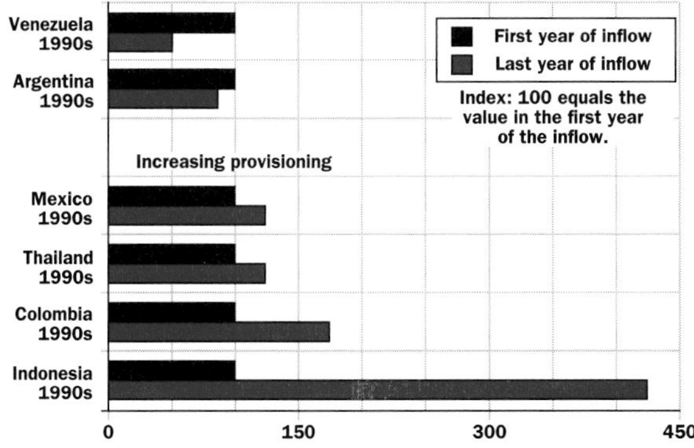

Figure 5.8 Exposure to Sectoral Risks
(percentage of loans to real estate and construction)

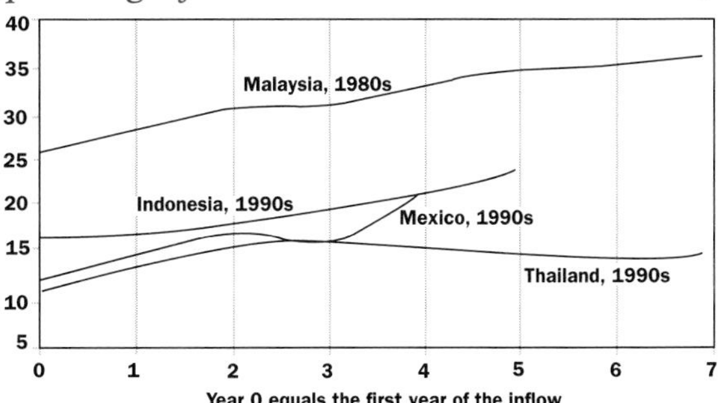

Note: In Indonesia sectoral risk is measured as the percentage of loans to the services sector.

Source: World Bank staff estimates using data from IBCA Ltd.; IMF, *International Financial Statistics* data base; Salomon Brothers; and reports from various national central banks.

a major economic and financial crisis after three years, while the second, which started exactly 10 years later, in 1989, has been extremely successful. In both cases Chile began the inflow period with a sound macroeconomic environment, with the only important difference between the two episodes being the exchange rate policy, a factor that resulted in banks increasing their foreign exchange exposure during the first inflow period but not during the second.[11] Nevertheless, on the microeconomic front the existence of a better regulatory and supervisory framework in Chile during the 1990s can explain the different pattern of indicators such as bank capitalization and provisioning. Belated attempts were made to strengthen these indicators in the earlier episode, but by then a crisis had become inevitable.[12]

Another conclusion suggested by the analysis is that initial conditions matter. This can be seen from the experience of those countries that have had two capital inflow episodes, and also by comparing countries in which external financial liberalization ended in a banking crisis with those that avoided a crisis. For example, the capitalization rate of banks in Malaysia at the beginning of its second capital inflow period (1987–88) was about twice that at the start of its first inflow period (1980), while banks' capital-asset ratios in the Philippines were also higher at the beginning of the second inflow period (1988) than at the start of the first (1979). Similarly, the average maturity of deposits was shorter at the beginning of the first inflow period than at the start of the second in the cases of Chile, the Philippines, and Thailand.

Finally, when comparing two groups of countries, it appears that those in which external financial liberalization led to a banking crisis started with lower capitalization rates than those in which a crisis was avoided—the initial bank capital-asset ratios in the former group of countries was in the range of 2 to 5 percent, while in the latter it was 6 percent or higher. Banks in countries where a crisis occurred also started with lower liquidity than those in which financial liberalization has been successful. Although these conclusions must be interpreted cautiously, since differences in accounting procedures and other rules can invalidate cross-country comparisons, it is clear that countries that have been able to strengthen their banking industries during a surge in inflows—or in a period between two episodes of inflows—have been able to avoid the difficulties that in 1995 affected Argentina, Brazil, and Mexico, and that during the 1980s affected Chile, Malaysia, and the Philippines.

Financial Sector Reforms in the Context of Integration: Policy Lessons

TO CONSOLIDATE THE LESSONS FROM THE PREVIOUS TWO sections, we have constructed financial and macroeconomic vulnerability indexes that summarize the developments which followed the surge in capital flows in a number of countries. These indexes are illustrated graphically in figure 5.9. A positive number in the chart means a deteriorating situation, and a negative number means an improving one.[13]

Our analysis found that financial sector conditions and macroeconomic conditions generally deteriorated in tandem, that banking crises occurred in countries where macroeconomic vulnerabilities increased or remained constant, and that no banking crises occurred during capital inflow episodes in which macroeconomic vulnerabilities were contained. These conclusions are consistent with the view that developments in the financial sector are, in general, a mirror image of developments in the real economy, and that the banking sector amplifies shocks that have already occurred in the real economy.[14] Indeed, none of the country episodes included in figure 5.9 show an increase in macroeconomic vulnerabilities along with an improvement in the financial sector, and none of the banking crisis cases show a worsening in banking sector vulnerabilities with an improvement in macroeconomic conditions.

The evidence therefore suggests that maintaining a strong macroeconomic stance may be critical to avoiding a banking crisis. In particular, the cases of Indonesia (1990–94), the Philippines (1988–94), and Thailand (1988–94) suggest that having strong macroeconomic fundamentals may enable an economy to escape or at least temporarily dodge a crisis even when financial conditions are deteriorating (box 5.5). Specifically, the need to curb the lending boom and to apply counterbalancing macroeconomic policies to prevent overheating when receiving large capital inflows appears as a very clear message. Because of the long time—usually several years—that it takes to put in place a sound and reliable regulatory and supervisory framework for banks, countries can help make financial integration less destabilizing by maintaining prudent macroeconomic performance. This does not, however, obviate the need for strong macroeconomic *and* financial sector conditions to avoid a banking crisis in the long run.

Figure 5.9 Macroeconomic and Financial Sector Vulnerabilities during Capital Inflow Episodes, Selected Countries and Years

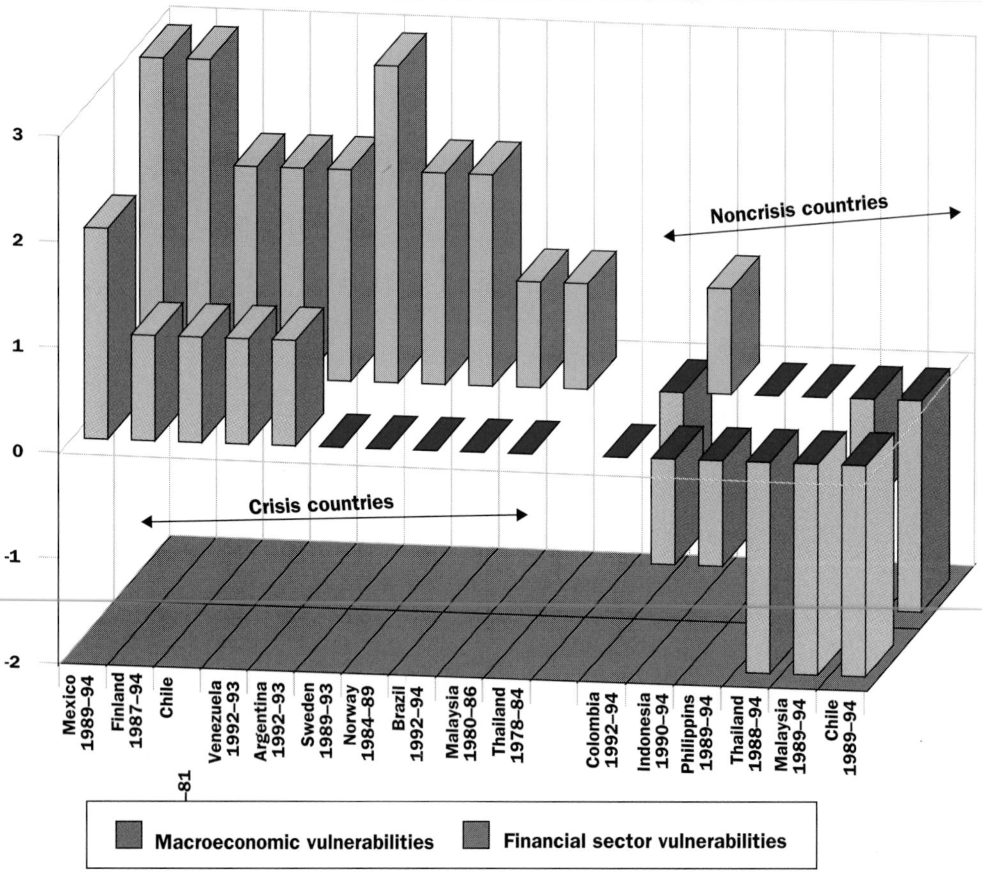

Source: World Bank staff estimates.

Banking crises generally occur in countries where macro- and microeconomic vulnerabilities increase during capital inflow episodes.

Next, we examine policy options that emerge from the discussion above, as well as from previous studies, on the implementation of financial sector reforms in different countries. Our analysis adds to previous studies by introducing the issue of integration.

In considering various policy options, it is important to understand how financial integration may affect the banking sector in countries receiving large capital flows. Financial integration may result in:

- increased competition in the form of, for example, new entrants and financial disintermediation

- new risks in the form of new investment opportunities and instruments, and risks created by a potentially more volatile environment, including the risk that flows will be suddenly reversed
- access to a larger pool of foreign and domestic capital (savings), which will enable banks to increase lending.

These three effects, in conjunction with conditions in the financial sector and the macroeconomy, will determine the outcome of increased financial integration. Although financial integration may be beneficial for developing countries in the long run (chapter 3), potential risks and losses are greater if the process is poorly managed.[15] This is so because the size and speed of market reactions increase in an integrated economy, as is shown by the Mexican experience in early 1995 (Calvo 1996, Griffith-Jones 1995).

Financial Integration: Guiding Principles for Financial Sector Reform

As outlined above, financial integration makes it easier for banks to rapidly increase the riskiness of their portfolios and consequently incur sizable losses.[16] Moreover, standard supervision and monitoring tools become less effective with integration because of the increased speed and magnitude of market reaction. Thus, financial integration puts a premium on the need of developing countries to reform the institutional and regulatory framework governing their banking industries. Given the importance of macroeconomic stability for sustained reforms, and the possibility of increased macroeconomic swings in an open environment, these reforms need to be underpinned by supportive macroeconomic policies.

Past attempts by both developing and industrial countries to liberalize their domestic financial sectors have led to an evolving view of best practice in financial sector reform. In this section we review how financial integration affects the domestic financial sector reform agenda concerning both macroeconomic and microeconomic policies. The policy recommendations discussed below consist of a minimum set of conditions that, in an ideal world, should be satisfied before financial integration begins. For countries that have already embarked on the process of integration, improvements in these areas are critical to averting financial distress or banking crises. Table 5.2 summarizes the major findings.

Creating a macroeconomic environment to sustain financial sector reform. In a world of increasing financial integration policymakers need to pay

Table 5.2 Domestic and External Financial Sector Reform: Policy Recommendations

	Macroeconomic environment			*Microeconomic environment*		
Context of reform	*Overall stability*	*Real interest rates*	*Timing of reforms within economic cycle*	*Financial infrastructure*	*Incentive structure*	*Regulatory framework*
Domestic financial sector reform	Implement reforms when the economy is stable to avoid a shortening of maturities in banks' liabilities.	Avoid sharp increases in interest rates that will reduce borrowers' repayment capacity and banks' net worth. Control interest rates if they become too high.	Implement reforms during a recovery period to facilitate the adjustment of banks to the new environment.	Put in place adequate institutions and upgrade human capital in both banks and supervisory agencies before liberalization occurs.	Put in place a good system to screen potential bankers and limit deposit insurance coverage to small depositors only.	Impose high capital-asset ratios and proceed slowly with reforms to avoid a sharp fall in bank profits. Impose ceilings on self-lending within conglomerates.
Increased financial integration	The same recommen-dation applies: implementing reforms in a volatile environment will shorten the maturity of flows and induce more speculative flows. Emphasize achieving macro-economic stability and eliminating debt overhang.	Accelerate reforms if interest rates are expected to decline. However, controlling interest rates will be more difficult and costly.	Pursuing reforms after an economic slowdown may exacerbate the lending boom and overheating of the economy. However, other counteracting policies can be used to minimize this problem.	The same policy recommendations apply. However, because potential losses are much greater and markets react faster under integration, the need to move forward on these fronts is even greater. Increased financial integration puts a premium on reforming the regulatory and incentive structures in banking. In addition, the use of guarantees for foreign exchange should be limited.		

attention to at least three aspects of the macroeconomic environment to ensure successful banking sector reform: overall macroeconomic stability, the level of real interest rates, and the phase of the business cycle at the time reforms are implemented.

Macroeconomic stability. One of the central lessons that has emerged from the experience with domestic financial sector reform is the importance of macroeconomic stability as a prerequisite for sustained reform. Because of the undesirable effects of sudden reversals of capital flows, developing countries that liberalize their financial sectors while becoming financially integrated should therefore move quickly to achieve a stable macroeconomic environment, one in which large macroeconomic swings are avoided and where the volatility in some key prices, such as the exchange and interest rates, has been reduced to internationally comparable levels. In working toward stability policymakers should aim to build macroeconomic cushions such as holding an increased stock of international reserves and a reduction of the public debt (Goldstein and Turner 1996). Countries with a public debt overhang problem are more vulnerable than others to changes in market sentiment and changes in variables such as interest rates or aggregate output (chapter 4).

Real interest rates. The macroeconomic environment chiefly affects the outcome of financial sector reforms by changing borrowers' and banks' net worth through variations in the level of real interest rates (annex 5.2). For example, several authors have argued that the high real interest rates that prevailed in Chile in the late 1970s are partly responsible for the financial crisis of the early 1980s in that country (Hernández 1991). Accordingly, it has been argued that policymakers should carefully monitor interest rates and prevent them from reaching too high a level—for example, by imposing maximum rates (Stiglitz 1994; Hellmann, Murdock, and Stiglitz 1996).

The desirability of pursuing or delaying financial sector reforms in an integrated environment also depends on expectations about interest rates that can affect borrowers' and banks' net worth.[17] It is likely that real interest rates will be low under integration because of the increased supply of loanable funds and increased competition in banking, as a result of which, spreads will fall. These low rates will have a positive impact on borrowers' repayment capacity and through this on banks' net worth. Therefore delaying reforms because of interest rate considerations does not seem appropriate. Moreover, the ability of policymakers to control interest rates in a more integrated environment is greatly reduced, and the process becomes increasingly costly.

Phase of the business cycle. Experience with domestic financial sector reforms suggests that reforms should be accelerated in periods of fast economic growth and delayed when the economy slows down (Caprio, Atiyas, and Hanson 1994). The reason for this is that the banking sector—like every other economic sector—can adjust more easily to the structural changes brought by reform in periods of high profitability and growth. In the case of increased financial integration, however, this argument changes. In particular, the surge in flows that normally follows the implementation of reforms triggers a larger lending boom than in a less integrated economy. Moreover the possibility that the economy might start growing rapidly after reforms are introduced can reinforce market participants' high expectations about growth. This chain of events, as explained in previous sections, may induce additional lending and trigger overheating, which could exacerbate both macroeconomic and financial sector vulnerabilities.

It might therefore seem that in an integrating environment financial sector reforms should be pursued during an economic slowdown rather than during a recovery period, because overheating and overlending are likely to be less severe if the financial liberalization process starts in an economic peak rather than a trough. On the other hand, pursuing financial liberalization during a recession may lead to capital outflows rather than inflows. Therefore domestic financial reform should be accelerated in periods of fast economic growth and delayed when the economy slows down, and the problems of overheating and overlending should be addressed through other policies.

Creating a microeconomic environment to sustain financial sector reform. Three microfinancial areas need to be given special attention when liberalizing the financial sector in an integrated environment: financial infrastructure and institution building, incentive structure, and the regulatory and supervisory framework. Progress in all three areas—and in the macroeconomic stance as well—is necessary to ensure that the reform process leads to a safer and sounder banking industry.[18]

Financial infrastructure and institution building. One lesson that emerges from past episodes of financial sector reform is the need to establish an appropriate institutional framework, providing clear standards and rules for accounting, auditing, and legal procedures, all of which are necessary for adequate functioning of a market economy.[19] In addition, experience shows that bankers' management and risk assessment skills often become obsolete after reforms are introduced and need to be strengthened when the system is liberalized (Brock 1996; Caprio, Atiyas, and Hanson 1994; Caprio and Vittas 1995; and Caprio

1996). For example, the lack of staff with modern banking skills contributed to the banking crises in the Baltic republics of Estonia, Latvia and Lithuania (Fleming, Chu, and Bakker 1996). This is particularly important under integration because lack of knowledge in managing new instruments and assessing their risks increases the potential for losses caused by fraud or wrongdoing. Moreover, lack of experience and knowledge in supervising banks in the riskier new environment increases the likelihood that such problems will remain undetected. This has been a problem even in more advanced economies, for example, Finland, Norway, and Sweden, where the lack of supervision was a key factor in banking crises.

The incentive structure. One important reason that banks run into financial difficulties is the presence of distorted external incentives—policies that can be modified by domestic economic authorities and that induce bank managers to pursue unsound banking practices (box 5.6). An example of this, one particularly important in the context of increased financial integration, is the existence of explicit guarantees for foreign exchange. As shown by the Chilean experience of the early 1980s, and more recently by that of Mexico, these guarantee mechanisms induce banks to increase their exposure to foreign exchange risk (annex 5.2). Another possible distortion is a deposit insurance scheme that is not properly priced according to each bank's risk level, which may lead depositors to put their money into institutions paying the highest interest and holding the riskiest portfolios.[20] The solution is to correct the incentive structure and tighten bank supervision.

Increased financial integration may aggravate this problem by giving domestic banks access to a larger supply of funds from abroad, especially if foreign deposits are covered by implicit or explicit insurance. A simple way to minimize the risk that increased financial integration will exacerbate this problem is to limit deposit insurance, thus forcing large depositors to scrutinize banks carefully before deciding where to put their money; this should impose some degree of market discipline on banks. More important, by excluding foreign (or foreign-currency-denominated) deposits from the insurance mechanism, authorities will force foreign lenders (usually large foreign banks or institutional investors) to look very carefully at banks, exerting even more control over them. In this way market discipline complements the imperfect monitoring of banks by domestic supervisory agencies, which may be ill equipped to effectively control risks and monitor such areas as prof-

Box 5.6 Good Bankers Make a Safe and Sound Banking Industry

DISTORTED EXTERNAL INCENTIVES ALONE ARE not sufficient to create a financial crisis. Indeed, it has been argued that no matter how distorted the incentives, cautious bankers rarely bring their institutions to the brink of bankruptcy (De Juan 1987). Banking practices depend on both *external* incentives and *internal* factors, which are usually difficult to observe and not under the control of domestic authorities, such as management's reputation and moral track record. The main concern is that risk-taking and fraud-prone individuals could enter the banking industry after liberalization occurs. In the presence of distorted incentives these individuals—as opposed to more conservative and cautious bankers—may pursue unsound lending practices and thereby aggravate financial fragility in the banking sector. This is particularly true in the case of increased financial integration, which offers greater opportunities for fraud and wrongdoing. Thus, the problem consists of both carefully screening prospective bankers and correcting the *external* incentives facing bank managers.

The problem of screening prospective bankers makes it important to establish a clear and transparent application process for bank licenses, in which all high-level managers and owners of banks are subject to careful screening. One important lesson concerning this issue emerges from the experience with bank privatization in Chile in the early 1980s and Mexico in the early 1990s. In both episodes banks were privatized without attention being paid to the qualifications of the new owners or how they were financing the purchase. In some cases banks were bought with debt instead of equity, so the new bankers had greater incentives to make risky investments with depositors' money. Furthermore, reforms were introduced shortly after privatization occurred, giving the new management teams little time to learn how to do business in the new environment. These developments were partly responsible for the banking crises experienced by Chile in 1981 and by Mexico in 1995. Poor screening of new entrants also played an important role in the difficulties faced by the banking sector in Hong Kong in the late 1970s, and more recently in Poland and Russia.

itability, capitalization, and interlocking relationships between banks and the corporate sector. These issues are discussed below.

Regulatory and supervisory framework. When implementing financial sector reforms, policymakers should pay particular attention to banks' profitability and capitalization, cross-ownership between banks and corporations, and bank supervision.

Banks' profitability and capitalization. Experience shows that poorly capitalized and money-losing banks are more inclined to undertake excess risks than those that are well capitalized and profitable, because the owners of safe, healthy banks have more to lose if their risky investments turn out to be unsuccessful. Therefore, to limit excess risk taking by banks when implementing financial sector reforms, particularly in an integrated environment, authorities should raise capitalization requirements to levels consistent with international standards, and developing countries have already started doing so.[21] Such actions should be undertaken within a consistent and well-articulated incentive and regulatory framework. Moreover, some analysts have recently argued in favor of imposing higher capitalization rates for banks in developing countries because these banks operate in an especially volatile economic environment (Gavin and Hausmann 1996, Caprio 1996). If this proposal is followed, then developing countries will need to keep strengthening their banking sectors by raising capital requirements in banks, since these banks do not appear to have risk-based capital ratios significantly higher than those in larger industrial countries (IMF 1996, Goldstein and Turner 1996).

Financial reform in an integrated environment can trigger a lending boom and temporarily increase banks profits (and risks), but it can also reduce profits in the medium and long term. It does so by increasing market competition and giving nonbanks new business opportunities, a situation that can be aggravated if it precludes domestic banks from entering these new markets. In this context, a financial deregulation process that is not carefully managed may therefore reduce banks' net worth in the medium and long term and induce unsound bank practices. Policymakers in liberalizing economies should proceed slowly to avoid a sharp decrease in banks profits while allowing all market participants to compete on a level field (Stiglitz 1994). As argued earlier, the temporary rise in profits resulting from lending booms should be used to increase capitalization and provisions.

Cross-ownership between banks and the corporate sector. Experience shows that close relationships between the corporate sector and banks tend to distort the incentive for banks to protect depositors' money. More specifically, an interlocking relationship between a bank and a group of firms tends to bias the incentives of bank managers toward protecting the interests of the group of firms rather than those of depositors. In so doing, banks usually end up investing too much in the firms' assets—a phenomenon called connected lending or self-lending—and therefore do not diversify their portfolios adequately. This has contributed to banking problems in many countries such as Argentina, Bangladesh, Brazil, Chile, Indonesia, Malaysia, Spain, and Thailand. In Chile, for example, it has been estimated that self-lending for the most troubled banks at the peak of the crisis ranked between 20 and 45 percent of total loans (de la Cuadra and Valdés 1992). Moreover, an interlocking relationship between a bank and a group of firms renders standard regulatory and monitoring procedures less effective, particularly in cases of financial distress, because the ways a bank can channel money to firms—and hide losses—in a conglomerate multiply with the size of the conglomerate. This makes prudential supervision more difficult. These problems become even more complex when both banks and corporations gain access to offshore markets as a result of integration. To solve these problems, policymakers must set limits on both bank holdings of stocks and on lending to individual borrowers, the latter calculated on a consolidated basis.[22] More important, because of the difficulties in enforcing these regulations (especially during periods of financial distress), bank managers should be subject to severe penalties if found guilty of violating them.

Bank supervision. Any effort to limit risk taking by banks and promote sound banking will be ineffective if supervision and enforcement of regulations are weak. Supervision becomes more difficult in an integrated environment because of the larger pool of assets and risks involved and the fast-changing market conditions. Therefore, the need to upgrade the skill mix and the effectiveness of the supervisory agency in an integrating environment becomes even more urgent than in an isolated economy.

Two elements can make supervision more effective in an integrated environment: the development of prudential standards and cooperation in cross-border supervision. Although progress in developing prudential standards has been made in recent years, the standards adopted pertain mostly to capital requirements and were designed primarily for international banks in industrial countries. The rash of severe crises in developing countries over the past 15 years has, however, recently rekindled interest in developing more comprehensive guidelines. Indeed, supervisory and regulatory authorities are expected to issue such guidelines in the near future. As regards cooperation among supervisors, authorities in the home country bear the main responsibility for cross-border supervison, but authorities in host countries can help by monitoring specific aspects, such as liquidity, and, most important, by removing impediments to the exchange of relevant information between supervisory authorities.

The Pragmatic Approach: Containing the Lending Boom while Strengthening the Banking Sector

Although it would be ideal for the policy recommendations discussed above to be implemented before integration begins, most developing countries that are already financially integrated do not have all these prerequisites in place. This means that they need to move quickly to fix their institutional framework and put in place all the missing elements. Since doing so can take years, developing countries can implement other policies in the meantime to prevent vulnerabilities from being made worse. Curbing the lending boom is one remedy that is especially important in countries where the banking sector is weak and where private sector spending is biased towards consumption rather than investment. This subsection discusses some options for reducing the degree to which a lending boom can aggravate macroeconomic and banking sector vulnerability. A summary of the discussion is presented in table 5.3.

Macroeconomic policies. Fiscal, monetary, and exchange rate policies can all help to mitigate the lending boom. Tight fiscal policy can be highly effective in counterbalancing the overheating caused by the lending boom (box 5.5); at the same time it can prevent an increase in capital inflows by keeping domestic interest rates low (a desirable side effect). By contrast, a tight monetary policy, while containing the increase in aggregate spending, may induce additional capital inflows by raising domestic interest rates (Corbo and Hernández 1996). A larger volume of capital inflows will exert additional pressure on monetary balances and increase the quasi-fiscal deficit of the central bank when it attempts to sterilize the flows. Moreover the positive effect of sterilization on domestic interest rates may significantly worsen the fiscal balance for countries having a large stock of outstanding public debt (for example, India or Mexico). In the end, unless compensatory fiscal policies are implemented, the deteriorating financial position of the central bank—and the public sector in general if the outstanding stock of government debt is large—will cause a worsening of macroeconomic vulnerabilities. Furthermore, when banks have weak loan portfolios, an increase in domestic interest rates may aggravate their problems by increasing the stock of nonperforming assets. A recent example of this is Mexico during 1993–94.

Exchange rate policy, when directed toward maintaining competitiveness and supported by a tight fiscal policy, has proved to bias aggregate spending away from consumption and toward investment, particularly in the tradables sector (chapter 4). The use of the exchange rate as a nominal anchor, however, has often been associated with consumption booms, as in Argentina and Mexico. Not using the exchange rate as an anchor can also help to reduce the risk that banks will over-

Table 5.3 Containing Lending Booms: Policy Options

	Macroeconomic policies			
	Foreign exchange system	*Fiscal policy*	*Monetary policy*	*Imposing ceilings on commercial bank lending and external borrowing*
Main advantages	A semifloating exchange rate system (band) increases the market risk faced by banks and other domestic borrowers, thereby reducing overall external borrowing.	Reduces overheating and helps keep interest rates low.	Helps contain the lending boom and reduces overheating.	Limits the lending boom and the overheating. Most effective if directed toward specific uses of credit such as consumption loans, credit cards, and mortgages.
Main disadvantages			Exacerbates capital inflows by keeping domestic interest rates high. Also, in the medium term, it impairs the financial situation of the central bank—and of the public sector if the stock of outstanding debt is large—and damages macroeconomic fundamentals.	Creates a microeconomic distortion and gives nonbank financial institutions an advantage over banks.

lend. Indeed, the adoption of a semifloating exchange rate system (band), by increasing market participants' exposure to foreign exchange risk, induces a more cautious approach toward external borrowing, resulting in smaller capital inflows and less bank lending and overheating. This was in fact the experience of Chile during the 1990s, as compared with that in the early 1980s.

Overall, the experience of countries that have avoided overheating during the most recent surge in capital inflows—such as Chile, Indonesia, and Thailand—suggests that sound macroeconomic management requires using all three policies within a consistent framework. A tight fiscal policy is crucial for the policy mix to be sustainable, and sterilized intervention accompanied by exchange rate flexibility—in some cases

Microeconomic policies			
Increasing banks' reserve requirements	*Increasing banks' risk-adjusted capital-asset ratios*	*Imposing indirect (economy-wide) capital controls*	*Tightening other bank regulations (provisioning for nonperforming loans)*
Restricts credit growth and minimizes the risk of overlending.	Makes banks more resilient to shocks, induces sound banking practices, and may reduce the growth in lending.	Capital controls appear to change the composition of flows toward longer maturities. This may have the positive effect of biasing expenditures (and bank lending) toward investment rather than consumption.	Increasing provisions for future loan losses makes banks more resilient to shocks and reduces the availability of loanable funds.
If not remunerated, the increase in reserves may induce banks to invest in riskier projects.	An excessively high capital-asset ratio will reduce creditors' efforts to monitor bank managers and can erode banks' profitability. Capital requirements are difficult to monitor if bank supervision is weak, especially in periods of financial distress.	It seems that capital controls will quickly become ineffective because of the important arbitrage opportunities they create. Most important, these profits usually benefit other economic agents (nonbanks) and in the long term create distortions and cause economic inefficiencies.	Provisions against future loan losses are difficult to monitor when bank supervision is weak. This problem becomes more acute in periods of financial distress, when banks start rolling over bad debts and capitalizing past-due interest.

strengthened with the use of capital controls—can play an important role in avoiding overheating and reducing vulnerability, especially so in the early stages of capital inflows (chapter 4 and Montiel 1996).

Microeconomic policies. Microeconomic policies directed at containing the lending boom include increasing banks' capitalization and provisioning against future losses, raising reserve (liquidity) requirements, and imposing capital controls and ceilings on credit growth and external borrowing.

Increasing capitalization requirements. Unless weighted by the risk of banks' assets, increasing capitalization requirements does not guarantee that banks will pursue a more sound investment and lending strategy—in fact, it could have the opposite effect and induce bankers to increase the risk in their portfolios. Therefore countries should introduce risk-adjusted capitalization requirements such as those recommended by the Bank for International Settlements (annex 5.3). Introducing risk-adjusted capitalization rates, as Argentina and Chile recently did, would—along with the implementation of other reforms discussed in this section—help induce banks to shift their portfolios towards safer assets, thus making the entire banking industry more resilient.[23] Although this would not necessarily reduce overall bank lending, it would negatively affect lending to the riskiest activities, such as home mortgages, commercial real estate, and consumption credit.[24] Excessively high capital requirements, however, could reduce banks' profitability and create other economic inefficiencies, such as inducing financial disintermediation.[25]

Raising the minimum provisioning against future loan losses. This will improve banks' ability to absorb shocks. In addition, it may induce a portfolio shift toward safer assets—those with lower provisioning requirements—and thereby indirectly reduce overheating. More important, by reducing banks' net profits and capital, this policy will constrain the growth in bank lending, with a direct negative effect on credit growth. This policy has been recently applied, for example, in the Czech Republic, where in September of 1994 tighter norms were introduced that caused an increase in the recorded volume of bad loans in that year from 23 to 38 percent of outstanding credit.

One problem with relying on provisioning and capital requirements to contain a lending boom, however, is that especially during periods of financial distress bank managers tend to hide their problems by underestimating the stock of nonperforming assets. It has often been observed that during periods of financial distress, banks will roll over nonperforming loans and capitalize past-due interest. Both practices were standard in Chile and Colombia in the early 1980s, and more recently in Mexico. In the latter case these practices were facilitated by rules permitting banks to declare as nonperforming only a portion of a loan if the borrower was partially meeting his payments. A more cautious approach would have been to declare the entire loan nonperforming. As in Mexico, in a number of Asia-Pacific Economic Cooperation Council developing countries, loans are classified as nonperforming only after the loan has been in arrears for at least six months, and in some cases bank management itself—rather than bank supervisors—set the classification criteria (IMF 1995). This problem has been particularly difficult to monitor in situations where lending goes to related parties (self-lending), and it is especially acute in financially integrated economies where banks and corporations have access to offshore markets. Therefore, for provisioning and capital requirements to be effective, it is critical to have a strong bank supervisory agency with a highly qualified staff that is capable of uncovering a bank's actual financial situation.

Reserve requirements. Although normally understood as a device to prevent liquidity crises, reserve requirements directly affect the amount of funds banks have available to extend credit. Therefore, increasing minimum reserve requirements will help to dampen the lending boom. If, however, these requirements are unremunerated, they can act as a tax on banks (Brock 1996) and may induce them to pursue a riskier investment strategy. Reducing reserve requirements, on the other hand, may exacerbate the credit boom. This is illustrated by the contrasting experiences of Malaysia and Mexico. In the case of Malaysia, the authorities increased reserve requirements on banks and other financial intermediaries by one percentage point in 1991—from 6.5 to 7.5 percent—to dampen the monetary impact of capital flows. Overall, the cumulative increase in the statutory reserve requirement during the capital inflow period was 6 percentage points—from 5.5 percent in 1990 to 11.5 percent in 1994. In contrast, in the case of Mexico in early 1993 the authorities reduced reserve requirements de facto by allowing banks to meet this obligation through the sale of securities to the central bank under a repurchase agreement. A direct consequence of this policy was increased market liquidity and a rise in lending by small, and riskier, banks that exacerbated further both macroeconomic and financial vulnerabilities in Mexico. Other countries that have increased bank reserve requirements recently are Colombia, the Czech Republic, Indonesia, and Sri Lanka (IMF 1995).

Ceilings on commercial bank lending. Imposing ceilings on commercial bank lending (or credit growth) has a direct negative effect on aggregate spending and therefore helps to reduce overheating. This type of policy is most effective in protecting against macroeconomic and financial sector vulnerabilities if directed toward particular types of credit, such as consumption loans, credit cards, and mortgages. In recent years countries such as Malaysia and Thailand have used these restrictions (Corbo and Hernández 1994). Countries that have such restrictions should consider leaving them in place while receiving large capital inflows, in order not to aggravate the overheating.

Restrictions on commercial banks' external borrowing. A similar rationale applies to imposing restrictions on commercial banks' external borrowing, such as those implemented in Indonesia in the early 1990s. The use of direct capital controls on banks can be justified also because of the existence of implicit or explicit deposit insurance (or a foreign exchange guarantee), which country authorities do not want to extend to foreign depositors (Dooley 1996). The increasing coverage of rising deposits may put in jeopardy the solvency of the deposit insurance scheme or, what is the same, the viability of the government budgetary program. The latter, in turn, can lead to a change in market sentiment toward the recipient country, trigger a reversal of flows, and cause a banking crisis (Brock 1996).

Although the last two types of policies—ceilings on commercial bank lending and foreign borrowing—can be justified by the fact that commercial banks are the largest intermediaries in most countries, it is important to note that they may also cause significant economic inefficiencies. By discriminating against commercial banks, these policies may induce financial disintermediation and thereby erode banks' profitability and increase their risk—the former because of the rise of other nonbank financial institutions and the latter because banks' prime clients start tapping into international capital markets for loans.

Indirect capital controls. Controls that apply to different types of foreign flows regardless of the agent intermediating the funds have been used in several countries, such as Brazil, Chile, and Colombia (chapter 4). They put a tax on the use of foreign funds and impose a wedge between domestic and foreign interest rates. Moreover they create important arbitrage opportunities that induce agents to look for ways to bypass the restrictions. Indirect capital controls may reduce overheating and vulnerabilities in the banking system to the extent that they affect the overall volume of intermediation, but this is a doubtful result (chapter 4). A more plausible result is that banks will increase their long-term lending, leading to an increase in investment rather than consumption. Nevertheless, because evasion is usually easier for nonbanks than for banks, in the medium and long term this type of restriction erodes banks' profitability and induces disintermediation.

In sum, a variety of macroeconomic and microeconomic policies can be used to contain the lending boom and minimize the impact of private capital inflows on macroeconomic and financial sector vulnerabilities (box 5.7). Nevertheless, discretion is advised because microeconomic policies could be distortionary and have an adverse effect on banking in the long run.

Crisis preparedness and management

As noted above, financial integration usually gets under way before countries possess all the elements necessary for their financial markets to function smoothly. During this transition period developing countries may experience strains in domestic financial markets that could, if not properly managed, lead to systemic crises. Because financial crises often cause the loss of several percentage points of GDP (box 5.1) and may cause the derailment of painfully achieved macroeconomic (fiscal) stability, it is very important for a country to be able to contain them. Accordingly, crisis preparedness and management form an important aspect of bank supervision and regulation.[26] This subsection reviews the main lessons that emerge from the analysis of actual banking crises and highlights their relevance in the context of increased financial integration. The main conclusion is that the need to act promptly is even more urgent under integration. Table 5.4 summarizes the discussion.

Among the objectives of banking crisis management are to quickly restore public confidence in the banking system in order to avoid severe reductions in liquidity, bank runs, and contagion effects, and to contain the extent and cost of a potential crisis, which is usually borne by taxpayers. Experience shows that to achieve these two objectives, policymakers need to act promptly and decisively and avoid policy reversals that increase market uncertainty. To do so, they need to identify ahead of time the areas of greatest vulnerability in the banking system and have a clear plan to deal with a crisis when it occurs.

Crisis preparedness. One lesson that emerges from past banking crises in developing countries is that policymakers, regulators, and bank supervisors need to have adequate information to realistically assess the nature and magnitude of the crisis. Since incomplete or misleading information may induce wrong policy actions, they need to emphasize data collection and use these data to identify the most critical areas of weaknesses. Common areas of concern are banks' poor risk assessment and management, self-lending, low capitalization and insufficient provisioning for future losses, poor portfolio diversification, foreign exchange exposure, and maturity mismatches.[27] Proper information in these areas will help in preparation of a crisis contin-

Box 5.7 Containing the Lending Boom: Taxation

ONE ARGUMENT GENERALLY OVERLOOKED IN the literature is that tax incentives may increase bank lending. Although taxes should not be intended to contain a lending boom, at the margin they can exacerbate (or ameliorate) its effects. Tax structures that artificially favor indebtedness in the corporate or household sectors—or that do not discourage it—may lead to increases in borrowing by either sector during financial integration, when credit becomes more easily available. In the presence of poor risk assessment, supervision, or management in the banking sector, such borrowing helps to increase financial and macroeconomic vulnerability. The experiences of Chile during the late 1970s and early 1980s, and those of Finland, Norway, and Sweden during the mid-1980s and early 1990s, each case ending in a banking crisis, clearly illustrate this point.

The tax system in effect in Chile during 1975–84 (after a major tax reform in 1974) provided a significant tax advantage to debt financing—as opposed to equity financing—for firms.[1] By taxing dividends twice, first at the corporate level, when companies paid taxes on profits, and then at the personal level, when individuals paid taxes on personal income, the Chilean tax system provided a disincentive for individuals to invest in equity and therefore hindered firms from financing their operations through equity. This disincentive to equity investment meant that individuals taxed at a 10 percent rate (marginal) would receive as much as 67 percent more disposable income—net of taxes—when investing in a bank deposit than when buying a stock rendering the same payoffs. This tax incentive for debt financing was eliminated in the tax reform implemented in 1984. Nevertheless, its presence during the first episode of financial liberalization and opening of the capital account, when credit became more easily available, facilitated the rapid growth of the banking sector and helped to aggravate both macroeconomic and financial fragility in the Chilean economy (Hernández and Walker 1993).

Similarly, the tax structure in effect in Finland, Norway, and Sweden when their domestic banking systems were liberalized, in the second half of the 1980s, provided incentives for household indebtedness at a time when credit became more easily available because of the reforms. In particular, in all three countries high marginal tax rates—above 60 percent

gency plan, which in turn can help reduce decisionmaking time, trial-and-error policies, market uncertainty, and the overall cost of a crisis. Chile's new banking law, which increased disclosure requirements on banks, represents a recent attempt to overcome this problem.

Because financial integration implies a higher speed of market reaction to any unusual developments, and wider swings in prices and quantities, the need to collect consolidated information on banks, assess their main weaknesses, and plan for possible contingencies becomes more urgent than it would be if the economy were isolated. In particular, bank supervisors need to carefully monitor off-balance and offshore operations and the extent to which these are used as a device to hide nonperforming assets and bypass domestic regulations. The practice of lending to third parties abroad—which then relend the in Finland—and full tax deductibility of interest payments led households to increase their borrowing for both mortgages and consumption loans. The increase in bank lending and household expenditure, in turn, reinforced the lending boom by raising real estate prices and collateral values and financing a construction boom. In the end, banks' portfolios became more exposed to cyclical sectors such as construction, real estate, and services, and to exchange rate risk—because of the increase in foreign-currency-denominated loans (Drees and Pazarbasioglu 1995).

Since their banking crises in the second part of the 1980s and early 1990s, all three Nordic countries launched reforms that reduced the tax rates on capital income and therefore the incentives for households to incur high indebtedness—Sweden in 1991, Norway in 1992, and Finland in 1993. Indeed, "all three countries currently impose a fairly low flat rate on capital income, and one can speak of a Nordic model of taxation of capital income" (Tikka 1993, p. 348). In the case of Finland, for example, starting in 1993 capital income was taxed at a flat 25 percent rate, and interest expenses are deductible from taxable income at the same flat rate, excluding interest paid on consumer loans other than those related to the purchase of a permanent residence. Other earned income, such as wages, is still taxed at an increasing marginal rate that goes above 60 percent. The new tax structure, however, eliminates tax arbitrage by incurring greater debt.

In sum, it is clear from these examples that at the margin tax incentives can exacerbate or ameliorate the effects of a lending boom, even though they should not be used as a main policy tool to contain a boom. Therefore such incentives can be thought of as a complement to enhance the effect of other, more permanent policies (such as fiscal policy and strong bank supervision) aimed at containing a quick expansion in bank lending.

1. The tax incentive for debt financing existed prior to the 1974 tax reform. However, the financial repression and credit rationing that existed in the Chilean economy until the mid-1970s reduce its importance for explaining the indebtedness in the corporate sector. For a more detailed analysis of these issues see Hernández and Walker (1993).

same funds to a related domestic party—has been used in some instances to bypass domestic regulations against self-lending. This occurred in Chile during the early 1980s and Venezuela during the 1990s. In the latter case, however, the Venezuelan authorities had no legal powers to supervise off-balance and offshore bank operations until 1994. Moreover, the recent Mexican and Venezuelan banking crises illustrate how off-balance transactions—involving financial derivatives—and offshore operations can become a very important source of losses (Garber 1996). In the case of Venezuela's Banco Latino, for example, it is estimated that one-third of the $3 billion in losses were registered off-balance (Celarier 1994). In contrast, Indonesia recently tightened the regulations and monitoring of offshore activities and borrowing by banks (1991) and nonbank financial institutions (1995).

Table 5.4 Banking Crisis: Policy Options

Policy option	*Major advantages*
No intervention	No cost to taxpayers. Strengthens market discipline.
Financial assistance and recovery	Avoids runs and disruptions in the payments system. Preserves the economic value of bank franchising (intangible assets).
Takeover and liquidation	Strengthens market discipline. Limits the cost of rescue operations to only insured deposits. Imposes higher losses on bank owners and managers (in the latter case only if it is possible to remove them.)
Takeover and assisted sale of failing institution	Avoids runs and disruptions in the payments system. Preserves the economic value of bank franchising (intangible assets). Imposes higher losses on bank owners and managers (in the latter case only if it is possible to remove them).

Major disadvantages	*Main effect of increased financial integration*
Not feasible or credible, especially when failing institutions are large or constitute a large segment of the market.	Induces depositors to put their money into offshore banks and, depending on the exchange rate regime, increases volatility either in capital flows and interest rates or in exchange rates.
May cause important economic losses if it leads to disruptions in the credit and payments system.	
Promotes unfair competition because it induces a de facto "too big to fail" doctrine.	
Promotes unfair competition (healthy banks have to compete for funds with failing institutions) and protects managers and stockholders of risk-taking institutions.	Increases the potential cost to taxpayers because of the greater possibilities for risk taking and increasing difficulties in monitoring.
Gives wrong incentives and signals that in the long run will exacerbate moral hazard problems.	
If left unconstrained, banks can continue investing in risky activities.	
May induce runs and disruptions in credit and payments if information leaks, a likely outcome in the case of large institutions.	May induce holders of unprotected deposits to go to offshore banks and, depending on the exchange rate regime, may increase volatility either in capital flows and interest rates or in exchange rates.
Destroys the franchise value of banks.	
Likely to lead to a "too big to fail" type of behavior; in the end it is strictly enforced only when the failure involves a small banking institution, since supervisors are afraid to liquidate large institutions for political reasons as well as to avoid panics and runs.	In an integrated environment, it may become easier to liquidate bank assets.
	More difficult to impose large losses on bank owners and managers—requires early intervention.
Usually leads to protecting all deposits because significant time is needed to assess the value of assets and work out a sale, a time during which unprotected depositors can withdraw their funds.	Increases the potential cost to taxpayers because of the greater possibilities for risk taking and increased monitoring difficulties.
If no cleanup of banks occurs before privatization, then a repetition of events leading to insolvency (and future intervention) is likely to occur.	It may become easier to implement in an integrated environment where foreigners are allowed to buy bank assets and failing institutions.
A delayed sale can reduce the value of the failing institution.	More difficult to impose large losses on bank owners and managers—requires early intervention.
Difficult to implement in developing countries because of shallow markets for bank assets and institutions, especially in the case of large banks.	
More expensive to implement when accounting standards are poor and bank liabilities are not accurately reported.	

Crisis management. Crisis management involves allocation of losses and management of failing institutions—whether and how to intervene in ailing banks. In an integrated environment, policymakers need to intervene promptly and decisively in ailing institutions in order to contain the crisis and impose losses on the parties responsible—the bank owners and managers (see below). In this regard a set of rigid policy rules, similar to those in the structured early intervention and resolution system proposed by Benston and Kaufman (1988) and incorporated into recent U.S. banking legislation (Federal Deposit Insurance Corporation Improvement Act), can be valuable in helping bank regulators to resist the opposition of interest groups affected by the intervention process. However, in many instances a set of rigid rules can have undesirable effects such as forcing the intervention and liquidation of viable institutions (Goldstein and Turner 1996). Thus, good judgment and discretion are needed in managing a banking crisis, and in many instances policymakers may choose to follow a more heterodox approach rather than a strict application of rules and pure orthodoxy (box 5.8).

Intervention strategies. Policymakers have four broad options for managing a banking crisis: (a) not intervening at all, (b) providing financial assistance to ailing institutions without restraining their activities, (c) taking over and liquidating ailing financial institutions, and (d) taking over and privatizing ailing banks. The first two policy options will, in most cases, aggravate the crisis and exacerbate moral hazard, a problem that becomes even more acute in financially integrated economies and that restricts their applicability even further (box 5.9). The second two policy options are more feasible and are discussed below.

- The strategy of taking over insolvent institutions and removing or restraining their management is intended to stop the practice of throwing good money after bad—that is, to prevent bankers from continuing unsound banking practices with depositors' money that, in turn, is insured by the government. This policy has been implemented in many instances in the past, for example, in Chile and Norway during the 1980s. In doing this it is important to act promptly after distress is detected, since delays tend to induce withdrawals of noninsured deposits, as well as additional risk taking by bank managers. One example where prompt action helped

Box 5.8 Orthodox versus Heterodox Bank Regulations

PRUDENTIAL BANK REGULATION IS GENERALLY structured around three orthodox principles regarding bank capital, supervision, and recapitalization or exit:

- Bank capital must be positive and sufficient to withstand most shocks to a bank's assets.
- A bank supervisory agency must have the capability to collect good information on banks' assets and liabilities.
- Bank supervisors must have the power and financial resources to either recapitalize bankrupt banks or to force their liquidation.

Underlying this orthodox approach to bank regulation is the idea that deposit insurance—which most countries have put in place to safeguard the payments system, protect small savers, and prevent bank runs—places government financial resources at risk. Regulation of bank capital, supervision of bank balance sheets, and the recapitalization or forced exit of bankrupt banks enable the government to control its exposure to financial risk related to such deposit insurance.

These orthodox principles of bank regulation have often been disregarded in economies that suffer from financial repression. In a financially repressed economy interest rates are controlled (often at negative real interest rates), portfolio guidelines are rigidly set, and much financial intermediation bypasses the banking system, often in the form of an unregulated curb market. The liberalization of a financial system marks a movement away from centralized control of financial resources and toward decentralized decisionmaking by agents in the private sector.

The move to a liberalized financial system, however, often takes place before orthodox banking regulations are implemented. Instead, the regulatory framework is often severely bent to accommodate the special circumstances surrounding the liberalization. A common problem during this time is a significant portfolio of bad loans, which can threaten banks' regulatory capital. Regulators are often tolerant of such problems because they hope that bank profits in the deregulated environment will allow the bank to make provisions for the bad loans. But equally important, most regulatory authorities adopt a policy of forbearance because intervention would involve an immediate large financial cost.

Low or negative net worth gives banks the incentive to undertake risky loans and investments, while liberalized access to funds gives them the means to overborrow. During the credit boom that often follows financial liberalization, authorities almost always pay lip service to orthodox regulatory policies, even while staffs of bank inspectors are kept small, poorly trained, and powerless to alter banks' lending or provisioning practices. In addition, if financial liberalization is accompanied by a trade reform, regulators will be reluctant to discourage high-risk loans to export-oriented activities for fear of derailing the government's reform program. During such a period the lack of orthodoxy is primarily due to neglect by the monetary authorities rather than an alternative set of policies.

When the gamble to let banks grow out of their problems fails, the formal commitment to orthodox banking regulations loses its credibility, and the inability to resolve systemic solvency and liquidity problems with standard measures forces monetary authorities to try to contain the crisis with ad hoc policies. Unlike orthodox policies, these heterodox policies vary widely from crisis to crisis, and their only common element is their attempt to distribute the costs of the crisis across different groups in the economy. Some of the policies are aimed at depositors: the imposition of capital controls prevents depositors from turning their assets into foreign assets (U.S. dollars). Other policies are aimed at debtors: preferential dollar exchange rates help debtors who borrowed in dollars, debt write-downs help firms and mortgage holders, and the swap of bad bank loans for central bank bonds helps banks improve their balance sheets. All heterodox policies to help

(Box continues on the following page.)

Box 5.8 (continued)

debtors and banks involve either a direct cost to the central bank or treasury or a postponement of the debt payment (or bailout).

The imposition of such policies is essentially an ad hoc bankruptcy process for much of the private sector. Unlike a formal bankruptcy process, these are often arbitrarily imposed and implemented with long lags after the crisis begins. The long lags are the result of poor information regarding the extent of portfolio problems, institutional inability to handle large-scale crises, and pressure by politically powerful groups to delay actions that would hurt members of the groups. The lags are often associated with high real interest rates that transfer wealth, in an accounting sense, from borrowers to lenders. This transfer complicates the implementation of policies to resolve the crisis, since the deadweight costs associated with the collection of taxes to pay for the transfer raise the social cost of the transfer above the narrow fiscal cost. The greatest difficulty with ad hoc policies is that the lack of rules can easily give rise to expectations that policies will be revised in the future in the direction of greater debt forgiveness. Such expectations may encourage a mass debtor default, even by debtors who are in a position to repay. In both Chile and Mexico, for example, programs to aid debtors proved insufficient to prevent the deterioration of debtors' net worth and later had to be revised with more generous terms (see below).

These considerations suggest that policies should be specified well in advance of any crisis. Much of Chile's 1986 banking law, for example, was motivated by the recognition that a special bankruptcy code for the banking system was needed to prevent a recurrence of the disorder that surrounded the 1983 financial crisis. Its intention was to deter risky behavior by specifying the policies that will be pursued in the event of a future crisis. In addition to improved supervision and bank capital requirements, that law specifies a number of mechanisms by which bank solvency problems can be resolved without a government bailout. These mechanisms include two different voluntary recapitalization plans, as well as a plan that permits depositors to choose one of two ways to convert deposits into bank equity. In addition, the law makes detailed provisions for the disposal of mortgages and other bank assets. The law was successfully tested in small ways when regulators intervened in the affairs of a medium-sized bank in the late 1980s.

Principal Heterodox Policies Used during Two Financial Crises: Chile and Mexico

Chile

Debt rescheduling, 1983–88. Two separate across-the-board debt rescheduling programs for firms and one across-the-board rescheduling for mortgage and

to reduce the cost of crisis is Malaysia in the mid-1980s. There the authorities devised rescue packages for the ailing financial institutions early in the crisis, in 1985, reducing total losses to only 2.4 percent of total deposits, and allowing the economy to start recovering only two years after the crisis started—in 1987.[28] In contrast, analysis of the 1980s savings and loan crisis in the United States, for example, suggests that delaying the closure of troubled institutions, by up to 38 months on average, doubled the cost of resolving the crisis (Dellas, Diba, and Garber 1996). In the case of consumer loans. The April 1983 program proved inadequate to solve the problem and was expanded in June 1984. Some loans were rescheduled again on a case-by-case basis by individual banks in 1986. Some mortgage loans were partially forgiven (up to 25 percent) in 1988 through a special refinancing facility set up by the central bank.

Purchase of risky loans by the central bank, 1982–87. The central bank purchased bad loans at par for up to 150 percent of capital and reserves of each bank. In exchange, banks were given central bank bonds indexed to the consumer price index that paid 7 percent in real terms. Banks were required to repurchase these loans out of earnings until 1996, when the central bank began negotiations that are expected to forgive about $1.5 billion of the outstanding debt.

Dollar loans, 1982–85. The central bank established a preferential exchange rate for the repayment of dollar-denominated loans. This was a costly rescue program for the central bank.

Recapitalization, 1985–87. Through a program called Capitalismo Popular, the government subsidized the purchase by small investors of new equity capital in banks that had undergone intervention.

Mexico

Debt restructuring, 1995–96. Commercial, mortgage, and consumer loans have been rescheduled into UDI (unit of investment, or CPI-indexed) loans. The UDI loans involve an interest subsidy to banks and can be carried at book value even though they might be sold at a loss.

Direct subsidies to borrowers, 1995–96. Under the September 1995 ADE program, created to neutralize the growing political importance of an organized debtors' movement, credit card and mortgage obligations receive a direct interest rate subsidy from the government for a year. The original ADE program failed to resolve growing arrears and was consequently expanded in April 1996.

Dollar loans, 1995. Following the December 1994 devaluation of the peso, commercial banks in Mexico had great difficulty rolling over dollar-denominated certificates of deposit. In response, the Mexican government established a special discount window for dollar loans to banks at penalty interest rates of 25 percent.

Recapitalization, 1995–96. Following an initial temporary recapitalization program, PROCAPTE, implemented in February 1995, FOBAPROA (the Bank Liability Protection Agency) instituted a loan purchase/capitalization program for the eight banks that had undergone intervention. In the program FOBAPROA purchases two dollars of nonperforming loans for each dollar of new capital infusion.

developing countries, where resolution costs appear to be higher (box 5.1), it becomes even more urgent to act promptly to contain the crisis, especially in an integrated environment, where bank managers have a number of channels through which they can undertake risky investments or commit fraud. Indeed, this occurred in the case of eight financial institutions that failed in Venezuela in the 1994 banking crisis, after the collapse of Banco Latino (box 5.9). In addition, in an integrated environment financial instability may lead to capital flight, which can increase macroeconomic

Box 5.9 Infeasible Policies in Banking Crisis Management

A POLICY OF NO INTERVENTION GENERALLY lacks credibility—and is therefore ineffective—unless the crisis is not systemic and involves only small financial institutions whose failure does not threaten the stability of the financial system. Moreover, intervention may be inevitable—even if it affects only small institutions—if there is in place a deposit insurance mechanism that allows banks to undertake risky investments with depositors' money and policymakers aim to minimize the cost of crisis to the taxpayers. In a financially integrated environment a policy of nonintervention will lead to capital flight whenever depositors suspect that even a small-scale financial crisis may occur. This, in turn, will lead to higher interest or exchange rate volatility—depending on the exchange rate system—which will exacerbate macroeconomic vulnerability. Moreover, a policy of nonintervention is self-defeating, since it will lead in the medium term to the establishment of large banks because markets tend to act as if the too-big-to-fail doctrine prevails.

A policy of providing financial assistance—for example, through emergency (soft) loans—to banks in distress without directly intervening in their operations, gives a competitive advantage to risky banks by subsidizing them and protecting the interests of their owners and managers. In addition, if no control mechanisms are established for the use of the emergency funds, this policy may increase risky lending and the associated losses. In this regard the experience during the second stage of the 1994 banking crisis in Venezuela (after the collapse of Banco Latino), which involved eight financial institutions, is instructive. Because the crisis occurred only weeks before a new administration took office, the authorities provided financial assistance to the ailing institutions but left any further action to the new administration. The delayed response in controlling bank actions exacerbated fraud and caused larger losses.

Thus, from an efficiency point of view the latter policy can be justified only if the ailing banks are economically viable—have a positive net worth—so that bankers have the incentive to invest the funds in a sound manner. For this to occur, intervention must take place at an early stage, before banks' net worth evaporates or becomes negative. On the other hand, from an equity point of view this policy can only be justified if bank problems are due to systemic risk and not to poor management; otherwise this policy will exacerbate moral hazard and discriminate against sound and well-managed banks. Financial integration increases the potential losses that may result from providing cheap financial assistance to ailing banks without intervention. This highlights the need for good information so that bank supervisors can quickly discriminate between solvent and insolvent institutions and provide financial assistance to only the former group. Nonviable financial institutions, on the other hand, need intervention, and their lending and risk-taking activities must be restricted.

vulnerability. In taking over insolvent institutions, bank regulators should seek to remove managers as a way of imposing on them part of the cost of the crisis (see below). Nevertheless, regulators may be unable to do so if manpower is scarce and there are no alternative teams capable of managing the ailing institutions (De Juan 1987). In this case, bank managers should be severely regulated and closely monitored, while perquisites and dividends should be drastically curtailed.

- The decision to liquidate or rehabilitate and sell an ailing financial institution should be based on the costs and benefits of each course of action. In general, the main benefit of rehabilitation and posterior sale—privatization—is that it preserves goodwill, while liquidation implies losing the economic value of the institution's intangible assets. Rehabilitation, therefore, may be more valuable in the case of large financial institutions with a large network of branches and some degree of specialization and know-how. On the other hand, the main advantage of liquidation is that it limits the cost of deposit insurance to only the amount of deposits covered by the insurance mechanism. Because rehabilitation and posterior sale is a lengthy process—especially if it involves a large and specialized financial institution—it usually leads to the protection of all deposits to prevent a withdrawal of funds and a disruption in credit and payments. In addition, rehabilitation and sale may be more difficult in developing countries, which lack specialized markets to dispose of financial institutions, while a delayed sale may destroy some of the economic value of the intervened bank. Liquidation, too, can be problematic, especially since in a financially integrated economy it can lead to capital flight and increased volatility in either exchange or interest rates, exacerbating macroeconomic vulnerabilities. On the other hand, the privatization of ailing institutions can be facilitated in an integrated environment if foreign banks can compete in the bidding process. Therefore, increased financial integration may bias the resolution of banking crises toward intervention and posterior sale of ailing banks. For this outcome to be preferable to liquidation, however, it is important to minimize the losses that result from risk-taking activities, which calls for early intervention and prompt action once problems are detected.

Although these conclusions are generally valid, they need to be considered or analyzed with caution. For example, rushing the privatization of banks may create future troubles if the buyers are not adequately screened. The purpose should not be to sell quickly but to sell to good bankers. Therefore, it is worthwhile to take the time to assess the new owners. This is illustrated by the recent experience in Mexico, where in the early 1990s state-owned banks were sold to inexperienced bankers who in many instances incurred large debts to finance their purchases (box 5.6). In an integrated environment the issue of carefully screening market participants acquires special relevance because of the potential for greater losses and the larger pool of market participants, including foreign-based institutions, which may enter the banking sector without the appropriate skills or incentives. The recent establishment of Russian-backed banks in some countries in Eastern Europe and the former Soviet Union—such as Hungary and Latvia—has been a matter of concern, for example, because in many cases these are only pocket banks of large state-owned enterprises and lack the expertise to function in a modern integrated economy (Fleming and Talley 1996; Fleming, Chu, and Bakker 1996).[29]

Also, because the restructuring and privatization of banks has proved to be unsuccessful—leading to second rounds of intervention and financial rehabilitation—when the macroeconomy has been in disarray, a macroeconomic stabilization program should be implemented prior to or at the same time that bank restructuring starts. Given the greater market response and the increased number of channels through which capital outflows can occur in an integrated economy, more emphasis and higher priority must be given to achieving and maintaining macroeconomic stability when managing a banking crisis and trying to rehabilitate failed banks. In the same vein, because of the potentially greater negative effects of financial distress on the macroeconomy in an integrated environment, a quicker response is needed to correct the underlying financial causes of the crisis.

Allocation of losses: guiding principles. The allocation of losses in a banking crisis is a difficult political problem. There are four groups that can be targeted: stockholders and bank managers, depositors, borrowers, and taxpayers.

- Bank owners and managers should suffer maximum losses—their institutions should be taken over and they should be removed from management. As argued earlier, however, this may be difficult to implement in countries where banking skills are scarce and supervisors lack experience in banking. Moreover, to effectively impose losses on owners and managers, intervention must take place at an early stage—before losses reach several times the institution's capital and the owners (using depositors' money) have moved funds offshore while managers have been overpaid. Imposing losses on owners and managers in an integrated environment requires early detection and prompt action.

- Depositors rarely bear a part of the losses, especially in the case of large banks (the "too-big-to-fail" syndrome), although there are exceptions to this rule. For example, in Côte d'Ivoire in 1991 depositors lost about 15 percent of their deposits, in Chile during 1982–84 depositors in banks that were liquidated (small banks) lost 70 percent of theirs, and in Estonia in 1993 depositors lost about 40 percent of their deposits.[30] It is politically costly to impose losses on depositors, although ideally governments would like to impose losses on large depositors to enhance market discipline. Trying to tax depositors in an integrated environment, however, will most likely lead to capital flight and exacerbate macroeconomic and financial problems.
- Borrowers should be targeted to the extent that seeking repayment from them does not distort their incentives to invest and undertake new projects. They should not be left with a debt overhang problem that would deter new investment and cause economic growth to decline (box 5.1). Alternatively, in an integrated environment borrowers may seek to start new businesses offshore.
- Taxpayers will bear less of the cost of a crisis the sooner the crisis is detected and contained. The cost to taxpayers results from the need to restore confidence in the market by bailing out borrowers and protecting depositors. The difficulties encountered in managing a banking crisis—for example estimating its actual cost and resolving incentive and other institutional problems—tend to delay policy responses and increase market uncertainty. Therefore, a prompt policy response will reduce the cost of the crisis shared by taxpayers. To the extent possible, however, the tax revenues raised to pay for the bailout should not deter economic growth in the medium and long term—for example, the authorities should avoid increasing tax collection through inflation.

In an integrated environment the allocation of losses will most likely be biased toward the less protected and informed groups—small depositors, small shareholders, and taxpayers—since large depositors, bank owners, and managers will often be able to move funds offshore. Thus, the need to intervene promptly is even more urgent if the objective is to impose maximum losses on the largest market participants, those who have greater incentives to be well informed and for whom it is cheaper—proportional to their investment—to move funds from onshore to offshore locations.

In sum, financial integration puts a premium on the need for good and reliable information, prompt decisionmaking, and swift corrective action by bank supervisors. Given the greater volatility and responsiveness of financial markets in an integrated environment, and the potential for larger losses, the need to detect and contain a banking crisis at an early stage becomes even more urgent. Special attention must be paid to offshore and off-balance transactions and to the screening of potential bankers, as well as to the need for economic authorities to put in place a contingency plan and provision adequate funding while, at the same time, maintaining macroeconomic stability. Indeed, analysis of past episodes shows that lack of appropriate funding has led bank supervisors not to intervene but to let distressed financial institutions remain in business, a course that in the end increases the cost of crisis. A sound macroeconomic stance and other aspects of bank regulation become even more important when managing a banking crisis under more stringent conditions, such as in the presence of a currency board. Two recent experiences of banking crises under a currency board, in Argentina and Hong Kong, are briefly discussed in annex 5.4.

Annex 5.1 Capital Inflows, Lending Booms, and Banking Crises: Country Episodes

THE ANALYSIS IN THIS CHAPTER IS BASED on a subsample of the country episodes studied in previous chapters. In particular, we study a set of countries that have experienced a surge in private capital flows at some point during the past 20 years while, at the same time, attempting to implement reforms in their financial sectors. Country episodes were selected on the basis of the importance of the banking sector in determining the outcome of the financial liberalization and integration experiment. In other words, the sample includes country episodes in which the banking sector has played a significant role in the observed outcome. The sample selection was partly influenced by the attention that each country experience has attracted in the relevant literature. The sample comprises both industrial and developing countries, and in the case of some developing countries more than one episode is analyzed. In particular, we include episodes occurring in the early 1980s, prior to the debt crisis, and compare them with those occurring in more recent years. The list of country episodes included in our sample is shown in table 5.5, on the next page.

Several features of the country episodes analyzed here are worth discussing. First, in all the episodes—except Sweden during 1989–93—the country involved received significant private capital inflows (measured in terms of GDP). Indeed, the sample average for all the episodes (including Sweden) is almost 5 percentage points of GDP. Second, more than half of the country episodes ended in a banking crisis (14 out of 20). This validates the point argued earlier that the outcome of the liberalization and integration experiment was largely affected by developments in the banking sector. Third, economic growth was significantly reduced in the years following a banking crisis—except for the cases of Brazil during the 1990s and Thailand during the early 1980s.[31] Moreover, in most cases economic growth during the years following a banking crisis was either negligible or negative. Fourth, in all the cases where a banking crisis occurred, credit to the private sector—from either banks or other financial institutions—grew in real terms at very high rates in the years before the crisis, with rates of growth usually several times that of real output. Furthermore, these periods of high growth were followed by years of very low or even negative credit expansion.

Table 5.5 Capital Inflows, Lending Booms, and Banking Crises, Selected Countries and Years

				Average percentage of growth					
Country	*Inflow period*	*Inflow as a percentage of GDP*	*Banking crisis years*	*Bank credit (inflow period or precrisis years)*	*Bank credit (crisis and postcrisis years)*	*Nonbank credit (inflow period or precrisis years)*	*Nonbank credit (crisis and postcrisis years)*	*GDP (inflow period or precrisis years)*	*GDP (crisis and postcrisis years)*
Argentina	1979–82	1.98	1980–82	14.64	13.19	6.57	−20.38	4.36	−1.79
	1992–93	4.03	1994–95	16.94	14.86	45.56	24.91	7.34	1.34
Brazil	1992–94	2.19	1995	52.57	—	17.41	—	3.00	3.35
Chile	1978–81	12.68	1981–83	43.26	10.29	71.55	−33.22	8.09	−3.45
	1989–94	5.48	no crisis	7.46	—	21.79	—	6.96	—
Colombia	1992–94	3.84	no crisis	15.23	—	15.15	—	5.03	—
Finland	1987–94	4.18	1991–93	11.99	−7.67	—	—	3.65	−1.94
Indonesia	1990–94	1.22	no crisis	18.59	—	—	—	6.92	—
Malaysia	1980–86	6.66	1985–88	16.53	6.32	23.41	7.18	6.87	3.52
	1989–94	9.75	no crisis	12.76	—	11.92	—	8.75	—
Mexico	1979–81	5.27	1982–83	14.58	-25.19	−1.82	−11.38	8.47	-2.42
	1989–94	5.15	1994–95	33.47	—	15.16	—	3.06	−1.79
Norway	1984–89	2.04	1988–89	18.71	2.22	0.02	1.49	4.29	0.19
Philippines	1978–83	4.57	1982–87	9.18	−10.84	12.48	−22.95	4.95	−0.37
	1989–94	4.17	no crisis	11.92	—	18.67	—	2.56	—
Sweden	1989–93	0.77	1991–93	7.54	−11.98	28.67	−1.96	1.87	−1.77
Thailand	1978–84	4.42	1983–87	7.92	14.31	9.43	7.55	6.34	6.19
	1988–94	9.34	no crisis	21.35	—	21.43	—	10.01	—
Venezuela	1975–80	7.81	1980	15.13	−2.14	16.99	3.31	4.97	−1.84
	1992–93	2.65	1994–95	−7.97	−26.81	−13.45	−31.95	3.13	−0.32

— Not available.

Note: Comparisons across countries are not valid because periods differ in length.

Source: IMF, *International Financial Statistics* data base; *World Economic Outlook* data base; Caprio and Klingebiel (1996); Kaminsky and Reinhart (1996).

Annex 5.2 Government Guarantees, High Real Interest Rates, and Banking Sector Fragility

A FINANCIAL SYSTEM INTERMEDIATES funds between savers and investors, determines the quality of investments undertaken in the economy, and provides the means of payment for many transactions. When the financial system is working well, these functions increase output in the short run, as well as the level and productivity of the capital stock in the longer run. The functions of the financial system are, in fact, so important that virtually all governments provide explicit or implicit guarantees to participants in the system. These guarantees may simply take the form of protection to otherwise solvent banks during a run on deposits, without protecting depositors in the event that banks turn out to be insolvent (lender of last resort). Or the guarantees may be extended to small savers, on the assumption that they are not sophisticated enough to monitor bank owners and managers (limited deposit insurance); or they may cover banks whose failure is judged to pose a threat to the financial system. This "too big to fail" guarantee usually covers all the liabilities of larger banks while leaving liabilities of smaller banks at some risk. Often governments extend—at least implicitly—blanket guarantees for all banks, which shift private risk associated with bank liabilities to the government.

Guarantees

The advantage of government financial guarantees is that they protect the payment system, prevent bank runs, and protect depositors against losses. The dark side of these guarantees is that they may promote risk taking and give overambitious bank owners access to financial resources with which to gamble on future economic growth. This can occur because a guarantee operates in the same way as a put option on a bank's assets: if the value of the bank's assets falls below the value of its liabilities, the guarantee makes up the difference. As with a put option, an increase in the riskiness of the asset portfolio raises the value of the guarantee to bank owners (and possibly to bank executives), since greater risk increases the potential for large up-side profits while the government guarantee insures depositors against downside losses. Without a countervailing force, therefore, guarantees will be a source of financial instability, since banks will end up attempting to maximize the value of the guarantees.

The incentives for risk taking associated with deposit guarantees can be counteracted by ensuring that the value of a bank as an ongoing operation, including the value of specialized human capital, is positive. When a bank has high franchise value and a healthy balance sheet, it will generally protect itself against risk, since the value of the government's guarantee to a banker is relatively small. If, on the contrary, the franchise value of the bank decreases, then bankers will pursue risky strategies that depend on the government guarantee. When banks have an incentive to maximize the value of the guarantee, the result can be a banking crisis that may involve a fiscal cost of up to 8 percent of GDP, as happened recently in Mexico. This cost, moreover, can easily be doubled by the deadweight costs of taxation, bankruptcies, and the interruption of new lending. Given the large potential cost associated with government guarantees, therefore, it is important for policymakers to keep track of variables that may signal an environment in which banks have the incentive and opportunity to maximize the value of the guarantee.

Interest Rates

A substantial rise in real interest rates almost always results in a deterioration of bank balance sheets because of the term transformation done by banks—deposits are short term, while bank assets are longer term—and because higher real loan rates cause an increase in nonperforming loans. If the high real rates are only transitory, then healthy banks will not be unduly affected. But if the high rates persist, banks' net worth may be so compromised that the banks try to grow out of their problems with risky loans and investments. To understand why interest rates can be high in a country, it is useful to look at two primary interest rate spreads: the *deposit rate spread* (the difference between the nominal domestic deposit rate and the sum of the relevant nominal international rate—usually the three-month U.S. treasury bill rate—and the actual change in the exchange rate), and the *loan rate spread* (the difference between the loan rate and the deposit rate). The table below separates the deposit and loan rate spreads into their respective parts and shows the economic reasons for these spreads.

Typically, a high deposit rate spread is accounted for by forecasting errors resulting from a prediction of domestic inflation that turns out to be too high or expectations of exchange rate depreciation. Furthermore, if the real deposit rate (the nominal rate adjusted by actual inflation) appears low, while the deposit rate spread appears high, there has usually been an appreciation of the real exchange rate combined with expectations of a future discrete depreciation, the so-called peso problem. The peso problem is important because expectations of future exchange rate depreciation will drive up interest rates even when the government has no intention of making a sharp exchange rate adjustment. Such high rates, if maintained over a long period, will erode the net worth of both banks and companies, pushing bankers to behave according to the incentives created by the dark side of the government deposit guarantees. For example, some analysts have argued that fixing the exchange rate signals an implicit government commitment to promote and guarantee the safety of long-term international borrowing at that exchange rate. This implicit guarantee makes the open capital account look inviting to foreign lenders and may encourage overborrowing in dollars when domestic interest rates are high.

Remaining factors that raise the deposit rate spread, grouped under the heading of deviations from interest rate parity, can be caused by exchange rate risk, country risk, or imperfect capital mobility. In addition, the risk that the government may not

Deposit rate spread $i_d - i^* - \Delta e$	*Macroeconomic factors*
Expected depreciation	Lack of monetary/exchange rate credibility
Deviations from interest rate parity	Exchange rate risk, imperfect capital mobility, default risk associated with government debt, guarantor risk associated with banking system
Loan rate spread $i_l - i_d$	***Microeconomic factors***
Taxes on intermediation	Reserve requirements, directed credit programs
Net spread	Default risk, industry structure

Note: i_d = deposit rate; i^*= international rate; Δe = change in the exchange rate; i_l= loan rate.

stand by its implicit, or even explicit, guarantees to the banking system will increase the differential between the domestic deposit rate and the international rate of interest. For example, if there is a perception that the government is likely to render dollar-denominated deposits inconvertible, the interest rate spread on dollar-denominated deposits will rise to reflect that probability.

The loan rate spread can be decomposed into two components, the first due to taxes on financial intermediation, and the second, the *net spread*, due to the banking system itself—its structure, its costs, and its information and incentive structure. The net spread reflects the costs of banking. When banks have been sheltered from international competition for many years, net spreads are generally high. Opening the capital account will tend to lower net spreads but may also cause formerly profitable banks to become unprofitable and, therefore, to undertake risky activities, as noted above.

To summarize, sustained high real deposit rates and loan rates are a strong signal of future trouble because such rates are usually accompanied by a rise in nonperforming loans. In an integrated environment, when high real rates and weak bank balance sheets are matched with government guarantees that permit banks to borrow internationally, then the stage is set for a credit boom in which rapid credit expansion both masks underlying portfolio problems and creates the opportunity for high-risk loan strategies. During such a boom—as occurred in Chile in the late 1970s and early 1980s, the U.S. savings and loan industry in the 1980s, and Mexico in the early 1990s—it is difficult not to get caught up in the euphoria associated with the economic growth financed by bank credit. But if the boom reflects the dark side of government banking guarantees, then there will be a fiscal reckoning at the boom's end.

An Illustration of Spread Analysis

The analysis of interest rate spreads is most useful when dollar deposit rates exist. In that case expected depreciation can be approximated by the difference between the domestic currency interest rate and the dollar deposit rate. Deviations from interest rate parity will then be picked up by the difference between the dollar deposit rate and the three-month treasury bill rate.

The behavior of interest rates in Chile during its transition to democracy in 1989–90 can be used to illustrate the analysis of interest rate spreads. In Chile many of the events of 1989 revolved around the upcoming December election, in which a candidate approved by the military was opposed by an alliance of various parties. The alliance won and took power in March 1990. Between March 1989 and February 1990 the annualized nominal deposit rate rose from 12.5 percent to 45 percent, and the nominal loan rate rose from 19.5 to 57 percent. This rapid rise in interest rates appears to have reflected concerns about inflation as a result of expansionary macroeconomic policies during 1989, as well as uncertainty about the economic policies of the new government. Interest rates remained high during most of 1990 and did not come down until the beginning of 1991. The deposit rate spread became positive in July 1989 and stayed positive through January 1991, reaching a sustained level of around 20 percent during most of 1990.

During this period, the central bank was attempting an uneasy tradeoff between fighting inflation and preventing an appreciation of the real exchange rate. This tradeoff was especially marked at the beginning of 1990, when the central bank raised interest rates on its long-term indexed debt from 6.9 to 9.7 percent in order to dampen aggregate expenditure. This high interest rate policy pro-

Figure 5.10 Exchange and Interest Rates in Chile, 1988–91

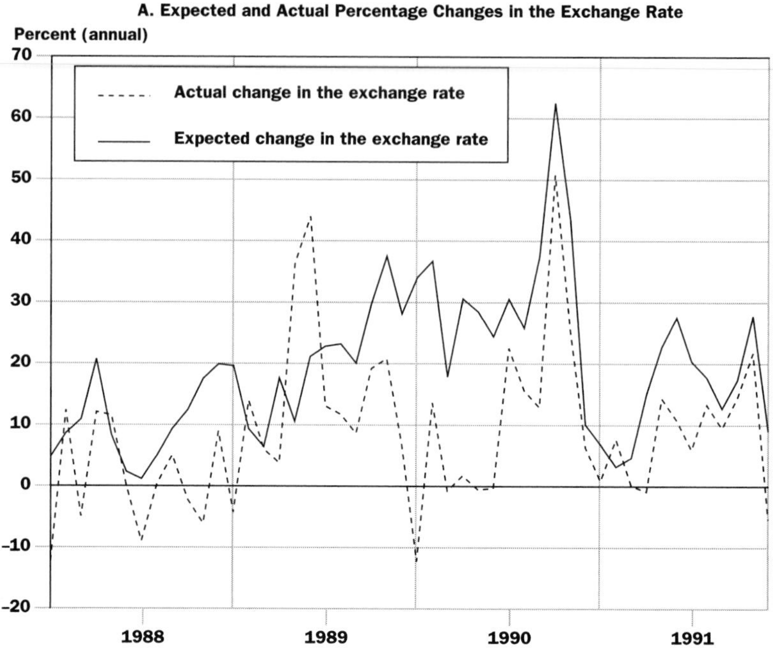

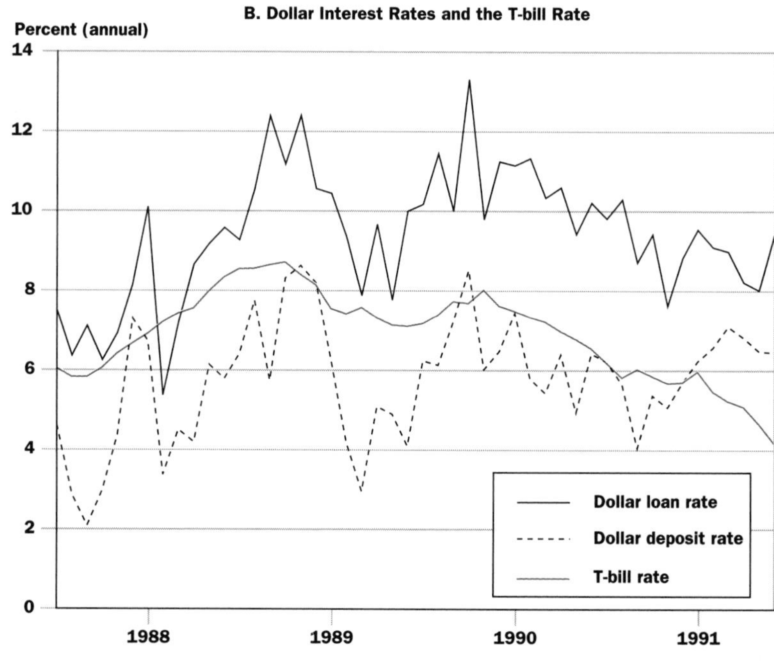

Source: Brock (1996).

duced an immediate appreciation of the currency (to the bottom of the central bank's preestablished exchange rate band) as well as short-term capital inflows which the central bank sterilized.

In terms of the spreads, figure 5.10A shows the difference between the expected change in the exchange rate (calculated from the peso and dollar deposit rates) and the actual annualized change in the exchange rate. The figure shows that from July 1989 to January 1991 the expected change in the exchange rate exceeded the actual change, often by 30 percentage points on an annualized basis. During this period market participants were betting that the central bank would ultimately reverse its inflation-dampening policy and actively depreciate the exchange rate in order to prevent a real appreciation. The expectation proved correct; the exchange rate was allowed to depreciate at the end of 1990. After this episode, the monetary authorities revised their policy in two ways: first, the nominal exchange rate was allowed to appreciate in several discrete steps; second, a 20 percent unremunerated reserve requirement was imposed on capital inflows in June 1991.

Figure 5.10B shows the position of dollar interest rates in Chile relative to the T-bill rate. It is easy to detect the upward shift in the dollar loan rate relative to the T-bill rate that took place at the end of 1989. This upward shift was initially sustained by the central bank's sterilization policy and then later by the reserve requirement on capital inflows. In terms of the spread analysis, this was a deviation from interest rate parity caused by imperfect capital mobility. Note, however, that the size of this component of the deposit rate spread was very small compared with the difference between the expected and actual exchange rate shown in figure 5.10A.

Chile 's high interest rate policy also affected the loan rate spread. In 1988 the loan rate spread averaged 6.06 percent, while it rose to 8.19 percent in 1989 and 8.56 percent in 1990. This increase, had it continued, could have increased the fragility of the banking system, but following the exchange rate depreciation at the end of 1990 and the change in stabilization policies by the central bank, the loan rate spread fell to 6.23 percent in 1991, or approximately its level in 1988.

Annex 5.3 Risk-Adjusted Capital-Asset Ratios: The BIS Classification of Risky Assets

IN DECEMBER 1987 THE BASLE COMMITTEE OF bank supervisors, operating under the auspices of the Bank for International Settlements (BIS), published proposed guidelines for the measurement and assessment of the capital adequacy of banks operating internationally. The guidelines were approved in July 1988 by bank supervisors of 12 industrial countries comprising the Group of Ten (G-10) plus Luxembourg and Switzerland.[32] Under the July 1988 agreement, bank supervisors of these nations were obliged to impose a minimum risk-adjusted capital-asset ratio of 8 percent on all banks operating under their jurisdiction by the end of 1992. Supervisory authorities in each country were given significant discretion in the interpretation and implementation of the new rules.

The main purpose of the new capitalization rules was to put internationally operating banks under common regulatory conditions to prevent unfair competition by banks with lighter regulatory burdens. The new capital-asset ratio guidelines addressed only one aspect of banking regulation, however: the capital requirements needed to protect depositors against credit risk. The guidelines accordingly dealt with the identity of banks' debtors but did not address other sources of risk, such as interest rate risk, exchange rate risk, equities risk, or banks' overall portfolio risk—all of which implies taking into account the correlation among different types of bank assets and liabilities. Furthermore, the new capitalization rules generally did not advance the use of market prices to evaluate bank assets and liabilities.[33]

Although the Basle Accords concerned only international banks and had other limitations, the capitalization guidelines have been voluntarily adopted by an increasing number of countries around the world, and have been extended to the regulation of other financial institutions. For example, the European Union extended the guidelines to all credit institutions in 1989, and the United States has extended them to bank holding companies and their subsidiaries.

The major innovations concerning capital requirements introduced in the accords are:

- The accords assigned percentages for weighting each asset category according to its credit risk.
- They redefined the composition of a bank's primary capital by, for example, excluding general loan loss reserves.
- They initiated a procedure to equate off-balance-sheet items (standby letters of credit, swaps, options, futures contracts, and other contingent assets or liabilities) to asset equivalents based on the type of item and the initial contract terms.

Risk-based capital requirements under the Basle Accords are generally expressed as: $ACB \geqslant 0.08$ *TOWRA*, where *ACB* and *TOWRA* stand for adjusted capital base and total weighted risk assets, respectively. *ACB* is the sum of allowable components of primary (tier 1) and secondary (tier 2) capital, subject to prescribed limits and deducting certain items. For example, goodwill is excluded from primary capital, and term-subordinated debt included in secondary capital cannot exceed 50 percent of primary capital. *TOWRA*, on the other hand, is the weighted sum of on-balance and off-balance items as shown in the following expression:

$$TOWRA = \sum_{i=1}^{s}\sum_{j=1}^{t}(A_{ij}W_j) + \sum_{i=1}^{w}\sum_{j=1}^{v}\sum_{k=1}^{w}(B_{ijk}X_kW_j)$$

where A_{ij} is the value of the ith asset with risk weight W_j, and B_{ijk} is the notional principal amount of off-balance-sheet activity i with risk weight W_j and conversion factor X_k. Table 5.6 summarizes the main risk categories for on-balance sheet items as recommended in the Basle Accords and the conversion factors for off-balance sheet transactions as applied by Japan, the United Kingdom, and the United States.

Table 5.6 BIS Risk Categories of Bank Assets

BIS-recommended risk weight (percent)	*On-balance asset item*
0	Cash, gold, or loans to or fully guaranteed by OECD central governments and central banks; claims fully collateralized by cash; loans to or fully guaranteed by non-OECD central governments or central banks when denominated and funded in local currency.
Less than 20	Holdings of fixed interest securities issued or guaranteed by OECD central governments and floating rate or index-linked OECD central government securities; claims fully collateralized by OECD central government fixed interest securities and similar floating rate securities; holdings of non-OECD central government securities when denominated and funded in local currency.
20	Claims on multilateral development banks (or claims fully guaranteed by or fully collateralized by the securities issued by these institutions), claims on credit institutions incorporated in the OECD countries and claims guaranteed or endorsed by OECD-incorporated credit institutions, claims on or guaranteed by non-OECD incorporated credit institutions when they have a residual maturity of up to one year, claims on or guaranteed by OECD public sector entities (excluding the central government), cash items in the process of collection.
50	Loans fully secured by mortgage on residential property owned or rented out by the borrower.
100	Claims on the nonbank private sector, claims on credit institutions incorporated outside the OECD with residual maturity of more than one year, claims on or guaranteed by non-OECD governments and central banks that are not denominated in local currency and funded locally, claims on public sector enterprises, fixed assets, capital instruments issued by other banks, real estate and trade investment and all other nonspecified assets.
Conversion factor applied in Japan, the United Kingdom, and the United States (percent)	*Off-balance-sheet transaction*
100	Direct credit substitutes, including general guarantees of indebtedness, standby letters of credit, acceptances, and endorsements; sale and repurchase agreements and asset sales with recourse where credit risk remains with the bank; forward agreements to purchase assets, including financial facilities and commitments with certain drawdown.
50	Certain transaction-related contingent items not having the character of direct credit substitutes (performance bonds, bid bonds, warranties, and standby letters of credit related to particular transactions); note issuance facilities and revolving underwriting facilities; other commitments (such as credit lines) with original maturities of more than one year.
20	Short-term, self-liquidating, trade-related contingent items (for example, documentary credits collateralized by the underlying shipments).
0	Similar commitments with original maturity of up to one year or commitments that can be unconditionally canceled at any time, endorsements of bills that have previously been accepted by a bank.

Source: Hall (1994).

Annex 5.4 Crisis Management in a Constrained Setting: The Case of Currency Boards

A CURRENCY BOARD IS A MONETARY REGIME in which the domestic authority is precluded by law from issuing liabilities—high-power money—unless the issue is backed by an equivalent amount of international reserves. Under this system the monetary authority basically relinquishes its right to grant credit to the public or private sector, and therefore, fiscal imbalances cannot be financed through an inflation tax. Although a currency board works as a fixed exchange rate system, it is more credible because a fixed exchange rate system can always be abandoned and is subject to discrete devaluations of the currency, so there is no guarantee that the value of the domestic currency in terms of foreign currency will remain constant through time. The main goal of a currency board, by contrast, is precisely to guarantee the full convertibility of domestic into foreign currency at a constant rate.

The main purpose of a lender of last resort, on the other hand, is to guarantee the full convertibility of a subset of bank liabilities—usually those with the shortest maturities—into domestic currency at their face value. Having such a mechanism in a fractional reserve banking system prevents bank runs and liquidity crises. Such crises could reduce the value of bank assets and lead to insolvency, causing disruptions in the payment and credit systems and great economic losses. Bank runs and liquidity crises lead to insolvency because bank assets are of longer maturity than bank liabilities, and because of asymmetries of information in banking that make bank assets illiquid (Diamond 1984). Therefore, in a fire sale bank assets are usually heavily discounted, causing important losses for the selling bank. Bank depositors, who understand the risk of suffering a loss if a run occurs, tend to withdraw their money as soon as they suspect that a large number of other depositors may do the same. In this context, an otherwise solvent bank may become insolvent if it is unable to contain a run on its deposits and is forced to sell assets at a large discount.[34] Thus, banks are intrinsically unstable institutions subject to self-fulfilling confidence crises that may lead them into insolvency (Diamond and Dybvig 1983).

To overcome the problem of self-fulfilling confidence crises in banking, countries rely on a lender of last resort to provide emergency loans to banks and guarantee full convertibility of deposits into domestic currency at face value; they thereby prevent some of the economic costs associated with bank crises that can affect otherwise solvent institutions. Although the lender of last resort can be any public entity capable of lending to troubled financial institutions, in practice this function in most countries is performed by the domestic monetary authority, which does it by creating money. Therefore, unless a foreign government, central bank, or (multilateral) credit institution is willing to provide a credit line in foreign currency, a currency board will be limited in the amount that it can lend to domestic banks during a liquidity crisis. In particular, it will be able to extend credit to banks only if it holds reserves in excess of the amount required to guarantee the value of the domestic currency at the established exchange rate. In sum, the adoption of a currency board implies that the monetary authority relinquishes its role as a lender of last resort, and unless an alternative entity assumes that role and provides the same type of insurance to bank depositors, the banking system will become more vulnerable to liquidity crises.

The experiences of Hong Kong during the mid-1980s, and more recently of Argentina during 1994–95, provide interesting cases in which a banking crisis occurred under a currency board (a quasi-currency board in the latter case). In both cases the local monetary authority was limited in the amount of credit it was permitted to extend to banks having financial difficulties, and in the end had to resort to alternative mechanisms to contain the crisis.

In Hong Kong several financial institutions faced difficulties starting in 1982, because of the slowdown in economic activity and the dive in stock and property prices from their peaks in 1980–81 (property prices fell between 60 and 90 percent and stock prices by 50 percent). In addition, the uncertainty surrounding the Sino-British talks on the political future of Hong Kong, and the currency crisis that unfolded in 1983, led to the reintroduction of the currency board system, with the Hong Kong dollar pegged to the U.S. dollar, in October of that year.[35] However, increasing financial difficulties in several banks and deposit-taking companies forced the Hong Kong government to intervene to protect depositors. Interventions occurred during 1982–86 and consisted of the government's taking over three medium-size commercial banks, arranging financial support packages for other financial institutions, and providing guarantees against additional irrecoverable debts when the troubled banks were sold to private entities. Although the Hong Kong Monetary Authority could not act as a lender of last resort, the government responded by using reserves held in excess of those in the Exchange Fund, a fund whose main purpose is to stabilize and protect the value of the Hong Kong dollar. Indeed, in April 1986, after several government-led banking rescues had occurred, the total reserves were estimated to be at least HK$35 billion, HK$1.4 billion above the minimum required in the Exchange Fund.[36]

The banking crisis in Argentina started in late 1994, when depositors began withdrawing funds from small and provincial banks and making deposits in larger banks (which were perceived as less vulnerable or "too big to fail"), a shift that led to the bankruptcy of several small financial entities and the crisis in the provincial banks. Initially the shift affected mainly peso-denominated deposits, reflecting a loss of confidence in the currency, but as the crisis deepened it also affected dollar-denominated deposits, reflecting lack of confidence in the banking system. The crisis resulted in total withdrawals of about US$8 billion between December 1994 and April 1995, equal to about 16 percent of total bank deposits, and the central bank's losing about US$4 billion in international reserves. In addition, the number of financial institutions decreased from 201 in December 1994 to 157 a year later, mainly through mergers and acquisitions. At the same time there was a shift toward U.S.-dollar-denominated deposits in large banks. Thus, between November 1994 and June 1995, the 10 largest banks increased their share in total private deposits from 49 to 57 percent, while of the increase in total deposits during the second half of 1995, about 80 percent was in U.S.-dollar-denominated accounts.

Argentine authorities responded to the crisis by significantly reducing bank reserve requirements to permit an increase in liquidity in the system, negotiating a financial assistance package with the multilateral institutions and creating a privately financed limited deposit insurance mechanism. Reserve requirements were reduced so that the 25 largest banks were able to buy assets from the smallest ones. Thus, out of the approximately US$8 billion in deposit losses occurring between the end of December 1994 and mid-May 1995, about US$3.4 billion (41 percent) was compensated with a fall in reserve requirements, and only US$1.1 billion (13 percent) with a credit cut (other sources of liquidity were external credit lines, repos, and central bank loans to banks).

Three features of the Argentine banking system that helped reduce the impact of the crisis are worth noting. First, banks were highly capitalized. Indeed, although an 11.5 percent risk-adjusted capital-asset ratio is required for Argentine banks, when the confidence shock hit the economy, banks had a capital-asset ratio of 13.4 percent nominal and 18.2 percent when adjusted by risk (Fernández and Schumacher 1996). Second, the increased dollarization of the economy had created a bimonetary system. Thus, by the end of 1994 about half of total deposits were dollar denominated (compared with only 21 percent at the end of 1989), and dollar-denominated loans represented about 57 percent of the total. Third, banks had high reserve requirements—although after the crisis these were changed for maturity-related liquidity requirements ranging from 5 to 15 percent of bank liabilities. Indeed, since 1993 demand and savings deposits were subject to a uniform 40 percent reserve requirement, and the stock of liquid resources held at the central bank at the time of the crisis was about US$9.4 billion, approximately 20 percent of total deposits.

In sum, in order to achieve stability in the value of the domestic currency and in the value of a subset of bank liabilities, authorities in financially integrated economies must rely on policy instruments that can complement the role played by international reserves and can help ensure more resilient banks. High reserve and capitalization requirements, although effective in increasing depositors' confidence, may reduce banks' profitability. Liquidity requirements seem to be a more efficient instrument, as illustrated by the recent change of policy in Argentina. Although holding excess international reserves also seems effective in containing a banking crisis, it is important to note that such a policy is equivalent to the government's having a sound fiscal stance (a surplus) that allows it to have permanent access to the international credit market.

Notes

1. Increased competition occurs because of new—foreign—banks and other nonbank financial intermediaries, while new risks appear in the form of new instruments and investment opportunities. The new sources of risk comprise not only credit risk but also currency, settlement and payments, interest rate, and country risks. Also among the new risks are external shocks, such as a crisis in a neighboring country, that can affect market sentiment negatively, triggering a capital outflow and causing a squeeze in liquidity.

2. The country episodes analyzed here include Argentina 1979–82 and 1992–93, Brazil 1992–94, Chile 1978–81 and 1989–94, Colombia 1992–94, Finland 1987–94, Indonesia 1990–94, Malaysia 1980–86 and 1989–94, Mexico 1979–81 and 1989–94, Norway 1984–89, the Philippines 1978–83 and 1989–94, Sweden 1989–93, Thailand 1978–84 and 1988–94, and Venezuela 1975–80 and 1992–93.

3. It is important to distinguish conceptually the term of an investment from its liquidity. A long-term investment (long-term bonds or stocks) can be liquid if investors can sell their holdings without forcing the dismantling of the factory that was financed with the securities.

4. This school of thought highlights the importance of bank credit as a channel of monetary transmission. This theory assigns a more relevant role to banks than standard macroeconomic (IS-LM) models do. See Bernanke 1983, Bernanke and Blinder 1988, Bernanke and Gertler 1989.

5. For a more detailed explanation see Kindleberger 1978, Calomiris and Gorton 1991, Hubbard 1991, Feldstein 1991, Calomiris 1995, and Minsky 1995.

6. In the case of inflows that enter the recipient country not through banks but through a different channel, such as portfolio investment, the first effect will be felt through an increase in asset prices, which will, in turn, increase the value of collateral and the financial wealth of the private sector. Later on, as the inflows increase the monetary base, the volume of funds being intermediated by the domestic banking system will grow.

7. The country episodes showing the greatest appreciation of the real exchange rate are Brazil (1992–94), Chile (1978–81), and Mexico (1979–81, 1988–94).

8. It is important to note that lending booms are not the primary cause of banking crises. However, large lending booms, in the presence of weak macroeconomic and financial sector conditions, can be an important factor leading to situations of distress (and in the extreme, crisis) in the banking sector.

9. The boom-bust in asset prices has been an outcome of financial liberalization—and has had a significant effect on the macroeconomy—in many country episodes other than those in our sample: for example, Japan, the United Kingdom, and the United States during the 1980s. (Schinasi and Hargraves 1993.)

10. The banking crisis in Argentina, triggered by the devaluation of the Mexican peso, affected mainly small provincial banks and was compounded by the lack of a deposit insurance scheme and a lender of last resort. Its effects were, however, contained by a strong macroeconomic response adopted by the authorities and by the takeover of weak institutions by the stronger ones.

11. During the first surge in capital inflows (1979–82), the authorities used the exchange rate as a nominal anchor to reduce domestic inflation, while during the most recent episode (1989–95), they used a crawling band of increasing width.

12. For a detailed discussion of the Chilean experience see Valdés-Prieto 1994, Larraín 1989, de la Cuadra and Valdés 1992.

13. Both indices can take positive and negative values. The macroeconomic vulnerability index is constructed by adding the scores of countries (in each episode), which are based on their performance in terms of the current account deficit, consumption, and investment growth. For example, a country receives a score of −1 (or 0) in terms of consumption growth if consumption growth in that episode was smaller than (or equal to) that predicted by the size of the country's capital inflow. A country that scores a 3 on the macroeconomic front is one in which all macroeconomic variables indicated an increase in vulnerability. A country that scores a negative number (or 0) is one in which macroeconomic conditions improved (or stayed constant) over the period of inflows (relative to the size of the country's capital inflow). The financial index is constructed following a similar methodology. Countries' scores on the basis of the financial behavior are added. Countries that score a positive number are those in which financial conditions deteriorated over the period of inflow. The opposite is true in countries where the value of the financial index is negative. Although the indices are on a numeric scale, they should be interpreted as qualitative indicators more than as quantitative ones. In other words, the sign of both indices is more relevant than their absolute value.

14. Using different samples, other authors observe situations of financial distress and bank insolvency that persist for some time, without a significant deterioration in the macroeconomy, or situations of financial distress accompanied by balance-of-payments crises (Caprio and Klingebiel 1996, 1997; Lindgren, Garcia, and Saal 1996, Kaminsky and Reinhart 1996). However, in our sample we have intentionally focused on those country episodes where a surge in capital flows, and associated intermediation by the banking system, played an important role.

15. One clear example of increased potential risk is the opening of the banking sector to foreign competition. Although increased competition leads to greater efficiency in the long term, an abrupt change of regime that erodes the franchise value of banking will aggravate moral hazard and lead to more risk taking by domestic banks. Hence,

there may be problems in increasing foreign competition too quickly (Stiglitz 1994).

16. This does not contradict the view that in the long term financial integration is beneficial. In particular, it increases competition and enhances efficiency in banking, and permits greater diversification of bank portfolios.

17. The level of interest rates also depends on expectations of devaluation. A highly appreciated real exchange rate can lead to sustained high real interest rates (ex post) that undermine the health of the banking system (chapter 1 and annex 5.2).

18. Regarding the incentive structure, for example, the incentives of all market participants must be taken into account: bank owners and managers, depositors, and bank regulators. Appropriate tools to do this include capital-asset ratios and extended (or unlimited) liability for the first group—prior to the mid-1930s double liability was routinely imposed on U.S. bank shareholders and managers—limited deposit insurance for the second, and appropriate funding, greater accountability, and political independence for the last group.

19. Without these basic institutions the financial system as a whole, and the banking sector in particular, will not perform the function of intermediating funds properly and will be more prone to fraud.

20. Properly pricing a deposit insurance scheme is not an easy task, mainly because the composition of a bank's portfolio can change much faster than a regulator can realistically assess its risk level. Also, bank regulators should continually update their pricing mechanisms to incorporate market developments and financial innovations. Although imperfect, however, a variable (adjusted by risk) deposit insurance premium can help to induce safer banking practices if other mechanisms, such as risk-adjusted capital-asset ratios, limited deposit insurance, unlimited (or extended) liabilities for managers, limited foreign exchange risk insurance, are put into place.

21. According to a recent survey of the Basle Committee, 92 percent of countries apply a Basle-like risk-weighted capital approach (although not necessarily at the 8 percent ratio). For details on the Basle Accord guidelines see annex 5.3.

22. Most countries impose rules of maximum exposure to a single borrower as a percentage of capital and other reserves of the lending bank. For each of the following examples, the percentage is shown in parentheses: Argentina (15–25), Brazil (30), Chile (5–30), Colombia (10), Germany (25), Hong Kong (25), India (25), Indonesia (10–20), Israel (15), Japan (20–40), Korea (15), Malaysia (30), Singapore (25), Thailand (25), the United States (15), and Venezuela (10). From Goldstein and Turner (1996).

23. The Argentine approach differs from others—in particular, the guidelines of the Basle Accord—in that it uses the interest rate applied to each credit as a measure of the risk associated with that operation.

24. According to current risk-based capital regulations in the United States, family residential mortgages are in the 50 percent risk category, while other real estate loans and loans to individuals are in the 100 percent risk category (Grenadier and Hall 1995). See also annex 5.3.

25. For a detailed analysis of the pros and cons of capital requirements see Berger, Herring, and Szego (1995).

26. This does not mean that banks should not be allowed to fail or that the likelihood of a banking crisis should be reduced to zero. The need for preparation arises because banks are bound to frequently encounter financial problems and, for reasons related to market discipline, *should* encounter such problems. The authorities should try to keep these problems from becoming systemic crises. Also, it can be argued, based on a cost-benefit analysis, that the likelihood of a banking crisis should not be reduced to zero.

27. Two risk areas that tend to be overlooked are the repayment capacity of public enterprises and payment and settlement risk. Concerning the former, the implementation of macroeconomic stabilization packages aimed at reducing fiscal deficits have led public enterprises (for example, in Venezuela) to default on their debt, thereby compounding bank difficulties. Regarding the latter, industrial countries have recently begun to establish mecha-

nisms aimed at addressing this problem (IMF 1996), but developing countries still have a long way to go.

28. By contrast, the losses in other nonbank deposit-taking institutions, which were lightly supervised, reached 40 percent of total deposits.

29. One way to minimize this risk is to permit entry to only a few well-known international firms and banks with good reputations. However, this may be difficult to do in Eastern Europe and the former Soviet Union, where economic activity is partly motivated by historical links.

30. Sources: Fleming, Chu, and Bakker (1996); Baer and Klingebiel (1995).

31. The case of Brazil can be partially explained by the recovery of the economy after economic reforms were introduced following several years of stagnation.

32. The G-10 comprises Belgium, Canada, France, Germany, Italy, Japan, the Netherlands, Sweden, the United Kingdom, and the United States.

33. An amendment to the 1988 Capital Accords, approved by the Basle Committee in 1995, adjusts banks' capital requirements to incorporate market risk as a variable in its calculation. The amendment takes effect in 1997 (IMF 1996).

34. The number of withdrawals needs to be large enough for the bank to run out of reserves and be forced to liquidate assets at a discount.

35. Hong Kong used a currency board, pegging the Hong Kong dollar to the British pound, up to 1972.

36. The fund is required to maintain assets equal to at least 105 percent of the stock of debt certificates and Hong Kong dollar notes issued. The total spent in helping Hong Kong's troubled banks was estimated to be less than 10 percent of the fund's total assets as of April 1986 (*Far Eastern Economic Review,* April 10, 1986, pp. 78–79).

CHAPTER 6

Preparing Capital Markets for Financial Integration

ONE OF THE CHARACTERISTICS OF THE CURRENT phase of international financial integration, as noted in chapter 1, is that—given the changing investor base—a growing proportion of flows to developing countries is being channeled through their capital markets in the form of portfolio equity capital. This trend will continue and even intensify over the medium term.[1] These investments represent an important opportunity for developing countries and have been accompanied by a spectacular increase in activity in the equity markets in these countries. Although the improvements in many emerging markets have been remarkable, most of these markets are still in the early stages of development and need to close the gap between themselves and the more advanced capital markets to be able to compete. Emerging markets are also increasingly competing among themselves for new issues and investors. To attract additional portfolio flows, therefore, developing countries need to address investor concerns regarding the attributes of their capital markets that raise transaction costs and risks, especially the reliability and efficiency of the infrastructure and trading systems, and transparency and fairness. By focusing on these concerns, policymakers can also reduce their own fears that financial integration will increase volatility in their capital markets and the risk of a financial crisis. This chapter will discuss the implications of financial integration for the functions and efficiency of domestic capital markets, and how policymakers can reconcile their concerns with the concerns of foreign investors.

The Main Issues

WHILE CAPITAL MARKET DEVELOPMENT IS A KEY ELEMENT of the policy agenda for developing countries as financial integration deepens, it is not a prerequisite in the same sense as a strong macroeconomic policy framework and a sound banking system. The robustness of the macroeconomic and banking sector conditions in developing countries, and how these countries deal with overheating pressures and reduce macroeconomic and banking sector vulnerability, will determine whether they enter a virtuous rather than a vicious cycle of financial integration, and reduce the potential for large reversals. Capital market development, however, plays less of a role in minimizing these downside risks but is essential to maximize the upside potential of financial integration.

The Benefits of Financial Integration

Growth in market capitalization and activity. In parallel to the surge in portfolio equity flows, the capitalization of equity markets in many developing countries has been expanding rapidly since the mid-1980s.[2] As shown in table 6.1, by the end of 1996 the combined market capitalization of 18 major developing countries included in the IFC Emerging Market Global Composite Index was 14 times larger than in 1985, rising from US$95 billion to US$1,371 billion. As a ratio to GDP, the average market capitalization of these countries had increased from 7 to 49 percent. This growth has been much more rapid than in developed markets. While market capitalization in emerging markets is, on average, still much smaller than in industrial countries, that difference declined substantially during the past decade. Because of this growth, equity markets in some of the more dynamic emerging markets, particularly in East Asia, have become increasingly important in domestic financial intermediation relative to banks, despite the continued growth of bank deposits. For example, in Malaysia and Thailand, the share of equity markets in the stock of financial savings increased, respectively, from 49 percent and 9 percent at the end of 1985 to 79 percent and 56 percent at the end of 1994.[3] In Chile, the equity market share in savings increased from 32 to 80 percent during the same period.

Table 6.1 Stock Market Growth in Selected IFC Index Countries, 1985–96

Country	*Stock market capitalization (billions of dollars)* 1985	1996	*Stock market capitalization (percentage of GDP)* 1985	1996	*Trading value (billions of dollars)* 1985	1996	*Trading value (percentage of market capitalization)* 1985	1996
Emerging markets								
Argentina	2.0	44.7	2.3	15.3	0.6	4.4	31.0	9.8
Brazil	42.8	217.0	19.2	30.9	21.5	112.1	50.2	51.7
Chile	2.0	65.9	12.2	92.7	0.1	8.5	2.8	12.8
Colombia	0.4	17.1	1.3	20.4	0.0	1.4	7.2	7.9
Hungary	0.0	5.3	0.0	11.3	0.0	1.6	—	31.1
India	14.4	122.6	6.9	36.2	5.0	26.6	34.5	21.7
Indonesia	0.1	91.0	0.1	41.2	0.0	32.1	2.6	35.3
Korea	7.4	138.8	7.8	28.9	4.2	177.3	56.4	127.7
Malaysia	16.2	307.2	52.0	323.6	2.3	173.6	14.4	56.5
Mexico	3.8	106.5	2.1	37.6	2.4	43.0	61.9	40.4
Pakistan	1.4	10.6	4.4	17.6	0.2	6.1	17.2	56.9
Peru	0.8	13.8	4.4	22.6	0.0	3.8	5.0	27.5
Philippines	0.7	80.6	2.2	97.5	0.1	25.5	16.6	31.6
Poland	0.0	8.4	0.0	6.2	0.0	5.7	—	68.0
Sri Lanka	0.4	1.8	6.2	13.3	0.0	0.1	0.8	7.2
Thailand	1.9	99.8	4.8	53.1	0.6	44.4	30.6	44.4
Turkey	—	30.0	0.0	17.5	0.0	36.8	—	122.7
Venezuela	1.1	10.1	1.8	16.7	0.0	1.3	2.7	12.7
Total	95.3	1,371.4	7.2	40.5	37.0	704.3	38.8	51.4
Developed markets								
France	79.0	585.9	15.1	37.6	14.7	859.0	18.6	146.6
Germany	183.8	664.8	29.7	27.9	71.6	1,405.4	38.9	211.4
Japan	978.7	3,019.7	72.9	65.1	330.0	933.1	33.7	30.9
United Kingdom	328.0	1,711.2	70.8	151.5	68.4	1,319.4	20.9	77.1
United States	2,324.6	8,478.0	55.6	111.8	997.2	7,265.6	42.9	85.7
Total	3,894.1	14,459.7	54.6	83.6	1,481.8	11,782.4	38.1	81.5

— Not available.

Note: End-of-year stock market capitalization figures are used. Japan includes only the Tokyo Stock Exchange.

Source: IFC Emerging Markets data base; data from International Federation of Stock Exchanges (FIBV).

In parallel to the growth in market capitalization, the volume and value of stocks traded have also risen dramatically. The combined annual value of shares traded in the IFC Index countries increased from US$37 billion in 1985 to US$792 billion in 1994 but declined to US$704 billion in 1996. Since this simple measure of trading activity is affected by changes in share prices, perhaps a better measure of trading activity is the turnover ratio—that is, the annual value of trades normalized by market capitalization. This ratio indicates that trading activity in emerging markets roughly doubled between 1985 and 1994, about the same increase as in industrial countries. The turnover ratio in emerging markets has since declined to 51 percent in 1996 but still remained significantly higher than in 1985. Combined with the growth in market capitalization, the increase in the volume of shares traded suggests that liquidity has significantly improved in emerging markets.

Increase in the foreign presence in domestic markets. Foreign investors have made a significant contribution to these improvements. While the sources are not fully reliable, the data do show that the share of foreign investors in trading volume and market capitalization was very large in most major emerging markets in 1995 (table 6.2). Since meaningful foreign involvement in these markets is a recent phenomenon starting in many cases only in the early 1990s, it is clear that the increasing foreign activity played an important role in improving the depth and liquidity in emerging markets. One of the few countries for which time-series data on foreign activity are available is Thailand. In 1986, the year preceding its capital inflow episode, foreign investors accounted for 8 percent of the trading turnover in Thailand. By 1990,

Table 6.2 Estimates of Foreign Presence in Emerging Stock Markets, 1995
(percent)

Market	*Foreign share in market capitalization*	*Estimate by*	*Foreign share in trading*	*Estimate by*
Argentina	35	National securities commission	—	
Brazil	—		35	Stock exchange
India	—		25	Local brokers
Indonesia	—		75	Local brokers
	29	Stock exchange	81	Stock exchange
Korea	13	Securities and exchange commission	6	Securities and exchange commission
Malaysia	—		50	Local brokers
Mexico	25	Stock exchange	—	
Pakistan	—		50	Local brokers
Peru	—		60	Local brokers
Philippines	38	Local brokers	50	Local brokers
Poland	—		25	Stock exchange
Thailand	21	Stock exchange	26	Stock exchange

— Not available.
Note: Most figures represent rough estimates of foreign participation, since few countries document flows.
Source: IFC data.

they accounted for 15 percent of turnover in the Thai stock market. This share declined during 1991–92, but rose again to 26 percent by 1995 and to about 32 percent during the first quarter of 1996.

Increase in access to foreign markets. Increasing financial integration has also enabled developing country corporations and banks to gain direct access to equity and bond markets in industrial countries. Many developing country firms have been able to cross-list in the world's major equity markets through global and American depository receipts (GDRs and ADRs, respectively). The growth in these instruments has been very rapid: at the end of 1995 there were some 228 ADRs and GDRs issued by firms from 26 developing countries with an original market value of about US$34 billion. On the debt side, since 1990, both corporations and banks have been able to issue paper in international markets, as well as in the U.S., Japanese, and some European markets. In addition to large sovereign issues, the amount of capital raised by the private sector from developing countries through international issues of debt during 1989–95 amounted to some US$52.4 billion. The number of countries whose issuers were able to gain access to international markets through these instruments also increased.

The Challenges of Integration for Emerging Markets

Increasing competition. With the benefits of financial integration have come challenges for the integrating capital markets. Just as domestic issuers gain direct access to foreign capital markets, so must domestic markets compete with industrial country exchanges for listings and new issues. As noted above, the growth in these alternative means of channeling funds to developing countries has been enormous. By the end of 1995, ADRs and GDRs represented 6 percent of the underlying market capitalization of the IFC Emerging Market Investable Index. And as can be seen from table 6.3, this average 6 percent ratio hides a large variation among countries, with some having surprisingly high ratios. In some of these cases, the success of ADRs and GDRs is explained in part by the weaknesses of developing country capital markets. Weaknesses in these markets may cause foreign investors to acquire shares of a developing country firm through depository receipts rather than directly, particularly if transaction costs and delays in the market in question are high or investor protection is poor. For example, foreign participants in the Indian stock markets report that inefficiencies in these markets' clearance, settlement, and depository systems are a key reason for their interest in Indian GDRs. As can be seen from table 6.3, the value of outstanding Indian depository receipts relative to the value of shares that foreign investors can acquire (that is, the market capitalization of the IFC Investable Index) is among the highest of the 20 countries included in the table. With regard to the Chinese markets, foreign investors report concerns regarding the quality of disclosure and corporate governance practices of listed firms. Since depository receipts need to meet the regulatory standards of the industrial country where they are issued, in this case too they are preferred by foreign investors. Depository receipts are also preferred in the case of Argentina, where the domestic market is

Table 6.3 Issues of American and Global Depository Receipts, 1989–95
(millions of dollars)

	Total issues[a]		*Corrected issues/market capitalization (percent)*[b]	
Country	*Uncorrected*	*Corrected*	*Global index*	*Investible index*
Argentina	4,204	3,898	10.3	17.7
Brazil	1,286	1,281	0.9	2.0
Chile	1,538	1,996	2.7	17.8
China	1,717	1,466	6.0	77.3
Colombia	329	277	3.3	3.4
Czech Republic	32	32	0.3	0.7
Hungary	362	330	41.5	75.9
India	3,859	2,650	2.1	19.6
Indonesia	2,162	2,267	3.4	11.5
Korea	3,102	3,175	1.7	18.6
Mexico	10,567	6,698	7.4	12.1
Pakistan	1,143	771	8.3	15.9
Peru	51	56	0.5	0.8
Philippines	1,015	1,295	2.2	7.6
Poland	51	51	1.1	2.6
South Africa	477	498	0.3	0.3
Sri Lanka	33	20	1.0	2.6
Thailand	358	314	0.2	1.1
Turkey	540	435	2.1	3.2
Venezuela	187	86	2.3	3.6
Total	33,013	27,596	2.3	6.1

a. This excludes some $700 million issued by firms from six countries not included in the IFC indexes.

b. Figures are corrected for changes in stock prices between the date of issue and the end of 1995 using the IFC Global Indexes (IFCG). Refers to market capitalization as measured by the IFCG and IFC Investable indexes, respectively.

Source: IFC, *Emerging Stock Markets Factbook 1996*; World Bank data.

perceived as very illiquid and has been losing volume to industrial country markets. In 1995, for example, the volume traded in New York of ADRs of Yacimientos Petroliferos Fiscales, a recently privatized Argentine oil company, was 25 times higher than the volume traded on the Buenos Aires market. In Korea the domestic market has been more restricted to foreign investors, and the high depository receipts–market capitalization ratio is an indicator of repressed foreign demand for equity.

Addressing investor concerns. To compete in an increasingly integrated world, developing countries need to make their markets more attractive to foreign investors. As explained in box 6.1, investors are concerned about the unreliability of emerging markets in three main areas: market infrastructure that results in delays in settlement and failed trades; lack of protection for property rights, including those of minority shareholders; and lack of transparency and fairness of markets, because of insufficient disclosure of accurate information that would enable investors to assess the merits of alternative investments and because of insider trading and other abusive practices. In addition, despite recent progress, emerging markets remain significantly less liquid than capital markets in industrial countries. In an illiquid market, investors fear they will not be able to liquidate their interests quickly without incurring a substantial loss.

The concerns of developing countries. For their part, policymakers in developing countries also have a number of concerns about growing international integration. Perhaps most important, they fear that financial integration may increase volatility in their capital markets. As discussed in chapter 2, financial integration makes developing countries more susceptible to external shocks. In addition, foreign investors may add to excess volatility in asset prices in emerging markets through herding behavior or contagion effects.[4] Policymakers are also concerned about the increasing vulnerability to financial crises as foreign investors become more important in both trading activity and market capitalization. In particular, they fear that foreign investors, because of herding, fads, or momentum trading, may increase the likelihood or magnitude of market bubbles, with securities prices rising far above the underlying fundamentals, followed by an inevitable market crash.

Policymakers in developing countries are also concerned about the equity implications of increasing foreign ownership of domestic firms. Some officials perceive foreign portfolio investors as fair-weather

Box 6.1 Investors' Viewpoint: Risks and Transaction Costs in Emerging Markets

THE HIGHER RETURNS THAT CAN BE EARNED BY capital in developing countries are the fundamental force driving investor interest in these countries. However, the stylized attributes of emerging markets (shallow, illiquid, and opaque markets; high transaction costs; and weak regulatory frameworks) and the underlying developing economy (larger, more frequent macroeconomic shocks and less mature, undercapitalized firms) mean that risks are also high. In particular, both domestic and foreign investors in developing countries are subject to very large risks and costs not directly related to the underlying investment.

Nonmarket risks. These nonmarket risks mainly regard the *lack of reliability* in four basic areas:

- Investors require a reliable system to settle transactions, with either cash or securities, to reduce principal risk and the opportunity cost of a delay.
- Investors demand reliable systems that record ownership, ensure safe custody of securities, and protect property rights. Investors require that securities truly represent a claim on a future income stream and that claims be enforceable by law. Related to this is protection against abuse by management or majority shareholders, which could reduce the value of the investment.
- Investors also want reliable systems to ensure that they pay or receive a fair price for a security and, most important, that ensure disclosure of material information to evaluate investment choices.
- Investors desire liquidity to be able to liquidate securities or change the composition of their portfolios without incurring high costs. Liquidity, to a large extent, is an endogenous variable—that is, the result of capital markets having the right attributes to be able to attract large numbers of buyers and sellers. Liquidity needs to be nurtured; it cannot be bought or created by decree.

Investors will be concerned about these risks to different degrees, depending on their risk-return preferences and investment strategies. For example, value investors who do not inordinately turn over their portfolios would be concerned about company disclosure practices but would be less concerned with transaction costs and liquidity.

Settlement and operational risks and costs. Capital market infrastructure in many emerging markets is still in a nascent stage, and investors are subject to high settlement risks, both operational and counterparty. Risks that a party will default on payment or delivery obligations are large, and failed trades or long delays in settlement are widespread. The long delays reduce liquidity and increase market risk. For example, a Templeton fund bought shares in India that subsequently rose by 150 percent. The fund was not able to make good on the potential profit because by the time the original transaction had settled and the fund could sell, the stock price had declined back to its original level (Seeger 1996). Failed trades expose investors to counterparty risks if the settlement system does not ensure that shares are only delivered versus payment (DVP—that is, that the final delivery of securities takes place if and only if final payment is made). Most emerging market do not conform to DVP. Failed trades can have

friends, interested in benefiting from large short-term capital gains and dividends but contributing little to the long-run health of domestic firms and the development of the economy—and selling at the first hint of trouble. Perhaps more important, there is a perception in many systemic consequences for a securities market, since they may produce a chain reaction of failures. Investors also desire reliability in postsettlement actions, particularly the timely payment of dividends to reduce opportunity costs and market risk, such as an unfavorable change in the exchange rate.

Legal and custodial risks and costs. A key risk investors face in emerging markets is that securities purchases may not be recorded in the legal registry, providing them no way to prove ownership. If the omission is deliberate, recourse to the courts may be costly and lengthy, with an uncertain outcome if property rights are not well defined. Real or perceived bias by the judiciary against foreign interests, or the lack of adequately functioning arbitration and legal systems, would further increase uncertainty. These risks are especially prevalent in transition economies where the concept of private property, let alone legal protection for it, is very recent. For example, Dmitry Vasilev, chairman of Russia's Federal Stock Commission, commented in May 1996: "Current legislation does not defend shareholders. Confidence in the stock market has been bruised by secret company meetings at which share registers have been altered and new issues voted on" (Seeger 1996, p. 15). Even if securities are registered, it may be only with a lengthy delay with a loss of dividends and other shareholder rights. Operational risks such as loss of shares or counterfeit securities are another concern. There have been instances of counterfeit securities in India, Indonesia, Malaysia, and Turkey. A recent scandal involved Russia's Minfin bonds.

In addition, investors are widely concerned about their rights as minority shareholders. In developed markets, decisions that would significantly affect the value of the firm, and practices such as dealings with insiders, need to be submitted to a vote by shareholders. There is a fear that in developing country firms such protections may be lacking or not effectively enforced, especially since many of these firms are closely held and managed directly by majority shareholders.

Informational and regulatory risks and costs. Lack of quality information on firms, combined with high asset price volatility, is another prime concern for investors. One reason why the information base is lacking in emerging markets is that the accounting and auditing systems and standards are weak, and that there are not enough qualified accountants and auditors, as shown by numerous World Bank reviews. More to the point, the regulatory systems in many of these markets are weak in terms of quality, quantity, and frequency of information disclosure. Foreign investors and fund managers feel particularly at risk, believing domestic investors to be better informed. Another concern, which is also related to protection of minority shareholder rights, is insider trading. For example, the International Organization of Securities Commissions (IOSCO) reports that only about one-half of its developing country members require disclosure of securities transactions made by company insiders. Even in the more advanced emerging markets, such as Thailand, insider trading is perceived to be difficult to control despite the strong monitoring and enforcement powers of the Thai Securities Commission.

Source: Authors' interviews with fund managers and advisers, Gray (1996), IOSCO (1992a), Mobius (1995), Seeger (1996).

developing countries that foreign and domestic investors are not competing on a level playing field, that foreign investors, because of their wealth, will be able to buy a large share of the equity of domestic firms, to the detriment of long-term national income.

Finally, integration and globalization are raising new issues for capital market regulators in developing (and industrial) countries. For example, integration increases systemic risk, since the failure of a financial intermediary overseas could have an impact on domestic markets. In addition, globalization may reduce the effectiveness of monitoring and supervision of financial intermediaries because of difficulties in assessing the financial status of firms that are active in many markets, and because of potential gaps in the responsibilities of regulators in different countries. And two parallel global trends, the development of derivative products and financial conglomerates, are making financial markets even more opaque. The Barings affair of 1995 is a good example of these new problems: a securities subsidiary of a U.K. bank located in Singapore was taking positions in the Nikkei futures index. Who was responsible for monitoring what and where?

The Policy Agenda

In summary, developing countries will be able to benefit from increased investment, and from the deepening and improved liquidity of their capital markets, only if they put in place the institutional and policy prerequisites to attract capital inflows, and reduce the risks of instability. To this end, developing countries face three main tasks:

- Capital markets—especially equity markets, given the expected composition of capital flows—must be made more attractive to foreign investors. While investors are attracted by the potential for rapid growth and high returns, they are discouraged by operating inefficiencies and lack of reliability of market institutions and infrastructure, and by regulatory frameworks that increase transaction costs and reduce transparency.
- Developing countries need to implement policy reforms and strengthen institutions to reduce the risks of instability. As explained below, improvements that increase the attractiveness of emerging markets for foreign investors also serve to reduce volatility and risks.
- Authorities in developing countries also need to deal with the new regulatory concerns resulting from globalization. These concerns are shared by industrial countries, and their resolution will be greatly facilitated by international initiatives.

These institutional and policy reforms are not only prerequisites for successful financial integration but are also essential to develop capital markets in a more closed economy. Domestic and foreign investors generally share the same concerns, and hence both would welcome the same institutional and policy improvements. Similarly, measures that reduce volatility and risks that originate from foreign shocks would generally also be beneficial for domestic sources of volatility. Financial integration increases the urgency of these reforms: developing countries need to act quickly to take full advantage of the substantial opportunities offered by financial integration.

Organization of the chapter. These issues are developed in the remainder of the chapter. The next section discusses whether financial integration facilitates the role of capital markets in investment. It also reviews how integration might exacerbate inefficiencies in domestic capital markets as a result of information asymmetries and price volatility. The third and fourth sections review the reforms and improvements required for emerging capital markets to operate and develop in an increasingly integrated world—that is, measures that enhance the attractiveness of domestic capital markets to foreign investors and reduce potential volatility and address regulatory concerns regarding globalization.[5] The third section will focus on market infrastructure (that is, microstructures, clearance, settlement, and depository systems), and the fourth on the regulatory and legal frameworks. Each of these sections will discuss alternative institutional and policy options in their respective areas, and establish, to the extent possible, best practice, as well as describe the constraints typically encountered in implementing these reforms.[6] Each of these two sections will also describe the progress of the more dynamic emerging markets in achieving the desired institutional and regulatory attributes. Finally, the last section will be a summary that offers conclusions.

Capital Markets and Financial Integration

Capital markets in a market economy fulfill three functions:

- First, capital markets serve as a source of long-term capital for financing investment.

- Second, capital markets expand the menu of financial instruments available to domestic savers, allowing risk diversification and encouraging resource mobilization.
- Finally, capital markets—especially equity markets—continuously monitor the corporate sector, serving both as a signaling device for the allocation of capital and as a means of corporate control, thereby promoting managerial and organizational efficiency. However, informational asymmetries, including principal-agent problems in the area of corporate control, as well as price volatility, may impede equity markets from correctly fulfilling their monitoring and signaling functions.[7]

The basic questions we will address in this section are whether and how financial integration facilitates the first and third functions and exacerbates volatility. The impact of financial integration on risk diversification and resource mobilization was discussed in chapter 3.

How Financial Integration Helps Foster Investment

Properly functioning capital markets help increase investment by affecting both the supply of and demand for capital in several ways. First, they are a cost-efficient way to attract savings from a large group of small savers, thereby reducing the cost of capital for firms through economies of scale. Second, capital markets have two risk-sharing and diversification properties that promote the financing of riskier but higher-return investments: they reduce the vulnerability of firms to interest rate and demand shocks by facilitating the process of raising equity by firms, and they reduce risks faced by investors by easing portfolio diversification. Finally, capital markets, like banks, perform a term transformation function. Many investments require a long time span to generate returns, while investors generally wish to commit funds for a shorter period. With liquid and active secondary capital markets, both requirements can be met simultaneously, since investors feel assured that they will have access to their funds quickly and without paying an excessive price.

The benefits of financial integration. Financial integration enhances this role of capital markets in several ways. Most directly, integration expands the supply of investment resources by tapping foreign sources, increasing the demand for domestic securities. The increased demand will drive up the price of domestic securities, raising the price-earnings ratio and reducing the cost of capital. Less directly, internationally integrated stock markets allow wider risk diversification and thereby facilitate the implementation of higher-return but riskier projects (for example, see Levine and Zervos 1996b). Finally, as noted above, increased foreign activity improves the depth and liquidity of domestic capital markets, key ingredients for these markets to perform their term transformation function. The fact that a growing share of foreign investment is accounted for by institutional investors could magnify the positive impact on liquidity, since institutional investors are very active traders.[8] With improved liquidity in domestic markets, investors will lower their demands for higher yields, reflecting their ability to sell securities at declining costs, and the cost of capital will decline. These favorable effects should lead to changes in the behavior of domestic agents. The declining cost of capital and the enhanced risk diversification should induce the corporate sector to issue initial public offerings (IPOs) and additional shares, including offerings and shares in emerging sectors, such as private infrastructure projects. In addition, as liquidity in domestic capital markets improves, new domestic investors will be attracted to these markets.

The data support the hypothesis that financial integration enhances the role of capital markets as a source of investment finance. As discussed in chapter 3, the growth in both stock market capitalization and turnover in the major emerging markets is correlated with the level of foreign activity, as measured by the magnitude of portfolio equity inflows. And most important, the analysis in chapter 3 also suggests that foreign activity has had significant positive spillovers to domestic activity, including the level and growth of domestic trading activity and the number of new listings.

All of this rise in activity in emerging markets has real and positive implications for investment and growth prospects in developing countries. While conventional wisdom based on industrial country data suggests that capital markets are not a large source of investment financing (see Mayer 1989), there is increasing evidence that they are much more important for this purpose in developing countries. For example, analyzing data on the 100 largest corporations listed on the stock market in 10 developing countries during the 1980s, Singh (1994) finds that these corporations relied strongly on external sources for financing, and in particular on equity markets (41 percent of total financing, on average).[9]

In addition, there is growing empirical and theoretical support for the idea that development of the stock market has positive implications for economic growth. Levine and Zervos (1996b), for example, find a strong positive long-run empirical association between stock market development and the increase in per capita GDP.[10]

Financial Integration and Improvements in Corporate Governance

As noted above, one means through which equity markets increase investment efficiency is by serving as a mechanism for corporate control. In essence, shareholders can exercise their right to change the management of the firm if they perceive that it is not acting in their best interest. In addition, investors can react to weak management performance by selling (or by refraining from buying) shares, actions that can lead to a decline in share prices. In turn, low or declining share prices can influence owners and managers to change their behavior and improve corporate performance. Indeed, underperforming firms will have share prices that are low relative to their underlying value and hence will be more vulnerable to takeovers.[11] However, the academic literature is divided on how well the market for corporate governance works. For example, shareholders may not be able to monitor management without incurring high costs because of information asymmetries. The incentives for individual shareholders (unless their holdings are large) to incur these monitoring costs may be perverse because of the free-rider problem.[12] Information vendors and analysts play an important role in reducing these information asymmetries and enhancing the effectiveness of the market as a means of corporate control.

Corporate governance and institutional investors. Another issue widely discussed in the literature is whether the principal-agent problem improves or worsens as institutional investors come to account for a larger share of a firm's market capitalization.[13] Some authors believe that institutional investors, with their strong professional background, will be able to monitor corporate performance effectively. On the other hand, their incentives to monitor management behavior may not be strong because they turn over their portfolios quickly. In addition, the free-rider problem mentioned above can also affect institutional investors, given prudential regulations that limit the concentration of the portfolios of institutional investors in an individual firm. According to Samuel (1996), the evidence, based on U.S. data from the 1980s, is that there is no discernible effect of institutional ownership on corporate performance but that the monitoring activities of institutional investors may be functioning as a substitute for the disciplinary role traditionally played by the providers of debt financing.[14] However, these empirical analyses do not capture the full impact of the recent sharp increase in shareholder activism by institutional investors, which in some instances has forced key firms in the United States and some European countries to improve their structures for corporate governance. Some of these experiences have been pathbreaking, in particular the influence of the California Public Employees Retirement System during the board shakeup at General Motors in 1995.

Foreign investment and corporate governance. This discussion suggests that increasing foreign participation in domestic stock markets in developing countries would have both negative and positive implications for corporate governance. On the negative side, overseas investors, because of information asymmetries, would seem to lack the familiarity with local conditions needed to be effective monitors of management. In addition, foreign, especially institutional, investors may not have strong incentives to participate actively in corporate governance functions; they may be more interested in liquidity (if unhappy with performance, they sell) than in control. On the other hand, as discussed in chapter 2, the nature and objectives of foreign investment change as emerging markets mature. During the period in which foreign investors follow an index-based approach, they take little interest in the underlying companies. But as they become more selective and pick stocks more carefully, they may take a more active role in corporate governance. In addition, to attract increased foreign funds, and as foreign practices are adopted by domestic shareholders, financial integration may lead domestic companies to improve corporate governance. This demonstration effect may prove to be quite important in the medium term, as suggested by the experience of the large Indian development-investment bank described in box 6.2.

Preventing an Increase in Volatility

If capital markets, in particular equity markets, are to function as a signaling device for the allocation of capital, information markets need to work efficiently so that asset prices reflect all material information. Obvious impediments to efficiency are lack of information, delays in its

Box 6.2 Corporate Governance in India

FOREIGN PORTFOLIO INVESTMENT HAS LED TO radical changes in corporate governance at the Industrial Credit and Investment Corporation of India (ICICI), one of India's largest development-investment banks. While foreign portfolio investors in developing countries are generally not considered demanding, and tend to vote with their feet rather than at board meetings, ICICI's experience probably presages the future. Indeed, the changes that are taking place at ICICI parallel those of a growing number of corporations in developed countries.

ICICI's ongoing experiment with corporate governance started with the issue of several GDRs in the early 1990s, which led to a change in the ownership structure of the company. Today, ICICI still has more than half a million shareholders, but some 34 percent of the shares are held by foreigners, especially large institutional investors, and 41 percent by large domestic institutions, including the central government. Foreign investors were critical of the company's activities in several areas, including substandard IPOs, diversion of funds into nonproject areas, poor accountability and transparency, preferential allotment of shares to promoters, and, more generally, little concern for managing the company to increase the value of shares. Foreign investors joined large domestic investors in voicing these concerns at board meetings and were instrumental in having management accept sea changes in corporate governance. In turn, ICICI has pushed for similar changes in its many client companies. Recognizing the value of these changes, the government has been a passive but approving spectator.

Based on the Cadbury Committee's recommendations on corporate governance in the United Kingdom, the main reforms implemented at ICICI regard the role and composition of the board of directors, including having a distinct chairperson who is separate from the chief executive officer. The reforms have created a more balanced, responsible, and independent board, with greater participation by the independent external directors. To further increase the sense of responsibility toward shareholders, directors now have a fiduciary responsibility. Complementing these reforms at the board level, the risk management and internal audit departments have been strengthened and made more independent, and a new key performance indicator for middle management is the impact of their work on shareholder value.

Some developing countries are uneasy about the presence of foreign investors on the boards of their largest firms. But if developing country governments wish to encourage long-term investors with buy-and-hold strategies, they must be prepared to accept their demands for increased transparency and control to ensure the value of their investment. Judging from the Indian experience, foreign representation on the board has had significant and positive impact on corporate governance. Indeed, this may prove to be one of the more important and long-lasting contributions of foreign investment to emerging markets.

Source: Kamath (1996).

dissemination, information asymmetries among market participants, and weak analytical capacity of market participants. Some authors (for example, Kyle 1984) have argued that the potential to make a profit in the stock market on the basis of new information promotes research by market participants. But this self-correcting mechanism seems to work best in active and liquid markets, where the potential for profit is higher. Another impediment to efficiency is volatility in asset prices, which makes it difficult for market participants to distinguish whether changes in equity prices are due to noise or to new material information on fundamentals such as dividends or interest rates.[15] Another source of volatility and inefficiency comes in the form of speculative bubbles, which Stiglitz (1990) defines as asset prices departing from values justified by fundamentals because of expectations about future additional price increases. Volatility and lack of information may feed on each other. Without information, some investors and market makers are less likely to make bets against the market, a fact that could exacerbate price movements.

The impact of financial integration on market efficiency and volatility. In theory, financial integration has both positive and negative implications for the price discovery process in domestic capital markets. On the positive side, foreign investment increases depth and liquidity in domestic capital markets, thereby reducing volatility. (Shallow markets are more prone to volatility since even small trades in these markets have a disproportionate effect on prices.) In addition, increasing foreign participation in domestic capital markets may induce improvements in accounting, information, and reporting systems, as well as increase the analytical sophistication of the domestic securities industry. There is, in fact, strong anecdotal evidence that this spillover effect of financial integration has been quite important in some developing countries. These two benefits should interact and reinforce each other: improved liquidity and profit-making opportunities should lead to increased research and better information systems, which in turn should provoke additional investor interest and activity.

On the negative side, however, other factors suggest that financial integration may lead to an increase in the volatility of domestic asset prices and returns. This is because, with financial openness, domestic capital markets are exposed to new external financial shocks (or these shocks may be transmitted more quickly across borders), such as changes in global interest rates, spillover effects from foreign stock markets, and investor herding. As discussed in chapter 2, some of these external shocks, particularly changes in global interest rates and certain stock market spillover effects, make asset prices and returns more volatile by affecting the fundamentals of an emerging market. But other shocks, such as investor herding and pure contagion effects, may change investment in a country even though its fundamentals are unaffected. These shocks are often the result of foreign portfolio investors having little access to information, worsening information asymmetries. Perversely, the improvements in liquidity noted earlier in this chapter may make emerging markets more susceptible to external financial shocks, since better liquidity reduces transaction costs and makes it easier for foreign investors to open and liquidate positions. Given the high share of foreign investors in the major emerging markets, these potential external sources of volatility are important.

Information asymmetries may also increase volatility through interaction effects between domestic and foreign investors. For example, a defensive reaction by local investors to the sale of domestic securities by foreign investors, who in turn are responding to events overseas, may magnify the impact of foreign stock market spillover effects on the domestic market. Since local investors generally do not know why foreign investors are changing their holdings of domestic securities, they may react to such changes even though the fundamentals of the domestic market have not changed. Similarly, information asymmetries could result in foreign investors magnifying the impact of the behavior of domestic agents.

What does the empirical evidence say? Most recent empirical studies have concluded that asset price volatility in emerging markets is generally higher than in developed countries but that volatility did not increase during the current inflow period.[16] For example, Richards (1996) found no evidence to support the hypothesis that volatility in emerging markets increased in recent years concurrent with the boom in portfolio inflows. Indeed, his results suggest a decline in absolute volatility. IMF (1995) also found that absolute volatility of stock market returns did not increase during periods of high and volatile portfolio inflows in Korea, Mexico, and Thailand. Bekaert and Harvey (1995), as well, observe that the volatility of returns remained unchanged or declined in 13 out of their sample of 17 countries after liberalization of their capital markets.

How can these reassuring empirical results be reconciled with the theoretical predictions that volatility may increase? A possible explanation is as follows. As shown in figure 6.1, volatility may originate from both domestic and international sources, as well as result from changes in country fundamentals or market inefficiencies. Although emerging markets became more susceptible to external financial shocks during the 1990s as they opened their economies, they were also undertaking

Figure 6.1 Factors Affecting Volatility of Asset Prices in Emerging Markets, 1990s

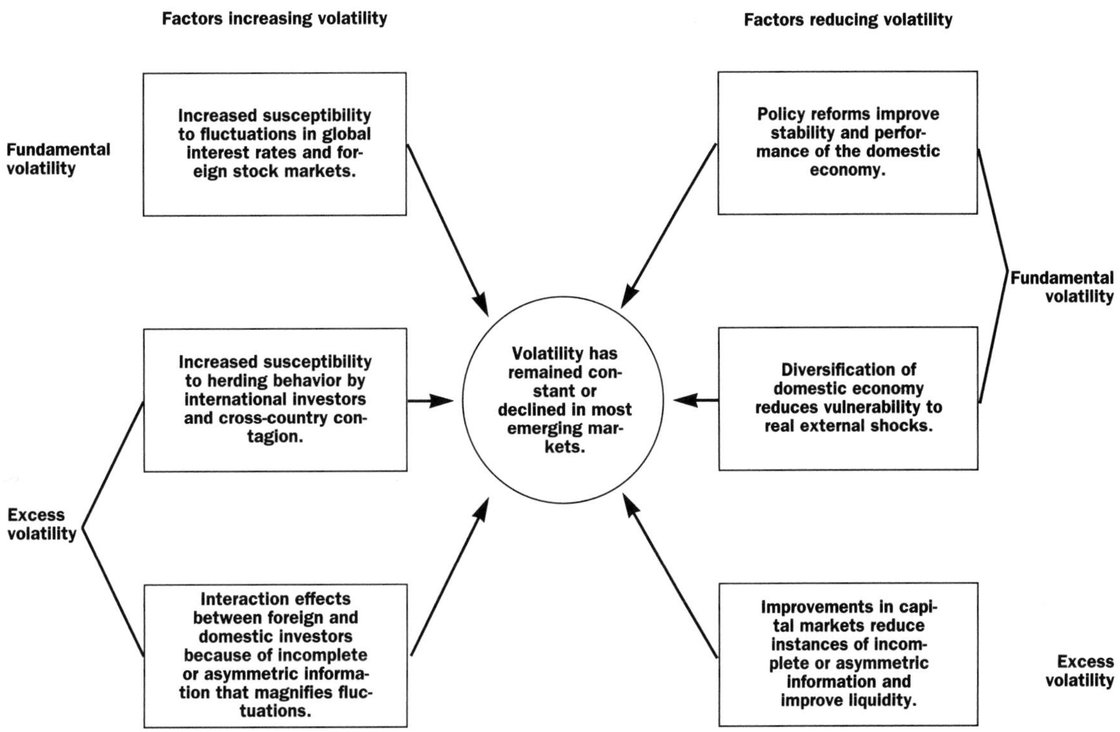

policy reforms aimed at improving domestic fundamentals and stabilizing their economic policies. These economic reform programs also led to the diversification of their economies, which reduced vulnerability to traditional external shocks such as changes in terms of trade. In addition, many developing countries during this period also improved their capital markets, reducing excess volatility arising from information asymmetries and other market imperfections, including foreign investor herding and pure contagion that as noted above may be caused by incomplete or asymmetric information. All of these effects have reduced fundamental volatility from traditional sources of shocks and may have moderated the potential for volatility arising from new sources. Indeed, chapter 2 concluded that although there is evidence of herding behavior by foreign investors, it is not robust enough to warrant the commonly held view that foreign investors destabilize emerging markets. Chapter 2 also concluded that the contagion effects do

Despite the increased susceptibility to external sources of volatility, improvements in macroeconomic management and capital market attributes may lead to a decline in overall volatility.

exist but that they appear to be relatively short-lived. In fact, the most significant corrections in developing country stock markets—for example, Mexico in 1994 and Thailand in 1996—have resulted not from external shocks but from shifts in the perceptions of domestic and foreign investors regarding domestic fundamentals.

As shown in figure 6.2, the improvements in capital markets have been a significant factor in reducing volatility. Figure 6.2, which relates excess volatility with an index of market development, suggests that market development is strongly associated with lower volatility, although the direction of causation can run both ways. Later in this chapter, we will explain in detail how the index was constructed. For the moment, it suffices to say that the index takes into account the depth and liquidity of a market, the efficiency of its infrastructure, and some additional variables that measure by proxy institutional development.

Improvements in capital markets can reduce excess volatility.

Figure 6.2 Excess Volatility and Market Development

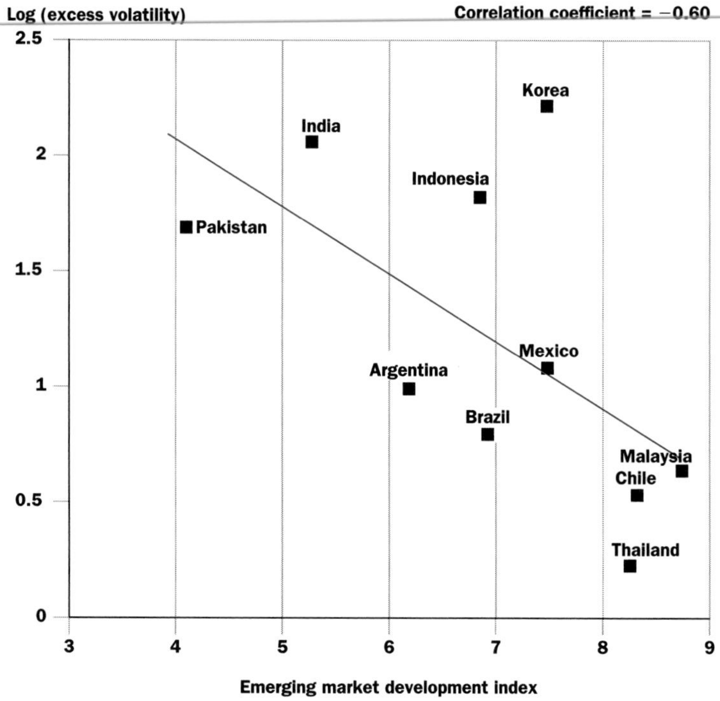

Log (excess volatility)
Correlation coefficient = −0.60
2.5
2
1.5
1
0.5
0
Korea
India
Indonesia
Pakistan
Mexico
Argentina
Brazil
Malaysia
Chile
Thailand
3
4
5
6
7
8
9
Emerging market development index

Source: World Bank staff estimates.

Conclusions

Two basic conclusions can be drawn from this discussion:

- First, liberalizing foreign access to domestic capital markets can bring substantial benefits to developing countries. Liberalization enables countries to tap into large overseas pools of capital, bringing in foreign portfolio investment that increases price-earning ratios and the depth and liquidity of the domestic capital market. This, in turn, reduces the cost of capital for domestic firms. Moreover, foreign participation may have important spillover effects on emerging markets in the form of improved accounting and disclosure practices and human capital. To realize these benefits, however, developing countries need to reduce transaction costs and take other actions to increase the attractiveness of their markets.
- Second, asset prices in developing countries are more volatile than in developed markets, and financial integration may increase volatility even further. Volatility and lack of information interact with each other and together constitute a major impediment to the price discovery process in emerging markets. Information asymmetries will, in addition, increase the agency cost for foreign investors. Volatility tends to decline, however, as emerging markets become less prone to fundamental shocks through improved economic policies and diversification. But, excess volatility resulting from information asymmetries and deficiencies will have to be tackled through reforms and improvements in the attributes of the capital markets themselves.

Improving Market Infrastructure

WHAT IS MARKET INFRASTRUCTURE? MARKET INFRAstructure comprises the systems and institutions that facilitate the trade and custody of securities. These functions can be subdivided into matching buyers and sellers, determining price, exchanging securities for good funds, registering securities to the new owners, and collecting dividends and other custody functions.[17]

A good way to understand the main components of market infrastructure is to follow the main steps in a market transaction. A transaction begins with the instructions of a buyer and a seller to their respective brokers to buy or sell a security. Market infrastructure kicks in when the market microstructures (that is, the trading system) match buyers to sellers and facilitate the price discovery process. The details of the trade are confirmed with the two counterparties by the trade comparison system before any further processing takes place. Then, the clearance system determines what the counterparties are to deliver and receive at settlement. Then comes settlement, when the transaction is completed and the securities and funds change hands.[18] The depository provides for safekeeping of securities but, more important, can facilitate the settlement process and other aspects of custody such as reregistration and payment of interest or dividends. Box 6.3 illustrates the main components of market infrastructure using the example of Thailand.

Why does it matter? During the 1990s, the exchanges, the governments, and the securities industry in emerging markets have all emphasized the need to develop capital market infrastructure, in response to long-standing concerns of foreign investors. When the infrastructure systems work well, as they usually do in developed markets, trading flow and custody seem painless. But in many developing countries, inefficient infrastructures have often been unable to handle the rapidly expanding volume of cross-border portfolio flows, in particular equity flows. The unreliability of market infrastructure has led to delays and failed settlements, the loss of principal because shares were not registered to the new foreign owners, and difficulties in exercising entitlements such as subscription rights and collecting dividends. Since these problems were discouraging many investors from entering their markets, the authorities in developing countries made improving infrastructure one of their top priorities. In developed markets, the importance of these functions became most recently apparent with the settlement problems that arose during the 1987 stock market crash.

Improving market infrastructure is a means not only to attract potential investors and issuers, but also to reduce systemic risk. The major sources of systemic risk in capital markets are volume and volatility surges, the default of a major market player, and operational breakdowns. Because of weaknesses among financial intermediaries, emerging markets are already prone to defaults by market players, to which integration adds increasing volume and creates the potential for increased volatility. A well-designed infrastructure will not only reduce the risk of operational breakdowns but can also make a significant con-

Box 6.3 Clearance, Settlement, and Depository Functions in Thailand

THAILAND'S CLEARANCE AND SETTLEMENT (C&S) system is a good example of the basic mechanisms often used to clear and settle transactions in securities markets. The concepts used in this box are explained in detail in the main text.

The C&S of transactions on the Stock Exchange of Thailand (SET) are handled by a subsidiary of SET—the Thailand Securities Depository Co. (TSD). TSD also functions as the central depository for equities listed on SET. The chart describes the main steps in the process.

- Trade instructions are received and executed by the brokers at time T.
- On T+2 days, matching is completed via telephone among market participants.
- C&S takes place on the afternoon of T+3. Although the system is presented as DVP, payments are made by check and these take one day for clearing.
- C&S in Thailand is the responsibility of the central depository—TSD. This arrangement simplifies C&S, since the estimate of what is owed by each counterparty and the transfer of shares from the seller to the buyer can be done within the same institution.
- With regard to the depository function, since September 1992, the securities market in Thailand has been moving toward a dematerialized environment, with stocks transferred directly between accounts of the members of the depository, instead of physical delivery of share certificates. Investors can also ask for physical delivery of shares if desired. In the case of physical settlement, the selling client must deliver the share certificates no later than 1,400 hours on T+3.
- There are no fixed C&S practices for bonds and other securities not traded on the SET.

Source: ISSA (1996), author's analysis of data from Citibank and Bank of New York.

Box Figure 6.3

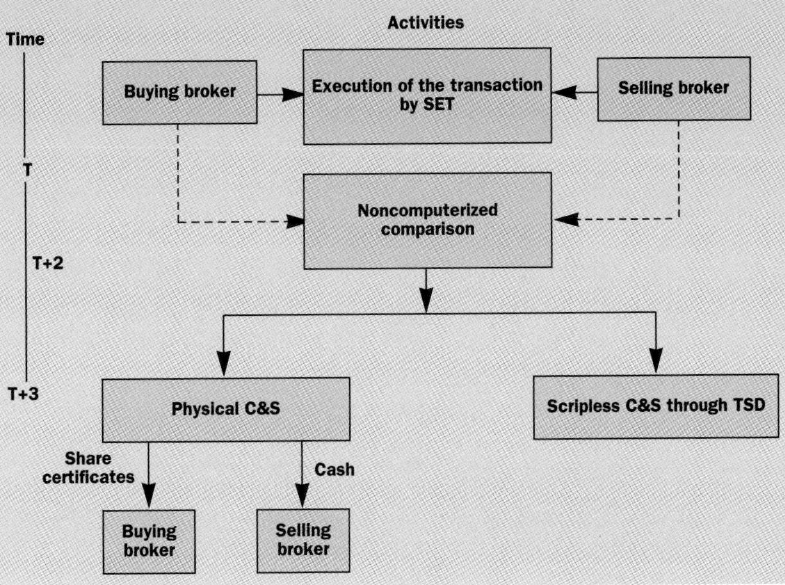

tribution in reducing the potential systemic impact of the other sources of risk.

International norms. Given increasing cross-border flows and the efforts by many developing countries to improve their infrastructures, a central issue during the late 1980s was to establish best practice and harmonize systems across countries. The landmark effort in this area was the G-30 initiative in 1989 that established what was to become best practice in trading and settlement for some six years.[19] Many developing and industrial countries, as well as international industry associations and organizations such as the International Federation of Stock Exchanges (FIBV in French) and IOSCO, endorsed the G-30 recommendations.[20] In 1995, the International Society of Securities Administrators (ISSA) organized a series of workshops to update the G-30 recommendations, taking into account changing technological capabilities and evolving views in the industry.[21] Annex 6.1 lists the original recommendations and the suggested ISSA revisions, to which we will turn when best practice is described below.

This section will discuss four aspects of market infrastructure that have been the focus of foreign investor concerns in emerging markets: the trade, comparison, clearance and settlement (C&S), and depository systems. The design of these systems, especially the last three, is also critical for reducing systemic risk.

Why Emerging Markets Improve Their Trading Systems

Functions and characteristics of trading systems. A good trading system should reduce transaction costs, ease the price discovery process by facilitating the incorporation of information into the price of securities, reduce volatility, and increase liquidity. There is no best system; rather, each system seems to work best in attaining one or two of these four market attributes, sometimes at the cost of the others.[22] Annex 6.2 describes the main typology of trading systems and the basic tradeoffs among them. Whether a particular trading system should be adopted depends on the circumstances of the market and the objectives. Because different systems have different advantages, equity markets are increasingly adopting two or more trading systems, depending on the characteristics of the stock being traded or the investor. Indeed, there seems to be a growing consensus on the desirability of having several trading systems in a market. However, the market and regulatory institutions need to be capable of handling the potentially complex interrelationships between the different systems and ensure transparency and fairness for all investors.

The impact of financial integration. Financial integration does not change these basic tradeoffs and affects the choice of the system only indirectly, in four ways. First, the trading system should be able to cope with the surge in activity that accompanies financial integration. Second, foreign investors may add their (powerful) voices to those of domestic market participants who are concerned about transparency of the market, most likely small investors and the regulatory authorities. This concern for transparency reflects a perception on the part of foreign investors that they are less informed than domestic participants and thus are more likely to be hurt by abusive practices such as front-running and insider trading. Third, foreign investors are likely to undertake large trades relative to the size of many emerging markets and prefer systems that add most to liquidity and immediacy so they are able to conduct transactions rapidly and at a lower cost. Given these preferences, market authorities face a dilemma, since the systems that maximize transparency are not the same ones that most enhance liquidity and immediacy. And fourth, given the premium placed by foreign investors on efficient market infrastructure, market microstructures should facilitate other aspects of market infrastructure, in particular trade comparison and C&S.

The Need for Improvement in Comparison Systems

A comparison system facilitates the comparison of trade details between the counterparties, and if the details do not match, the trade is not allowed to settle. The comparison system, by facilitating C&S as well as by being a prime source of information about market transactions, is a basic building block of a well-functioning capital market.[23] The key match criteria are trade date, security traded, face value or number of shares, and price and currency.[24] To accelerate the settlement flow, a good matching system should work quickly. The G-30 recommendations indicated that trade matches between direct market participants should be accomplished by trade date plus one (T+1). ISSA has revised the norm to T+0, that is, the same day of the trade. A good system, however, also needs to be accurate to avoid failed trades at settlement. For some emerging markets, it may be more cost-effective to compare trades at T+1 or even later to ensure accuracy. The ratio of compared to unmatched trades and the speed with which unmatched trades are resolved are good indicators of the quality of the matching system.

The other key norms and practices for trade comparison are:

- A centralized system by which the two counterparties submit information on the match criteria to a central agency that does a two-sided comparison. The system is usually operated by the exchange or a central clearing agency that integrates matching with the C&S systems, enhancing efficiency through standardization and computerization. Computers are cost-efficient for all but the smallest markets, allowing quick and accurate matching of many trades and criteria.
- Locked-in trades (trades compared at execution) are the norm in markets using a computerized system for trade execution. Locked-in trade systems are especially efficient in markets with many retail investors.
- An efficient one-sided system for large (institutional) investors that are not members of the two-side system—that is, of an exchange or clearing agency. In these cases, the broker or custodian acts as intermediary and requests confirmation of trade details from the investor. However, large investors are increasingly using the central system or an electronic confirmation system. Both ISSA and the G-30 recommend that all indirect market participants be members of a trade comparison system that achieves positive affirmation of trade details by T+1.

The Need for Improvement in Clearance and Settlement Systems

Desirable characteristics of C&S—the investors' perspective. From the point of view of market participants, these systems should facilitate settlement by:

- Reducing counterparty risks by ensuring DVP, preferably with same-day funds (that is, funds that are available the same day they are deposited).[25] A central depository (see below) linked with a payments system would facilitate achieving DVP. This link can be achieved by locating all systems within the same institution and making simultaneous transfers or by linking the systems. In the latter case, assets would be provisionally deposited in the buyer's account, pending receipt of funds through the payments system. ISSA has recently defined more precisely the desirable characteristics of a DVP system.[26]

- Reducing operational risk and problems (lost transactions, bad record-keeping, computer and power problems) that disrupt the C&S process. The settlement time frame adopted by a market will affect operational and market risks. Some markets use an account day cycle by which all trades for a given period are scheduled to settle on a given day. Other markets use rolling settlement, by which trades are scheduled for settlement a certain number of days after execution. Rolling settlement has the advantage of effectively limiting the number of outstanding clearances and reducing the time between trade and settlement dates. Both G-30 and ISSA recommend rolling settlement at T+3. In addition, the clearing system should have backup systems capable of completing the daily processing the day after a failure and good data security.
- Minimizing the movement of money and securities, thereby reducing transaction costs. This is usually achieved by instituting netting between market participants for both securities and cash, rather than relying on a trade-for-trade system that independently clears and settles each individual trade. Netting can be daily bilateral or multilateral, or continuous net settlement, in which open positions at the end of a day are offset against the next day's trade until settlement. A multilateral netting system requires a central C&S entity that acts as a guarantor of all trades, taking on the postnetting counterparty risk. In other words, a member's net obligations to deliver securities or funds are to the central agency, not to the original counterparty. A key point is that these systems require a legal framework that accepts and enforces net obligations transferred to a third party.

In building a C&S system there may be a difficult tradeoff between reducing transaction costs through netting and reducing counterparty risks. In a trade-for-trade gross settlement system, exposure to each party can be tracked, but the system can be prone to breakdown as volume increases, and cash requirements and cost are large. While the recent development of communication and computer technology has made gross settlement feasible in the more sophisticated markets, netting could bring significant savings for markets with growing or already high volume, and with currently high settlement costs and trade failure rates.[27] According to Stehm (1996), multilateral netting reduces the volume and value of settlements by 70 to 98 percent, depending on trading patterns. However, multilateral netting increases uncertainty, since the final counterparty is unknown, a fact that has a chilling effect on the market. Even with trade-for-trade settlement, the market may suffer from similar uncertainties if market participants are unable to evaluate each other's financial position because of lack of information. A central clearing agency that acts as a guarantor may reduce the uncertainty faced by individual participants but may increase systemic risk.

Risk management techniques. From the point of view of the authorities responsible for market development and regulation, and indeed for the market as a whole, a key design issue for a central clearing agency is risk reduction, since the purpose of the agency is to concentrate settlement risks. In addition, if it acts as a guarantor of all transactions, the incentives for market participants to evaluate prudently counterparty risk are weak, since the central agency is guaranteeing the transaction.

Clearing agencies have developed several methods to reduce settlement risk. One form of risk reduction is to set stringent standards for membership in the central clearing agency, although there is a potential tradeoff between achieving economies of scale and promoting broad participation and competition within the market. In addition, in many emerging markets, given inadequate information and weak disclosure standards, the clearing agency may have only a limited ability to develop a comprehensive picture of its members. Risk reduction can also be achieved through net debit caps that limit the net exposure of the clearing agency to each participant and require collateral for some types of exposure. For either procedure to be effective in containing risk, however, the clearing agency must develop a risk control system that marks to market and monitors, in real time, the exposure of its members.[28] More important, the clearing agency should design its procedures so that participants themselves have more of an incentive to manage and contain the risks they bear. For example, loss-sharing rules among participants in the event of a default could be established with a view to increasing the incentives for participants to assess prudently counterparty risk.[29] In addition, loss-sharing rules should also clearly define the potential liabilities of the central agency and participants to reduce uncertainty during periods of market stress. Finally, as a last defense, the central clearing agency should have quick access to sufficient liquidity and be adequately capitalized.

Reflecting the increasing concern with systemic risk, international norms in this area have been modified since the G-30 issued its recommendations in 1989. While the G-30 encouraged the adoption of netting in a high-volume market to enhance market efficiencies and to reduce counterparty risk, ISSA stresses reducing overall settlement risk. ISSA recommends real-time gross settlement or a netting system that fully meets the Lamfalussy Recommendations for multilateral netting systems.[30] Among the most important of these recommendations is that the netting system should be capable of completing daily settlement in the event of the default of the largest single net-debit position. Its procedures should also encourage participants to monitor and contain their own credit exposure.

The Need for Improvement in Depository Systems

Central depository systems have four main functions:

- They maintain facilities for the deposit, withdrawal, and safekeeping of securities. A registry maintains a record of who owns the shares whereas the depository maintains records of ownership for market participants. Good coordination between the two is essential, in particular in maintaining records regarding the securities held in the nominee name of the depository.
- They facilitate achieving settlement on a DVP basis by easing the delivery or recording the book entry transfer of securities against simultaneous payment between members (in accordance with members' instructions or resulting from a netting system), and maintaining an institutional delivery system that allows brokers and dealers to deliver securities to indirect market participants.
- They simplify postsettlement actions such as registration, payment of interest and dividends, and other corporate actions.
- They maintain links with depositories in other markets. However, these linkages are too complex and costly and have not really developed (Stehm 1996).

Physical transfer versus book entry. One key distinguishing characteristic among depository systems is whether or not settlement involves the physical transfer of securities. Book entry is the process of settlement without the physical movement of securities. It requires that physical documents or certificates be either immobilized (stored and lodged at the depository) or dematerialized (when no physical securities are issued at all), with transfer of property taking place as a book (or computer) entry only.[31] Immobilization can result in large savings for the entire industry, especially when securities are fungible and the depository can act as a nominee for the beneficial owners. Dematerialization can further reduce costs by eliminating the costs of custody of physical securities and of maintaining records of ownership on a segregated certificate basis. Legal constraints and adverse investor reaction can be a barrier to immobilization and dematerialization, as will large numbers of certificates from many issuers.

Direct versus indirect holding systems. Another important distinguishing characteristic is whether the beneficial owners (that is, the investors) hold their securities directly at the registry or through the accounts of financial intermediaries.[32] In an indirect system, the most common, an investor's securities are held at the depository in the nominee name of the investor's custodian. In turn, the depository's holdings are registered in its nominee name. In a direct system, the holdings of investors are registered directly at the registry or the depository, which can be merged into one institution. Both systems have disadvantages: most important in an emerging market context, while direct holding systems may discourage competition among custodians and brokers to provide quality services to investors, indirect systems may be plagued with investor protection issues that arise when financial intermediaries hold shares on behalf of their clients.[33] The two systems, however, can be combined or tailored to attenuate these problems. In the short term, what is crucial to attract foreign, in particular institutional, investors, is that there be financial institutions of high quality that can provide good and safe custodial services. Successful emerging markets have welcomed the establishment of global custodians within their borders or encouraged strong links between these custodians and domestic financial institutions.

The Experience in Emerging Markets

There are four key conclusions that can be drawn from the experience in emerging markets in the area of market infrastructure. First, market infrastructure in most emerging markets still compares unfavorably with that in mature markets. Second, infrastructure standards in the more dynamic emerging markets in East Asia and Latin America are, however, approaching international norms, and a number of these markets meet many of the G-30/ISSA standards. As described in box 6.4, East Asia has the made the most progress in market infrastructure in recent years and is on its way to becoming the region with the best market infrastructure. Efforts to upgrade infrastructure are, however, ongoing in almost all markets, and the situation is rapidly evolving. Third, progress has been weakest in adopting those standards designed to reduce counterparty and systemic risk, especially in achieving DVP. Fourth, many emerging markets, in particular in Asia, have adopted computerized automatic matching trading systems to enhance market transparency, despite the fact that these systems are not the best suited to increasing liquidity for large orders.

The gap between emerging and mature markets. There is still a gap between emerging markets and mature markets such as the United States. Figure 6.3 compares, for a selected group of developing and industrial countries in 1995, the reliability of settlement and the efficiency in collecting dividends and reregistering securities—two key custody functions. In all three areas, industrial countries are shown to be more efficient—by a factor of 10 to 1 regarding the average number of days it takes to collect dividends, 20 to 1 regarding the average number of days to register, and between 2 and 3 to 1 regarding trades that settle with a delay. There is also a wide range of performance among emerging markets. For some countries, such as India, the gap with industrial markets is very striking—the proportion of trades that settle after the contractual settlement date is about 75 percent, compared with 10 percent or less in most industrial country markets. Other markets, such as Korea and Mexico, have a performance close to or even better than that of industrial markets.

Meeting the G-30 recommendations. Emerging markets now meet many of the G-30 standards, as shown in table 6.4. Developing countries, in particular in Asia, as described in box 6.4, are upgrading their infrastructures very quickly, trying to keep up with rapidly growing trading volumes, by leapfrogging to state-of-the-art systems. For example, 12 out of the 16 markets included in the table have central depositories, and the remaining 4—India, Indonesia, Pakistan, and the Philippines—are all scheduled to have central depositories by mid-

Box 6.4 Developing Capital Market Infrastructure in Asia and Latin America

ASIA HAS MADE REMARKABLE PROGRESS OVER the last four years in improving capital market infrastructure. For example, as shown above, the efficiency of Malaysia's infrastructure (based on a measure that takes into account the ease and reliability of settlement and postsettlement actions) just about doubled between 1992 and the first quarter of 1996. Indonesia's performance was almost as good. India's successful effort to set up from scratch the National Stock Exchange (NSE) in about two years is another good example of this progress. The early focus of the NSE was on improving the transparency of trading, developing liquidity, and shortening settlement cycles and risk. To do so, the NSE instituted a computerized trading system and a clearing corporation, while a central depository is expected to be operational in India during the next six months. The NSE has also introduced a weekly settlement cycle and a large settlement fund, with rolling settlement expected to be launched within weeks.

The figure suggests that in contrast to those of Asia, the more advanced capital markets in Latin America started the decade with relatively well functioning infrastructures and have maintained this performance throughout the decade. In some cases, such as Argentina and Chile, however, the surge in trading volume has been smaller than in East Asia, so market infrastructure has not been under the same stress. As a result, there has been less urgency to upgrade these systems and adopt G-30 benchmarks. Indeed, although Chile's C&S system is capable of implementing netting, this has not been done so that the authorities can monitor compliance with capital controls (Bank of New York 1996). This is not the case for Brazil and Mexico, which have had larger increases in volumes.

1997. These improvements in market infrastructure are remarkable. Some five years ago, most developing markets were just beginning to improve their market infrastructure, and many market analysts thought that central depositories were only pipe dreams.

Table 6.4 suggests that shortening the settlement cycle to the G-30 benchmark of T+3 through more efficient comparison systems, netting, and central depositories has been a key focus of all this effort. Many of the countries that do not meet the T+3 objective are now close to it, some settling at T+4 (Indonesia and the Philippines) or T+5 (Malaysia and Sri Lanka). But this emphasis on speed may not be fully justified. Foreign investors do not necessarily demand G-30 speed standards, but rather reliability: they prefer a system that settles in five days but in a predictable process with no undue backlogs and failed trades to one that is faster but less reliable. Malaysia, one of the more successful emerging markets, makes this point very well: although only settling at T+5, as figure 6.3 suggests, it has been able to achieve one of the more reliable settlement systems in the developing world.

Box Figure 6.4 Market Infrastructure in Asia and Latin America

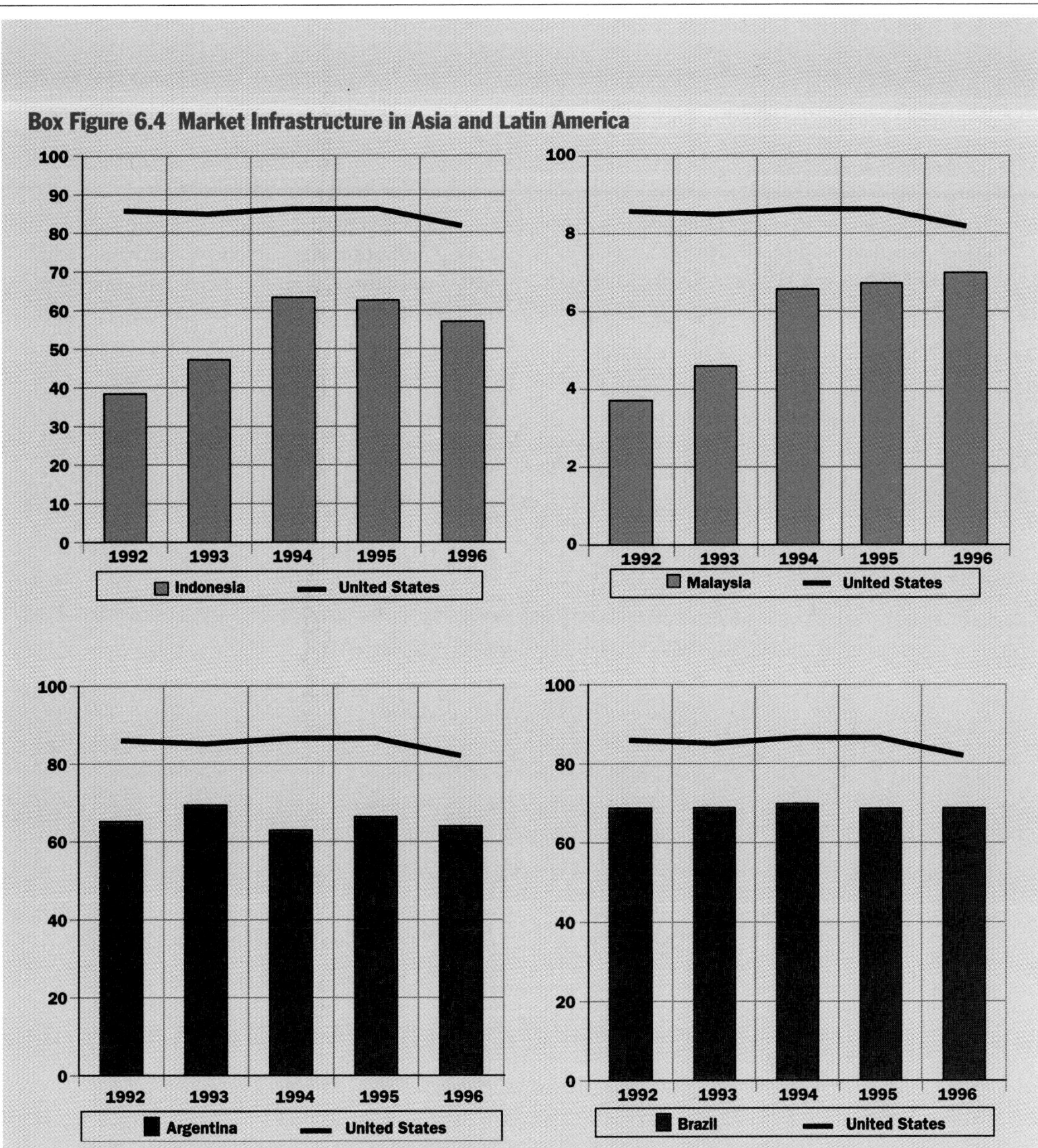

Note: The operational benchmark plotted above is a score out of a maximum of 100. A higher score indicates higher settlement and postsettlement efficiency and a lower overall operational risk associated with the market. Efficiency is measured taking into account the number and operational costs of failed and delayed transactions, the cost of administrative effort, the complexity of the market, and compliance with the recommendations of the Group of Thirty. The date for 1996 refers to the first quarter.

Source: Global Securities Consulting Service, Ltd.

Figure 6.3 Settlement and Postsettlement Efficiency, Selected Emerging and Developed Markets, 1995

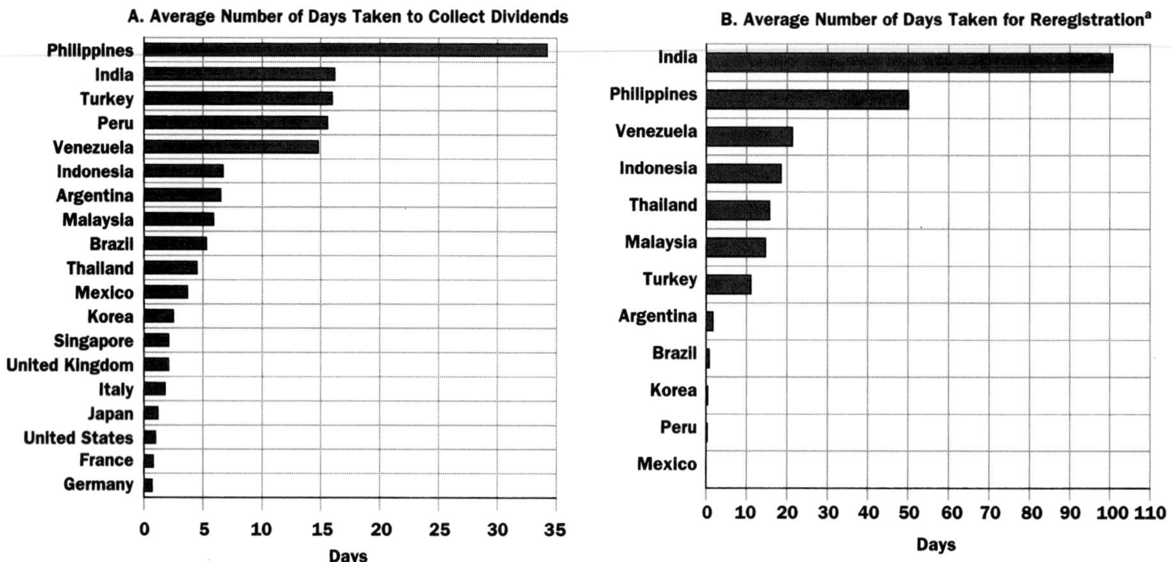

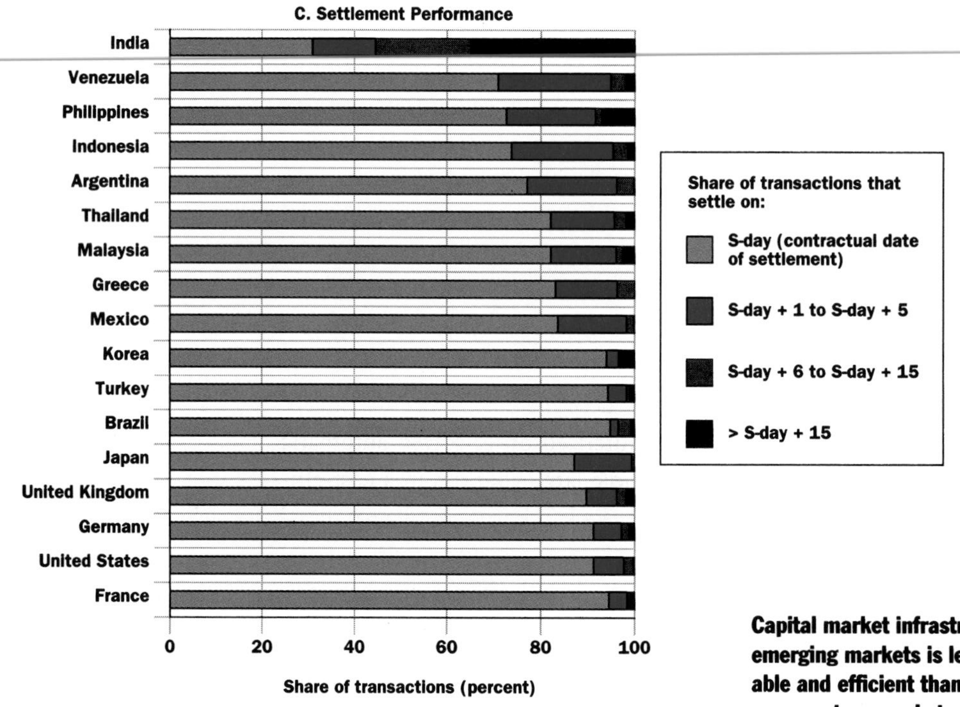

Capital market infrastructure in emerging markets is less reliable and efficient than that of more mature markets.

a. In most developed markets, reregistration is immediate.

Source: Global Securities Consulting Service, *Review of Emerging Markets* and *Review of Major Markets.*

Table 6.4 Conformity with the Group of 30 Recommendations

	Trade comparison system (T + 1)							
Country	*Direct participants*	*Indirect participants*	*Central depositories*	*Trade netting*	*Delivery versus payment*	*Same-day funds payment*	*T + 3 rolling settlement*	*Securities lending*
Argentina	Yes		Yes			Yes	Yes	Yes
Brazil	Yes	Yes	Yes	Yes	Yes		Yes	Yes
Chile			Yes		Yes		Yes	
China	Yes	Yes	Yes	Yes		Yes	Yes	
India	Yes							
Indonesia				Yes	Yes			
Korea	Yes	Yes	Yes	Yes	Yes	Yes	Yes	
Malaysia	Yes		Yes	Yes		Yes		Yes
Mexico	Yes		Yes	Yes[a]	Yes[a]	Yes	Yes	
Pakistan					Yes	Yes		
Philippines								
Poland			Yes	Yes			Yes	
Russia			Yes					
Sri Lanka	Yes		Yes	Yes				
Thailand	Yes		Yes	Yes	Yes		Yes	
Turkey	Yes		Yes	Yes	Yes	Yes		

a. See box 6.5.
Source: Data from Bank of New York and Citibank, ISSA (1995).

Least progress has been accomplished in achieving DVP in the settlement process. With central depositories, the delivery side of the equation is generally working well. It is on the payment side that DVP seems to fail, perhaps because of weaknesses in the domestic banking and payment systems.

Emerging markets are computerizing. As described in annex 6.2, many emerging markets have adopted computerized order-driven automatic matching systems. Computers can handle large volumes in a cost-efficient manner and can trade around the clock. They also enhance transparency by generating a detailed audit trail as well as voluminous real-time information regarding market transactions. However, computerized systems are not good at handling large orders in a market with little liquidity. The fact that many developing countries have adopted such computer-based order-driven systems suggests that this concern is outweighed by its advantages, including its facilitation of other aspects of market infrastructure such as trade comparison and C&S.

Best Practice and Lessons from Country Experience

The G-30 recommendations and the revisions suggested by ISSA are a good indication of what constitutes best practice for infrastructure in securities markets, for both stocks and fixed income securities. However, the discussion above also indicates that benchmarks need to be tailored to the needs and possibilities of each emerging market. In particular, policymakers and market participants need to carefully consider the tradeoffs that arise from adopting particular institutional arrangements, taking into account local circumstances when deciding, for example, whether to set up a central clearing agency. With this important caveat, the main conclusions on best practice for improving market infrastructure are:

- *Matching*: the matching system should be integrated with the C&S system, and all trades by direct and indirect (institutional) participants should be matched at most by T+1.
- *Clearance and settlement*: settlement should be accomplished by a DVP system with same-day funds; there should be real-time gross settlement or a netting system that meets stringent risk control standards, depending on the characteristics of the market; and the rolling settlement system should have final settlement occur by T+3.
- *Depository*: there should be one independent central depository managed for the benefit of the industry, broadly defined; there should be an independent registry or registries; and immobilization and dematerialization should be encouraged, and the legal framework revised, if necessary, to permit them.[34]

Mexico is a good example of how countries are adapting these standards to local circumstances. One peculiarity of the Mexican infrastructure is that while securities are settled on a gross basis, the central bank (Banco de Mexico) functions as the central clearing agency for the money side of market transactions. Banco de Mexico basically functions as the guarantor of the netting system, although it has recently introduced several measures to reduce systemic risk and change the incentives for market participants. Box 6.5 describes the Mexican experience in more detail.

The G-30/ISSA benchmarks do not say very much about the dynamics of constructing well-functioning capital markets. The problem with formulating specific recommendations on how to facilitate this process is that market and country circumstances are critical for deciding policy and institutional reform priorities. For example, in India the authorities decided that the most cost-effective manner of improving market infrastructure would be to construct from scratch a modern equities exchange, with the expectation that competition would promote improvements in the other exchanges. But this approach may not be advisable in markets where existing exchanges are able to overcome vested interests and adopt modern systems. Notwithstanding this caveat, basing our conclusions on both country experience and the work undertaken to develop international benchmarks, we can make the following recommendations:

- The G-30/ISSA benchmarks are objectives to be attained over time. While it is possible and in some cases advisable to leapfrog to modern systems, efficiency and reliability rather than speed of settlement should be the primary objectives. The example of Malaysia shows that investors and issuers will not be discouraged if the market does not fully conform to these benchmarks.
- Reducing systemic risk should, from the start, be an important objective in the design of market infrastructure. The stylized attributes of emerging markets suggest that they are more prone to systemic problems than are developed markets.[35] This suggests early attention to the interface with the banking and payments systems to facilitate attaining DVP. More controversial is the recommendation that, despite the possible negative consequences for market development, it may be advisable to have strict membership criteria for exchanges and clearinghouses, at least during the transition period, until other risk reduction systems are in place and domestic investment firms become financially stronger. Opening up domestic markets to well-capitalized foreign intermediaries may be a way of increasing competition in the market without increasing systemic risk.
- Country experience suggests that setting up a central depository should be encouraged early. While it is possible to have a well-functioning C&S system without one, a depository brings large benefits by reducing transaction costs and operational risks and facilitating DVP. That all the countries in table 6.3 have or soon will have central depositories reveals a strong preference for central depositories by the most dynamic emerging markets. However, an essential prerequisite for a central depository is the legal basis for nominee ownership.[36] In addition, there must be sufficient volume for the central depository to be cost-effective.

Box 6.5 The Anatomy of Bolsa de Mexico's Clearance, Settlement, and Depository System

MEXICO HAS BEEN ABLE TO GRADUALLY IMPROVE its clearance, settlement, and depository systems, moving toward international norms while taking into account local conditions. This process is a good example of how to apply in practice some of the principles of a good infrastructure.

First, Mexico has rationalized and consolidated the institutional structures of the clearance, settlement, and depository systems. One institution, Indeval, is the sole depository for equities, private bonds, commercial paper, and bank acceptances, as well as the clearinghouse for these instruments. It shares the latter responsibility with the Central Bank (Banco de Mexico) and the Mexican Stock Exchange (Bolsa de Mexico), which are responsible for the money side of transactions. As the sole depository, Indeval has succeeded in minimizing the continual movement of documents, thereby reducing the risk of loss, destruction, or forgery. As the sole clearinghouse, Indeval processes all transactions, whether executed on Bolsa de Mexico or outside it, and settles them operation by operation. Hence, all settlement operations involving securities are internal to Indeval, reducing operational risks.

Indeval has also been gradually improving its efficiency as a depository. It was founded in 1978 as a state-owned institution but was privatized in 1987. Today, it is owned by financial institutions, including banks, brokerage firms, and insurance companies, on a nonprofit basis. Since 1984, all Mexican securities have had to be in registered form, and these securities are transferred by Indeval either by book entry or by physical delivery. The transaction is registered in the name of the current stockholder, and, if physical delivery is made, the stockholder's name must appear on the stock certificate. Indeval then advises the corporation about the changes to be made in its stockholders' register. The long-term objective of Indeval is to dematerialize all securities. To this end, it is promoting the use of jumbo or global certificates. Indeval also provides extensive postsettlement services for securities owners and custodians, as well as issuers. In an effort to simplify cross-border transactions, it has established a link

Country experience, in particular that of Asia, also brings good news to nascent markets. A key lesson that can be drawn from this experience is that while these markets need to develop appropriate infrastructure to prepare for international financial integration, with a sustained and well-organized effort they can achieve rapid progress.

The Regulatory Challenges of Financial Integration

WHAT ARE THE OBJECTIVES OF THE LEGAL AND REGULATORY framework? The legal framework is the basis on which capital (and other) markets function. Essentially, it should provide for the effective enforcement of private contracts with Cedel and the International Securities Clearing Corporation in the United States, and it is also studying options with similar institutions in other countries.

In regard to the settlement system, in April 1995, Banco de Mexico implemented structural changes to reduce settlement risk. The objectives of these changes were to attain a DVP environment and reduce systemic risk by instituting better risk control procedures and increasing the incentives of market participants to monitor their counterpart exposure. To this end, Banco de Mexico implemented a new payment system that monitors the ability of a participant to effect payments, as a function of the participant's cash, collateral, and line of credit at Banco de Mexico. These risk control measures should prevent participants from effecting payments in excess of their credit lines. They are also linked to Indeval's clearing system, so securities will be credited to a participant only if the participant can pay for them. Securities will be transferred on a real-time basis, while cash will be netted throughout the day. Banco de Mexico will make one net debit or credit to each financial institution's account at the Banco de Mexico at the end of the processing cycle. With regard to incentives, if a participant's account at Banco de Mexico is overdrawn in terms of cash and collateral for three business days, Banco de Mexico will debit the accounts of all market members who gave settlement lines to the participant under stress. The debit will be proportional to the settlement lines. Industry sources, however, report that the trading system does not allow identifying easily who counterparties are.

While Mexico's clearance and settlement system is effective, it does not fully conform with the G-30 recommendations in two respects. The system does not permit trade comparison for indirect market participants, and the practice of securities lending and borrowing is not operational, although it recently received regulatory approval.

Source: ISSA (1996), author's analysis of data from Citibank and Bank of New York.

and form the foundation for instruments and practices necessary to the functioning of modern capital markets.[37] Building on the legal infrastructure, the regulatory authorities must make markets fair, efficient, and safe. The presumption is that without regulations, capital markets would not result in a socially efficient outcome because of market imperfections (such as incomplete or asymmetric information) and negative externalities (systemic risk). Fair markets are those in which the investor is protected from abuse and fraud and similar market participants are treated equally. Efficient markets are competitive and have efficient infrastructure and information systems. The regulatory framework should promote and protect competition by ensuring that market practices and rules do not impose any unnecessary burden on competition, unless required for the pursuit of the other regulatory goals. Safe markets are those protected against systemic risk.

Best practice. There is a convergence in many emerging markets toward a regulatory model based on public disclosure and on self-imposed market and industry discipline, along with better internal risk management by financial firms themselves.[38] The premises of the model, and associated key regulations, are discussed below.

- First, the goals of the regulator are not to substitute for the market in making investment decisions, but to ensure that the incentives and structure of the market are consistent with efficiency, fairness, and safety. The regulatory framework should ensure that timely and accurate information is available so that investors can judge the merits of alternative investments, hence the regulatory emphasis on disclosure and eradicating fraud. The regulator should prohibit insider trading for fairness reasons and because such practices have the negative externality of discouraging investors and savers from participating in capital markets.
- Second, market participants, rather than government, should be mainly responsible for establishing and enforcing market rules and regulations. The rationale is that participants have an interest in ensuring that markets are fair and efficient, and are better able to judge how to make them so. In practical terms, this means that self-regulatory organizations (SROs) such as the exchanges, broker-dealer associations, and accounting and auditing associations will bear much of the responsibility for the regulation and surveillance of securities markets and auxiliary supporting services. For the system to work correctly, the official regulator must have sufficient regulatory oversight to ensure that the SROs enforce securities regulations as well as their own market conduct rules and that they act to minimize potential conflicts of interest and restraints on competition.
- Third, concerns about systemic risk in capital markets do not justify prudential regulations and monitoring as intense as those in the banking sector. As a rule, investment firms are less vulnerable than banks, on both the asset side and the liability side, to liquidity and solvency crises, and are less prone to contagion.[39] An exception to this rule regards clearance and settlement arrangements, discussed above. However, with the increasing integration

of banks and securities businesses, there is a much stronger rationale for intensifying prudential rules and oversight of the latter.[40]

- Fourth, the protection of investors' assets from loss and the insolvency of investment firms is another rationale for prudential rules and oversight of investment firms. Since investors may not be able easily to evaluate the riskiness of financial institutions through which they conduct business and hold assets, such rules and monitoring would promote market confidence.[41] To this effect, investment firms are often required to meet capital adequacy standards, segregate investors' assets, and meet minimum standards with regard to internal mechanisms for identifying, accounting for, and safeguarding client assets.[42] In addition, the legal system should provide the legal basis for segregating investors' assets. Some markets also make provisions to compensate clients for losses resulting from the insolvency of the firm holding their assets (for example, investor protection funds). Disclosure to investors of the level and types of risks to which their assets are exposed, as well as the status of financial institutions, is essential for market discipline to play a role in reducing these risks.[43]
- Fifth, financial innovation, in particular the development of a wide variety of derivative products, is leading to some important changes in how financial firms are regulated. Although derivative trading still involves price risk, the speed with which these risks can be transformed and the opacity of the transformation process make it difficult for regulators to assess the degree of exposure of financial firms. The regulatory response to this lack of transparency has been to focus on the ability of each firm to manage these risks and to create incentives for financial firms to put in place appropriate risk control procedures. This is a relatively new area of concern in emerging markets, since derivative products are not widely used (except in Brazil and Malaysia) or may actually be proscribed. However, as financial integration intensifies, domestic financial firms may trade in these instruments overseas.

Regulatory agencies in many industrial and developing countries are also mandated to promote the development of domestic capital markets. Obviously, the functions and key regulations described above are essential to foster market confidence and growth. In some cases, however, the regulator needs to carefully assess the potential short-term tradeoff between investor protection and safety on the one hand, and market development or liquidity on the other. More broadly, the cost of a regulation and its enforcement needs to be weighed against its benefits. In addition, in order to promote market development, regulatory agencies will sometimes need to perform functions outside their strictly defined regulatory responsibilities. Box 6.6 lists some of the most important development tasks and describes how certain countries have avoided a common regulatory-development tradeoff.

Preparing for financial integration. Financial integration brings increased urgency to the task of constructing and reinforcing the regulatory framework in emerging securities markets. As with building market infrastructure, this task is essential if developing countries are to compete in an integrating world, attract foreign investors, and reduce systemic risk. For example, investors want both macro data on economic prospects and micro data on corporate performance, to be able to make informed investment choices. Improving disclosure will not only address investor concerns but will also reduce the susceptibility of the market to volatility resulting from incomplete or asymmetric information.

Moreover, financial integration brings new challenges for the regulatory authorities. Globalization of financial transactions and intermediaries will require regulators to find new tools and approaches to monitor effectively market risk and the financial soundness of market participants. Domestic financial firms will be exposed to new market and counterparty risks as they increase their international activities, and new foreign intermediaries may become active in domestic markets. In addition, developing countries have political economy concerns regarding foreign ownership of domestic firms, and some of them have responded through restrictions on foreign investment that seem to have little economic justification.

Given this background, this section will first address four main issues: the costs and benefits of direct restrictions on foreign investment in domestic capital markets, the special regulatory issues that arise from the globalization of financial intermediaries and transactions, the most important concerns of foreign investors regarding the regulatory framework, and enforcement and the role of SROs. Finally, the section will describe some cross-country findings on how emerging markets are dealing with these issues.

Box 6.6 The Regulator and Market Development

REGULATORY AGENCIES THAT FOSTER MARKET development also perform other functions; these include establishing the legal and regulatory prerequisites for domestic institutional investors, encouraging the development of financial institutions and infrastructure (such as credit-rating agencies), and human capital formation. With regard to the last, well-qualified SROs can play a critical role by training, testing, and licensing their members, in particular exchanges and broker-dealer organizations. SROs can effectively provide such training and testing services because of their knowledge of the industry and their self-interest in developing and maintaining the investor public's trust. For example, the Korean and Malaysian securities dealers associations offer a wide range of training programs. For broker and dealers, training in the following areas is particularly important: general knowledge of securities markets and regulations, customer relations (including suitability requirements and sales practices), and back office matters (management of customer funds, record-keeping, and so forth). Good practices build the confidence of both domestic and foreign investors. Investor education is another critical task, in particular so that investors understand the risks and rewards of investing in securities and how to make informed investment decisions.

One of the most common tradeoffs between investor protection and market development regards listing requirements imposed by regulators to ensure that companies traded on an exchange meet minimum standards. If listing requirements are too stringent, few firms will be able to list and the market will not be liquid. One solution to this dilemma is to segregate the market, allowing firms with less-established track records to list in a special, perhaps over-the-counter, market for less risk-averse investors. This system has worked well in industrial countries; one example is NASDAQ in the United States. Emerging markets have also successfully segregated their markets. Korea's stock market, for example, is divided into two trading sections, with newly listed stocks automatically listed in the second section for at least one year. The Korean stock exchange evaluates the annual reports of all listed companies to determine whether second section firms meet the requirements to be promoted to the first section, as well as whether first section firms should be moved back into the second. The key requirements for the first section are that the stock is widely held and that the company has a demonstrated track record. Korea also has an over-the-counter market with even less rigorous listing requirements. Other countries with similar practices include Mexico and Poland.

Restrictions on Foreign Ownership

Typology and rationale. Restrictions on foreign investment are not uncommon in emerging securities markets. Typically, there is a ceiling on the proportion of a firm's equity that can be owned by a single foreign investor plus an aggregate ceiling on ownership by all foreigners. Ceilings may vary among sectors, generally with lower limits for banks, financial firms, and certain strategic sectors. In some emerging markets, a firm can impose even more restrictive limits for its own shares. There may also be differential treatment by type of foreign investor, with institutional investors often being given preference. Foreign investors may also be subject to special registration requirements, which, depending on their severity and on the efficiency of the process, could restrain foreign investment. In addition, controls or administrative requirements that delay the repatriation of capital gains and dividends could severely curtail foreign participation in a country's capital markets.[44]

Restrictions are generally imposed because of political economy concerns about domestic firms being owned by foreigners and because of the need to ensure a level playing field among investors. Part of the fear is that if foreign investors were not restricted, they would capture the great majority of the increases in capital gains and dividends that rapid growth brings, to the detriment of national income.

Are restrictions justified? The economic justification for restricting foreign ownership is weak. If the limits are binding, they curtail foreign portfolio investment, denying the market the additional liquidity, as well as constrain the issuing of IPOs by firms that are unable to mobilize enough local capital to remain within the ceiling. In addition, ownership restrictions on foreign investors have negative implications for corporate governance. Confined to being small shareholders, foreign investors are often reluctant to spend resources to monitor management because of the free-rider problem of the benefits accruing to others. Finally, often the restrictions are not effective because foreigners can avoid the limits through nominee ownership, which further exacerbates the corporate governance problem. This is widely believed to be the case in both Indonesia and Thailand.

Any elimination or softening of these restriction on foreign ownership needs to take the political economy concerns into account to be sustainable. Some countries, such as Mexico, have instituted investment trusts consisting of shares without voting rights for foreigners who wish to acquire shares of a firm over and above the ceiling. Thailand is considering a similar system. While this solution allows foreigners to hold more shares, however, corporate governance remains an issue.

Creating a domestic investor base. The best solution to these concerns regarding foreign ownership is to develop a strong domestic institutional investor base. Such investors will be able to mobilize significant amount of resources, increase liquidity in domestic capital markets, and thereby serve as a counterweight to foreign investors. They also reduce the vulnerability of domestic capital markets in the event of a rapid liquidation of assets by foreign investors. With their deep pockets, they would be able to act as an automatic market stabilizer by bottom fishing and value picking when foreign investors as a group are selling. Moreover, active domestic institutional investors, by increasing depth and liquidity in domestic markets, would reduce the sensitivity of domestic markets to small trades. In addition to serving as a counterweight to foreign investors, pension and mutual funds strongly benefit domestic savers by reducing transaction costs and facilitating portfolio diversification. Furthermore, these instruments are managed by professionals who help overcome the information constraints faced by households.

Developing a domestic institutional base requires reforming and expanding the legal and regulatory framework, in particular in the area of investor protection. Investment fund regulation addresses prudential rules, custodial arrangements to protect investors if the management company becomes insolvent, and rules to prevent fraud and enhance transparency with regard to a fund's objectives and fees, as well as to protect against self-dealing. Expanding the domestic institutional investor base, especially pension funds, also requires reform in a wide variety of policy areas. Box 6.7 describes some recent initiatives undertaken in Latin America to establish domestic institutional investors and the obstacles encountered.

The Regulatory Implications of Globalization

The new risks and challenges. Financial integration leads to rapid increases in three types of a ctivities in financial markets: the activities of multinational financial institutions in foreign financial markets, transactions between financial intermediaries in different countries, and the cross-border delivery of financial services. These activities affect the nature and magnitude of the underlying market, and counterparty and systemic risks in the domestic capital market. In particular:

- As domestic financial firms engage in cross-border investments, they may incur new market or price risks from open positions in exchange- and interest-rate-sensitive foreign assets.
- Domestic residents engaging in cross-border transactions will be exposed to new counterparty risks with foreign investors and firms. Multinational firms that become active in domestic mar-

kets constitute another new source of counterparty risks for domestic residents. In addition, integration exposes domestic residents to foreign jurisdictional risks not under their control.

- Systemic risks also increase with financial integration. Most immediately, the effects of the collapse or insolvency of a financial firm in another country may be transmitted to domestic markets, either directly, if the firm has established itself in the domestic market, or through the payments and settlements systems. Systemic risk also rises because of higher operational risks due to increasing volumes and different hours of operation among payment systems; this can complicate the achievement of a DVP environment and delay settlement. More broadly, integration subjects the home country to more sources of external disturbances and increases the speed at which these disturbances are transmitted across markets.

These activities and associated risks are creating new and interrelated regulatory challenges in two broad areas. First, the most obvious challenge is to contain these new sources of systemic and counterparty risk at the same time that globalization is also rendering the regulatory environment more imperfect. Indeed, with integration, domestic residents, including the regulators, may find it difficult to assess comprehensively the risks incurred by foreign counterparties if they engage in multiple cross-border activities around the globe. Integration will also create similar difficulties in assessing domestic intermediaries as they increase their multinational activities. And there is also a danger that financial integration could blur the lines of supervisory responsibility between domestic and foreign regulators. Second, globalization is magnifying the importance of regulatory issues that arise from cross-country differences in regulations. One important concern of national governments is to ensure a level playing field so that these differences in regulations do not distort the competitive positions of firms and financial centers in different countries. Another concern is the possibility that financial intermediaries will engage in regulatory arbitrage—that is, seek to take advantage of differences in regulations and their coverage between countries.

Two other trends in international financial markets are interacting with globalization, significantly magnifying the regulatory challenge. First, as discussed above, financial firms are increasingly becoming financial conglomerates, combining traditional banking with securities operations and other nonbank financial activities. Second, financial innovation has resulted in a vast array of new derivative instruments and markets. The main regulatory issue with these instruments is that they permit financial firms to change their risk profiles very quickly and in very complex manners. The combined impact of globalization and these two trends is making the assessment of the financial status and risk profile of financial firms very difficult. This lack of transparency is undermining the ability of the market to police itself and of the authorities to regulate.

The international regulatory response. National regulatory authorities have recognized that reducing these risks and challenges of globalization requires stronger international cooperation. This is particularly true with regard to controlling systemic risk, since national regulatory frameworks in this area clearly have an impact across borders. Indeed, there seems to be growing concern among national authorities, heightened by the failure of Barings in 1995, regarding the dangers of unregulated or underregulated financial activities of global firms.[45] But even in the investor protection area, where national preferences have less of an effect across borders, there have been long-standing efforts to harmonize regulations across countries and promote international cooperation in enforcement. These efforts have been undertaken in part to reduce transaction costs and increase market efficiency, and they are motivated by pressure from institutional investors and international issuers. In addition, these efforts at convergence also address fears of competition between financial centers resulting in a regulatory race to the bottom, and of investors practicing regulatory arbitrage.

As the focus of international cooperation among securities regulators, IOSCO has played a key role in these endeavors to reduce transaction costs and systemic risk. Its main activities have been as follows:[46]

- To promote regulatory convergence and reduce transaction costs, IOSCO has issued reports and resolutions on best practice, making recommendations in such areas as curbing and punishing securities fraud, disclosure standards, clearance and settlement, and investor protection (which is also important in reducing systemic risk). Its efforts to improve disclosure and reduce transaction costs by promoting accounting uniformity are particularly im-

Box 6.7 Promoting Domestic Institutional Investors

THERE IS CONSIDERABLE SCOPE FOR PROMOTING the growth of securities markets through the development of domestic mutual and pension funds. These funds have become an important form of financial intermediation in the 1980s in industrial countries, but in emerging markets they have reached respectable sizes only in Brazil, Chile, and Mexico in Latin America, and in Malaysia and Thailand in East Asia. In South Asia, the Unit Trust of India is one of the largest mutual funds in the world in terms of number of investors, but overregulation of asset management has reduced its beneficial impact on Indian capital markets. As is well known, Chile has one of the most developed private pension fund industries among developing countries, managing some 45 percent of GDP in assets.

To be able to develop such funds, there needs first to be the legal basis for practices, such as beneficial ownership, novation, and trusts, that are central to their development. And second, in order to promote confidence in funds, the investor needs to be protected through investment management legislation that is adequately enforced. The legislation should:

- Ensure that investors are well informed about the funds' investment objectives and risk profiles and the quality and costs of fund management.
- Ensure fair valuation of investors' purchases and redemptions.
- Define prudential and fiduciary standards. The extent to which regulation includes detailed investment rules regarding the composition of fund portfolios (types of assets and their shares in the total) varies among countries.
- Define, discourage, and regulate improper practices such as self-dealing.
- Protect the integrity of the funds' assets. These rules generally segregate the funds' assets from those of the management company (to ensure that investors do not suffer in the case of insolvency of the management company) and ensure proper custody arrange-

portant and are described in more detail elsewhere in this chapter. In addition, given the strong representation of emerging markets at IOSCO, its resolutions, reports, and accompanying discussions have served as a conduit for the transfer of expertise and experience between countries.[47]

- IOSCO has also been quite active in the area of systemic risk, especially during the 1990s. One key focus has been to contain the systemic risks arising from derivative activities. In this regard, IOSCO and the Basle Committee on Banking Supervision have collaborated on several reports during 1994–95 on best practice in disclosure of both qualitative and quantitative information of derivative activities (for example, Basle Committee and IOSCO, 1995a, 1995b).[48] IOSCO is also fleshing out the recommendations made in May 1995 by the regulators of most major futures and options markets (the Windsor Declaration), including protection of customer positions and assets, and strengthening default procedures.

ments. Management legislation usually also requires independent directors on the board of the fund.

In certain Latin American countries, capital markets have received a huge boost from the reform and privatization of social security. However, the benefits of these reforms and the development of mutual and pension funds have been delayed by problems regarding the structure of the industry as well as excessive regulation. Throughout the region, competing intermediaries such as banks play a dominant role in the mutual fund industry and have not pursued the development of the industry aggressively. In Mexico, banks have reportedly redirected fund investors into deposits. Custodial arrangements also tend to be costly, with only a few institutions, mainly banks, being allowed to act as custodians.

But among the most important obstacles to the development of mutual funds are the design and prudential regulation of private pension funds. These design and prudential rules have created barriers in the provision of financial management services and perverse incentives, and reduced the potential development of equity markets. Typically, pension funds must be new and specially licensed to manage mandated retirement savings (excluding existing intermediaries) and guarantee a certain return. The guaranteed return is defined as a certain percentage of the average return of the pension fund industry. The exclusion of mutual funds has limited their growth and their ability to attain economies of scale. The return guarantee has led pension fund managers to offer virtually identical portfolios, limiting competition, which in turn has led to high upfront commissions. These problems have been compounded by regulatory restrictions limiting equities to 20 to 30 percent of pension fund portfolios. Remedial action should introduce greater competition and portability of these mandated savings, offering greater freedom to savers to choose among different portfolios of approved products.

- Finally, given that its recommendations are advisory and nonbinding to its members, IOSCO has strongly encouraged coordination among members, in particular through bilateral agreements (memorandums of understanding) regarding information sharing and enforcement.[49] While there has been a sharp increase in the number of these bilateral agreements these last few years, many of these understandings have been between industrial countries, some between industrial and developing countries, and only a few between developing countries. The exceptions to this rule are the Latin American countries, which have established a network of such understandings, and, in Asia, Hong Kong, which has signed agreements with many emerging markets in the region. Recently, in response to the Windsor Declaration, exchanges, clearinghouses, and regulators of the major global futures and option markets have signed information-sharing agreements.

Other efforts at international collaboration in capital markets have focused on clearance, settlement, and payment systems, and regulating financial conglomerates. In the payments area, settlement and systemic risk have been reduced by harmonizing regional payments standards and increasing the overlap of hours of operation of different payment systems. With regard to financial conglomerates, securities, banking, and insurance regulators have been collaborating in developing principles for the supervision of financial conglomerates and for collaboration among the three different types of regulators.[50] Finally, given that the settlement and payment systems are among the most important sources and channels of transmission of systemic risk in securities markets, there is an ongoing debate on the desirability of reaching minimum standards for clearinghouses.

Policy implications for emerging markets. The above discussion suggests several implications for policymakers responsible for emerging securities markets. First, there seems to be a high payoff in information-sharing and enforcement agreements, both between emerging and industrial country markets, and among developing countries themselves. Given the Latin America example, agreements between emerging markets in the same region may be especially useful since they are likely to share financial intermediaries and investors and be exposed to common sources of external shocks. These collaborative arrangements should also include advance agreements on how to handle a crisis (Oyens 1996). Second, given the increased complication in assessing counterparty risk and the enhanced probability of contagion from other markets, governments and markets would do well to concentrate on improving prudential rules and operating procedures of the securities clearing agency, as discussed in the previous section.

The Regulatory Framework Is Critical for Attracting Foreign Investors

Three functions of the regulatory framework are critical for attracting foreign portfolio investment and reducing the potential costs associated with financial integration: ensuring accurate disclosure of all material information, eradicating insider trading, and improving corporate governance.

Improving disclosure. Among the most critical functions of a regulatory framework is to increase transparency in the market by mandating public disclosure, both at the initial phase, when a firm issues securities to the public, and continuously thereafter. As emphasized earlier in this chapter, such information is critical for foreign investors, indeed all investors, if decisions are to be more than just uninformed gambles. Hence, investors shun capital markets with weak disclosure. Inappropriate disclosure also undermines the more macroeconomic benefits of capital markets, in particular the efficiency of the market as a signaling device for the allocation of capital.

Over time, three types of disclosure requirements have developed in capital markets:

- Listing requirements—that is, the disclosure required for a firm to list in a securities market or trade publicly. Listing requirements typically include minimum thresholds regarding the number of shareholders and the value and volume of public shares, earnings, and balance sheet criteria over a number of years; an assessment of the potential of the firm and industry it belongs to; qualitative criteria regarding corporate governance; and credible documentation of the above criteria. Most markets also have continuing listing or maintenance requirements. In addition, to avoid a regulatory race to the bottom among competing exchanges in a country, there should be a baseline on disclosure imposed by the official regulator for all securities traded publicly on these exchanges, or through other means.[51]
- Initial offering requirements—that is, the disclosure mandated for a firm to issue new securities. This involves two types of information. First, information that allows investors to evaluate the overall condition of the firm issuing the securities, including risk factors and prior performance. Second, more specific information about the new issue: amount of capital to be raised and its intended purpose, dilution, how the offering price was determined, distribution plan, underwriters, and other market-making activity. The information for initial offerings is usually distributed to the public in the form of a prospectus.
- A general requirement to disclose all material information on a timely basis. Even though issuers may be complying with periodic reporting requirements, they are also obligated to disclose all important corporate developments as they occur—that is, developments that may have an effect on the company's business or the stock price. These include mergers and acquisitions, stock divi-

dends, and changes in capital. In some cases, the exchange may suspend trading in the security when the event is announced to allow time for dissemination and analysis by the market.

There may be additional disclosure requirements for companies in special industries, for example, mining, banking, and others. Also, in both industrial and developing countries, private offerings have less of a disclosure burden than public offerings. And finally, in industrial countries, there is the concept of the "sophisticated" investor, usually a high-net-worth individual or institution, that is presumed to be well informed. Disclosure for securities sold to these investors is also less stringent.

Differences in disclosure requirements among countries are not insignificant. They arise because of different legal frameworks and regulatory approaches, including the assignment of institutional responsibilities both within governments and between governments and the SROs. In industrial markets, while there is widespread agreement on the general categories or criteria that need to be disclosed, the specifics vary, as do the methods by which disclosure is made. In some countries, regulators rely on market practice and the general obligation to disclose all material information rather than on specific disclosure requirements. Australia, for example, has moved sharply in this direction in the 1990s. The United States, by contrast, has more specific requirements. But while this distinction is important in theory, in practice what is disclosed may be similar because of the generalized requirement to report all material events. With regard to how disclosure is made, some industrial countries rely more on the disclosure of material events and offering documents than on periodic reporting. Again, in practice the differences in what is actually disclosed may not be large. In emerging markets, since market practice may not be very widespread and the ability of regulators to monitor and enforce disclosure may be weaker than in more mature markets, it seems prudent to be quite specific on disclosure and reporting requirements.

Harmonizing disclosure standards. The international community has been trying to harmonize disclosure requirements to facilitate cross-border trade. To this end, IOSCO prepared in 1991 a special report on the different disclosure requirements in member industrial countries to facilitate discussion of the issuance of securities in multiple jurisdictions with a single set of documentation. Then, in 1992, IOSCO published a survey of disclosure requirements in some 23 emerging markets and in

Singapore and Taiwan (China). Finally, in 1993, IOSCO prepared guidelines for disclosure in corporate offerings. In 1994, the Council of Securities Regulators of the Americas (COSRA) issued a framework for full and fair disclosure including when, what, and how disclosure should be provided and enforced and stated its intention to implement and maintain a system based on these principles. Both the COSRA framework and the IOSCO guidelines are good blueprints, but emerging markets need to adapt them to local conditions. The caveat is critical. For example, the best means and periodicity of disclosure and the treatment of small companies will depend on country circumstances. In addition, adopting such standards may require significant revisions in a country's legal framework, since in many countries disclosure requirements are defined piecemeal in a variety of laws and decrees.

Accounting standards. Disclosure will be effective only if the financial information provided by the company is based on sound accounting principles and practices that are well understood by investors. Common accounting standards are essential for investors to be able to evaluate the financial performance of a company on both an absolute and a relative basis. In parallel, auditing standards and practices also need improvement to ensure the reliability of disclosed information.

Major cross-country differences in accounting and auditing standards are an impediment to cross-border issues and to portfolio equity flows to the extent that financial statements are not transparent for international users.[52] IOSCO and the International Accounting Standards Committee (IASC) are working together to harmonize accounting standards. The approach adopted is to develop a revised set of international accounting standards toward which national standards could converge. To this end, the IASC hopes to develop a core set of international accounting standards by 1998. By 1995, 15 out of 31 norms had been developed. Upon successful completion of the project, IOSCO would recommend to its members that they accept these standards in cross-border filings. The IASC's most important challenge is to develop a comprehensive core set of standards that can portray accurately the very different circumstances that firms in different countries deal with and that measure consistently their performance. Another challenge is to ensure that these international standards are not adopted at the cost of excessive discretion in comparison with national standards.

Private standard-setting bodies have played an extremely important role in the more advanced emerging markets in developing sound accounting and auditing principles and practices, and in offering continuing education for accountants and auditors. The IASC's international standards have been used by these organizations in many cases as benchmarks. For example, in Malaysia, regulation of the accountancy profession is vested in the Malaysian Institute of Accountants (MIA). The MIA requires all limited companies to comply with local accounting standards and helps ensure compliance by regularly reviewing samples of published financial statements. If a statement falls short of the requirements, the member responsible for preparing or auditing the statements is asked to provide an explanation and take appropriate follow-up action. With regard to international standards, the MIA reviews on a regular basis the standards issued by the IASC to determine their applicability in Malaysia. If the new standard does not conflict with local law or accounting practices, it will be issued under the heading of an international accounting standard. The MIA has, to date, adopted 24 of the 31 international standards without alteration. With regard to the others, Malaysia has its own alternative requirements, which are generally consistent with international standards.

Insider legislation. Another critical function of the regulatory framework necessary to develop confidence among investors is to eradicate insider trading—that is, the trading of securities while in possession of material nonpublic information obtained in breach of fiduciary duty or duty of confidentiality. Insider rules typically define what information is considered illegitimate—usually all facts that can have an impact on a company's business and the performance of its stock, who is subject to insider trading rules, the reporting requirements for insiders, and what types of companies are subject to these rules. In some industrial countries, owners of more than a certain amount of a certain stock are considered insiders and are required to file reports on their trading activities. Insider legislation also defines insiders' responsibilities: respecting strict confidentiality and not using the information for the benefit of self or others.

Typically, civil and administrative penalties for insider offenses include loss of profits, warnings, fines, and temporary suspension or cancellation of registration. Criminal penalties can include jail terms. Judging from U.S. experience, Strahota (1996) suggests that emerging markets should not try to eliminate insider trading by relying solely on criminal prosecution. It is more effective to have the full range of sanctions (civil, administrative, and criminal), since criminal prosecutions require a burden of proof that is not easy to establish in the financial area, in particular in emerging markets, where the police and courts may not be experienced in these types of cases. To further facilitate enforcement, insider rules should include incentives for market participants to monitor compliance, such as making managers and firms responsible for breaches of insider rules committed by their subordinates or employees, requiring security houses to institute internal control procedures, and holding responsible both the giver and receiver of information. These recommendations regarding the range of sanctions and incentives are important enforcement principles that can be applied over a wide array of regulatory areas.

Minority shareholder rights and corporate governance. Effective corporate governance involves essentially the promotion of shareholder rights and responsibilities, including those of minority shareholders. The two basic principles are fair treatment for all shareholders and shareholder approval of key corporate decisions. The latter is directed more at the potential conflicts between management and shareholders, while the former regards more minority shareholder rights.

Fair treatment for shareholders implies that voting power, dividends, tender or exchange offers, and redemption should be proportional to the number of shares held, and that disclosure announcements should not discriminate among shareholders. Shareholder approval will in the first instance be indirect, through the election of an independent board of directors that approves the most significant corporate decisions made by senior management. But in addition, certain outstanding decisions that can have a material effect on the financial value of the corporation or its shares should be approved by the majority of the shareholders.[53] Moreover, it is becoming common practice in industrial countries, especially in the United Kingdom and the United States, for management compensation to be determined by a committee of independent board members and for independent directors to establish an audit committee. Shareholders in industrial countries are also mandating changes in management compensation (for example, linking compensation to share price) and other incentives that encourage management to maximize shareholder value.

Laws and regulations that promote these criteria make a capital market significantly more attractive for both foreign and domestic investors. To this end, some developing countries have begun to mandate by law the appointment of independent directors and other measures to improve corporate governance. Indonesia, for example, has recently introduced the requirement that issuers grant preemptive rights to existing shareholders in the case of new equity issues, as is common in Europe and Latin America.[54] In Malaysia, one listing requirement is that there be a board audit committee composed of independent directors. In Korea, too, authorities are very much aware of the concerns of foreign institutional investors regarding shareholder rights and are considering ways of promoting corporate governance principles through capital market regulations (Hong 1996). However, it is not clear to what extent each of these principles should be regulated rather than enforced through shareholder pressure that leads to changes in corporate practices. The example of ICICI in India discussed in box 6.2 is a good example of how market pressures can improve governance without changes in regulations.

More broadly, corporate governance also refers to shareholders and their representatives at the board being more independent and active in corporate affairs, monitoring and demanding more transparency from management. This shareholder activism and emphasis on corporate governance is increasing in many OECD countries, including Australia, Canada, France, the United Kingdom, and the United States, where, as noted earlier in this chapter, certain institutional investors have played a key role.[55] One focus of these efforts has been to strengthen board membership criteria, in particular, to redefine what constitutes outside directors and to increase their role on the board. In some companies, outside directors now evaluate formally the chief executive officer, actively engage in succession planning, and more generally are instrumental in preparing and implementing a long-term strategy for the company.

The Role of SROs in Enforcement

While laws and regulations based on international norms and best practice are one pillar of an effective regulatory framework, the other essential component is enforcement. The importance of enforcement cannot be stressed sufficiently. Without enforcement, neither domestic nor foreign investors will have confidence in the capital markets, which will remain undeveloped.

Effective enforcement requires clarifying the mandate and powers of the different regulatory institutions. With regard to the official regulator, the consensus is that one independent institution should be responsible for the oversight of capital markets. The benefits of this regulatory structure are well known and will not be discussed further here, although there are some exceptions to this rule. For example, government debt markets are in many countries the responsibility of the central bank. And given the SRO model that is being adopted by many developing countries, effective enforcement also requires defining the functions of SROs and their interrelationships with the official regulator.

Self-regulation in industrial markets. The role of self-regulation in securities markets varies across developing and industrial markets. Where this concept is most developed, in the United Kingdom and the United States, much of the responsibility for regulating the securities markets lies with SROs, which include the exchanges, the professional organizations, and the clearing and depository organizations. The SROs develop rules for their members and ensure compliance with these rules and with securities laws. Self-regulatory responsibilities can encompass regulation of market transactions (listing requirements, market surveillance, trading regulations, clearing and settlement, and disclosure of information), which is usually the responsibility of an exchange; regulation of market participants (licensing of broker-dealers and other professionals, capital and probity requirements, and business and ethical codes), typically done by professional organizations; and dispute resolution and enforcement actions, including those that deal with insider trading.[56]

This regulatory model, based on disclosure and self-regulation, has been the result of a long evolutionary process in industrial countries. In the United States, for example, the self-regulatory organizations were the only regulators until the creation of the Securities and Exchange Commission after the crash of 1929. Self-regulation is based on the premise that it is in the long-term self interest of the industry to develop fair and efficient markets in order to attract capital and investors to the markets. The model presupposes competition among intermediaries and that different segments of the industry will have the incentive to monitor one another. Given the stylized attributes of capital markets in developing countries, however, the question is whether it is possible and desirable for these countries to have the same kind of market-based disclosure system for their capital markets.

Applying the SRO model to developing countries. There are, in fact, several reasons why the SRO regulatory model can face problems in emerging markets:

- Since the structure of the securities markets is imperfect because of limited competition, self-regulation may not be enough to ensure fair and efficient markets. Korea, for example, has fixed commission rates, while membership in Indian exchange and clearance organizations is restricted.
- The institutional and human capital may be insufficient to ensure that two pillars of the system—self-regulation and disclosure—result in fair and efficient markets. For example, accounting standards may be deficient, the investor public may be uninformed, and reporting and disclosure practices may be weak or nonexistent. In addition, the accounting SROs may not have the ability to perform the oversight function effectively.
- Finally, there may be short-term tensions between the regulatory and market development objectives of the authorities or the SROs. For example, care needs to be taken that new listings are not discouraged by excessive listing requirements; these perhaps should be tightened progressively or modulated according to the market on which the security will be traded. Alternatively, listing requirements may be too loose because the exchange may be seeking to increase business to the detriment of long-term confidence in capital markets.

Despite these problems, however, the benefits of a self-regulatory structure to an emerging capital market are substantial, and such a structure seems the best alternative. As discussed above, because of its first-hand experience, the industry is more able than government to formulate good rules and procedures, and to keep them current with new technology and industry practices. For the same reasons, the industry will generally also be better able to monitor compliance. In addition, self-imposed rules are usually better accepted than rules mandated from the outside. Finally, excessive government oversight or regulation may create different but just as serious governance issues through increased rent-seeking behavior. In any case, self-interest is central to all regulatory systems, not only to the self-regulatory model. Any well-designed system has to be based on creating the right incentives for market participants. If the incentives are not right, it is probably just a matter of time before the rules are broken, even with intense and effective monitoring.

The evolving role for SROs in emerging markets. Given these concerns, some forethought on the sequencing of responsibilities is necessary.

Three criteria seem important for deciding which regulatory functions should be transferred to the SROs and at what speed:

- Most obviously, the transfer of responsibilities should be modulated according to the institutional capacity of the SRO. In Indonesia, for example, in the absence of strong professional associations, the official regulator, BAPEPAM, continues to license both legal and accounting professionals to work in the securities area.
- The governance structure of the SROs should also be considered in allocating regulatory responsibilities, and it may be necessary to review the SRO's governance arrangements to minimize potential conflicts of interest. These issues are not unique to developing countries. For example, in both the United Kingdom and the United States there has been increasing concern about the ability of professional associations to monitor compliance by members with professional and ethical codes of conduct. In addition, governance issues may change over time, and as markets develop, new conflicts of interest may arise. Box 6.8 describes the reforms implemented in 1996 in both these countries to reduce these conflicts of interest while preserving the SRO model.
- The comparative advantage of the industry relative to the official regulator in performing different regulatory functions should also be taken into account. Even if the SRO is not fully developed, it still might do a better job in certain areas than the official regulator.

According to these criteria, functions regarding regulation of market transactions—market surveillance, the provision of information, and trading regulations for the securities market—should be transferred first to the SRO (the exchange). Not only does the exchange have a large comparative advantage over the official regulator, but potential conflicts of interest seem less serious. For example, members of the exchange have an incentive to ensure compliance with rules regarding the release of price-sensitive information, and to control and punish manipulative practices. Members of an exchange would also wish to have an efficient trading system. Potential conflicts of interest would seem more intense in licensing members, ensuring compliance with codes of conduct and listing requirements. Many regulators, however, believe that the prosecution of insider trading should be the responsibility of the official regulator because the SROs may not be willing to

Box 6.8 Effective Governance of SROs in the United Kingdom and the United States

IN RESPONSE TO INCREASING CONCERNS ABOUT potential conflicts of interest in two key SROs, the National Association of Securities Dealers (NASD) in the United States and the Institute of Chartered Accountants (ICA) in the United Kingdom, independent commissions made far-reaching proposals to change the structure and governance of both SROs in 1996. These proposed reforms illustrate how conflicts can be resolved while preserving the benefits of a self-regulating system.

NASD is the only registered securities association in the United States, and every broker or dealer conducting a public securities business is required to become a member. Hence, it oversees the activities of more than 5,400 securities firms, more than 57,000 member branch offices, and nearly 500,000 professionals. As an SRO, it has certain defined obligations regarding the oversight and discipline of its members. NASD is, as well, the primary regulator, and owner, of the NASDAQ stock market and is mandated to adopt rules that promote a fair, efficient, and safe market. NASD has therefore three missions. It is first a membership association. It is also entrusted with ensuring responsible professional conduct of brokers and dealers. Finally, it is also the overseer of the NASDAQ market. The Securities and Exchange Commission oversees NASD, and reviews and approves NASD rules and procedures.

NASD's three-prong mission required it to mediate among conflicting interests. For example, NASD was the primary regulator of NASDAQ, in particular of the trading and reporting practices of NASDAQ market makers, who were also members of NASD. It was a membership association but was responsible for handling public complaints against its members. NASD attempted to meet the needs of these different constituencies by including representation of issuers and investors in association affairs. However, its decentralized administration, heavy reliance on volunteer member leadership, and the fact that one professional staff was responsible for all three missions made fulfillment of its responsibilities increasingly difficult. In 1995, an independent select committee—the Rudman Committee—was asked to assess NASD's corporate governance structure. The select committee found that structure not adequate to fulfill its responsibilities.

In 1996, NASD undertook a fundamental restructuring following the committee's recommendations. NASD was restructured so as to put substantial "daylight" between the membership association, the NASDAQ market, and the broker-dealer regulator, with

prosecute a member, especially if competition in the broker-dealer industry is not strong.

Another way of approaching the sequencing of the transfer of responsibilities to SROs is to distinguish between types of SROs rather than regulatory functions. Certain SROs—the exchanges, clearinghouses, and depositories—can be considered "natural," that is, those whose members have strong and immediate incentives to develop and enforce rules of behavior in order to minimize transaction costs and risks. Indeed, in many industrial and developing countries these SROs were developed naturally by self-interested market participants before securities commissions were established. In the case of other SROs—

three separate governing bodies whose compositions are tailored to the particular requirements of their respective missions. Regulation of the broker-dealer profession was separated from NASD into NASD-Regulator (NASDR), and NASDAQ was given an independent governing board. The professional staff members were also separated, even though all governing boards and staff remain associated within a single SRO structure. The restructuring also placed significant emphasis on disciplinary proceedings and internal review. Finally, the reforms also emphasize increased public representation on the NASD's governing bodies (50 percent public members), which not only will provide useful public feedback to NASD but should also bolster confidence in the NASD's policies.

In the United Kingdom, there was concern whether the ICA was adequately managing the innate tensions arising from acting as the advocate for the interests of members and as a fiduciary administering a code of conduct. After considering complaints by members and others about the effectiveness and reliability of the institute as a regulator, the ICA established the Regulation Review Working Party. The report of the working party states that it was guided by two objectives: to maintain public confidence in regulation and to establish confidence among members that regulation would be sensible.

The working party proposed the creation of a Public Oversight Board (POB) and the separation of the Office for Professional Standards (OFPS) from the institute's other functions. Its proposal parallels the NASD initiatives designed to separate functional responsibilities and to introduce transparency into the system via public participation. The POB would consist of a few independent nonaccountants, not chosen by the institute, charged with reviewing the effectiveness of regulation, reviewing public expectations, assessing the extent to which expectations are met, and reporting in public to ensure redress of shortcomings and encourage public confidence. All the institute functions related to regulation would be grouped within the OFPS, which would be distanced from the institute's other activities, in particular its representative function. The disciplinary aspect of members in business and the setting of ethical standards will not be incorporated within the OFPS. These areas would remain the responsibility of committees and tribunals consisting largely of members.

Source: NASD (1995), ICA (1996).

broker-dealer and other professional organizations—self-interest is not as strong a motivating force for complying with rules. The benefits of complying with rules may become fully apparent only in the long term, and may accrue not only to the institution complying with the rule but mainly to the profession or market as a whole (for example, business and ethical codes of conduct). The implication is that regulatory responsibilities can be transferred first to natural SROs, since they would be better able and more willing to develop and monitor rules of conduct. The two approaches to looking at the transfer of responsibilities to SROs are not contradictory, and imply similar sequencing priorities. The very fact that natural SROs were able to develop and enforce rules of conduct suggests that conflicts of interests are not intense between their members. What regulators need to watch out for are conflicts of interest between the members of a natural SRO and the market as a whole, in particular anticompetitive behavior.

Improvements in the Regulatory Framework in Emerging Markets

There are three key findings regarding the state of regulatory frameworks in emerging markets. First, as discussed above, many emerging markets are restricting foreign ownership of domestic stocks in their markets. However, the prevailing trend is a gradual softening of these restrictions, even in Asia, where they are most prevalent. Second, the regulatory frameworks of the more dynamic emerging markets have improved significantly in recent years, as have accounting standards. However, progress in this area is difficult to measure, since a judgment would need to take into account the completeness and soundness of the legal and regulatory frameworks, and effectiveness of enforcement. It is also difficult to generalize across countries, with remaining concerns varying very much by region. Third, emerging markets are converging to a disclosure-based, self-regulated framework. The self-regulatory model has been adapted, however, to the particular circumstances of each country, and the resulting systems range from those that give primary and extensive powers to the official entity, to those that rely heavily on SROs, subject to oversight by the official regulator. As described in box 6.9, generally the influence of the state remains stronger in Asia than in Latin America.

The gradual softening of investment restrictions. As shown in table 6.5, many emerging equity markets are not fully open, with some economies imposing restrictions on foreign investment or the associated foreign exchange movements. These restrictions are much more prevalent in Asia than in other parts of the developing world, in particular Latin America. Except for Malaysia and Pakistan, all other major Asian emerging markets have some form of control. Korea and Taiwan (China), which require registration procedures and impose very tight foreign investment ceilings, seem the most closed. Notwithstanding the continued existence of controls, as discussed in chapter 1, the prevailing trend is one of gradual opening, with the number of countries that can be categorized as fully open increasing sharply since 1991. In Asia, for example, Korea and Taiwan (China) relaxed their

Box 6.9 The Role of the State in Capital Markets in Asia and Latin America

THERE IS A GROWING CONSENSUS IN DEVELOPING countries on the proper role of the state in developing and regulating capital markets. At a general level, the consensus is that the state plays a key role in creating an enabling environment for the growth of private sector activity, including activity in capital markets. A supportive environment includes prudent economic management, and sound and transparent legal and regulatory frameworks that protect property rights and enforce contracts. With regard to capital markets, there is also consensus that the role of the state should change from one of direct intervention in development and regulation to one of support and oversight. As noted before, the plurality of emerging markets have adopted the disclosure and self-regulatory model, and are at various stages in the process of gradually increasing the role of the SROs. There are, however, some important differences between Asia and Latin America.

In Asia, despite the self-regulatory model, the role of the state in capital markets seems stronger than in industrial countries. In the minds of the authorities, certain characteristics of Asian capital markets justify this stronger role for the state, at least for the moment. The most important are:

- The generally more paternalistic view regarding the role of the state in economic and social development, coupled with weak investor education.
- The Asian tradition of closely held family businesses, which results in weak disclosure practices and the lack of protection of minority shareholder rights.
- More concentrated and financially weaker capital market intermediaries and less developed human capital among the SROs.
- "Reputational" risk: these markets are all developing and are more susceptible to a situation in which a problem involving an issuer or intermediary spills over and affects the reputation of the market more generally.

As a result, Asian SROs are generally less independent than their industrial country counterparts and have fewer regulatory responsibilities.

In contrast, although their markets share many of the characteristics of Asian markets, Latin American securities regulators frequently have weaker powers than in industrial markets in critical areas such as certification of broker-dealers and exchanges and disciplining violators of trading rules. In many countries, exchanges and other SROs predate a securities commission by many decades; derive their influence from special, older statutes than those establishing the commissions; and have significant political and financial influence. As a result, noncompetitive practices, such as obstacles to wider membership in exchanges, inadequate capital adequacy provisions for broker-dealers, and undesirable trading practices are more common in Latin America than in industrial markets. In addition, vested interests have delayed the adoption of more modern market infrastructures.

investment ceilings in 1996, and Korea has announced a program to abolish the ceilings by the year 2000.

Where do developing countries stand? As noted above, emerging markets have made progress in developing their regulatory frameworks. All the major emerging markets now have in place the basic building blocks of a framework; for instance, they have enacted securities laws (Russia most recently) and established independent securities commissions.

Table 6.5 Investment Restrictions in Emerging Equity Markets, 1995

	Restrictions on foreign investment		*Restrictions on foreign exchange movements* [b]	
Market	*Freedom of entry* [a]	*Investment ceilings (percent)*	*Repatriation of income*	*Repatriation of principal*
Argentina	Free	None	Free	Free
Brazil	Free	49 for common stocks, none for preferred stocks	Free	Free
Chile	Some restrictions	None	Free	After one year
China	Only special classes of shares	None for B and H shares	Free	Free
India	Only authorized (institutional) investors	24 in general	Free	Free
Indonesia	Some restrictions	49 in general	Some restrictions	Some restrictions
Korea	Some restrictions	15 in general	Free	Free
Malaysia	Free	None	Free	Free
Mexico	Free	None	Free	Free
Pakistan	Free	None	Free	Free
Philippines	Only through B shares	40 in general and 30 for banks through B shares	Free	Free
Poland	Free	None	Free	Free
Sri Lanka	Some restrictions	49 for banks	Some restrictions	Some restrictions
Taiwan (China)	Only authorized investors	15 in general	Some restrictions	Some restrictions
Thailand	Some restrictions	10–49	Free	Free
Venezuela	Some restrictions	None	Some restrictions	Some restrictions

a. "Some restrictions" implies that some registration procedures are required to ensure repatriation rights.
b. "Some restrictions" implies that registration or authorization of foreign exchange control authorities is required.
Source: IFC, *Emerging Stock Markets Factbook 1996.*

The latter is a relatively recent phenomenon in many Asian countries, where independent commissions replaced the ministry of finance and the central bank as the primary regulator of securities markets only in the early 1990s. Somewhat surprisingly, the accounting standards of many emerging markets have also strengthened considerably. Industry sources say that financial-reporting practices (a key component of disclosure) in several emerging markets are based on internationally recognized standards and are as comprehensive as in the United Kingdom and the United States.[57] Studies conducted for the IASC also show that accounting standards in developing countries have been improving over time and are now on the whole either based on or consistent with international standards.[58] These results do not contradict the more negative World Bank assessments mentioned earlier, since the Bank assessments refer to actual accounting practices. Accounting practices are more influenced by the lack of a sufficient number of qualified accountants and auditors, a common problem in many emerging markets, than are standards. Finally, most major emerging markets also have regulations defining disclosure standards and listing requirements.

Where the gap between developing countries and their industrial counterparts is still wide is in the more detailed but still critical aspects of a sound regulatory framework. For instance, although the data are not fully reliable, about half of the emerging markets included in table 6.6 have not established the legal and regulatory basis for dealing with compensation funds, takeovers, and insider trading.[59] More to the point, many emerging markets have not yet instituted the legal and regulatory basis for dealing with domestic institutional investors, as described in box 6.7. In addition to these common sources of fragility, there are other, rather general concerns that are shared by the regulatory frameworks of countries within the same region. As discussed in box 6.9, in Asian countries the common danger is overregulation, which may stifle market development and repel foreign investors. In Latin America, the danger seems to be underregulation or the lack of effective enforcement. In Eastern Europe and the Commonwealth of Independent States, the main task is to establish the basic legal and regulatory framework for capital market development.

Despite these difficulties, it is clear that the regulatory authorities and SROs in many emerging markets are undertaking significant initiatives to be able to fulfill their responsibilities and improve enforcement. These initiatives are particularly striking in Asia. For instance, the Philippine Stock Exchange has set up new surveillance and audit departments, and has instituted a new computerized trading system to provide the raw material for surveillance. The Stock Exchange of Thailand has set up similar departments and instruments for market surveillance. At the same time, the Securities and Exchange Act of 1992 granted the Securities Commission of Thailand wide powers to pursue and prosecute securities offenses. These include the power to subpoena witnesses and documentary evidence, and to inspect premises and records of securities intermediaries, including bank accounts. Since the commission is not able to prosecute, it has established a special legal unit to work jointly with the police and the courts to prosecute securities wrongdoings. It is

Table 6.6 Legal and Regulatory Initiatives in Emerging Markets

Country	*Securities laws*	*Established SEC*	*Disclosure regulation*	*Listing requirements*	*Insider trading regulation*	*Compensation fund*	*Takeover regulation*
Argentina	Yes	Yes	Yes	Yes	Yes	Yes	Yes
Brazil	Yes	Yes	Yes	Yes		Yes	Yes
Chile	Yes	Yes	Yes	Yes	Yes	Yes	Yes
China	Yes	Yes					
India[a]	Yes	Yes	Yes		Yes		Yes
Indonesia	Yes	Yes	Yes	Yes	Yes		
Korea	Yes	Yes	Yes	Yes	Yes	Yes	Yes
Malaysia	Yes	Yes	Yes	Yes	Yes	Yes	Yes
Mexico	Yes	Yes	Yes	Yes	Yes	Yes	Yes
Pakistan	Yes	Yes		Yes			
Philippines	Yes	Yes	Yes	Yes		Yes	
Poland	Yes	Yes	Yes	Yes	Yes		Yes
Russia	Yes	Yes					
Sri Lanka	Yes	Yes	Yes	Yes	Yes		Yes
Thailand	Yes	Yes	Yes	Yes	Yes	Yes	Yes
Turkey	Yes	Yes	Yes	Yes			

Note: The table has been constructed from secondary sources that have not been validated by an independent search. In addition, emerging markets are undertaking new initiatives on an ongoing basis. A blank means either that the country does not have regulation in that area or that it was not possible to establish from the secondary sources whether a country had such regulation.

a. In India, there are listing requirements but they are solely informational.

Source: Latin Finance, various issues; International Bar Association; ISSA.

also seeking to increase investor confidence and reduce systemic risk by instituting capital adequacy rules based on risk factors that take into account the specific types of risks faced by security firms.

Summary and Conclusions

IN THE NEW INTERNATIONAL ENVIRONMENT, AN INCREASING proportion of private capital flows will be channeled through capital markets. This represents an important opportunity for developing countries to tap into large overseas pools of capital. To attract this capital, developing countries need to rapidly develop their capital markets. There is a growing consensus on the principles that should guide such reform, and rapidly evolving country experience on which policymakers can draw. Addressing the priority agenda of foreign investors will have large spillover benefits for domestic markets and will reduce volatility and other market risks—two of the main concerns that developing countries have about increased financial integration. Indeed, this policy agenda to maximize the net benefits from financial integration largely overlaps with that considered essential to develop capital markets in a more closed economy setting.

Foreign investors have already made an important contribution to capital market development in the more rapidly integrating developing countries. From no foreign presence in the mid- to late 1980s, the share of foreign investors in trading and market capitalization has risen sharply, and is now quite significant in most major emerging markets. Based on this impetus, developing country capital markets, especially equity markets, have made large strides: average market capitalization of 13 key emerging markets rose from 7 percent of GDP in 1985 to 43 percent in 1994, and trading activity roughly doubled during the same period. Foreign participation may also have important spillover effects on emerging markets through improved accounting and disclosure practices, corporate governance, and human capital.

Despite these benefits, however, developing countries are concerned that financial integration may increase volatility and the risk of bubbles. Although it is true that asset prices in emerging markets are more volatile than in developed markets, there is, in fact, little evidence that volatility increases during capital inflow episodes. But we do find evidence of a negative cross-country correlation between excess volatility and the level of market development. Domestic capital market reforms that reduce information asymmetries and thereby promote liquidity can help reduce excess volatility, vulnerability to reversals, and inefficiencies.

Developing countries show considerable variation in the capital market attributes needed for financial integration. The most aggressive have readily responded to increased interest by the foreign investor community by pursuing rapid and wide-ranging reforms. Others are making needed reforms more slowly, while most are still in a preemerging stage. Table 6.7 is an index of the overall level of development of the major emerging equity markets. It is based on the three essential aspects of market development that have been the main focus of investor concerns: market infrastructure, institutional development, and market structure and liquidity. The infrastructure subindex measures the efficiency of the market in settlement and postsettlement actions; the institutional development subindex is based on the quality of financial reporting, the protection of investor rights, and the openness of the market to foreign investment; and the market structure subindex is a weighted average of desirable market characteristics such as depth, lower volatility, and level of activity, relative to an industrial country benchmark. Annex 6.3 describes in more detail how the index was constructed.

The most dynamic emerging equity markets, where progress has been particularly intense during the last five years, include most of high-growth Asia (Korea, Malaysia, and Thailand, with Indonesia and the Philippines not far behind), and two markets in Latin America (Chile and Mexico, with Brazil also ranking well). The East Asian markets stand out for their depth and liquidity, and because of efforts undertaken in the 1990s their market infrastructures are now equal to those in Latin America. The lagging emerging markets in the sample are in South Asia (India, Pakistan, and Sri Lanka) and China. Generally, these countries need to continue to improve their market infrastructure, as well as their institutional development. But even in the most advanced markets, the outstanding agenda is large. In the infrastructure area, for example, about 20 percent of all securities trades in Malaysia and Thailand do not settle on the contractual settlement date—four times more than in the United States.

The potential gains for developing countries from improving their capital markets are also illustrated by the significantly wider bid-ask spreads in emerging versus industrial country equity markets. Bid-ask spreads measure liquidity and reflect a wide gamut of infrastructure and regulatory factors that affect transaction costs and risks, and promote investor interest in a market. Based on 1996 data, figure 6.4 illustrates that even in the more dynamic emerging markets such as Brazil, Indonesia, Mexico, the Philippines, and Thailand, average spreads range from 130 to 170 basis points, compared with 67 basis points in the United Kingdom. The differences remain just as striking for the most actively traded stocks in these markets for which the average spreads ranged from 70 to 125 basis points compared with 28 points in the United States. Hence, through policy reforms and institutional improvements, emerging markets could reduce the cost of equity in their economies by some 100 basis points or more by replicating the performance of industrial countries, spurring investment and growth.[60]

To close the gap, emerging markets should pursue the following policy agenda:

- *Infrastructure*: Emerging markets should implement well-synchronized comparison, clearance and settlement, and central

Table 6.7 Capital Market Development in Emerging Markets, 1995

	Subindex			
Country	*Market structure*[a]	*Market infrastructure*[b]	*Institutional development*[c]	*Overall index*
Argentina	4.0	8.7	8.2	6.2
Brazil	5.6	9.1	7.5	6.9
Chile	8.4	10.0	6.6	8.3
China	4.1	7.6	3.9	5.0
India	6.1	3.8	5.2	5.3
Indonesia	5.9	8.1	7.5	6.9
Korea	6.7	8.7	7.7	7.5
Malaysia	8.7	8.6	9.0	8.7
Mexico	6.4	8.4	8.8	7.5
Pakistan	4.3	1.0	7.8	4.1
Philippines	8.5	6.3	6.2	7.4
Poland	4.7	7.5	7.3	6.1
Sri Lanka	2.9	7.0	8.2	5.3
Thailand	8.6	8.7	7.1	8.3
Turkey	4.8	9.3	8.0	6.7

Note: The index ranges from 1 to 10 with higher numbers representing a higher level of market development. See annex 6.3.

a. Based on a weighted average of market characteristics, including market capitalization, volatility, market concentration, and level of activity, relative to an industrial country benchmark.

b. Based on measures of efficiency in settlement and postsettlement actions.

c. Based on measures of the quality of financial reporting, protection of investor rights, and market openness.

Source: IFC, *Emerging Stock Market Factbook 1996*; Global Securities Consulting Service, *Review of Emerging Markets* and *Review of Major Markets*.

depository systems, with the goal of meeting G-30/ISSA guidelines. However, achieving the G-30 recommendation of a T+3 settlement cycle should not be at the expense of reliability. Emerging markets should also pay close attention to reducing systemic risk by developing sound links with the banking and payment systems. In addition, the risk control procedures of a central clearing agency, if such an agency is required, should meet BIS guidelines, and a central depository should be established early in the integration process. The immobilization and dematerialization of securities should also be encouraged, but not mandated, since such systems require a lengthy lead time because of investor habits and legal impediments.

- *Property rights*: The legal and regulatory framework should include two basic principles of shareholder governance: fair treatment for all

Figure 6.4 Bid-Ask Spreads in Emerging and Industrial Country Equity Markets, 1996

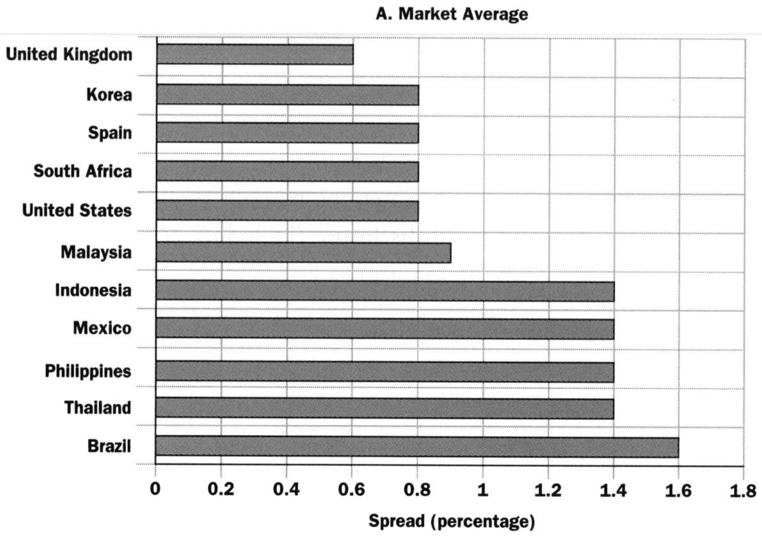

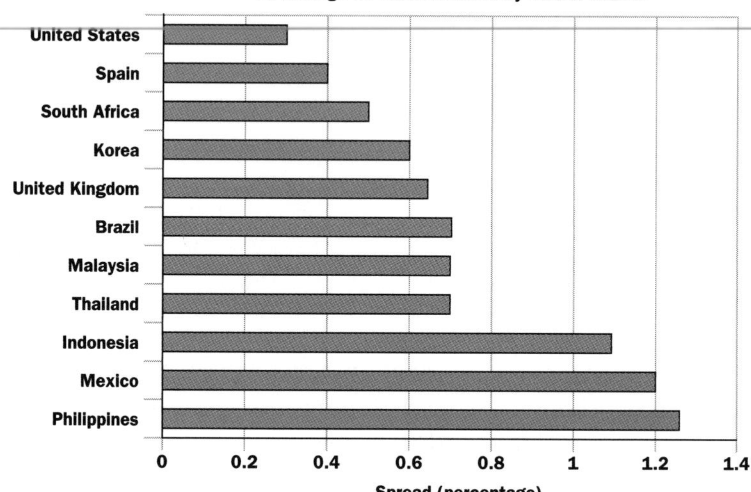

There is great potential for improved efficiency in secondary markets in developing countries.

Note: Values are based on the closing bid-ask spreads for the first 15 trading days in December 1996, taken from the Bloomberg stock quotation system. The market average is based on a sample of 20 stocks from the IFC Investable Index for each country, except for Spain, the United Kingdom, and the United States, for which the stocks were selected from the MADX, FT-SE 100 and the S&P 500, respectively. The stocks were selected to try to replicate the distribution of market capitalization across the respective index. The average for the most actively traded stocks is based on the five most traded shares.

Source: IFC, *Emerging Stock Markets Factbook 1996.*

shareholders and shareholder approval of key corporate decisions. Some of these principles can be mandated in company bylaws or promoted through regulation, and will also spill over to emerging market firms through the increasing presence of foreign investors on their boards of directors. Also, in transition economies, it is essential to establish an independent registry so that records cannot be manipulated by management or shareholders.

- *The regulatory framework.* Emerging markets should adapt international best practice on disclosure (including accounting) and self-regulation to local conditions, and improve enforcement of these rules. Government regulatory functions (starting with oversight of trading activities) should be devolved to SROs as quickly as practicable, taking into account potential conflicts of interest and the SROs' capabilities.

Better infrastructure, protection of property rights, and a well-conceived and -enforced regulatory framework are essential to promote investor interest and liquidity, and reduce systemic risks and volatility. They are the three legs of an efficient and safe capital market, each complementing the beneficial impact of the others. Indeed, progress in only one of these areas would be difficult to achieve. For example, risk reduction measures for central clearing agencies will be effective only if they are backed up by legal and regulatory practices that allow counterparty risk to be transferred to third parties and the market exposure of broker-dealers to be effectively monitored. Similarly, the eradication of insider trading and other illegal trading practices will be greatly facilitated by market microstructures that simplify audit trails.

While the construction of equity markets has been emphasized in many developing countries, there is increasing interest in the development of fixed income markets. On the domestic side, policymakers are turning to domestic bond markets as a means of mobilizing domestic savings to fund large investments, in particular in the infrastructure sector, with a more balanced mix of debt and equity. International investors are becoming more interested in emerging market domestic debt as macroeconomic and financial sector conditions continue to improve in developing countries. As explained in box 6.10, bond markets have specific constraints that need to be addressed, although many elements of market development are common to both fixed income and equity instruments.

Box 6.10 Developing Local Bond Markets

INTERNATIONAL INVESTORS HAVE BEEN LESS INterested in developing country fixed income instruments than in local equities. While net portfolio debt flows to developing countries have increased from $2 billion in 1990 to $46 billion in 1996, most of these resources have been raised through international bond issues. In addition, investments in local debt securities have mainly been on the short end of the market, in money market instruments.

Foreign investors have preferred developing country equities to bonds from these nations for two main reasons. First, debt markets in most developing countries are generally smaller and less liquid than equity markets because of lack of supply and demand. On the supply side, borrowers may favor equity over debt so that they can share the downside risk in the high-return, high-risk environment of an emerging market. On the demand side, investors are concerned with several issues, including the higher sensitivity of bond returns to macroeconomic instability, and a generally weaker debt market infrastructure. In addition, in many emerging markets, domestic institutional investors, such as pension funds and insurance companies, whose counterparts in industrial countries invest heavily in debt securities, are weak and sometimes restricted to purchasing only public sector securities. Foreign institutional investors prefer securities that allow them to capture the large up-side potential in emerging markets and not just share the many risks common to equity and debt. Second, some governments have restricted foreign transactions in domestic debt to minimize interest rate and exchange rate volatility.

Now, however, there is growing domestic interest in developing local debt markets as well as foreign interest in domestic currency debt instruments from developing countries. In developing countries, the main driving force is the need to fund large investments, especially in the infrastructure sector, with a more balanced financing structure. Internationally, the number of developing country closed- and open-end mutual funds dedicated to emerging market debt has increased, and in parallel, the investment firm J. P. Morgan and other organizations, such as the IFC, have or are establishing performance benchmarks for this new emerging market asset class. As emerging markets consolidate macroeconomic and financial sector policies and institutions, interest in bonds and money markets from both investors and issuers will continue to rise.

Much of the policy and institutional agenda for equity markets analyzed in this chapter is shared by debt markets, since many elements of market development, for example, regarding market infrastructure, domestic institutional investors, and the regulatory framework, are the same. The experience of the Bond Dealers Club (BDC) in Thailand illustrates the benefits that well-functioning market infrastructure can bring to the bond market. BDC dealer members are strong financial institutions licensed to trade bonds, and they set up BONDNET, a transparent and dedicated electronic screen trading network, in 1994. BDC has also facilitated market development

Finally, emerging markets should also promote the development of domestic institutional investors that, by mobilizing significant resources, can serve as a counterweight to foreign investors and thereby assuage fears of excessive foreign presence. Institutional investors can ensure that a large pool of dedicated money will be available for bottom with net clearing and settlement on a scripless and DVP basis. After the first two years of its operation, the registered debt securities in BDC increased from 29 issues with an outstanding volume of $1.3 billion to 116 issues with an outstanding volume of $5.7 billion, an increase of 330 percent. The trading volume through BONDNET has increased from a monthly average of $37 million in 1994 to $676 million in 1996, an annual increase of 300 percent.

However, bond markets have specific development constraints that are not shared with equity markets; among the most important is the need for a benchmark to price securities with different risk profiles regarding default. In industrial country markets, risk-free government paper has traditionally served as the benchmark, but in many developing countries, the price and yield of domestic treasury and other public debt securities are controlled for fiscal and debt management reasons and are not market based. Establishing a price benchmark based on public instruments would hence require deregulating public debt markets, as well as fiscal consolidation to make the reforms sustainable. Ironically, in other countries, in particular across much of Asia, the rapid decline in outstanding public debt as a result of strong fiscal positions has led to similar difficulties in establishing adequate price benchmarks. The approach taken by the Hong Kong authorities is to issue government securities, regardless of budgetary needs, on a regular basis. By gradually lengthening the maturity of these issues, authorities have been able to establish a yield curve stretching for 10 years. In Malaysia, however, the market benchmark is securitized mortgage obligations issued by CAGAMAS, the major public mortgage bank. This suggests that the benchmark security should have stable and well-known risk properties but need not be risk-free government paper. In Thailand, the market may in time find its own benchmark among the high-grade corporate paper being traded in the Bond Dealers Club.

Various forms of securities are rated by outside agencies, but such ratings are more important for bonds than for equities. Bond ratings help investors estimate the risk premiums to compensate for varying probabilities of default on debt payments; hence rating agencies reduce information asymmetries between issuers and investors, thereby promoting efficiency and liquidity in primary and secondary debt markets. Ratings are also beneficial to issuers, especially those of less risky securities, since investors without access to ratings may demand higher risk premiums than otherwise or not differentiate between securities. These benefits are particularly important in emerging markets, where risk assessment skills are probably less abundant and advanced than in industrial country markets. Emerging markets are aware of these advantages, and many of them (such as Argentina, Chile, India, Indonesia, Korea, Malaysia, Mexico, Pakistan, the Philippines, Sri Lanka, and Thailand) have ratings agencies, most of them recently established.

Source: Chow (1996), Hoonsiri (1996), J. P. Morgan (1996), World Bank data.

fishing and value picking, reducing the vulnerability of domestic capital markets to a rapid liquidation of assets by foreign investors. In addition, domestic institutional investors will increase the depth and liquidity of domestic capital markets, enabling the markets to absorb the benefits that integration can produce.

Annex 6.1

Table 6.8 G-30 Recommendations and Suggested ISSA Revisions

G-30 recommendations	*ISSA revisions of the G-30 recommendations*
By 1990, all comparisons of trades between direct market participants (that is, brokers, broker-dealers, and other exchange members) should be accomplished by T+ 1 (the day after the trade date).	All comparisons of trades between direct market participants (that is, brokers, broker-dealers and other exchange members) should be accomplished by T+ 0. Matched trade details should be linked to the settlement system.
By 1992, indirect market participants (such as institutional investors or any trading counterparties that are not broker-dealers) should be members of a trade comparison system that achieves positive affirmation of trade details.	Indirect market participants (such as institutional investors and other indirect trading counterparties) should achieve positive affirmation of trade details on T+1.
Each country should have an effective and fully developed central securities depository (CSD), organized and managed to encourage the broadest possible industry participation (directly and indirectly), in place by 1992.	Each country should have in place an effective and fully developed central securities depository, organized and managed to encourage the broadest possible direct and indirect industry participation. The range of depository-eligible instruments should be as wide as possible. Immobilization or dematerialization of financial instruments should be achieved to the utmost extent possible.
	If several CSDs exist in the same market, they should operate under compatible rules and practices with the aim of reducing settlement risk and enabling efficient use of funds and available cross-collateral.
Each country should study its market volumes and participation to determine whether a trade netting system would be beneficial in terms of reducing risk and promoting efficiency. If a netting system would be appropriate, it should be implemented by 1992.	Each market is encouraged to reduce settlement risk by introducing either real-time gross settlement or a trade netting system that fully meets the Lamfalussy Recommendations of the BIS.

G-30 recommendations	*ISSA revisions of the G-30 recommendations*
Delivery versus payment (DVP) should be employed as the method of settling all securities transactions. A DVP system should be in place by 1992.	Delivery versus payment (DVP) should be employed as the method of settling all securities transactions. DVP is defined as follows: simultaneous, final, irrevocable, and immediately available exchange of securities and cash on a continuous basis throughout the day.
Payments associated with the settlement of securities transactions and the servicing of securities portfolios should be made consistent across all instruments and markets by adopting the "same day" funds convention.	No change.
A "rolling settlement" system should be adopted by all markets. Final settlement should occur on T+ 3 by 1992. As an interim target, final settlement should occur on T+ 5 by 1990 at the latest, except where it hinders the achievement of T+ 3 by 1992.	A rolling settlement system should be adopted by all markets. Final settlement for all trades should occur no later than by T+ 3.
Securities lending and borrowing should be encouraged as a method of expediting the settlement of securities transactions. Existing regulatory and taxation barriers that inhibit the practice of lending securities should be removed by 1990.	Securities lending and borrowing should be encouraged as a method of expediting the settlement of securities transactions. Existing regulatory and taxation barriers that inhibit the practice of lending and borrowing securities should be removed.
Each country should adopt the standard for securities messages developed by the International Organization of Standardization (ISO Standard 7775). In particular, countries should adopt the ISIN numbering system for securities issues as defined in the ISO Standard 6166, at least for cross-border transactions. These standards should be universally applied by 1992.	Each country should adopt the standard for securities messages developed by the International Organization of Standardization (ISO Standard 7775). In particular, countries should adopt the ISIN numbering system for securities issues as defined in the ISO Standard 6166.

Source: ISSA (1995).

Annex 6.2 Market Microstructures

IN RECOGNITION OF THE IMPORTANT ROLE that they can play in a securities market, there has recently been a good deal of interest and activity in trading systems, or market microstructures.[61] For example, recently, the London exchange instituted an order-driven trading system for its larger-volume stocks. Many European and emerging equity markets have adopted computerized trading systems, in contrast to the New York Stock Exchange (NYSE), which has used computers to improve and complement rather than replace open outcry floor trading.[62] Emerging markets are also exploring alternative trading systems to increase the liquidity of the smaller-volume stocks quoted in their markets.[63] Microstructures are also being modified to reduce volatility. For instance, after the 1987 crash, many markets instituted an automatic halt to trading when equity prices change by more than a predetermined amount.

Characteristics of a good trading system. A good trading system should encourage the positive attributes of markets, those that enhance returns or decrease risk. First, the system adopted should reduce transaction costs. Second, microstructures should ease the price discovery process, facilitating the rapid and accurate incorporation of information into the price of securities. When prices do not correctly reflect information, market risks are higher, again discouraging investor interest. Third, microstructures should contribute to reducing volatility in asset prices. As discussed in the main text, excess volatility confounds the information content of market prices, increasing market risk. Finally, microstructures should enhance liquidity.

While these functions are not controversial, the net benefits of adopting a particular trading system will depend on the circumstances of the market and the objectives of the market authorities. Since there is no one optimal trading system, but rather each system works best in attaining one or two of the different functions described above, market authorities may face difficult dilemmas. For example, adopting a dealer system for the smaller-volume stocks may increase liquidity, but only at the cost of higher bid-offer spreads, particularly because in many emerging markets there may be little competition among dealers. To help clarify the options that can be used to improve market microstructures, this annex analyzes the properties of alternative microstructures. However, this is a very wide area, and it will be possible only to touch upon the more important tradeoffs and issues.

The Typology of Trading Systems

Markets in industrial and developing countries use a wide array of methods to match buyers and sellers. A first distinction is between auction-call markets and continuous markets. In a call market, orders are batched together for simultaneous execution at a prespecified time at a single price. The price is determined through an algorithm that maximizes the number of trades that can be executed, with a time priority rule or a pro rata system to determine which orders are executed first.[64] In a continuous market, orders are processed continuously, interacting with changing prices. In turn, continuous markets can be subdivided into order- and quote-driven markets. Quote-driven markets are dealer markets, in which a finite number of competitive dealers quote prices at which they are willing to buy or sell the securities they wish to trade. In an order-driven, or auction, market, orders are consolidated in an auction type of environment. Some auction markets also have market makers, or specialists, as they are called on the NYSE, who are charged by the exchange with "maintaining a fair and orderly market" in the stock for which they are responsible. Finally, all of these markets may be computerized. Figure 6.5 illustrates the typology of markets.

The Basic Tradeoffs

Call markets versus continuous markets. The basic tradeoff between a call market and a continuous market is between liquidity and immediacy. Call markets have characteristics that make them especially appropriate for markets or stocks with little liquidity or with information asymmetries. The periodic auctions of call markets collect orders and therefore facilitate liquidity. By creating these pools of liquidity, a call market stabilizes the prices of infrequently traded issues. At the same time, since all transactions are executed at the same price, investors

Figure 6.5 Major Types of Trading Systems

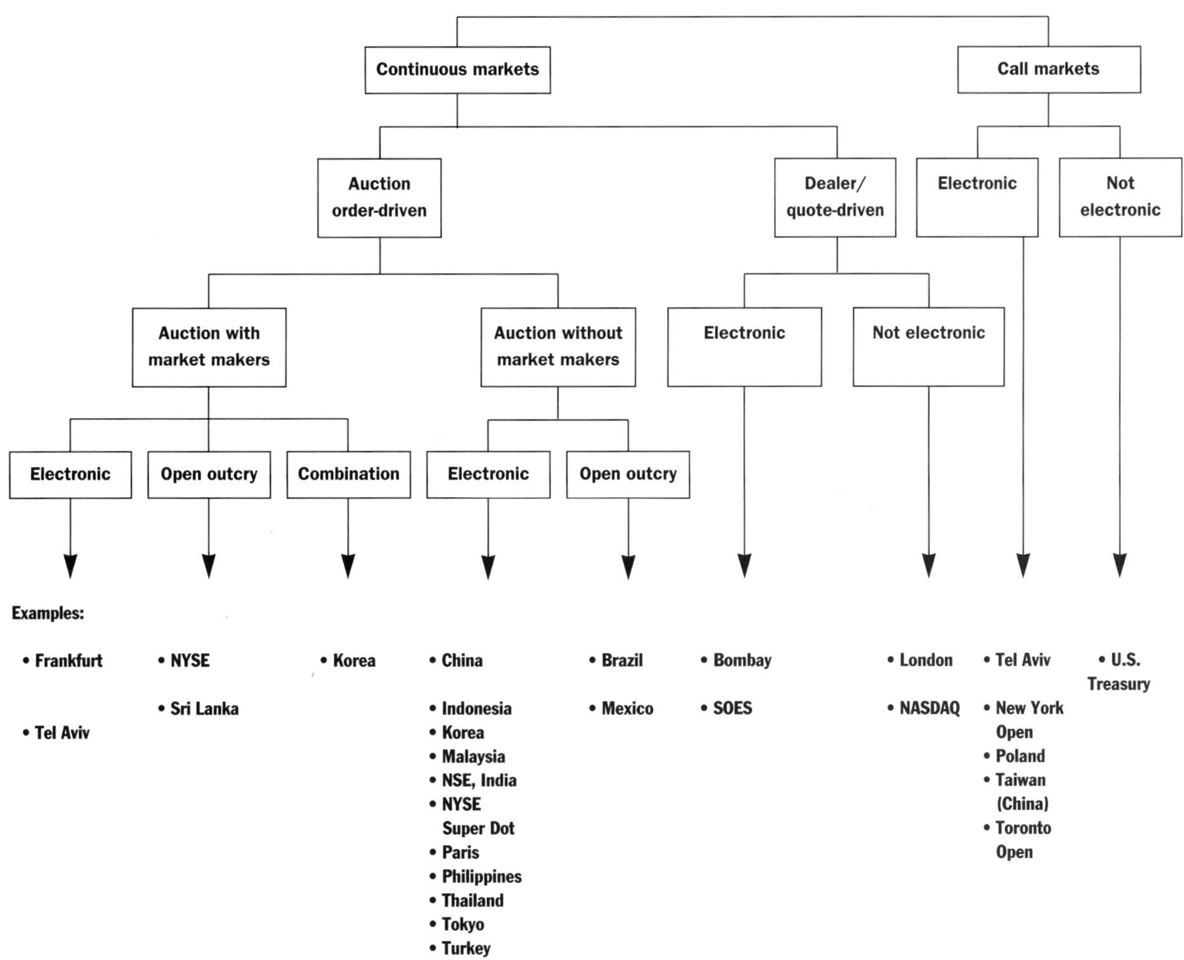

Abbreviations: NASDAQ: National Association of Securities Dealers Automated Quotation; NSE: National Stock Exchange; NYSE: New York Stock Exchange; SOES: Small Order Execution Service of the National Association of Securities Dealers.

with less information will not be at a disadvantage. Another positive characteristic of a call market, if appropriately structured, is that it efficiently incorporates available information into the price. In this sense, it is a good system for determining opening prices in a market or for determining the price of a stock whose trading has been temporarily halted because of the announcement of new information. Many markets use call auctions for these purposes. Finally, call markets generally result in lower execution and settlement costs, mainly because transactions execute at the same price and in one batch. On the negative side, in contrast to continuous markets, call markets provide no immediacy, that is, the ability of buyers and sellers to transact promptly. Other problems are that call markets provide no price information between sessions and may result in incomplete order execution.

The lack of immediacy in a call market may be a significant deterrent to foreign portfolio managers, who quite actively change the composition of their portfolios. For many of the larger-volume, more active stocks in emerging equity markets, a call auction system would add little liquidity and sacrifice both immediacy and information. A combination of the two systems may be attractive to some equity markets, with a call market for the smaller-volume, less liquid stocks and a continuous market for the others. There is no technical impediment to having two systems; indeed, as noted above, many equity markets use a call auction to determine the opening price. Another good example is the Tel Aviv stock market, which has an electronic call market for the less capitalized stocks and a semicontinuous order-driven market for the most liquid stocks.[65]

Order-driven markets versus quote-driven markets, and the role of market makers. The basic tradeoff is between higher liquidity in quote-driven dealer markets versus lower transaction costs and higher transparency in order-driven markets. The greater liquidity in dealer markets is a consequence of having dealers "making a market" in the security, in contrast to one specialist, or none at all, in order-driven markets. By standing ready to buy and sell at their quoted prices and committing their own capital, dealers add liquidity and immediacy to a market. In addition, dealers' profits increase with order flow, and they have an incentive to promote the securities they are trading, creating more liquidity. However, dealers provide these liquidity services at a cost, in particular the expense of holding an inventory of the security, labor and technology costs, and losses incurred in trading. These costs will be reflected in the dealer's bid-offer spread. In contrast, transaction costs in order-driven systems generally will be smaller, since traders can conduct transactions directly with each other. In a quote-driven market, competition among dealers is essential to ensure a high-quality market. Recently, in industrial countries, private proprietary trading systems that facilitate direct interaction among traders are becoming an additional source of competition for dealer markets.

In general, with regard to both pretrade and post-trade information, dealer markets provide less information and are less transparent than order-driven markets. In a quote-driven market with more than one dealer, the information on order flow will be segmented. This contrasts with order-driven systems, which consolidate efficiently all information when determining prices. In many order-driven markets, the order book is available for all to see, while in quote-driven markets, only the dealers have a good sense of the order flow and the price of execution. This lack of transparency in quote-driven markets is compounded by the fact that many trades, especially the larger ones, are not transacted at the quoted price, but are negotiated between the dealer and the trader. The effective transaction price may not be reported in a timely manner. For example, a recent investigation by the Securities and Exchange Commission of the United States revealed instances of less than competitive dealer quotations and pricing as well of dealers declining to honor quotes in the NASDAQ stock market (U.S. Securities and Exchange Commission 1996).

The choice among systems depends on particular circumstances and objectives, and financial integration does not make choosing any easier. For example, different types of investors may prefer different types of market systems. In particular, large-volume traders, and most foreign traders will fall into this category, are usually concerned about the price impact of their order. Other things remaining equal, they would prefer a system that creates the most liquidity and immediacy, and through which they are better able to control the degree of disclosure about the prospective transaction. Retail investors, on the other hand, are more concerned about getting the best price and would prefer a mechanism that gives their orders the widest exposure. Hence, a trading system that accommodates this concern of foreign investors may be to the interest of some but not all of the domestic investor community.

On the other hand, for some foreign investors, the most important concern may be transparency. As noted above, foreign investors believe that they are at a disadvantage with respect to access to information and are concerned about trades with a better-informed domestic dealer. In this case, they may prefer the more transparent order-driven systems to a dealer market. The support of many foreign investors for computerized markets arises out of this concern for transparency.

Computerized markets. Figure 6.5 shows that many of the most dynamic emerging equity markets have computerized their trading systems. The term "computerized" can be misleading. While a dealer market such as NASDAQ is computerized, what a computerized market is usually understood to mean is an order-driven system where an algorithm matches buyers and sellers automatically, replacing the traditional floor open outcry trading. This trend in emerging markets is based on the need to increase the capacity of the market to handle larger volumes, as well as to increase transparency. Electronic markets can trade around the clock and can handle large volumes in a cost-efficient manner. With regard to transparency, computers simplify market monitoring by creating a detailed audit trail, and have the capacity to generate and disseminate huge amounts of information on market transactions on a real-time basis. And very important, the automatic matching system helps ensure that investors are treated fairly. Computer-based systems work best in markets with a large volume of retail trading, simplifying the matching process and helping small investors get the best price.

The main problem computerized systems have is that of processing large orders in a market with insufficient liquidity. To address these concerns, many equity markets have adopted a mixed system in which small orders are executed automatically through the electronic system, while larger trades can be executed by a more traditional system operating in tandem. For example, NASDAQ in the United States has an automated system that directs small orders automatically to the best quote, while the larger trades can be negotiated over the phone with a dealer. Argentina also has two systems, an open outcry continuous auction and an electronic market for smaller trades.

Annex 6.3 Construction of the Emerging Markets Index

THE EMERGING MARKETS INDEX (EMI) IS intended to serve as a rough estimate of the overall level of development of emerging equity markets from the investors' perspective. The EMI is a weighted average of three subindexes measuring three essential aspects of market development:

- a *market structure* subindex that measures depth, liquidity and volatility
- a *market infrastructure* subindex that measures the efficiency of the market in terms of settlement and custody
- an *institutional development* subindex that measures institutional aspects of market development—for example, the quality of financial reporting, the protection of investors' rights, and the openness of the market to foreign investment—that are important determinants of investor interest in a market.

This annex describes the EMI's construction methodology, including variable selection and weights.

Guiding principles and issues. In developing the EMI, we were guided by several general criteria:

- The use of well-defined, measurable, and objective variables that capture the critical aspects of market development.
- The use of information that is uniform across countries, including standardized information such as the Global Securities Consulting Services, Inc., (GSCS) benchmarks on clearance and settlement.
- Weighting (ideally) based on investor concerns, as revealed through a survey. In the absence of such data, however, we use equal weights in both the subindexes and the main index, unless there is a strong reason to believe that one variable dominates the others.
- The use of benchmarks, or reference points, in calculating the subindexes. Variables in the subindexes are evaluated on the basis of how far they deviate from a benchmark, typically defined as the value of the variable in an industrial country market.

Despite these principles, the EMI suffers from several problems. First, given the lack of a formal investor survey, the weights—both those assigned to the three subindexes in calculating the overall EMI and those allocated to the underlying variables used to estimate the subindexes—are somewhat arbitrary. To increase the transparency of the index, as noted above, we have used equal weights unless there is a strong reason to believe other values should be used. The second problem regards the choice of benchmarks against which to evaluate emerging market development and how much to penalize countries for deviations from the benchmark. We have used the U.S. market as a benchmark for simplicity and because the use of other industrial markets (or an average) does not change relative country rankings significantly. Basing our methods on investor preferences, we have tended to penalize larger deviations from the benchmark proportionally more than smaller ones—that is, investors are willing to adjust to small problems in a market but may become more sensitive to market constraints when these constraints cross a certain threshold. Another significant problem is the lack of systematic, standardized cross-country information regarding the quality and completeness of the regulatory framework in emerging markets. Hence the

EMI does not incorporate this critical aspect of market development.

These problems suggest that EMI should be used only as a rough indicator of market development and that small differences between countries are not significant. The results are, however, reassuring, in the sense that the EMI rankings shown in table 6.7 are broadly consistent with foreign investors' preferences among emerging markets as revealed to the authors.

The overall weights. The structure subindex is given a 50 percent weight in the EMI; the trading infrastructure and institutional infrastructure subindexes are each weighted at 25 percent. The structure of the market has been given a higher weight because liquidity and depth are two characteristics highly desired by foreign investors. In addition, and perhaps more important, since liquidity and depth are endogenous variables, their presence indicates that the market in question is perceived favorably by investors.

The structure subindex. The market structure is calculated using the following ratios or variables:[66]

1. market capitalization/GDP (weighted at 50 percent)
2. turnover ratios (weighted at 12.5 percent)
3. new issues/market capitalization (weighted at 12.5 percent)
4. volatility as measured by the coefficient of variation (weighted at 12.5 percent)
5. market concentration (weighted at 12.5 percent).

Each of the five variables is rated on a scale of 0 to 10. A cumulative score of 10 implies that the particular market is highly advanced. The rating may be performed using either a rating function or a schedule. Items 1 to 4 are rated according to their deviations from their benchmark values in the United States.

Specifically for items 1 to 3, the rating function is:

$$S_j = 10\left[1 - \frac{(b - x_j)^2}{b^2}\right], \quad x_j \leq b$$

$$S_j = 10 \qquad \textit{otherwise}$$

where b is the value of the selected variable for the reference market and x_j is its value in the emerging market j. We chose the quadratic function to accentuate the penalties for increasing divergence from the benchmark (the b^2 term in the denominator is for scaling purposes), as noted above.

The coefficient of variation is also rated with respect to its benchmark value in the United States according to the following schedule:

Deviation of coefficient of variation from benchmark (percent)	*Rating*
0 to 10	9
10 to 30	8
30 to 50	7
50 to 70	6
70 to 100	5
100 to 150	4
150 to 250	3
250 to 500	2
500 to 800	1
over 800	0

This schedule gives the highest rating to markets for which the coefficient of variation differs up to 10 percent from the benchmark. If the deviation is from 10 to 70 percent, we apply a linear rating. As the deviation goes beyond 70 percent, ratings decrease, but at a diminishing rate. This rating procedure differs from the one used previously because investors expect high levels of volatility in emerging markets and because they probably do not distinguish among very high levels of volatility relative to the United States benchmark.

Market concentration is measured by the ratio of two shares: the share of the 10 largest stocks in total market capitalization divided by the share that these stocks represent in the total number of stocks. Concentration is then rated according to the following schedule:

Concentration measure	*Rating*
0 to 5	9
5 to 10	8
10 to 20	7
20 to 30	6
30 to 40	5
40 to 60	4
60 to 80	3
80 to 90	2
90 to 100	1

This schedule rates markets linearly if the concentration measure ranges from 5 to 80, while penalizing the more extreme levels of concentration (80 to 100). We did not identify any benchmark for the market concentration figures.

Trading infrastructure subindex. The trading infrastructure is determined by assigning equal weight to the settlement benchmark and the safekeeping benchmark established by GSCS. The settlement benchmark measures settlement efficiency as indicated by the number and operational costs of failed and delayed transactions, administrative complexity, and compliance with G-30 recommendations. The safekeeping benchmark measures the efficiency of different markets in terms of the collection of dividends and interest, reclamation of withheld taxes, and protection of rights in the event of a corporate action.

The benchmarks are expressed as a score ranging to 100; the lower the score, the higher the effective operational costs and administrative efforts involved in any given market. Because GSCS in assigning values already captures deviations from a theoretical benchmark, using 100 as the highest score, we do not adjust for a developed market. One simplification for our purposes is that markets which have negative values for either of the benchmarks are assigned a value of zero instead. Since GSCS does not estimate safekeeping benchmarks for Chile, China, Pakistan, Poland, and Sri Lanka, the settlement benchmark becomes in effect the infrastructure subindex.

Institutional infrastructure subindex. The institutional infrastructure is determined by assigning equal weight to the following criteria:

1. financial reporting standards, using the CIFAR Index from the Center for International Analysis and Research
2. foreign taxation, using the IFC's assessment
3. investor protection, using the IFC's assessment
4. openness to foreign investors, using the IFC's assessment.

The CIFAR Index, with a maximum score of 100, measures the quality of the reporting standards against an ideal and implicitly allows direct comparisons between those prevailing in different capital markets. Because of lack of information, Indonesia and Poland are excluded from the assessment of accounting standards, and that weight is redistributed equally among the remaining elements.

The foreign taxation rating is based on the IFC data on withholding taxes for emerging markets. We first calculate the average tax rate from the three forms of taxation—on interest income, dividends, and long-term capital gains on listed shares—and then rate the taxation policy of emerging markets according to the following schedule:

Average tax rate (percent)	*Rating*
0	10
0 to 5	9
5 to 10	8
10 to 15	7
15 to 20	6
20 to 25	5
25 to 30	4
30 to 100	2

This schedule is justified strictly from an investor's point of view; the classes used in our rating schedule are relatively parsimonious under the assumption that the presence of any taxation policy acts as a strong disincentive to foreign investment.

The investor protection rating is based on the IFC classification, available as of the end of 1994. We convert the IFC classification according to the following terms: a good program scores a 9, an adequate one receives a 6, and a poor scheme is rated at 2.

Openness to foreign access is rated using the IFC summary of regulations for entering and exiting emerging markets. The rating schedule is as follows:

Foreign access classification	*Rating*
Free	10
Relatively free	7.5
Restrictions to special classes	5
Authorized investors	2.5
Closed	0

Notes

1. As explained in chapter 2, portfolio flows are expected to increase because emerging markets are still underrepresented in the portfolios of industrial country investors, and investments in emerging markets would result in a significant improvement in the return-risk ratio of these investors. In addition, it is expected that an increasing share of savings in industrial countries will be intermediated by institutional investors and that these investors will continue to increase the share of emerging market equities in their portfolios.

2. Market capitalization is the value of the shares quoted in the market at market prices. It is a measure of the size of a market.

3. The stock of financial savings can be defined as the sum of the stock of deposits in commercial banks and the capitalization of the stock market.

4. As defined in chapter 2, excess volatility (in flows or asset prices) is volatility not due to changes in fundamentals.

5. Given the interest of foreign investors in emerging market equities, the chapter focuses on improvements in domestic stock markets in developing countries. With regard to emerging market debt, foreign investors have been mainly attracted to paper issued in international or industrial country markets, rather than to domestic issues in developing countries. However, over time, the development of domestic bond markets will become increasingly important. The interest of foreign investors in domestic debt instruments will undoubtedly rise, and debt will play an increasing role in financing investment in emerging markets, especially in the infrastructure sector. While many development issues discussed in this chapter with respect to market infrastructure and the regulatory framework are common to equity and debt markets, others, such as domestic rating agencies and market price benchmarks, are more specific to bond markets.

6. A key question that will arise with regard to the regulatory and legal frameworks is the role of the state in facilitating the transition process in capital markets as financial integration deepens.

7. The principal-agent problem to which we refer is the result of information asymmetries between management and the shareholders of a corporation. Shareholders, who

may not have easy access to all material financial and operational information regarding the firm, are concerned whether managers are operating to maximize shareholder value. However, to acquire such information, shareholders will incur a cost. The higher the cost, the more potential investors will be deterred from buying shares in the firm, leading to a suboptimal level of investment. Institutional factors and regulations also affect the problem; for example, it may not be worthwhile for a small shareholder to incur the search cost since better monitoring will mostly benefit other shareholders. In addition, small shareholders may not be able to effectively organize themselves to contest management. On the other hand, improvements in corporate governance would help shareholders to monitor management. Blommestein and Spencer (1993) review this issue in the context of transition economies, where the principal-agent problem is particularly severe.

8. There is strong empirical evidence from the United States that institutional investors are very active traders. For example, see Samuel (1996).

9. Demirgüç-Kunt and Maksimovic (1994) and Glen and Pinto (1994) present additional evidence. Samuel (1996) found that Indian firms use external sources of finance more than their counterparts in industrial countries because of higher reliance on debt.

10. Their findings are based on pooled cross-section (41 countries) time-series (1976–93) regressions, controlling for the more traditional macroeconomic and human capital variables that past studies have found to be significant in explaining growth. Atje and Jovanovic (1993) reach similar conclusions.

11. There is wide disagreement in the literature regarding the causes and consequences of takeovers. In any case, takeovers are not common in developing countries.

12. It may not be worthwhile for a small investor to incur these costs because the benefits of better monitoring will accrue mainly to other shareholders. See note 5.

13. See Samuel (1996) for a summary of the literature.

14. A related issue is whether institutional ownership puts too much short-term profit-maximizing pressure on firms to the detriment of investment and research and development expenditures. The empirical work on this question based on U.S. data suggests that institutional ownership does not affect investment but may reduce research and development expenditures (see Samuel 1996).

15. For example, Summers (1986) found evidence of such inefficiencies because of volatility in industrial country markets.

16. Levine and Zervos (1996a), which found that external liberalization increased asset price volatility, is an exception.

17. It is not uncommon in the literature to include the legal framework, accounting standards, and rating institutions as part of market infrastructure. We discuss the legal system and accounting standards together with the regulatory framework, to which they are closely related, in the next section of this chapter. Rating agencies are reviewed in box 6.9.

18. To be more precise, the clearance and settlement of trades in organized markets involve relationships between brokers that are members of the exchange. These broker-broker relationships are referred to the "street," or market, side of a trade, while the investor-broker relationships are referred to as the "customer" side. This review of market infrastructure mainly focuses on the street side, although we will discuss some investor-broker issues in the section dealing with custody functions and central depositories.

19. See Group of 30 (1989).

20. For example, see IOSCO (1992b).

21. See ISSA (1995).

22. Glen (1994) reviews how microstructures influence these market attributes.

23. There are no significant differences between matching systems for fixed-income and for equity instruments, except the match criteria.

24. Other criteria could include counterparty and clearing broker, buy-sell instructions, settlement date, and so forth.

25. DVP is the most effective yet simple way of reducing principal risk, whether involving physical or dematerialized securities, or for transactions that are settled through a central C&S system or directly between buyer and seller.

26. Stehm (1996) discusses these characteristics in some detail.

27. High trade failure rates, however, are not only the result of inefficiencies in the C&S system but also, for instance, of undercapitalized or inefficient broker and dealers.

28. Effective risk monitoring would also require the central clearing agency to correctly value or revalue the collateral, including the credit standing of the issuer of the collateral, and any legal impediments on it.

29. BIS (1990) and Stehm (1996), for example, suggest allocating losses to the surviving participants prorated with their level of activity with the defaulting participant. Since individual participants may have the same problems as the clearing agency in evaluating the financial strength of the counterparty, the proposed measure may reduce market activity.

30. See annex 6.1 and BIS (1990).

31. The terminology in this area can be confusing. Some experts refer to all book entry systems as dematerialized and to systems where certificates are not issued as uncertificated.

32. Other important differences concern ownership and governance of the depository and whether or not there is more than one depository.

33. Other advantages of indirect holding systems are that investors need to deal with only one institution for all purposes and that they reduce broker-investor settlement risk. On the other hand, direct systems facilitate the accounting and control of the number of shares outstanding, as well as the communication between the issuer and investors. Morgenstern (1996) has an excellent review of the two systems.

34. If more than one exists, all the depositories should not only be interlinked, but also well managed, capitalized, and regulated. If not, the better depositories would insist that interdepository settlement take place only in "good securities"—that is, in the accounts of the registrar or a top-tier depository, potentially slowing the settlement process (Morgenstern 1996).

35. As noted above, compared with intermediaries in mature markets, intermediaries in emerging markets are more likely to be financially weak, and volatility is generally higher, while financial integration may bring large surges in volume. In addition, the systemic consequences of the failure of an intermediary may be larger if the industry is more concentrated, as some analysts believe it to be in emerging markets.

36. Nominee ownership is not required when the securities-holding system is a direct system. For example, in China, the central depositories of the two main markets directly record the ownership of securities by beneficial owners and also act as registrars.

37. Laws important for the functioning of the financial system include: a company law that adequately promotes corporate governance; banking and commercial laws that give firms a legal basis for practices (such as beneficial ownership, notation, trusts, collateral, and so forth) that are central to financial markets; bankruptcy laws that clearly define the rights of different asset owners in a liquidation; and competition laws. An essential component of the legal infrastructure is a set of well-functioning institutions that enforce these laws.

38. Strahota (1996) describes how this model could be applied in emerging markets.

39. The assets of an investment firm consist of marketable securities that in a crisis can be liquidated at close to their book value, which is not the case for bank assets. Similarly, liabilities of investment firms are less liquid than bank liabilities, especially deposits, which can be withdrawn quickly. Dale (1996) discusses this rationale for regulation in some detail.

40. There are other methods to address this concern. For example, the approach taken by regulatory authorities in the United States has been to raise funding fire walls between banks and nonbanks to insulate the former from

solvency or liquidity problems in the latter. See Dale (1996) for a discussion of the regulatory response to functional integration in the European Union, Japan, and the United States.

41. In an indirect holding system for securities, investors' assets would be held by brokers and custodians.

42. The collapse of Barings in 1995 illustrates the importance of arrangements that permit clearinghouses to identify separately proprietary positions taken by investment firms from those taken on behalf of their clients.

43. IOSCO (1996) reviews and makes recommendations about the main techniques that regulators can use to achieve a satisfactory level of client asset protection.

44. In some cases, for example, Chile, these controls are imposed not to constrain foreign ownership but to influence the amount and composition of capital inflows for macroeconomic management reasons and to restrain lending booms. The advantages and costs of such restrictions are discussed in chapters 4 and 5.

45. The regulatory implications of the failure of Barings are discussed in Dale (1996) and IMF (1995).

46. See Dale (1996), Goldstein (1996), and IMF (1995 and 1996) for more details. The *International Securities Regulation Report* is an even more detailed source.

47. The securities regulators of 73 countries, or about 95 percent of countries with stock exchanges, are members of IOSCO. Interestingly, IOSCO also has affiliate and associate members, in particular stock exchanges and other self-regulatory organizations, as well as some international organizations. IMF (1996) describes IOSCO's internal committee structure.

48. Previously, IOSCO had issued recommendations regarding internal control and auditing arrangements for financial institutions dealing in derivatives (IMF 1996).

49. These memorandums usually include all or a subset of the following: routine sharing of general information, sharing of certain information on firms operating in the two markets, access to official information held by the counterpart regulator that may help in an investigation or an enforcement action, approval of certain investigative powers of the domestic regulator in the counterpart country, and the obligation to report to the other party that a firm is experiencing financial difficulties.

50. See IMF (1996).

51. Listing requirements, to the extent that they are not solely informational, seem to contradict the basic premise that investors should be responsible for their investment decisions. There are two reasons for such requirements. First, because of lack of experience and financial expertise, investors may not be able to judge the relative merits of alternative investments. Second, because of the negative externalities resulting from investors' losing confidence in the market, caused in general by the bad performance of a listed firm.

52. See IASC (1993) for a description of the key differences in accounting standards.

53. Among the decisions often submitted for shareholder approval are acquisition or transfer of ownership of, say, 20 percent of the shares of the company, limitation of shareholder rights, sale of corporate assets, or the incurring of significant new debt liabilities. See Seeger (1996).

54. Preemptive rights are the entitlement of existing shareholders to subscribe to new share issues for cash. For issuers, it may raise the cost of capital if the sale is made at a substantial discount from market price, as is common practice to maintain attractiveness during the subscription period. Existing shareholders are either able to maintain their ownership interests if they subscribe or are compensated for the resulting dilution if they choose to sell their subscription rights. The pros and cons of this practice are still being debated.

55. Some key documents of this trend are the General Motors (1995) and Cadbury (Committee on the Financial Aspects of Corporate Governance 1992) reports. For a comparison of the corporate governance initiatives in the OECD, see Millstein and Gregory (1996).

56. See International Capital Markets Group (1992) for a good summary review of self-regulatory activity.

57. According to the International Financial Reporting Index constructed by the Center for International Analysis and Research (an investment adviser located in the United States), Chile, Malaysia, Mexico, Pakistan, and Sri Lanka have reporting standards comparable to those in industrial countries. Argentina, Korea, and Thailand are also ranked relatively highly, and only Brazil, India, the Philippines, and Turkey lag behind the industrial countries. The index is based on the reporting practices of major domestic corporates with regard to 85 disclosure variables.

58. IASC (1996).

59. Compensation funds protect investors from losses arising from the failure of broker-dealers (not market risks), while takeover rules protect the rights of minority shareholders in a target company for a takeover.

60. There are two reasons why the bid-ask spreads for emerging markets in figure 6.4 are probably biased downward. First, for the markets included in the figure, the average spreads are based on a sample of stocks included in the IFC Investable Index and hence are among the most liquid. Second, it is likely that bid-ask spreads in many of the emerging markets for which data were not available will be wider than those of the countries included in the figure. This is because many of the omitted countries are, according to the index on capital market development, somewhat behind in developing their markets.

61. Microstructures refers to the way securities are traded and the influence that trading systems have on key market attributes.

62. For example, see Freund (1996).

63. For example, in Thailand, the stock exchange is considering having dealers try to make a market for the less active stocks.

64. In turn, call markets can be distinguished by the type of auction or algorithm that is used to determine prices—for example, whether or not bids are public. See Aggarwal (1996).

65. Another example of mixed systems very prevalent in emerging markets regards government debt instruments. Primary markets for these instruments are usually call markets, while secondary markets are usually over-the-counter dealer markets.

66. Practically all data are from the IFC; data for new equity issues are from FIBV (the International Federation of Stock Exchanges) sources and supplemented by IFC data. Market capitalization is at year-end. The coefficient of variation is that of the monthly percentage change in the IFC Global Total Return Indexes. The benchmark is the corresponding coefficient of variation for the S&P 500.

Bibliography

The word "processed" describes informally reproduced works that may not be commonly available through libraries. Abbreviations: BIS, Bank for International Settlements; IADB, Inter-American Development Bank; IMF, International Monetary Fund; ISSA, International Society of Securities Administrators; MIT, Massachusetts Institute of Technology; NBER, National Bureau of Economic Research; OECD, Organisation for Economic Co-operation and Development.

Adler, Michael, and Bernard Dumas. 1983. "International Portfolio Choice and Corporation Finance: A Synthesis." *Journal of Finance* 38(June): 925–84.

Aggarwal, Reena. 1996. "An Evaluation of Market Microstructures." Background paper prepared for *Private Capital Flows to Developing Countries.* World Bank, International Economics Department, Washington, D.C.

Aitken, Brian. 1996. "Have Institutional Investors Destabilized Emerging Markets?" IMF Working Paper 96/34. Washington, D.C.

Aitken, Brian, and Ann Harrison. 1992. "Does Proximity to Foreign Firms Induce Technology Spillovers?" MIT, Cambridge, Mass. Processed.

Aiyer, Sri-Ram. 1996. "Anatomy of Mexico's Banking System during the Peso Crisis." Report 45. World Bank, Latin America and the Caribbean Technical Department, Regional Studies Program. Washington, D.C.

Andersen, P. S., and William R. White. 1996. "The Macroeconomic Effects of Financial Sector Reforms: An Overview of Industrial Countries." BIS, Basle, Switzerland.

Arrow, Kenneth. 1964. "The Roles of Securities in the Optimal Allocation of Risk Bearing." *Review of Economic Studies* 31(April): 91–96.

Atje, Raymond, and Boyan Jovanovic. 1993. "Stock Markets and Development." *European Economic Review* 37(April): 632–40.

Backus, David, Patrick Kehoe, and Finn Kydland. 1992. "International Real Business Cycles." *Journal of Political Economy* 100(4): 745–75.

Baer, Herbert, and Daniela Klingebiel. 1995. "Systemic Risk when Depositors Bear Losses: Five Case Studies." In George G. Kaufman, ed., *Banking, Financial Markets, and Systemic Risk.* Greenwich, Conn.: JAI Press.

Bagehot, Walter. 1880. *Economic Studies.* London: Longmans, Green.

———.1924. *Lombard Street.* Reprint of 1st ed. London: John Murray.

Bank of New York. 1996. "Current Profiles." New York.

Barro, Robert, and Xavier Sala-i-Martin. 1995. *Economic Growth.* New York: McGraw-Hill.

Basle Committee on Banking Supervision and IOSCO (International Organization of Securities Commissions). 1995a. *Framework for Supervisory Information about the Derivatives Activities of Banks and Securities Firms.* Basle, Switzerland.

——. 1995b. *Public Disclosure of the Trading and Derivatives Activities of Banks and Securities Firms.* Basle, Switzerland.

Baxter, Marianne, Urban Jermann, and Robert King. 1995. "Nontraded Goods, Nontraded Factors, and International Non-Diversification." NBER Working Paper 5175. Cambridge, Mass.

Bayoumi, Tamim. 1990. "Saving-Investment Correlations: Immobile Capital, Government Policy, or Endogenous Behavior?" IMF Working Paper 90/66. Washington, D.C.

——. 1993. "Market Integration and Investment Barriers in Emerging Equity Markets." Working Paper. Stanford Graduate School of Business, Stanford, Calif.

Bekaert, Geert, and Campbell R. Harvey. 1995. "Emerging Equity Market Volatility." NBER Working Paper 5307. Cambridge, Mass.

Bencivenga, Valerie, and Bruce Smith. 1991. "Financial Intermediation and Endogenous Growth." *Review of Economic Studies* 58(April): 195–209.

Bencivenga, Valerie, Bruce Smith, and Ross Starr. 1995. "Equity Markets, Transaction Costs, and Capital Accumulation" Policy Research Working Paper 1456. World Bank, Policy Research Department, Washington, D.C.

Benston, George, and George Kaufman. 1988. "Regulating Bank Safety and Performance." In William S. Haraf and Rose Marie Kushmeider, eds., *Restructuring Banking and Financial Services in America.* Washington, D.C.: American Enterprise Institute.

Berger, Allen, Richard J. Herring, and Giorgio P. Szego. 1995. "The Role of Capital in Financial Institutions." *Journal of Banking and Finance* 19 (3–4, June): 393–430.

Berger, Allen, William C. Hunter, and Stephen G. Timme. 1993. "The Efficiency of Financial Institutions: A Review and Preview of Research, Past, Present, and Future." *Journal of Banking and Finance* 17(April): [22]-49.

Bernanke, Ben S. 1983. "Nonmonetary Effects of the Financial Crisis in the Propagation of the Great Depression." *American Economic Review* 73(3, June): 257–76.

Bernanke, Ben S., and Alan S. Blinder. 1988. "Credit, Money, and Aggregate Demand." *American Economic Review* 78(2, May): 435–39.

Bernanke, Ben S., and Mark Gertler. 1989. "Agency Costs, Net Worth, and Business Fluctuations." *American Economic Review* 79: 14–31.

Bernstein Research. *The Future of Money Management in America.* New York: Sanford C. Bernstein.

Bhattacharya, Amar, Peter Montiel, and Sunil Sharma. 1996. "Private Capital Flows to Sub-Saharan Africa: An Overview of Trends and Determinants." World Bank, International Economic Department, Washington, D.C. Processed.

Beveridge, Stephen, and Charles R. Nelson. 1981. "A New Approach to Decomposition of Economic Time Series into Permanent and Transitory Components with Particular Attention to Measurement of the Business Cycle." *Journal of Monetary Economics* 7(2, March): 151–74.

BIS (Bank for International Settlements). 1990. *Interbank Netting Schemes of the Central Banks of the Group of Ten Countries.* Committee on Payment and Settlement Systems Report 10. Basle, Switzerland.

——. 1996. *66th Annual Report.* Basle, Switzerland.

Bisignano, Joseph. 1994. "The Internationalisation of Financial Markets." *Cahiers Economiques et Monétaires* (France) 43: 9–77.

Blanchet, Marie-Christine, Peter Burridge, Stijn Claessens, and Maxwell Fry. 1995. "Foreign Direct Investment, Other Capital Flows, and Current Account Deficits." Policy Research Working Paper 1527. World Bank, Policy Research Department, Washington, D.C.

Blommestein, H. J., and Michael G. Spencer. 1993. "The Role of Financial Institutions in the Transition to a Market Economy." IMF Working Paper 93/75. Washington, D.C.

Blomström, Magnus, Robert E. Lipsey, and Mario Carlos Zejan. 1992. "What Explains Developing Country Growth?" NBER Working Paper 4132. Cambridge, Mass.

Böhm-Bawerk, Eugen von. 1891. *Positive Theory of Capital.* London: Macmillan.

Borensztein, Eduardo, José de Gregorio, and Jong-Wha Lee. 1995. "How Does Foreign Direct Investment Affect Economic Growth?" NBER Working Paper 5057. Cambridge, Mass.

Börsch-Supan, Axel. 1996. "The Impact of Population Aging on Savings, Investment and Growth in the OECD Area." In OECD, *Future Global Capital Shortages: Real Threat or Pure Fiction.* Washington, D.C.

Bovenberg, Lans, and Roger Gordon. 1994. "Why Is Capital So Immobile Internationally?" NBER Working Paper 4796. Cambridge, Mass.

Brock, Philip L. 1996. "High Real Interest Rates and Guarantor Risk in an Open Economy: A Case Study of Chile, 1975–83." University of Washington, Department of Economics, Seattle. Processed.

Buckberg, Elaine. 1996. "Institutional Investors and Asset Pricing in Emerging Markets." IMF Working Paper 96/2. Washington, D.C.

Burchill, Andrew. 1996. "Is Russia Ready for Mutual Funds?" *Institutional Investor* 21(March): 85–89.

Calomiris, C. W. 1995. "Financial Fragility: Issues and Policy Implications." *Journal of Financial Services Research* 9(3).

Calomiris, C. W., and Gary Gorton. 1991. "The Origins of Banking Panics: Models, Facts, and Bank Regulation." In R. Glenn Hubbard, ed., *Financial Markets and Financial Crises.* Chicago: University of Chicago Press.

Calvo, Guillermo. 1990. "The Perils of Sterilization." IMF Working Paper 90/13. Washington, D.C.

——. 1996. "Capital Flows and Macroeconomic Management: Tequila Lessons." *International Journal of Finance and Economics* 1(July): 207–23.

Calvo, Guillermo, Leonardo Leiderman, and Carmen M. Reinhart. 1993. "Capital Inflows and Real Exchange Rate Appreciation in Latin America: The Role of External Factors." *IMF Staff Papers* 40(1): 108–51.

Campbell, John Y., and Robert J. Shiller. 1987. "Cointegration and Tests of Present Value Models." *Journal of Political Economy* 95(October): 1062–88.

Caprio, Gerard, Jr. 1996. "Bank Regulation, The Case of the Missing Model." Policy Research Working Paper 1574. World Bank, Policy Research Department, Washington, D.C.

Caprio, Gerard, Jr., and Daniela Klingebiel. 1997. "Bank Insolvency: Bad Luck, Bad Policy, or Bad Banking?" In Michael Bruno and Boris Pleskovic, *Annual World Bank Conference on Development Economics 1996.* Washington, D.C.

——. 1996. "Bank Insolvency: Cross-Country Experience." Policy Research Working Paper 1620. World Bank, Policy Research Department, Washington, D.C.

Caprio, Gerard, Jr., and Dimitri Vittas. 1995. "Financial History: Lessons of the Past for Reformers of the Present." Policy Research Working Paper 1535. World Bank, Policy Research Department. Washington, D.C.

Caprio, Gerard, Jr., Izak Atiyas, and James Hanson, eds. 1994. *Financial Reform, Theory and Practice.* Cambridge, U.K.: Cambridge University Press.

Caprio, Gerard, Jr., Michael Dooley, Danny Leipziger, and Carl Walsh. 1996. "The Lender of Last Resort Function under a Currency Board, The Case of Argentina." Policy Research Working Paper 1648. World Bank, Policy Research Department, Washington, D.C.

Cardenas, Mauricio, and Felipe Barreras. 1996. "On the Effectiveness of Capital Controls in Colombia." World Bank, International Finance Division. Washington, D.C. Processed.

Celarier, Michelle. 1994. "How the Bankers at Banco Latino Stole the Bank." *Global Finance* 7(9, September): 130–35.

Center for International Financial Analysis and Research. 1995. *International Accounting and Auditing Trends, 1995.* Princeton, N.J.

Chevalier, Judith A., and Glenn D. Ellison. 1995. "Risk Taking by Mutual Funds as a Response to Incentives." NBER Working Paper 5234. Cambridge, Mass.

Chinn, Menzie, and Michael Dooley. 1995. "Asia-Pacific Capital Markets: Integration and Implications for Economic Activity." NBER Working Paper 5280. Cambridge, Mass.

Chow, Paul. 1996. "Debt in the Asia Pacific Region—Hong Kong's Role" (paper presented at the conference on Private Capital Flows: Implications for Asian Capital Markets, Bali, Indonesia, October 18–20). Processed.

Chuhan, Punam. 1994. "Are Institutional Investors an Important Source of Portfolio Investment in Emerging Markets?" Policy Research Working Paper 1243. World Bank, Policy Research Department, Washington, D.C.

Chuhan, Punam, Stijn Claessens, and Nlandu Mamingi. 1993. "Equity and Bond Flows to Latin America and Asia: The Role of Global and Country Factors." Policy Research Working Paper 1160. World Bank, International Economics Department, Washington, D.C.

Chuppe, Terry, and Michael Atkin. 1992. "Regulation of Securities Markets: Some Recent Trends and Their Implications for Emerging Markets." Working Paper 829. IFC, Economics Department, Washington, D.C.

Citibank. 1996. "Country Profiles." New York.

Claessens, Stijn, and Sudarshan Gooptu, eds. 1993. *Portfolio Investment in Developing Countries.* World Bank Discussion Paper 228. Washington, D.C.

Claessens, Stijn, Michael P. Dooley, and Andrew Warner. 1995. "Portfolio Capital Flows: Hot or Cold?" *World Bank Economic Review* 9(1): 153–74.

Cohen, Daniel. 1995. "Foreign Finance and Economic Growth." In Leonardo Leiderman and Assaf Razin, eds., *Capital Mobility: The Impact on Consumption, Investment, and Growth.* Cambridge, U.K.: Cambridge University Press.

Cole, Harold, and Maurice Obstfeld. 1991. "Commodity Trade and International Risk Sharing." *Journal of Monetary Economics* 38: 3–24.

Committee on the Financial Aspects of Corporate Governance. 1992. *The Cadbury Report.* London: Her Majesty's Stationery Office.

Corbo, Vittorio, and Leonardo Hernández. 1994. "Macroeconomic Adjustment to Capital Inflows: Latin American Style versus East Asian Style." Policy Research Working Paper 1377. World Bank, Policy Research Department, Washington, D.C.

——. 1996. "Macroeconomic Adjustment to Capital Inflows: Lessons from Recent Latin American and East Asian Experience." *World Bank Research Observer* 11(1, February): 61–85.

——. 1997. "Private Capital Inflows and the Role of Economic Fundamentals." Background paper prepared for *Private Capital Flows to Developing Countries.* World Bank, International Economics Department, Washington, D.C.

Council of Securities Regulators of the Americas. 1994. "Framework for Full and Fair Disclosure in the Americas." Quebec.

Dailami, Mansoor, and Michael Atkin. 1990. "Stock Markets in Developing Countries: Key Issues and a Research Agenda." Policy Research Working Paper 515. World Bank, Country Economics Department, Washington, D.C.

Dale, Richard. 1996. "Regulating the New Financial Markets" (paper prepared for conference on Globalization: What It Is and Its Implications, São Paulo, Brazil, May).

Davis, E. P. 1991. "International Diversification of Institutional Investors." *Bank of England Discussion Papers* 44(September): 1–53.

——. 1993. "The Structure, Regulation, and Performance of Pension Funds in Nine Industrial Countries." Policy Research Working Report 1229. World Bank, Financial Sector Development Department, Washington, D.C.

de Gregorio, José, and Pablo Guidotti. 1995. "Financial Development and Economic Growth." *World Development* 23: 3–24.

de Juan, Aristobulo. 1987. "From Good Bankers to Bad Bankers: Ineffective Supervision and Management Deterioration as Major Elements in Banking Crises." World Bank, Financial Policy and Systems Division, Washington, D.C.

de la Cuadra, Sergio, and Salvador Valdés. 1992. "Myths and Facts about Financial Liberalization in Chile: 1974–1983." In Philip L. Brock, ed., *If Texas Were Chile: A Primer on Banking Reform.* San Francisco: ICS Press.

de Larosière, Jacques. 1996. Per Jacobsson Lecture, September 29, IMF, Washington, D.C.

De Ryck, Koen. 1996. "European Pension Funds: Their Impact on European Capital Markets and Competitiveness." European Federation for Retirement Provision, London.

Dellas, Harris, Behzad Diba, and Peter Garber. 1996. "Resolving Failed Banks: The U.S. S&L Experience." Discussion Paper Series 96–E–22. Bank of Japan, Institute for Monetary and Economic Studies, Tokyo.

Demirgüç-Kunt, Asli, and Ross Levine. 1996a. "Stock Markets, Corporate Finance, and Economic Growth." *World Bank Economic Review* 10(2, May): 223–39.

——. 1996b. "Stock Market Development and Financial Intermediaries: Stylized Facts." *World Bank Economic Review* 10(2, May): 291–321.

Demirgüç-Kunt, Asli, and Vojislav Maksimovic. 1994. "Capital Structures in Developing Countries: Evidence from Ten Countries." Policy Research Working Paper 1320. World Bank, Policy Research Department, Washington, D.C.

Denton, Nicholas. 1996. "Banks Plan Grip on World Debt Market." *Financial Times* (July 10).

Dermine, Jean. 1993. "The Gains from European Banking Integration: A Call for an Active Pro-Compassion Policy." In Hans Genberg and Alexander Swoboda, eds., *World Financial Markets after 1992.* London: Kegan Paul International.

Devereux, Michael, and Gregor Smith. 1994. "International Risk Sharing and Economic Growth." *International Economic Review* 35(August): 535–50.

Devlin, Robert, Ricardo Ffrench-Davis, and Stephany Griffith-Jones. 1994. "Surges in Capital Flows and Development: An Overview of Policy Issues." In Ricardo Ffrench-Davis and Stephany Griffith-Jones, eds., *Coping with Capital Surges: The Return of Finance to Latin America.* Boulder, Colo.: Lynne Rienner.

Diamond, Douglas. 1984. "Financial Intermediation and Delegated Monitoring." *Review of Economic Studies* 51(3): 393–414.

Diamond, Douglas, and Philip Dybvig. 1983. "Bank Runs, Deposit Insurance, and Liquidity." *Review of Economic Studies* LI: 393–414.

Diaz-Alejandro, Carlos. 1985. "Good-Bye Financial Repression, Hello Financial Crash." *Journal of Development Economics* 19: 1–24.

Domowitz, Ian. 1990. "The Mechanics of Automated Trade Execution Systems." *Journal of Financial Intermediation* 1(June): 167–94.

Dooley, Michael P. 1994. "Are Recent Capital Inflows to Developing Countries a Vote for or against Economic Policy Reforms?" Policy Research Working Paper 295. University of California, Santa Cruz.

——. 1995. "A Survey of the Academic Literature on Controls over International Capital Account Transactions." NBER Working Paper 5352. Cambridge, Mass.

——. 1996. "Capital Controls and Emerging Markets." *International Journal of Finance and Economics* 1(July): 197–205.

Drees, Burkhard, and Ceyla Pazarbasioglu. 1995. "The Nordic Banking Crisis: Pitfalls in Financial Liberalization?" IMF Working Paper 95/61. Washington, D.C.

El-Erian, Mohammed, and Manmohan S. Kumar. 1995. "Emerging Equity Markets in Middle Eastern Countries." *IMF Staff Papers* 42(June): 313–43.

Fama, Eugene. 1991. "Efficient Capital Markets: II." *Journal of Finance* 46(December): 1575–617.

Far Eastern Economic Review. Hong Kong.

Feis, Herbert. 1964. *Europe, The World's Banker, 1870–1914.* New York: Kelley.

Feldman, Robert A., and Manmohan S. Kumar. 1995. "Emerging Equity Markets: Growth, Benefits, and Policy Concerns." *World Bank Research Observer* 10(2, August): 181–200.

Feldstein, Martin, ed. 1991. *The Risk of Economic Crisis.* Chicago: University of Chicago Press.

Feldstein, Martin, and Charles Horioka. 1980. "Domestic Saving and International Capital Flows." *Economic Journal* 90(June): 314–29.

Fernández, Roque, and Liliana Schumacher. 1996. "Does Argentina Provide a Case for Narrow Banking?" (paper presented at the conference on Preventing Banking Crises in Latin America, World Bank, Washington, D.C., April 15–16). Processed.

Fernández-Arias, Eduardo. 1994. "The New Wave of Private Capital Inflows: Push or Pull?" Policy Research Working Paper 1312. World Bank, International Economics Department, Washington, D.C.

——. 1996. "The New Wave of Private Capital Inflows: Push or Pull?" *Journal of Development Economics* 48(March): 389–418.

Fernández-Arias, Eduardo, and Peter J. Montiel. 1995. "The Surge in Capital Inflows to Developing Countries: Prospects and Policy Response." Policy Research Working Paper 1473. World Bank, International Economics Department, Washington, D.C.

FIBV (Fédération Internationale des Bourses de Valeurs). 1996. "Clearing and Settlement: Best Practices." Paris. Processed.

Fieleki, Norman S. 1994. "International Capital Transactions: Should They Be Restricted?" *New England Economic Review* (March–April): 27–39.

——. 1996. "International Capital Movements:

How Shocking Are They?" *New England Economic Review* (March–April): 41–60.

Fischer, Bernhard, and Helmut Reisen. 1994. "Financial Opening: Why, How, When." Occasional Paper 58. International Center for Economic Growth. San Francisco, Calif.

Fleming, Alex, and Samuel Talley. 1996. "The Latvian Banking Crisis: Lessons Learned." Policy Research Working Paper 1590. World Bank, Enterprise and Financial Sector Division, Washington, D.C.

Fleming, Alexander, Lily Chu, and Marie-Renee Bakker. 1996. "The Baltics—Banking Crises Observed." Policy Research Working Paper 1647. World Bank, Enterprise and Financial Sector Division. Washington, D.C.

Folkerts-Landau, David, and others. 1995. "Effects of Capital Flows on the Domestic Financial Sectors in APEC Developing Countries." In Mohsin Khan and Carmen Reinhart, eds., *Capital Flows in the APEC Region.* Occasional Paper 122. Washington, D.C.: IMF.

Frankel, Jeffrey. 1993. *On Exchange Rates.* Cambridge, Mass.: MIT Press.

Frankel, Jeffrey, and Chudozie Okongwu. 1996. "Liberalized Portfolio Capital Inflows in Emerging Markets: Sterilization, Expectations, and the Incompleteness of Interest Rate Convergence." *International Journal of Finance and Economics* 7(March): 1–23.

Frankel, Jeffrey, and Andrew K. Rose. 1996. "Currency Crashes in Emerging Markets: Empirical Indicators." NBER Working Paper 5437. Cambridge, Mass.

Frankel, Jeffrey, and Sergio L. Schmukler. 1996. "Crisis, Contagion, and Country Funds: Effects on East Asia and Latin America" (paper delivered at a conference at the Center for Pacific Basin Monetary and Economic Studies, San Francisco). Processed.

Freund, William. 1996. "Will New Technology Leave the Big Board behind the Times?" *Durell Journal of Money and Banking* (Winter).

Fry, Catherine. 1993. "Custodial Issues (Clearing and Settlement) of Equities in Emerging Markets." In Keith Park and Antoine Van Agtmael, eds., *The World's Emerging Stock Markets.* Chicago: Irwin.

Garber, Peter. 1996. "Managing Risks to Financial Markets from Volatile Capital Flows: The Role of Prudential Regulation." *International Jounal of Finance and Economics* 1(July): 183–95.

Gardener, E. P. M. 1991. "1992 and the Future of Asset Securitisation in Western Europe." In J. J. Norton and P. R. Spellman, eds., *Asset Securitisation: International Financial and Legal Perspectives.* Oxford: Basil Blackwell.

Gavin, Michael, and Ricardo Hausmann. 1996a. "Make or Buy: Approaches to Financial Market Integration" (paper presented at the conference on Safe and Sound Financial Systems: What Works for Latin America? IADB, September). Processed.

———. 1996b. "The Roots of Banking Crises: The Macroeconomic Context." In Ricardo Hausmann and Liliana Rojas-Suárez, eds., *Banking Crisis in Latin America.* Baltimore: Johns Hopkins University Press.

Gavin, Michael, Ricardo Hausmann, Roberto Perotti, and Ernesto Talvi. 1996. "Managing Fiscal Policy in Latin America and the Caribbean: Volatility, Procyclality, and Limited Creditworthiness." IADB Working Paper 326. Washington, D.C.

General Motors. 1995. "GM Board of Directors Corporate Governance Guidelines on Significant Corporate Governance Issues." Detroit, Mich.

Glen, Jack. 1994. *An Introduction to the Microstructure of Emerging Markets.* IFC Discussion Paper 24. Washington, D.C.: World Bank.

Glen, Jack, and Brian Pinto. 1994. *Debt or Equity? How Firms in Developing Countries Choose.* IFC Discussion Paper 22. Washington, D.C.: World Bank.

Glen, Jack, Yannis Karmokolias, Robert R. Miller, and Sanjay Shah. 1995. *Dividend Policy and Behavior in Emerging Markets: To Pay or Not to Pay.* IFC Discussion Paper 26. Washington, D.C.: World Bank.

Gokhale, Jagadeesh, Laurence J. Kotlikoff, and John Sebelhaus. 1996. "Understanding the Postwar Decline in U.S. Saving: A Cohort Analysis." *Brookings Papers on Economic Activity* 1: 315–407.

Goldfajn, Ilan, and Rodrigo O. Valdés. 1996. "Balance of Payment Crises and Capital Flows: The Role of Liquidity." Department of Economics, Brandeis University, Waltham, Mass. Processed.

Goldsmith, Raymond. 1969. *Financial Structure and Development.* New Haven, Conn.: Yale University Press.

Goldstein, Morris. 1996. "Regulation of Banking and Capital Markets: Key Issues." Background paper prepared for *Private Capital Flows to Developing Countries.* World Bank, International Economics Department, Washington, D.C.

Goldstein, Morris, and Michael Mussa. 1993. "The Integration of World Capital Markets." IMF Working Paper 93/95. Washington, D.C.

Goldstein, Morris, and Philip Turner. 1996. "Banking Crises in Emerging Economies: Origins and Policy Options." Economic Paper 46. BIS, Basle, Switzerland.

Gonson, Paul. 1996. "Securities Regulation in the United States." U.S. Securities and Exchange Commission. Washington, D.C.

Gray, Cheryl W., and Arnold Holle. 1996. "Bank-Led Restructuring in Poland: An Empirical Look at the Bank Conciliation Process." Policy Research Working Paper 1650. World Bank, Policy Research Department, Washington, D.C.

Gray, Philip. 1996. "Macroeconomic and Microeconomic Impediments to Foreign Portfolio Flows" (paper presented at the conference on Private Capital Flows: Implications for Asian Capital Markets. Bali, Indonesia, October 18–20). Processed.

Greenwood, Jeremy, and Boyan Jovanovic. 1990. "Financial Development, Growth and the Distribution of Income." *Journal of Political Economy* 98(October): 1076–107.

Greenwood, Jeremy, and Bruce Smith. 1993. "Finance in Development and Development of Financial Markets." *Journal of Economic Dynamics and Control.*

Grenadier, Steven R., and Brian J. Hall. 1995. "Risk-Based Capital Standards and the Riskiness of Bank Portfolios: Credit and Factor Risks." *Regional Science and Urban Economics* 26(June): 433–64.

Griffith-Jones, Stephany. 1995. "How Can Future Currency Crises Be Prevented or Better Managed?" Institute of Development Studies, University of Sussex, Brighton, U.K. Processed.

——. 1996a. "The Mexican Crisis and Its Causes." *CEPAL (ECLAC) Review* 60(December), Santiago, Chile.

——. 1996b. "Study of Movement of Funds on the Global Market." Study prepared for Grupo de analise e pesquisa, Presidencia de Republica, Brazil. Institute of Development Studies, University of Sussex, Brighton, U.K. Processed.

——. Forthcoming. *Global Capital Flows.* New York: Macmillan.

Griffith-Jones, Stephany, and Vassilis Papageorgiou. 1996. "Globalization of Financial Markets and Impact on Flows to LDCs: New Challenges for Regulation." Institute of Development Studies, University of Sussex, Brighton, U.K. Processed.

Grilli, Vittorio, and Gian Maria Milesi-Ferretti. 1995. "Economic Effects and Structural Determinants of Capital Controls." IMF Working Paper 95/31. Washington, D.C.

Grossman, Gene, and Elhanan Helpman. 1991. *Innovation and Growth in the Global Economy.* Cambridge, Mass.: MIT Press.

Group of 30. 1989. *Clearance and Settlement Systems in the World's Securities Markets.* New York.

Hall, Maximilian. 1994. *Banking Regulation and Supervision: A Comparative Study of the UK, USA and Japan.* Aldershot, U.K.: Edward Elgar.

Haque, Nadeem, Manmohan Kumar, Nelson Mark, and Donald Mathieson. 1996. "The Economic Content of Indicators of Developing-Country Creditworthiness." IMF Working Paper 96/9. Washington, D.C.

Harrison, Debbie. 1995. *Pension Fund Investment in Europe.* London: Financial Times Publishing.

Hausmann, Ricardo, and Michael Gavin. 1995. "Securing Stability and Growth in a Shock-Prone Region: The Policy Challenge for Latin America." IADB, Washington, D.C. Processed.

Hausmann, Ricardo, and Liliana Rojas-Suárez, eds. 1996a. *Banking Crisis in Latin America.* Baltimore: Johns Hopkins University Press.

———. 1996b. *Volatile Capital Flows: Taming Their Impact on Latin America.* Baltimore: Johns Hopkins University Press.

Helleiner, G. K. 1996. "Capital Account Regimes and the Developing Countries" (paper prepared for the Studies on International Monetary and Financial Issues for the Group of Twenty-four. United Nations Conference on Trade and Development, Geneva, Switzerland). Processed.

Hellmann, Thomas, Kevin Murdock, and Joseph Stiglitz. 1996. "Financial Restraint and the Market-Enhancing View" (paper presented at the International Economic Association conference in Tokyo, December 16–19). Processed.

Helpman, Elhanan, Leonardo Leiderman, and Gil Bufman. 1994. "New Breed of Exchange Rate Bands: Chile, Israel, and Mexico." *Economic Policy: A European Forum* 9(October): 260–306.

Hernández, Leonardo. 1991. "Credibilidad, problema 'peso,' y el comportamiento de las tasas de interés: Chile 1979–1982." *Cuadernos de Economía* (December).

Hernández, Leonardo, and Heinz Rudolph. 1995. "Sustainability of Private Capital Flows to Developing Countries: Is a General Reversal Likely?" Policy Research Working Paper 1518. World Bank, Policy Research Department, Washington, D.C.

Hernández, Leonardo, and Eduardo Walker. 1993. "Estructura de financiamiento corporativo en Chile (1978–1990): Evidencia a partir de datos contables." *Estudios Públicos* 51.

Hicks, John. 1969. *A Theory of Economic History.* Oxford: Clarendon Press.

Honeygold, Derek. 1987. *International Financial Markets.* New York: Nichols.

Hong, In-Kie. 1996. "The Impact of Foreign Capital Flows on Asian Capital Markets: An Overview of Key Issues" (paper presented at the conference on Private Capital Flows: Implications for Asian Capital Markets, Bali, Indonesia, October 18–20). Processed.

Hoonsiri, Jaroungpon. 1996. "The Development of the Thai Bond Market" (paper presented at the conference on Private Capital Flows: Implications for Asian Capital Markets, Bali, Indonesia, October 18–20). Processed.

Hubbard, R. G., ed. 1991. *Financial Markets and Financial Crises.* Chicago: University of Chicago Press.

IFC (International Finance Corporation). *Emerging Stock Markets Factbook.* Various issues. Washington, D.C.

IMF (International Monetary Fund). 1995. *International Capital Markets: Developments, Prospects, and Key Policy Issues.* World Economic and Financial Surveys. Washington, D.C.

——. 1996. *International Capital Markets: Developments, Prospects, and Key Policy Issues.* World Economic and Financial Surveys. Washington, D.C.

——. *International Financial Statistics.* Various issues. Washington, D.C.

——. *World Economic Outlook.* Various issues. Washington, D.C.

Institute of Chartered Accountants (U.K.). 1996. *Regulation Review Working Party.* London.

International Accounting Standards Committee. 1993. "Survey on the Use and Application of International Accounting Standards 1993." Geneva, Switzerland.

——. 1996. "Compliance with International Accounting Standards" (paper presented at the Intergovernmental Working Group of Experts on International Standards of Accounting and Reporting. Geneva, Switzerland, July). Processed.

International Securities Regulation Report. Various issues. Horsham, Pa.: LRP Publications.

Investment Company Institute. 1996. *Mutual Fund Fact Book.* Washington, D.C.

IOSCO (International Organization of Securities Commissions). 1990a. "Report to the 15th Annual Conference of IOSCO." Harmonization of Accounting and Auditing Standards Technical Committee. Montreal, Canada.

——. 1990b. "Report of the Technical Committee, International Accounting and Auditing Standards." Montreal, Canada.

——. 1990c. Cross-Border Investment Services in the 1990s: Positioning Transaction Services." Symposium Report. Montreal, Canada.

——. 1991. "Comparative Analysis of Disclosure Regimes." Montreal, Canada.

——. 1992a. "Survey of the Development Committee on Disclosure." Montreal, Canada.

——. 1992b. "Clearing and Settlement in Emerging Markets: A Blueprint." Montreal, Canada.

——. 1993. "Report of the Development Committee on Disclosure." Montreal, Canada.

——. 1996. "Client Asset Protection." Report of the Technical Committee. Montreal, Canada.

ISSA (International Society of Securities Administrators). 1995. *G-30 Review Report.* Zurich, Switzerland.

——. 1996. *Handbook: 1996–97.* Zurich, Switzerland.

J. P. Morgan Securities. 1996. "Introducing the Emerging Local Markets Index (ELMI)." Market Brief, Emerging Market Research. New York.

Johnston, Barry R., and Ceyla Pazarbasioglu. 1995. "Linkages between Financial Variables, Financial Sector Reform, and Economic Growth and Efficiency." IMF Working Paper 95/103. Washington, D.C.

Kamath, K. V. 1996. "Corporate Governance: An Indian Perspective" (paper presented at the conference on Private Capital Flows: Implications for Asian Capital Markets, Bali, Indonesia, October 18–20). Processed.

Kamin, Steven B., and Paul R. Wood. 1996. "Capital Inflows, Financial Intermediation, and Aggregate Demand: Empirical Evidence from Mexico and Other Pacific Basin Countries." Federal Reserve Board, Washington, D.C. Processed.

Kaminsky, G. L., and C. M. Reinhart. 1996. "The Twin Crises: The Causes of Banking and Balance of Payments Problems." Board of Governors of the Federal Reserve, International Finance Discussion Paper 544, March. Washington, D.C.

Kang, Jun-Koo, and Rene Stultz. 1996. "Why Is There a Home Bias." Ohio State University, Department of Economics, Columbus. Processed.

Khan, M. S., and D. M. Mathieson. 1996. "The Implications of International Capital Flows for Macroeconomic and Financial Policies." *International Journal of Finance and Economics* 1(July): 155–60.

Khan, M. S., and Carmen M. Reinhart. 1995. *Capital Flows in the APEC Region.* Occasional paper 122. Washington, D.C.: IMF.

Kiguel, Miguel, and Leonardo Leiderman. 1993. "On the Consequences of Sterilized Intervention in Latin America: The Cases of Colombia and Chile." World Bank. Processed.

Kindleberger, C. P. 1978. *Manias, Panics, and Crashes.* New York: Basic Books.

King, Robert, and Ross Levine. 1993. "Finance and Growth: Schumpeter Might Be Right." *Quarterly Journal of Economics* 108(August): 717–37.

Krugman, Paul. 1993. "International Finance and Economic Development." In Alberto Giovannini, ed., *Finance and Development: Issues and Experience.* New York: Cambridge University Press.

Kyle, Albert S. 1984. "Market Structure, Information, Futures Markets, and Price Formation." In Gary G. Storey, Andrew Schmitz, and Alexander H. Sarris, eds., *International Agricultural Trade: Advanced Readings in Price Formation, Market Structure, and Price Instability.* Boulder, Colo.: Westview.

Lakonishok, Josef, Andrei Shleifer, and Robert W. Vishny. 1992. "The Impact of Institutional Trading on Stock Prices." *Journal of Financial Economics* 32: [23]–43.

Larraín, Mauricio. 1989. "How the 1981–83 Chilean Banking Crisis Was Handled." Policy Research Working Paper 300. World Bank, Office of the Vice President, Development Economics, Washington, D.C.

Le Fort, Guillermo, and Carlos Budnevich. 1996. "Capital Account Regulations and Macroeconomic Policy: Two Latin American Experiences." *Studies on International Monetary and Financial Issues for the Group of Twenty-four, Report to the Group of Twenty-four.* Central Bank of Chile, Santiago. Processed.

Levine, Ross. 1991. "Stock Markets, Growth, and Tax Policy." *Journal of Finance* 46(September): 1445–65.

———. 1995. "Foreign Banks, Financial Development, and Economic Growth." World Bank, Policy Research Department, Washington, D.C. Processed.

———. 1996. "Financial Development and Economic Growth: Views and Agenda." Policy Research Working Paper 1678. World Bank, Policy Research Department, Washington, D.C.

Levine, Ross, and Sara Zervos. 1995a. "Stock Markets, Banks, and Economic Growth." World Bank, Policy Research Department, Washington, D.C.

———. 1995b. "Capital Control Liberalization and Stock Market Performance." World Bank, Policy Research Department, Washington, D.C. Processed.

———. 1996a. "Capital Control Liberalization and Stock Market Development." Policy Research Working Paper 1622. World Bank, Policy Research Department, Washington, D.C.

———. 1996b. "Stock Market Development and Long-Run Growth." Policy Research Working Paper 1582. World Bank, Policy Research Department, Washington, D.C.

Lewis, Karen. 1994. "Puzzles in International Financial Markets." NBER Working Paper 4951. Cambridge, Mass.

———. 1995. "What Can Explain the Apparent Lack of International Consumption Risk Sharing?" NBER Working Paper 5203. Cambridge, Mass.

———. 1996. "Consumption, Stock Returns, and the Gains from International Risk Sharing." NBER Working Paper 5410. Cambridge, Mass.

Lindgren, Carl-Johan, Gillian Garcia, and Matthew I. Saal. 1996. *Bank Soundness and Macroeconomic Policy.* Washington, D.C.: IMF.

Listfield, Robert, and Fernando Montes-Negret. 1994. "Modernizing Payment Systems in Emerging Economies." Policy Research Working Paper 1336. World Bank, Financial Sector Development Department, Washington, D.C.

Lo, Andrew, and A. C. MacKinlay. 1988. "Stock Market Prices Do Not Follow Random Walks: Evidence from a Simple Specification Test." *Review of Financial Studies.* 1(1): 41–66.

Madhavan, Ananth. 1992. "Trading Mechanisms in Securities Markets." *Journal of Finance* 47(June): 607–41.

Malas, Iyad. 1996. "Capital Markets Development: Securities, Market Regulation, and Market Infrastructure" (paper presented at the workshop on Financial Market Development. Arab Monetary Fund and the Economic Research Forum, Abu Dhabi, United Arab Emirates, May). Processed.

Mathieson, Donald J., and Liliana Rojas-Suárez. 1993. *Liberalization of the Capital Account: Experiences and Issues.* IMF Occasional Paper 103. Washington, D.C.

Mayer, Colin. 1989. "Myths of the West: Lessons from Developed Countries for Development Finance." Policy Research Working Paper 301. World Bank, Office of the Vice President, Development Economics, Washington, D.C.

McKinnon, R. I., and Hum Pill, 1995. "Credible Liberalizations and International Capital Flows: The 'Over-borrowing' Syndrome." Stanford University, Department of Economics, Stanford, Calif. Processed.

McKinsey Global Institute. 1994. *The Global Capital Market: Supply, Demand, Pricing, and Allocation.* Washington, D.C.

Micropal Directory of Emerging Market Funds. Glen Allen, Va.: Emerging Market Funds Research.

Milesi-Ferretti, G. M., and A. Razin. 1996. "Persistent Current Account Deficits: A Warning Signal." *International Jounal of Finance and Economics* 1(July): 161–81.

Millstein, Ira, and Holly Gregory. 1996. "Comparison of Materials on Board Guidelines" (paper presented at the SEC International Institute for Securities Market Development Program, New York, May). Processed.

Minsky, Hyman P. 1995. "Financial Factors in the Economics of Capitalism." *Journal of Financial Services Research* 9: 197–208.

Mishkin, Frederic S. 1984. "Are Real Interest Rates Equal across Countries? An Empirical Investigation of International Parity Conditions." *Journal of Finance* 39(December): 1345–57.

——. 1996. "Asymmetric Information and Financial Crises: A Developing Country Perspective." NBER Working Paper 3400. Cambridge, Mass.

——. 1997. "Understanding Financial Crises: A Developing Country Perspective." In Michael Bruno and Boris Pleskovic, eds., *Annual World Bank Conference on Development Economics 1996.* Washington, D.C.: World Bank.

Mobius, Mark. 1995. *The Investor's Guide to Emerging Markets.* New York: Irwin.

Montiel, Peter. 1994. "Capital Mobility in Developing Countries: Some Measurement Issues and Empirical Estimates." *World Bank Economic Review* 8(3, September): 311–50.

——. 1996. "Policy Responses to Surges in Capital Inflows: Issues and Lessons." In Guillermo Calvo, Morris Goldstein, and Eduard Hochreiter, eds., *Private Capital Flow to Emerging Markets after the Mexican Crisis.* Washington, D.C.: Institute for International Economics.

Morgenstern, Claudia. 1996. "Legal and Operating Principles for Market Infrastructure: Securities Custody, Clearing and Settlement Systems." Draft, IFC, Washington, D.C. Processed.

Mundell, Robert. 1968. *International Economics.* New York: Macmillan.

NASD (National Association of Securities Dealers). 1995. "Report of the NASD Select Committee on Structure and Governance." New York.

Nowakowski, C. A. No date. "Survival and Growth in Cross-Border Investment Services through 2001." Symposium Report on Cross-Border Investment Services in the 1990s: Positioning Transaction Services. ISSA, Zurich, Switzerland.

Nurkse, Ragnar. 1954. "International Investment Today in the Light of Nineteenth-Century Experience." *Economic Journal* 64: 134–50.

Obstfeld, Maurice. 1989. "How Integrated Are World Capital Markets?" In Guillermo Calvo, ed., *Debt, Stabilization, and Development.* Oxford: Basil Blackwell.

——. 1992. "Risk-Sharing, Global Diversification, and Growth." NBER Working Paper 4093. Cambridge, Mass.

——. 1995. "International Capital Mobility in the 1990s." In Peter Kenen, ed., *Understanding Interdependence: The Macroeconomics of the Open Economy.* Princeton, N.J.: Princeton University Press.

Oyens, Gerrit de Marez. 1996. "Improvements in Risk Management in Securities Trading" (paper presented at the conference on Private Capital Flows: Implications for Asian Capital Markets, Bali, Indonesia, October 18–20). Processed.

Pagano, Marco. 1993. "Financial Markets and Growth: An Overview." *European Economic Review* 37: [613]–22.

Papaioannou, M. G., and Lawrence K. Duke. 1993. "The Internationalization of Emerging Equity Markets." *Finance and Development* 30(September): 36–39.

Penati, Alessandro, and Michael Dooley. 1984. "Current Account Imbalances and Capital Formation in Industrial Countries, 1949–81." *IMF Staff Papers* 31(1): 1–24.

Perry, Guillermo, ed. 1997. *Currency Boards and External Shocks: How Much Pain, How Much Gain?* World Bank, Washington, D.C.

Pomerleano, Michael. 1996. "Infrastructure Development in Emerging Capital Markets: The Comparative International Experience." Background paper prepared for *Private Capital Flows to Developing Countries.* World Bank, International Economics Department, Washington, D.C.

Poterba, James M., and Lawrence H. Summers. 1988. "Mean Reversion in Stock Prices: Evidence and Implications." *Journal of Financial Economics* 22(October): 27–59.

Prebisch, Raúl. 1959. "Commercial Policy in the Underdeveloped Countries." *American Economic Review* 71(2, May): 251–73.

Purba, A Zen Umar. 1991. "Securities Laws in the Indonesian Capital Markets: Recent Developments" (paper presented at the Tenth Biennial Conference of the Section on Business Law, International Bar Association, London, September–October). Processed.

Quirk, Peter J., and Owen Evans. 1995. *Capital Account Convertibility: Review of Experience and Implications for IMF Policies.* IMF Occasional Paper 131. Washington, D.C.

Rajan, Raghuram, and Luigi Zingales. 1996. "Financial Dependence and Growth." NBER Working Paper 5758. Cambridge, Mass.

Ramakrishnan, Ram T. S., and Anjan V. Thakor. 1984. "Information Reliability and a Theory of Financial Intermediation." *Review of Economic Studies* LI: 415–32.

Reisen, Helmut. 1996. "Net Capital Inflows: How Much to Accept, How Much to Resist?" (paper prepared for the conference on Managing Capital Flows and Exchange Rates: Lessons from the Pacific Basin, September 26–27. Federal Reserve Bank of San Francisco). Processed.

——. Forthcoming. "Managing Volatile Capital Inflows: The Experience of the 1990s." *Asian Development Review* 43(1).

Review of Emerging Markets. Various issues. Global Securities Consulting Services Benchmarks, London.

Review of Major Markets. Various issues. Global Securities Consulting Services Benchmarks, London.

Richards, Anthony. 1996. "Volatility and Predictability in National Stock Markets: How Do Emerging and Mature Markets Differ?" *IMF Staff Papers* 43(September): 456–501.

Rodríguez, Carlos A. 1994. "Interest Rates in Latin America." Centro de Estudios Macroecónomicos de Argentina. Buenos Aires, Argentina. Processed.

Rojas-Suárez, Liliana, and Steven R. Weisbrod. 1994. "Financial Market Fragilities in Latin America: From Banking Crisis Resolution to Current Policy Challenges." IMF Working Paper 94/117. Washington, D.C.

——. 1996. "Towards an Effective Regulatory and Supervisory Framework for Latin America" (paper presented at the conference on Safe and Sound Financial Systems: What Works for Latin America? IADB, Washington, D.C., September). Processed.

Romer, Paul. 1990. "Endogenous Technological Change." *Journal of Political Economy* 98(October): S71–S102.

——. 1993. "Idea Gaps and Object Gaps in Economic Development." *Journal of Monetary Economics* 32(December): 543–73.

Rosen, Sherwin. 1981. "The Economics of Superstars." *American Economic Review* 71(5, December): 845–58.

Sachs, Jeffrey, and Andrew Warner. 1995. "Economic Reform and the Process of Global Integration." *Brookings Papers on Economic Activity* 1: 1–118.

Sachs, Jeffrey, Aaron Tornell, and Andrés Velasco. 1996. "Financial Crises in Emerging Markets: The Lessons from 1995." NBER Working Paper 5576. Cambridge, Mass.

Saint-Paul, Gilles. 1992. "Technological Choice, Financial Markets, and Economic Development." *European Economic Review* 36: 763–81.

Samuel, Cherian. 1996. "Stock Market and Investment: The Governance Role of the Market." Policy Research Working Paper 1578. World Bank, Operations Policy Department, Washington, D.C.

Sandmo, Agnar. 1970. "The Effect of Uncertainty on Savings Decisions." *Review of Economic Studies* 37: 353–60.

Saragih, Freddy, and Hamud Balfas. 1995. "Indonesia: Development of Equity and Bond Market/ History and Regulatory Framework" (country presentation at the Fifth Annual International Institute for Capital Market Development, U.S. Securities and Exchange Commission, Washington, D.C., April–May). Processed.

Scharfstein, D. S., and Jeremy C. Stein. 1990. "Herd Behavior and Investment." *American Economic Review* 80(June): 465–79.

Schinasi, Garry J., and Monica Hargraves. 1993. " 'Boom and Bust' in Asset Markets in the 1980s: Causes and Consequences." *Staff Studies for the World Economic Outlook,* World Economic and Financial Surveys. IMF, Washington, D.C.

Schmidt-Hebbel, Klaus. 1995. "Fiscal Adjustment and Growth: In and Out of Africa." World Bank, Policy Research Department, Washington, D.C.

Seeger, Charles M. 1996. "Securities Exchange Essentials." Background paper prepared for *Private Capital Flows to Developing Countries.* World

Bank, International Economics Department, Washington, D.C.

Segerstrom, Paul. 1991. "Innovation, Imitation, and Economic Growth." *Journal of Political Economy* 99(August): 807–27.

Sellon, Gordon H., Jr. 1992. "Changes in Financial Intermediation: The Role of Pension and Mutual Funds." *Economic Review* 77: [55]–70. Federal Reserve Bank of Kansas City.

Shaw, Edward S. 1973. *Financial Deepening in Economic Development.* New York: Oxford University Press.

Sheng, Andrew, ed. 1996. *Bank Restructuring: Lessons from the 1980s.* Washington, D.C.: World Bank.

Singh, Ajit. 1994. "How Do Large Corporations in Developing Countries Finance Their Growth?" *Finance and the International Economy.* New York: Oxford University Press.

Sobel, Andrew C. 1994. *Domestic Choices: International Markets—Dismantling National Barriers and Liberalizing Securities Markets.* Ann Arbor: University of Michigan Press.

Stehm, Jeff. 1996. *Clearance and Settlement Systems for Securities: Critical Design Choices in Emerging Market Economies.* World Bank Discussion Paper 321. Washington, D.C.

Stiglitz, Joseph E. 1990. "Symposium on Bubbles." *Journal of Economic Perspectives* 4(Spring): 13–18.

——. 1994. "The Role of the State in Financial Markets." In *Proceedings of the Annual World Bank Conference on Development Economics 1993.* Washington, D.C.: World Bank.

Stock Exchange of Thailand. 1996. "Thai Trust Fund: Concept and Current Status." Bangkok. Processed.

Strahota, Robert D. 1996. "Securities Regulation in Emerging Markets: Some Issues and Suggested Answers" (paper prepared for the SEC International Institute for Securities Market Development, Washington, D.C., April). Processed.

Summers, Lawrence H. 1986. "Does the Stock Market Rationally Reflect Fundamental Values?" *Journal of Finance* 41(July): 591–601.

Sundararajan, Vasudevan, and Tomás J. T. Baliño, eds. 1991. *Banking Crises: Cases and Issues.* Washington, D.C.: IMF.

Svensson, Lars. 1988. "Trade in Risky Assets." *American Economic Review* 78(June): 375–94.

Terell, H. S. 1986. "The Role of Foreign Banks in Domestic Banking Markets." In Hang-sheng Cheng, ed., *Financial Policy and Reform in Pacific-Basin Countries.* New York: Lexington.

Tesar, Linda. 1991. "Savings, Investment, and International Capital Flows." *Journal of International Economics* 31(August): 55–78.

——. 1995. "Evaluating the Gains from International Risksharing." *Carnegie-Rochester Conference Series on Public Policy* 42(June): 95–144.

Tesar, Linda, and Ingrid Werner. 1992. "Home Bias and the Globalization of Securities Markets." NBER Working Paper 4218. Cambridge, Mass.

Tikka, Karl S. 1993. "Finland: Fundamental Tax Reform—25 Percent Rate on Capital Income and Corporate Income." *Bank of Finland Bulletin* (June). Helsinki.

Topol, Richard. 1991. "Bubbles and Volatility of Stock Prices: Effect of Mimetic Contagion." *Economic Journal: Journal of the Royal Economic Society* (U.K.) 101(July): 786–800.

U.S. Federal Reserve System. 1992. "Clearance and Settlement in U.S. Securities Markets." Washington, D.C.

U.S. Securities and Exchange Commission. 1994. "Market 2000: An Examination of Current Equity Market Developments." Washington, D.C.

——. 1996. *Report pursuant to Section 21(a) of the Securities and Exchange Act of 1934 regarding the NASD and the NASDAQ Market.* Washington, D.C.

Valdés-Prieto, Salvador. 1994. "Financial Liberalization and the Capital Account: Chile—1974–84." In Caprio, Atiyas, and Hanson, eds., *Financial Reform, Theory and Practice,* Cambridge, U.K.: Cambridge University Press.

Valdés-Prieto, Salvador, and Marcelo Soto. 1996. "New Selective Capital Controls in Chile: Are They Effective?" Economics Department, Catholic University of Chile, Santiago. Processed.

van Wincoop, Eric. 1994. "Welfare Gains from International Risksharing." *Journal of Monetary Economics* 34(October): 175–200.

Velasco, Andrés. 1987. "Financial and Balance of Payments Crises: A Simple Model of the Southern Cone Experience." *Journal of Development Economics* 27(October): 263–83.

Wang, Jian-Ye. 1990. "Growth, Technology Transfer, and the Long-Run Theory of International Capital Movements." *Journal of International Economics* 29(November): 255–71.

Williamson, John. 1996. *The Crawling Band as an Exchange Rate Regime: Lessons from Chile, Colombia, and Israel.* Washington, D.C.: Institute for International Economics.

World Bank. 1989. *World Development Report.* New York: Oxford University Press.

——. 1993. "Regulatory Environments in Emerging Markets." IFC Capital Markets Department, Washington, D.C.

——. 1994. *Averting the Old Age Crisis: Policies to Protect the Old and Promote Growth.* New York: Oxford University Press.

——. 1996a. *Managing Capital Flows in East Asia.* Development in Practice Series. Washington, D.C.

——. 1996b. *Global Economic Prospects and the Developing Countries.* Washington, D.C.

——. 1997. *Global Development Finance 1997.* Washington, D.C.